AMERICA'S FASTEST GROWING EMPLOYERS

THE COMPLETE GUIDE TO FINDING JOBS WITH OVER 700 OF AMERICA'S HOTTEST COMPANIES

CARTER SMITH

EDITOR OF THE JOBBANK SERIES

BOB ADAMS, INC.
PUBLISHERS
Holbrook, Massachusetts

Managing Editor: Carter Smith
Associate Editor: Michelle Bevilacqua
Researchers: Mary Canavan, Madeline Pagan

Published by Bob Adams, Inc.
260 Center Street, Holbrook MA 02343

Cover design by Peter Gouck.

Manufactured in the United States of America.

ISBN: 1-55850-100-2 (Paperback)
ISBN: 1-55850-146-0 (Hardcover)

TABLE OF CONTENTS

Resumes and Cover Letters, 461

Advice on Creating a Strong Resume. Includes sample
resumes and cover letters.

Indexes, 479

Industrial and geographical indexes to help you
pinpoint the job for you.

PREFACE

General Motors to Lay Off 74,000 Workers....IBM to Lay Off 20,000....Unemployment tops 7 percent....Over 200,000 Lose Jobs in One Month Alone. So read the headlines that closed the economic door on a bleak 1991. At the same time, most Americans didn't need a newspaper to understand what they were already feeling in their pocketbooks. These days, the country's economic misfortunes are more than just news stories. In fact, according to a CBS/New York Times poll taken in late January, well over 50% of the American public felt that they were worse off in 1992 than they were four years earlier.

By February, many economists were forecasting that the hard times would continue at least through the mid-Summer, and then, ever so slowly, begin to turn around. From corporate boardrooms to shopping malls, predictions of a light at the end of the tunnel are being met with a wait-and-see attitude. After all, as most people remember, the economists have been wrong before.

In the midst of all this gloom, however, there are a number of surprising companies that are not only managing to keep afloat, but are surging ahead:

-- **Gateway 2000,** a direct-mail seller of IBM PC clones based in North Sioux City, South Dakota, has seen its annual revenues grow from about $1 million in 1986 to over $275 million in 1990, garnering for itself the top slot on *Inc.* magazine's 1991 list of the fastest growing private companies in America.

-- **Spaghetti Warehouse,** the Dallas-based owner of moderately-priced Italian restaurants, has grown from a single restaurant started by a retiring Tandy Corporation executive to a $43 million chain with locations in 20 cities, ringing up profits far above the restaurant industry average.

-- **SPI Pharmaceuticals,** a Costa Mesa, California distributor of pharmaceutical and nutritional products, almost doubled its revenues during the first three quarters of 1991 alone, largely because Hungarian health authorities have authorized SPI's parent company to market one of its products in that country to help in the fight against AIDS.

-- **Birmingham Steel Corporation,** a Birmingham, Alabama-based operator of mini-mills that produce reinforced bar steel products for the construction industry, is prospering in an industry whose long-term decline has become a symbol of waning American manufacturing might.

These success stories are just a small sampling of the companies you will find in *America's Fastest Growing Employers*. Over 700 firms are listed, from small software development companies employing under 75 people to companies like Wal-Mart Stores, which hired over 60,000 new employees during 1990 (making the retail discounter the private sector's biggest generator of new jobs). *America's Fastest Growing Employers* gives you an inside look at the companies that are leading the way out of tough economic times.

During the last several months of 1991, our researchers looked into just what companies qualified as the fastest-growing in the nation, how they had gotten there and where they were headed. Our research was done in several phases. The first was to compile an initial list of employers. In order to do this, we had to decide how to define the term "fastest-growing." For example, growth might refer to a company's rising profits, increasing revenues or sales, or, for investors, rising earnings per share. Or it can mean an increase in the size of the company's workforce.

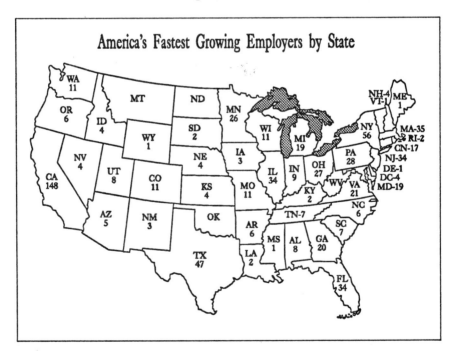

America's Fastest Growing Employers by State

For means of comparison, we've defined "growth" in terms of rising revenues and sales figures. Revenues can tell us about the short and long-term future of a company, not only as a growing business enterprise, but also as a place of employment. In the case of a manufacturing company, the opening of a new plant or distribution center does not always mean an increase in the number of professional, fast-track career opportunities. And while there is not necessarily a direct correlation between revenues and the number of new professional hires a company is planning, by looking at what events or strategies caused an increase in revenues, jobseekers looking for professional positions with room for advancement can uncover opportunities that may otherwise have gone undiscovered.

Nonetheless, because revenues can soar at a company that employs just 5 people and never hires new staff members, you will also find critical, specific information on how many people a particular company has hired over the past several years.

Each and every company listed in this book has been included only after meeting a number of minimum requirements:

- *Each employer must have shown a minimum 3-5 year revenue growth rate of 20%*

- *Each employer must have shown 1990 revenues of over $10 million*

- *Each company must employ at least 50 people*

- *Each must have been in business for a minimum of four years*

- *No company can have announced major layoffs at any time during the past twenty-four months*

After compiling our initial list of employers, we collected annual, 10-K, and 10-Q reports, product brochures, newspaper and magazine articles, and more, in search of the secrets behind the success stories. We kept a careful eye on the latest news on each firm, dropping those from our initial list that soared from 1986 to 1990, but struggled badly in 1991. We then mailed out questionnaires to each and every company, asking for information on who they were hiring, and how many.

Within these pages you will find the kind of vital information neccessary in any successful job search -- the names and addresses of the companies that are thriving, how many people each of these companies employs, and what each company's prospects are for the future. You'll also find that many of the company profiles in this book list the positions that the firm commonly hires for, backgrounds needed to fill those jobs, and a summary of the benefits that the company offers to its employees.

In addition to company profiles, you'll also benefit from the following:

Our chapter called "Ten Industries for the 1990's and Beyond," which takes a detailed look at the issues facing companies in industries such as Computers, Healthcare, Information Services, Retail, Entertainment, and Biotechnology, among others. Use this chapter to research the trends that will affect your job prospects in both the short- and long-term.

"A Job Search Primer" will help you map out your job search strategy. It's a condensed review of the most effective job search methods, including getting, preparing for, and succeeding in interviews.

The "Resumes and Cover Letters" chapter, which will help you write a winning resume and learn how to sell yourself most effectively on paper.

The industrial and geographical indexes of employers, which will help you form a target list of potential employers.

Although just a handful of "cutting edge" industries -- healthcare, computers, biotechnology, for example -- may come to mind when you think of America's fast-track growth sectors, we found that a surprising number of fast-growth companies are involved in much more "traditional" industries. From restaurants and video store chains to makers of sneakers and low-fat cheese, the growth companies listed here come in all shapes and sizes.

Another surprise uncovered by our research was the wide geographical distribution of growth firms. While it may be no surprise that California was the leading headquarters location for fast-track companies, less-populous states such as Arkansas, Idaho, and South Carolina are also represented. In fact, 44 states as well as the District of Columbia are homes to firms appearing in these pages.

In the new business climate of the 1990's, the most valuable currency is information. That holds true for companies in all industries, and for all levels of management and staff. And it is especially true for the jobseeker. By using the information provided in this book, you can separate yourself from the flock of candidates who answer help wanted advertisements hoping for a job. By using *America's Fastest Growing Employers* to supplement your own research, you'll be arming yourself with the kind of up-to-date inside information you need to land the fast-track-job that you desire.

PART I

The Company Profiles

A&W BRANDS
709 Westchester Avenue
White Plains, New York 10609
(914) 397-1700

Founded: 1986. **No. of Employees:** 175. **Revenues (1990):** $119 million. **Revenues (1986):** $40 million. **Five-Year Revenue Growth:** 197%.

Description: One of the nation's leading manufacturers of soft drinks. A&W Root Beer is the best selling brand of root beer in the world.

How they're growing/Recent developments: A&W Root Beer was first introduced in 1971, and within five years became the leading U.S. brand. The current company was formed in 1986. In that, A&W acquired Squirtco, the owner of Squirt, a citrus beverage. A&W now also produces Country Time Lemonade through an agreement with General Foods. For the nine months ending September, 30, 1991, revenues rose 1.4% year to year, aided by price increases, decreased raw material and packaging expenses and a decline in interest expense. Analysts believe that sales of Squirt will be particularly strong in 1992. Employment has grown from an estimated 130 in 1987 to 175 in 1991.

ABBOTT LABORATORIES
Abbott Park
North Chicago, Illinois 60064
(312) 937-6100

Founded: 1888. **No of Employees:** 43,770. **Revenues (1990):** $6.2 billion. **Revenues (1986):** $3.8 billion. **Five-Year Revenue Growth:** 62%.

Description: A diversified health care products and pharmaceuticals firm. Products include diagnostic equipment, nutritional products and consumer items like Similac brand infant formula, and Selsun Blue shampoo.

How they're growing/Recent developments: Abbott has seen continued growth in its established pharmaceutical, nutritional, and diagnostic product lines. Development of new products -- Abbott was first in the development of an AIDS antibodies test, for example -- has further strengthened the company. The company is currently at work on a treatment for hypertension, a blood gas monitor. In 1990, Abbott's new insomnia drug won approval from the Food and Drug Administration. Employment has grown from an estimated 36,000 in 1987 to 43,770 in 1991.

ACUSON
P.O. Box 7393
Mountain View, California 94039
(415) 969-9112

Contact: Ms. Judith Heyboer, V.P. of Employee Relations. **Founded:** 1981.
No. of Employees: 1,223. **Revenues (1990):** $283 million. **Revenues (1986):**
$64 million. **Five-Year Revenue Growth:** 342%.

Description: Manufacturers of ultrasound medical instruments.

How they're growing/Recent developments: In May, 1989, Acuson introduced its XP Xcelerator, and in July, 1990, it introduced the Acuson 128XP, a
second-generation system with new abilities. Employment has grown from an
estimated 293 in 1987 to 1,223 in 1991.

ADIA SERVICES
64 Willow Place
Menlo Park, California 94025
(415) 324-0696

Contact: Barbara Latour, Vice President, Human Resources. **Founded:** 1973.
No. of Employees: 2,500. **Revenues (1990):** $666 million. **Revenues (1986):**
$244 million. **Five-Year Revenue Growth:** 173%.

Description: The world's second-largest temporary and permanent employee
placement service.

Common positions include: Customer Service Representative; Branch Manager; Management Trainee; Personnel and Labor Relations Specialist; Sales
Representative.

Principal educational backgrounds sought include: Business Administration;
Communications; Economics; Liberal Arts; Marketing.

Company benefits include: Medical insurance; dental insurance; pension
plan; life insurance; tuition assistance; disability coverage; profit sharing.

Operations at this facility include: Regional headquarters; service; sales.

How they're growing/Recent developments: Although earnings were down
for the first quarter of 1991 due to the national recession, Adia has continued
to pursue the aggressive acquisitions policy that has fueled growth in recent

years. Employment has grown from an estimated 1,150 in 1987 to 2,500 in 1991.

ADOBE SYSTEMS
1585 Charleston Road
Mountain View, California 94043
(415) 961-4400

Founded: 1983. **No. of Employees:** 508. **Revenues (1990):** $169 million. **Revenues (1986):** $16 million. **Five-Year Revenue Growth:** 956%.

Description: Adobe is one of the nation's leading developers and marketers of custom software. The company's PostScript software is an industry standard, allowing users to integrate text and graphics with PCs and laser printers.

How they're growing/Recent developments: In October, 1991, Adobe announced that it would begin sales of a new computer chip which speeds up the process of printing and displaying text. In August, 1991, Adobe acquired a digital video-editing software product called ReelTime from SuperMac Technology. Apple accounts for 23% of Adobe's sales, and, in 1990, the two companies signed a licensing agreement. In more recent developments, Lotus agreed in May, 1991, to use Adobe's typeface software and Hewlett Packard has agreed to "bundle" Adobe's software with its newest printer. Employment has grown from an estimated 49 in 1987 to 508 in 1991.

ADVANCED LOGIC RESEARCH, INC.
9401 Jeronimo Road
Irvine, California 92718
(714) 581-6770

Founded: 1984. **No. of Employees:** 338. **Revenues (1990):** $171.9 million. **Revenues (1987):** $15.1 million. **Four-Year Revenue Growth:** 1,038%.

Description: Advanced Logic designs, manufactures and markets microcomputer systems that offer leading-edge performance and value for business and professional use.

How they're growing/Recent developments: The company was expected to introduce several new desktop and notebook products by late 1991. The company's high-end focus is currently on protecting its 30% gross margins from severe competition. Net sales for the six months ending March 31, 1991, totaled $110.2 million, up from $84.4 million a year earlier.

ADVANCED SCIENCES, INC.
2620 San Mateo NE, Suite D
Albuquerque, New Mexico 87110
(505) 883-0959

Founded: 1977. **No. of Employees:** 422. **Revenues (1990):** $38.7 million. **Revenues (1986):** $4.2 million. **Five-Year Revenue Growth:** 821%.

Description: Company provides commercial physical research, biological research, custom computer programming services and systems engineering.

How they're growing/Recent developments: Employment has grown from 96 in 1986 to 422 in 1991.

ADVANCED TELECOMMUNICATIONS CORPORATION
East Paces Ferry Road
Suite 2100
Atlanta, Georgia 30326
(404) 261-5885

Founded: 1983. **No. of Employees:** 1,405. **Revenues (1990):** $333 million. **Revenues (1986):** $46 million. **Five-Year Revenue Growth:** 623%.

Description: Provides long-distance service to over 300,000 customers in eleven Southeastern and Southwestern states.

How they're growing/Recent developments: Company operations have expanded in recent years thanks to an aggressive acquisitions policy. In August, 1991, the company won approval from New Mexico to provide intrastate long-distance service to that state's residents. Employment has grown from an estimated 160 in 1987 to 1,405 in 1991.

AGENCY RENT-A-CAR
30000 Aurora Road
Solon, Ohio 44139
(216) 349-1000

Founded: 1971. **No. of Employees:** 2,700. **Revenues (1990):** $274 million. **Revenues (1986):** $118 million. **Five-Year Revenue Growth:** 132%.

Description: Agency Rent-A-Car operates three separate divisions whose principal business is the rental of automobiles on a short-term basis to the insurance replacement market.

How they're growing/Recent developments: In August, 1991, the company announced that it had increased its fleet size by 9.3%, and had plans to make further increases in the third and fourth quarters of the year. Employment has grown from an estimated 1,200 in 1987 to 2,700 in 1991.

AIRBORNE FREIGHT CORPORATION
P.O. Box 662
Seattle, Washington 98111
(206) 285-4600

Founded: 1968. **No. of Employees:** 9,900. **Revenues (1990):** $1.2 billion. **Revenues (1986):** $542 million. **Five-Year Revenue Growth:** 121%.

Description: A leader in the domestic express delivery industry, specializing in door-to-door, next-morning deliveries of small packages and documents. Airborne also has an expanding international service.

How they're growing/Recent developments: Although the recession has slowed Airborne's growth slightly, the company has begun aggressive marketing of its new second day-service and thus actually improved its shipping volume. In addition, Airborne has formed a joint venture with Matsui & Co. and Tonami Transportation to promote operations in Japan. Employment has grown from an estimated 6,200 in 1987 to 9,900 in 1991.

AIRTRAN
7501 26th Avenue South
Minneapolis, Minnesota 55450
(612) 726-5151

Founded: 1981. **No. of Employees:** 978. **Revenues (1990):** $71 million. **Revenues (1988):** $29 million. **Five-Year Revenue Growth:** 145%.

Description: A regional airline providing service to 37 cities in the Upper Midwest. The airline serves the hub airports of Minneapolis-St. Paul and Detroit.

How they're growing/Recent developments: Revenues rose 11% for the three months that ended in June, 1991, due in part to increased passenger traffic in the Detroit systems, a higher yield per passenger mile and improved margins due to costs increasing at a slower rate than revenues.

A.L. LABORATORIES
One Executive Drive
P.O. Box 1399
Fort Lee, New Jersey 07024
(201) 947-7774

Founded: 1975. **No. of Employees:** 1,800. **Revenues (1990):** $275 million. **Revenues (1986):** $122 million. **Five-Year Revenue Growth:** 125%.

Description: A.L. Labs, 49% owned by Norwegian-based Apothernes Laboratorium A.S., manufactures generic pharmaceutical drugs, as well as animal health and human nutrition products.

How they're growing/Recent developments: The company's income grew 15% in the first half of 1991 alone, mainly from the sale of a number of trademarks. In August, 1991, the company acquired the right to manufacture chlortetracycline, an antibiotic used in animal feed, and a month earlier purchased the entire animal feed line from Solvay Animal Health. Employment has grown from an estimated 1,600 in 1987 to 1,800 in 1991.

ALASKA AIR GROUP
19300 Pacific Highway South
Seattle, Washington 98188
(206) 431-7040

Founded: 1944. **No. of Employees:** 6,183. **Revenues (1990):** $1 billion. **Revenues (1986):** $468 million. **Five-Year Revenue Growth:** 114%.

Description: Alaska Air is a holding company for the airlines Alaska Airlines and Horizon Air Industries. The two Seattle-based airlines serve the Western United States, as well as Mexico, Canada and Russia.

How they're growing/Recent developments: The company has dominated passenger travel to Alaska since the early 1970s. Alaska Air has an established loyal, customer base, which it rewards with greater leg room, free wine on every flight, and overall superior customer service. Although high fuel prices and fare discounting have hurt earnings in the past year, Alaska Air has recently begun service to Toronto and Russia. Employment has grown from an estimated 5,933 in 1987 to 6,183 in 1991.

ALBERTSON'S, INC.
250 Parkcenter Boulevard
Boise, Idaho 83726
(208) 385-6200

Founded: 1939. **No. of Employees:** 58,000. **Revenues (1990):** $8.2 billion.
Revenues (1986): $5.4 billion. **Five-Year Revenue Growth:** 52%.

Description: A supermarket and drug store chain operating in seventeen
Western and Southern states.

How they're growing/Recent developments: Albertson's places great emphasis on selecting the right locations for its new stores, and operates only a few
stores in each market, backed by a strong distribution network. Albertson's
spent over $200 million between 1987 and 1990 on its regional distribution
centers. Albertson's plans to open a total of 240 new stores within five years.
In addition, recent store computerizations have lowered operating expenses.
In 1990, the company introduced its own HOPE (Help Our Planet's Ecology)
line of environmentally safer paper products. The company also recently acquired Cullum's, a Texas-based chain. Employment has grown from an estimated 40,000 in 1987 to 58,000 in 1991.

ALCO HEALTH SERVICES CORPORATION
P.O. Box 959
Valley Forge, Pennsylvania 19482
(215) 296-4480

Founded: 1977. **No. of Employees:** 2,381. **Revenues (1990):** $2.3 billion.
Revenues (1986): $1.7 billion. **Five-Year Revenue Growth:** 35%.

Description: Parent company to a group of health service companies engaged
in pharmaceutical distribution, medical specialties and hair care, and cosmetic distribution. The company operates 15 separate divisions and four subsidiaries.

How they're growing/Recent developments: During the 1980's, Alco benefitted from the dramatic growth of the full-service drug wholesale industry.
Since 1988, when the company was acquired by AHCS Holdings Corporation,
management's focus has been to increase operating efficiency through a consolidation of company facilities, to expand market share in the areas the
company already serves, and to target growth opportunities by pursuing new
customers and selected acquisitions. Employment has grown from an estimated 1,900 in 1987 to 2,381 in 1991.

ALDUS CORPORATION
411 First Avenue South
Seattle, Washington 98104
(206) 622-5500

Founded: 1984. **No. of Employees:** 809. **Revenues (1990):** $135 million. **Revenues (1987):** $11 million. **Five-Year Revenue Growth:** 1,127%.

Description: Aldus develops computer software for Apple Macintosh and Windows and OS/2 compatible computers.

How they're growing/Recent developments: For the six-month period that ended June, 1991, sales rose 44% due to strong demand for retail and up-grade units of Aldus PageMaker 4.0 and Aldus FreeHand 3.0, as well as the introduction of Aldus Persuasion 2.0. During 1990, Aldus completed the acquisition of Silicon Beach Software, Inc., a microcomputer software publisher. The acquisition has allowed Aldus to extend its Macintosh-based product line, with the addition of SuperCard, Digital Darkroom, Super 3D and Personal Press. Employment has grown from an estimated 380 in 1987 to 809 in 1991.

ALFA CORPORATION
2108 East South Boulevard
Montgomery, Alabama 36116
(205) 288-3900

Founded: 1971. **No. of Employees:** 1500. **Revenues (1990):** $212.4 million. **Revenues (1986):** $51 million. **Five-Year Revenue Growth:** 316%.

Description: A financial services holding company. Alfa Corporation and its subsidiaries are closely affiliated with the Alfa Mutual Group of companies, and with them constitute the Alfa Mutual Group. Alfa Mutual Insurance Company and Alfa Mutual Fire Insurance Company together own approximately 50.8% of Alfa Corporation's common stock.

How they're growing/Recent developments: Alfa achieved record results for the first nine months of 1991. Premiums for the period increased 10% and total revenues were up 9.3%. In September, 1991, Alfa received recognition in *The National Underwriter* as one of the top 50 in its listing of Results of Outstanding Insurers, based on historical results, operating trends and soundness of the balance sheet.

ALL AMERICAN SEMICONDUCTORS
16251 NW 54th Avenue
Miami, Florida 33014
(305) 621-8282

Founded: 1964. **No. of Employees:** 175. **Revenues (1990):** $37 million. **Revenues (1987):** $14 million. **Four-Year Revenue Growth:** 164%.

Description: Distributors of a full range of semiconductors, including transistors, diodes, memory chips and microprocessors.

How they're growing/Recent developments: Net income for the nine-month period ending September 30, 1991, was $242,000. Employment has grown from an estimated 79 in 1987 to 175 in 1991.

ALLIANCE IMAGING
One Centerpointe Drive
La Palma, California 90623
(213) 921-7330

Founded: 1983. **No. of Employees:** 275. **Revenues (1990):** $45 million. **Revenues (1987):** $22 million. **Four-Year Revenue Growth:** 105%.

Description: Provides mobile diagnostic imaging equipment and support services for the health care and hospital industry.

Common positions include: Radiologic technologist.

How they're growing/Recent developments: Employment has grown from an estimated 150 in 1987 to the current 275.

ALLOU HEALTH & BEAUTY CARE
50 Emjay Boulevard
Brentwood, New York 11717
(516) 273-4000

Founded: 1962. **No. of Employees:** 137. **Revenues (1990):** $71 million. **Revenues (1986):** $34 million. **Five-Year Revenue Growth:** 109%.

Description: A distributor of health and cosmetics products to independent retailers in the New York metropolitan area.

How they're growing/Recent developments: Allou has profited from its expanding line of Allou Brands beauty products, and higher profits on fragrances and cosmetics. The company now has over 3,500 active accounts, including Sears and Wal-Mart. Revenues for fiscal 1991 climbed to $88.7 million.

ALLWASTE, INC.
3040 Post Oak Boulevard
Suite 1300
Houston, Texas 77056-6511
(713) 623-8777

Founded: 1980. **No. of Employees:** 2,759. **Revenues (1990):** $221 million. **Revenues (1986):** $4 million. **Five-Year Revenue Growth:** 5,425%.

Description: Providers of garbage collection and transport, asbestos removal and encapsulation, tank and boiler cleaning service and recycling of waste materials.

How they're growing/Recent developments: Allwaste expansion is backed by an aggressive acquisitions program. In fact, management expects 50% of the company's growth over the next year to be provided by acquisitions. By last July, the company had completed acquisition of five separate businesses in 1991, following the acquisition of 16 during fiscal 1990. Net income for the year ending August 31, 1991, was $3.16 million. Employment has grown from an estimated 167 in 1987 to the current 2,759.

ALPHA MICROSYSTEMS
3501 West Sunflower Avenue
Santa Ana, California 92704
(714) 957-8500

Founded: 1977. **No. of Employees:** 330. **Revenues (1990):** $56 million. **Revenues (1986):** $48 million. **Five-Year Revenue Growth:** 16%.

Description: A manufacturer of multi-user, multitasking computer systems.

How they're growing/Recent developments: In May, 1991, the company announced the acquisition of CAIR Systems' field services operations. Exports account for more than 25% of Alpha Microsystems' sales, Employment grew 8% between 1989 and 1990. Net income for the 26 weeks ending August 25, 1991, was $239,000. Employment has grown from an estimated 310 in 1987 to the current 330.

ALPINE LACE BRANDS
111 Dunnell Road
Maplewood, New Jersey 07040
(201) 378-8600

Founded: 1986. **No. of Employees:** 259. **Revenues (1990):** $141 million. **Revenues (1986):** $18 million. **Five-Year Revenue Growth:** 683%.

Description: Develops and markets low-salt, low-cholesterol cheeses.

How they're growing/Recent developments: In 1990, Alpine Lace introduced PreMonde Alpine Lace Free 'N' Lean cheeses and is currently negotiating with several food manufacturers and fast-food companies to use its cheese in pizza, salads, and crackers. The company is also moving into fat-free cheeses, following the acquisitions of patents pending from Gamay Foods.

ALTERA CORPORATION
2610 Orchard Parkway
San Jose, California 95134
(408) 984-2800

Contact: Sandra Berg, Senior Staffing Specialist. **Founded:** 1979. **No. of Employees:** 450. **Revenues (1990):** $78 million. **Revenues (1986):** $10 million. **Five-Year Revenue Growth:** 680%.

Description: Altera designs and markets programmable logic semiconductor chips and software tools

Common positions include: Accountant; Computer Programmer; Customer Service Representative; Ceramics Engineer; Electrical Engineer; Industrial Engineer; Public Relations Specialist.

Principal educational backgrounds sought: Computer Science; Engineering; Finance; Marketing; Physics.

Company benefits include: Medical insurance; dental insurance; life insurance; tuition assistance; disability coverage; profit sharing; savings plan.

Operations at this facility include: Manufacturing; research and development; administration; service; sales.

How they're growing/Recent developments: Altera manufactures full-custom semiconductor chips that allow customers to configure and program the chips using company-provided software. The key force behind Altera's success is the market penetration of its low-cost design tools, higher pin count and high density performance. Employment has grown from an estimated 147 in 1987 to the current 450.

AM-PRO PROTECTIVE AGENCY
P.O. Box 23829
Columbia, South Carolina 29223
(803) 741-0287

Founded: 1982. **No. of Employees:** 1,035. **Revenues (1990):** $29 million. **Revenues (1986):** $2 million. **Five-Year Revenue Growth:** 1,350%.

Description: Provides security services.

How they're growing/Recent developments: Employment has grown from an 180 in 1987 to the current 1,035.

AMBITECH ENGINEERING
800 Roosevelt Road, Building E
Suite 300
Glen Ellyn, Illinois 60137
(708) 858-8960

Contact: Elizabeth Miller, Manager of Human Resources; **Founded:** 1982; **No. of Employees:** 185; **Revenues (1990):** $11 million; **Revenues (1986):** $1 million; **Five-Year Revenue Growth:** 1,000%.

Description: A consulting engineering firm engaged in the engineering and design of petroleum refineries, chemical plants and petrochemical plants. Includes both new construction and retrofits.

Common positions include: Draftsperson; Civil Engineer; Electrical Engineer; Mechanical Engineer; Petroleum Engineer; Purchasing Agent.

Principal educational background: Engineering.

Company benefits include: Medical insurance; dental insurance; pension plan; life insurance; tuition assistance; disability coverage.

AMDAHL CORPORATION
1250 East Arques Avenue, MS 300
Sunnyvale, California 94088
(408) 746-6000

Contact: Joe Svancara, Director of Human Resources; **Founded:** 1972; **No. of Employees:** 9,500. **Revenues (1990):** $2.2 billion. **Revenues (1986):** $966 million. **Five-Year Revenue Growth:** 128%.

Description: Produces large scale mainframe computers that are IBM hardware and software compatible. American Stock Exchange.

Common positions include: Accountant; Administrator; Attorney; Buyer; Computer Programmer; Customer Service Representative; Electrical Engineer; Industrial Engineer; Mechanical Engineer; Financial Analyst; Branch Manager; Department Manager; General Manager; Operations/Production Manager; Marketing Specialist; Personnel and Labor Relations Specialist; Public Relations Specialist; Purchasing Agent; Reporter/Editor; Sales Representative; Systems Analyst; Technical Writer/Editor; Transportation and Traffic Specialist.

Principal educational backgrounds sought: Accounting; Business Administration; Communications; Computer Science; Engineering; Finance; Marketing.

Company benefits: Medical Insurance; Dental Insurance; Life Insurance; Tuition Assistance; Disability Coverage; Daycare Assistance; Profit Sharing; Employee Discounts; Savings Plan.

How they're growing/Recent developments: Amdahl expected to begin releasing of its next generation of mainframes in December, 1991. Prices will range from $3.2 million to $32.1 million, and revenues are predicted to advance strongly at that time, despite a competing new release from IBM. Employment has grown from an estimated 7,800 in 1987 to 9,500 in 1991.

AMERICAN BIODYNE
400 Oyster Point Boulevard
Suite 306
South San Francisco, California 94080
(415) 742-0980

Founded: 1985; **No. of Employees:** 425. **Revenues (1990):** $28 million. **Revenues (1986):** $3 million. **Five-Year Revenue Growth:** 833%.

Description: Provides mental health treatment programs.

How they're growing/Recent developments: In September, 1991, American Biodyne acquired Assured Health Systems, Inc., a vendor of employee assistance programs. American Biodyne's income for the year ending September 30, 1991 was $2.89 million. Employment has grown from an 60 in 1986 to 425 in 1990.

AMERICAN FRUCTOSE
250 Harbor Drive
Stamford, Connecticut 06904
(203) 356-9000

Founded: 1983. **No. of Employees:** 238. **Revenues (1990):** $196 million. **Revenues (1986):** $151 million. **Five-Year Revenue Growth:** 30%.

Description: Manufacturers of high fructose corn syrup.

How they're growing/Recent developments: The company's product is widely accepted as a sugar substitute in the food and soft drink industry. The recent expansion of a plant in Dimmitt, Texas, increased production by 29% Employment has grown from an estimated 217 in 1987 to 238 in 1990.

AMERICAN HOME PRODUCTS CORPORATION
685 Third Avenue
New York, New York 10017
(212) 878-5000

Founded: 1926; **No. of Employees:** 48,700. **Revenues (1990):** $6.8 billion. **Revenues (1986):** $5 billion. **Five-Year Revenue Growth:** 36%.

Description: A leading manufacturer of pharmaceuticals, over-the-counter medications, hospital supplies and food products. Well-known consumer products include: Anacin, Chap Stick, Chef Boyardee, Jiffy Pop, and Preparation H.

How they're growing/Recent developments: Sales have increased with the introduction of new products in the contraceptive line. American Home Products has also recently released Norplant, a groundbreaking birth control implant. In 1988, the company acquired A.H. Robbins, the makers of Robitussin, the foremost cough medicine in the United States, as well as Dimetapp. Employment has grown from an estimated 43,496 in 1987 to the current 48,700.

AMERICAN INTERNATIONAL GROUP
72 Wall, 6th Floor
New York, New York 10270
(212) 770-7000

Founded: 1967. **No. of Employees:** 34,000. **Revenues (1990):** $16 billion. **Revenues (1986):** $9 billion. **Five-Year Revenue Growth:** 77%.

Description: Operating in more than 130 countries, American International is one of the world's largest insurance organizations, providing property, casualty, marine, life, and financial guarantee insurance. The company also provides diversified financial services.

How they're growing/Recent developments: AIG's underwriting record has consistently been better than industry standard, largely because of the company's strict adherence to underwriting standards. At a time when most lines of commercial insurance have come under pricing pressures, AIG's leadership position in specialty lines and services has protected it from the cyclical nature of the property/casualty business. The company has also been expanding its Far East operations. Growth in financial services is due to the 1990 acquisition of International Lease Financing Corporation, an aircraft leasing concern. Employment has grown from an estimated 24,000 in 1987 to 34,000 in 1991.

AMERICAN MANAGEMENT SYSTEMS
1777 North Kent Street
Arlington, Virginia 22209
(703) 841-6000

Contact: Joanne Hoargan, Personnel. **Founded:** 1970. **No. of Employees:** 2,700. **Revenues (1990):** $279 million. **Revenues (1986):** $112 million. **Five-Year Revenue Growth:** 149%.

Description: The company is a developer of financial management and other administrative and systems software. Products are sold to the energy, telecommunications, financial, and insurance industries, and to institutions of higher learning and the government.

How they're growing/Recent developments: Exports account for up to 10% of sales. Net income for the quarter ending June 30, 1991, was $4.75 million. Employment has grown from an estimated 2,159 in 1987 to 2,700 in 1991.

AMERICAN MEDICAL ELECTRONICS
250 East Arapaho Road
Richardson, Texas 75081
(214) 918-8300

Founded: 1982. **No. of Employees:** 155. **Revenues (1990):** $19.5 million. **Revenues (1986):** $3.9 million. **Five-Year Revenue Growth:** 400%.

Description: A manufacturer of orthopedic medical devices.

How they're growing/Recent developments: Although the company was forced into bankruptcy back in 1987, it has emerged stronger than ever. In 1990, the company won FDA approval to market its Spinal-Stim unit, a non-invasive system for assisting the healing of spinal fusions. In July, 1991, the company received approval for its lightweight Physio-Stim product for treating hip fractures. Employment has grown from an estimated 22 in 1987 to 155 in 1991.

AMERICAN OIL AND GAS CORPORATION
333 Clay Street
Suite 2000
Houston, Texas 77002
(713) 739-2900

Founded: 1984. **No. of Employees:** 278. **Revenues (1990):** $441 million. **Revenues (1986):** $73 million. **Five-Year Revenue Growth:** 504%.

Description: Services oil and gas wells and transmits natural gas.

How they're growing/Recent developments: In November, 1989, American Oil and Gas expanded operations by acquiring Cabot Corporation, a gas pipeline business. The expansion will allow the company to market gas to West Coast, Midwest, and Northeast. Employment has grown from an estimated 24,000 in 1987 to 34,000 in 1991.

AMERICAN POWER CONVERSION
132 Fairgrounds Road
West Kingston, Rhode Island 02892
(401) 789-5735

Founded: 1981. **No. of Employees:** 477. **Revenues (1990):** $59 million. **Revenues (1986):** $2.5 million. **Four-Year Revenue Growth:** 2,260%.

Description: Manufactures uninterruptable computer power supply products that protect data in personal computers from disruptions caused by dips and/or surges in electrical power.

Common positions include: Customer Service Representative; Electrical Engineer; Mechanical Engineer; Sales Representative.

Principal educational background sought: Engineering

Company benefits: Medical Insurance; Dental Insurance; Tuition Assistance; Disability Coverage; Profit Sharing.

Operations at this facility: Manufacturing; Administration; Service; Sales.

How they're growing/Recent developments: American Power Conversion produces a product which virtually every company that uses computers and needs to protect data during power surges can use. In December 1990, the company was selected as a subcontractor to provide up to 42,000 UPS (uninterruptible power supply) units to defense installations, a contract that will provide up to $15 million over the next several years. Sales for the six months that ended in June, 1991, were up 50% over the same period of the previous year. The company was voted number 13 and 14 on *Forbes* magazine's 1990 and 1991 lists of the 200 best small companies in the United States.

AMERICAN PRECISION INDUSTRIES
2777 Walden Avenue
Buffalo, New York 14225
(716) 684-9700

Founded: 1946. **No. of Employees:** 646. **Revenues (1990):** $48 million. **Revenues (1986):** $34 million. **Five-Year Revenue Growth:** 41%.

Description: Manufactures industrial and electronic equipment.

How they're growing/Recent developments: Increased revenues have been generated from the company's industrial process equipment and electronics products. The company's products are used in a wide and varied number of applications, including telemarketing, aerospace, diagnostic medical equipment, and computers.

AMERICAN SOFTWARE
470 East Paces Ferry Road NE
Atlanta, Georgia 30305
(404) 261-4381

Contact: Ryan L. Lenox, Manager of Corporate Recruiting; **Founded:** 1970. **No. of Employees:** 830; **Revenues (1990):** $102 million; **Revenues (1986):** $38 million. **Five-Year Revenue Growth:** 168%.

Description: Develops, markets and supports applications software for use on mainframe and midframe IBM computers. The company's products consist of a variety of management systems, including forecasting, inventory management, purchasing and materials control, manufacturing resource planning and financial applications.

Common positions include: Accountant; Computer Programmer; Customer Service Representative; Marketing Specialist; Systems Analyst; Technical Writer/Editor; all data processing professionals.

Principal educational backgrounds sought: Accounting; Business Administration; Computer Science; Marketing; Mathematics.

Company benefits include: Medical insurance; dental insurance; life insurance; disability coverage; profit sharing; savings plan.

Operations at this facility include: Manufacturing; research and development; administration; service; sales.

How they're growing/Recent developments: The company's mainframe applications for IBM's ES/9000 series of mainframes are immediately available, and the company expects delivery during 1992 of a new warehouse management system. The fact that the company's mainframe software applications are compatible with IBM's DB2 database management system makes them even more attractive. The company is currently developing networks of sales agents throughout the Pacific Rim and Europe. Although the recession has dampened sales growth recently, sales picked up during the first quarter of the 1991-92 fiscal year. Employment has grown from an estimated 400 in 1987 to 830 in 1991.

AMGEN, INC.
1840 Dehavilland Drive
Thousand Oaks, California 91320
(805) 499-5725

Founded: 1980. **No. of Employees:** 1,400. **Revenues (1990):** $381 million. **Revenues (1986):** $30 million; **Five-Year Revenue Growth:** 1,170%.

Description: The nation's largest independent manufacturer of biotechnology products.

How they're growing/Recent developments: Amgen's rapid growth has been fueled by two new products -- Epogen and Neupogen -- that were created by using recombinant DNA, or gene-splicing. Epogen is used to treat anemia in renal dialysis patients and Neupogen is used to help produce white-blood cells in chemotherapy patients. The two products alone were expected to bring in at least $450 million in 1991. In addition, both products have recently won marketing approval in Europe. Amgen is currently involved in a joint research project with Regenon Pharmaceutical into the neurotropic factors which may be used to treat Alzheimer's and Lou Gehrig's diseases. Employment has grown from an estimated 260 in 1987 to 1,400 in 1991.

AMP, INC.
P.O. Box 3608
Harrisburg, Pennsylvania 17105-3608
(717) 564-0111

Founded: 1941. **No. of Employees:** 24,700. **Revenues (1990):** $3 billion. **Revenues (1986):** $1.9 billion. **Five-Year Revenue Growth:** 57%.

Description: The world's largest supplier of electrical and electronic connectors.

How they're growing/Recent developments: AMP is constantly developing new products -- over 20% of revenues are generated from products introduced since 1986. The company has poured money into developing fiber-optics technology and now has several products on the market. The company has also released cable and data communications products for LAN environments like Ethernet and IBM's Token Ring. Employment has grown from an estimated 22,000 in 1987 to 24,700 in 1991.

ANALYSTS INTERNATIONAL CORPORATION
7615 Metro Boulevard
Minneapolis, Minnesota 55439
(612) 835-2330

Founded: 1966. **No. of Employees:** 1,700. **Revenues (1990):** $108 million. **Revenues (1986):** $46.7 million. **Five-Year Revenue Growth:** 131%.

Description: Provides analytical and computer programming services to users and manufacturers of data processing equipment.

How they're growing/Recent developments: During 1990, Analysts International provided services to approximately 235 new clients and was engaged in approximately 2,200 projects, up from 1,900 in 1989. Recent clients include Federal Express and IBM, which accounted for more than 10% of the company's 1990 revenues. Employment has grown from an estimated 900 in 1987 to 1,700 in 1991.

ANTHEM ELECTRONICS
1040 East Brokaw Road
San Jose, California 95131
(408) 295-4200

Founded: 1968. **No. of Employees:** 582. **Revenues (1990):** $408 million. **Revenues (1986):** $149 million. **Five-Year Revenue Growth:** 174%.

Description: The sixth-largest distributor of semiconductors in the United States, with special emphasis on advanced technology products.

How they're growing/Recent developments: Although the recession has hurt Anthem's major markets, the company has continued to make major investments in training programs, operating systems and quality programs. Since May, 1991, Anthem has become an authorized distributor of Texas Instruments' semiconductor products throughout the United States. Anthem also recently began distributing Hewlett-Packard's disk mechanism products, as well as integrated circuits made by Dallas Semiconductor and Analog Devices. Employment has grown from an estimated 468 in 1987 to 582 in 1991.

APOGEE ENTERPRISES, INC.
7900 Xerxes Avenue South, Suite 1944
Minneapolis, Minnesota 55431
(612) 835-1874

Founded: 1949. **No. of Employees:** 5,377. **Revenues (1990):** $590 million. **Revenues (1986):** $250 million. **Five-Year Revenue Growth:** 136%.

Description: Apogee fabricates, distributes and installs energy-efficient window and glass products.

How they're growing/Recent developments: Apogee receives most of its revenues from the construction and automotive industries. In face of the national recession, annual revenue advances have slowed. Apogee expects, however, that its recent acquisition of Norment Industries, a leading detention and security systems integrator and contractor will spur continued growth. Employment has grown from an estimated 3,534 in 1987 to 5,377 in 1991.

APPLIED BIOSCIENCE INTERNATIONAL
Mettlers Road, Box 2360
East Millstone, New Jersey 08875
(908) 873-2550

Founded: 1986. **No. of Employees:** 1,300. **Revenues (1990):** $100 million. **Revenues (1986):** $26 million. **Five-Year Revenue Growth:** 285%.

Description: A broad-based research and development company that provides services to the pharmaceutical, agrochemical, chemical, and food industries. The company also offers environmental and risk management services.

How they're growing/Recent developments: In September, 1990, the company acquired Environ Corporation, through which it now provides chemical and environmental risk-assessment consulting. In July, 1991, Applied agreed to acquire Pharmaco Dynamics Research, a provider of contract clinical research and analytical chemistry. Pharmaco Dynamics had revenues of $30.5 million in fiscal year 1991. Employment has grown from an estimated 734 in 1987 to 1,300 in 1991.

APPLIED MATERIALS, INC.
3050 Bauer Street
Santa Clara, California 95054
(408) 727-5555

Founded: 1967. **No. of Employees:** 3,281. **Revenues (1990):** $567 million. **Revenues (1986):** $149 million. **Five-Year Revenue Growth:** 281%.

Description: Manufacturers of semiconductor wafer fabrication equipment. Products are sold to the computer, electronics and semiconductor industries. Systems are designed for chemical vapor deposition, dry plasma etching, epitaxial deposition, ion implantation and physical vapor deposition.

How they're growing/Recent developments: More than half of the company's revenues come from foreign sales. Sales for the nine months ending July, 28, 1991, increased 12% year to year. The company is one of the few remaining U.S. makers of semiconductor manufacturing equipment. Management plans to begin selling machines to produce ultra-thin PC screens, so-called thin-film transistors liquid crystal screens of LCDs. Employment grew 52% between 1989 and 1990. Employment has grown from an estimated 1,720 in 1987 to 3,281 in 1991.

ARCHER-DANIELS-MIDLAND COMPANY
4666 Faries Parkway, P.O. Box 1470
Decatur, Illinois 62525
(217) 424-5200

Founded: 1923. **No. of Employees:** 11,861. **Revenues (1990):** $7.751 billion. **Revenues (1986):** $5.336 billion. **Five-Year Revenue Growth:** 45%.

Description: A major processor, transporter, and marketer of agricultural products.

How they're growing/Recent developments: ADM is geared to play a growing role in the newly opening markets of Russia and the other Commonwealth of Independent States nations. ADM already has gained a major market role in Eastern Europe, with its 1990 acquisition of a 50% stake in Alfred C. Toepfer International. The company's other recent acquisitions include Collingwood Grain and Pfizer's Citric Acid division. Employment has grown from an estimated 4,875 in 1987 to 11,861 in 1991.

ARCHIVE CORPORATION
1650 Sunflower Avenue
Costa Mesa, California 92626
(714) 641-0279

Founded: 1980. **No. of Employees:** 3,367. **Revenues (1990):** $293 million. **Revenues (1986):** $79 million. **Five-Year Revenue Growth:** 271%.

Description: A leading manufacturer of data storage products used with PCs, workstations, multi-user systems, and mainframes.

How they're growing/Recent developments: Archive has expanded recently through the acquisitions of Maynard Electronics in 1989, and Cipher Data Products in 1990. Demand for Archive's products is up from both original equipment manufacturers and distributors. Employment has grown from an estimated 800 in 1987 to 3,367 in 1991.

ARCTIC ALASKA FISHERIES
P.O. Box 79021
Seattle, Washington 98199
(206) 282-3445

Contact: Kate Gaiser, Human Resources. **Founded:** 1987. **No. of Employees:** 850. **Revenues (1990):** $180 million. **Revenues (1988):** $121 million. **Five-Year Revenue Growth:** 49%.

Description: Operates the largest U.S.-owned catching and at-sea processing fleet in the North Pacific.

How they're growing/Recent developments: Arctic Alaska has benefitted from federal legislation encouraging development of the North Pacific's food resources by U.S. fishermen. In addition, September, 1989, saw the Japanese firm Nippon Suisan Kaisha Ltd. purchase 12% of Arctic Alaska, thus opening up the Japanese seafood market to the company. Income for the quarter ending June 30, 1991, was $4.01 million

ARTISOFT INC.
575 East River Road
Artisoft Plaza
Tuscon, Arizona 85704
(602) 293-6363

Contact: Ms. Margaret Bundy, Human Resources Manager. **Founded:** 1982. **No. of Employees:** 138. **Revenues (1990):** $41 million. **Revenues (1986):** $2 million. **Five-Year Revenue Growth:** 1,950%.

Description: A manufacturer of hardware and software for local area network communications, including operating systems, LAN software, network management software adapters and boards.

How they're growing/Recent developments: The company completed an initial public offering of stock in September, 1991. The company's strategy is to emphasize distribution contracts with large national, regional, and international computer equipment and software distribution companies. Employment has grown from an estimated 5 employees in 1987 to 138 in 1991.

ARTISTIC GREETINGS
One Komer Center
Elmira, New York 14901
(607) 733-5541

Founded: 1972. **No. of Employees:** 400. **Revenues (1990):** $44 million. **Revenues (1987):** $11 million. **Four-Year Revenue Growth:** 300%.

Description: A marketer of proprietary personalized products through direct mail advertising.

How they're growing/Recent developments: Revenues have advanced through increased sales of personalized products in co-op advertising, free-standing programs and catalog markets. Margins have also improved due to a greater concentration of direct mail sales, more effective labor management and lower postal expenses. In 1986, the company signed a licensing agreement with King Features Syndicate, Inc. to market personalized products which feature cartoon and comic strip characters such as Betty Boop, Popeye, and Felix the Cat. Employment has grown from an estimated 175 in 1987 to 400 in 1991.

ART'S-WAY MANUFACTURING COMPANY
Highway 9W
Armstrong, Iowa 50514
(712) 864-3131

Founded: 1956. **No. of Employees:** 228. **Revenues (1990):** $19 million. **Revenues (1986):** $10 million. **Five-Year Revenue Growth:** 90%.

Description: Manufacturers of farm and industrial machinery under its own and private labels. A subsidiary provides motor freight transportation, mainly for the company's own products.

How they're growing/Recent developments: Art's-Way has benefitted from improving production efficiency. The company has also recently expanded its engineering department. Employment has grown from an estimated 150 in 1987 to 228 in 1991.

ASSOCIATED NATURAL GAS COMPANY
900 Republic Plaza
370 17th Street
Denver, Colorado 80202
(303) 595-3331

Founded: 1983. **No. of Employees:** 360. **Revenues (1990):** $395 million. **Revenues (1986):** $51 million. **Five-Year Revenue Growth:** 675%.

Description: Company produces, transmits and distributes natural gas and mixed natural and manufactured gas. Also produces crude oil.

How they're growing/Recent developments: The company has expanded operations significantly through acquisitions. In April, 1991, Associated Natural Gas acquired a natural gas gathering and marketing company, which increased the miles of pipeline owned by 33% and doubled natural gas volume. Employment has grown from an estimated 214 in 1987 to 360 in 1991.

AST RESEARCH
16215 Alton Parkway
P.O. Box 19658
Irvine, California 92713-9658
(714) 727-4141

Founded: 1980. **No. of Employees:** 2,312. **Revenues (1990):** $534 million. **Revenues (1986):** $172 million. **Five-Year Revenue Growth:** 210%.

Description: The manufacturer of high-performance desktop computers, AST also sells memory enhancement and data communications products.

How they're growing/Recent developments: Revenues for fiscal year 1991 rose to $689 million and revenues for fiscal year 1992 are projected to advance another 25%, largely through increased sales of its notebook computer system, which was priced significantly below its competition. Employment has grown from an estimated 1,358 in 1987 to 2,312 in 1991.

ASTRO-MED, INC.
60 East Greenwich Avenue
Astro-Med Industrial Park
West Warwick, Rhode Island 02893
(401) 828-4000

Founded: 1969. **No. of Employees:** 230. **Revenues (1990):** $29 million. **Revenues (1986):** $11 million. **Five-Year Revenue Growth:** 164%.

Description: Manufacturers of specialty high-speed graphic recording systems used by the aerospace, medical, telecommunications and educational industries, among others.

How they're growing/Recent developments: During the past several years, Astro-Med's revenues have jumped sharply, spurred by the sales of new products. One of the most recent is the Dash 8, the world's first eight-channel field recorder capable of operating from an internal battery pack. Employment has grown from an estimated 200 in 1987 to 230 in 1991.

ATLANTIC SOUTHEAST AIR
1688 Phoenix Parkway
College Park, Georgia 30349
(404) 996-4662

Founded: 1979. **No. of Employees:** 1,577. **Revenues (1990):** $187.2 million. **Revenues (1986):** $92.3 million. **Five-Year Revenue Growth:** 103%.

Description: A regional air carrier providing regular service from hubs in Atlanta and Dallas/Ft. Worth. The airline has been part of the Delta Connection marketing program since 1984.

How they're growing/Recent developments: During the first seven months of 1991, paying passengers increased their travel miles on the airline by 17% over the same period of 1990. In addition, the airline is continuing to expand its fleet --- further increasing its passenger capacity. Employment has grown from an estimated 1,200 in 1987 to 1,577 in 1991.

AUTOCLAVE ENGINEERS
Fred Gasche Building
2901 West 22nd Street
P.O. Box 5051
Erie, Pennslyvania 16512-5051
(814) 838-5700

Founded: 1958. **No. of Employees:** 691. **Revenues (1990):** $85 million. **Revenues (1986):** $35 million. **Five-Year Revenue Growth:** 143%.

Description: Producer of equipment capable of withstanding extreme temperature and pressure, used in industrial research and production, materials forming, gas compression, defense applications and semiconductor production.

How they're growing/Recent developments: Although the recession has slowed Autoclave's growth, the company moved to make several cost-cutting measures to increase overall profitability.

AUTODESK, INC.
2320 Marinship Way
Sausalito CA 94965
(415) 332-2344

Contact: Kimberley C. Young, Director of Personnel. **Founded:** 1982. **No. of Employees:** 1,200. **Revenues (1990):** $267 million. **Revenues (1987):** $79 million. **Five-Year Revenue Growth:** 238%.

Description: Develops, markets, and supports a line of computer-aided design (CAD) software products for desktop computers and workstations.

Common positions include: Computer Programmer; Marketing Specialist; Quality Control Supervisor; Sales Representative; Systems Analyst; Technical Writer/Editor.

Principal educational backgrounds sought: Computer Science.

Company benefits include: Medical, dental, and life insurance; pension plan; tuition assistance; disability coverage; profit sharing; employee discounts; savings plan; stock option plan.

How they're growing/Recent developments: The company's primary software package is AutoCAD, which has experienced strong sales. The company plans to support the Windows operating environment and will thus be releasing an extension kit for AutoCAD that will allow customers to run AutoCAD on DOS, under Windows or in both. Employment grew 53% from 1989 to 1990.

AUTOMATIC DATA PROCESSING, INC.
One ADP Boulevard
Roseland, New Jersey 07068
(201) 994-5000

Founded: 1949. **No. of Employees:** 19,000. **Revenues (1990):** $1.7 billion. **Revenues (1986):** $1.2 billion. **Five-Year Revenue Growth:** 42%.

Description: The largest independent computing services firm in the United States, offering a wide range of data processing services.

How they're growing/Recent developments: During 1991, the employer services division of the company continued double-digit revenue growth -- with both payroll processing and tax filing services contributing strongly. The company also plans on expanding its automotive dealer and automobile collision repair services.

BABBAGES
10741 King William Drive
Dallas, Texas 75220
(214) 401-9000

Founded: 1983. **No. of Employees:** 1,300. **Revenues (1990):** $95 million. **Revenues (1986):** $5 million. **Five-Year Revenue Growth:** 1,800%.

Description: Operates 187 retail mall stores specializing in the sale of software for home computers.

How they're growing/Recent developments: Sales for fiscal year 1991 soared to $133 million, based largely upon the strong demand for video game software and systems. Leading the way have been Sega's Genesis, NEC's Turbografx 16 and Nintendo's Game Boy. Babbage's opened 19 stores in 1990-91 and plans to open another 20 in 1991-92. The company has succeeded by always offering up-to-date software and minimizing inventory investment.

MICHAEL BAKER
4301 Dutch Ridge Road, P.O. Box 280
Beaver, Pennsylvania 15009
(412) 495-7711

Founded: 1946. **No. of Employees:** 2,071. **Revenues (1990):** $127 million. **Revenues (1986):** $50 million. **Five-Year Revenue Growth:** 154%.

Description: An engineering services firm.

How they're growing/Recent developments: Michael Baker's revenues have climbed due to the acquisition of MO, Inc., a provider of offshore oil and gas platform maintenance services. In August, 1990, the company established a new subsidiary in Frankfurt, Germany, which will serve the company's interest in Europe. In more recent developments, the company received a $13 million contract in 1991 from the U.S. Navy contracts to renovate barracks, as well as a $100 million Navy contract for environmental cleanup services.

BALDWIN TECHNOLOGY
401 Shippan Avenue
Stamford, Connecticut 06904
(203) 348-4400

Founded: 1918. **No. of Employees:** 1,400. **Revenues (1990):** $183 million. **Revenues (1986):** $61 million. **Five-Year Revenue Growth:** 200%.

Description: The world's leading manufacturer of controls, instruments and accessory equipment for printing presses, with plants across North America, Europe and Asia.

How they're growing/Recent developments: Baldwin's sales have continued to rise, and the company continues to pursue an active acquisitions policy. In 1989, Baldwin acquired Ohio-based SPM, Inc., and established new subsidiaries in Hong Kong and Beijing, China. In 1990, the company acquired two subsidiaries of the Dyson-Kissner-Moran Co. Employment has grown from an estimated 571 in 1987 to 1,400 in 1991.

BALLARD MEDICAL PRODUCTS
12050 South Lone Peak Parkway
Draper, Utah 84020
(801) 572-6800

Founded: 1978. **No. of Employees:** 331. **Revenues (1990):** $29 million. **Revenues (1986):** $10 million. **Five-Year Revenue Growth:** 190%.

Description: Manufacturers of disposable medical products.

How they're growing/Recent developments: Ballard's products are meeting increased acceptance in the health care industry. New products in the respiratory and critical care area have done especially well. Employment has grown from an estimated 220 in 1987 to 331 in 1991.

BANCTEC, INC.
4435 Spring Valley Road
Dallas, Texas 75244
(214) 450-7700

Founded: 1979. **No. of Employees:** 1,810. **Revenues (1990):** $186 million. **Revenues (1986):** $76 million. **Five-Year Revenue Growth:** 145%.

Description: BancTec manufactures computerized systems for processing documents, including checks, remittance advices and sales drafts.

How they're growing/Recent developments: BancTec recently received about $18 million in orders from Bankgiro of Sweden, the Royal Bank of Canada and SSBA, a Dallas-based credit-card processor. Employment has grown from an estimated 950 in 1987 to 1,810 in 1991.

BANDAG, INC.
2905 North Highway 61
Muscatine, Iowa 52761-5886
(319) 262-1400

Founded: 1957. **No. of Employees:** 2,411. **Revenues (1990):** $586 million. **Revenues (1986):** $370 million. **Five-Year Revenue Growth:** 58%.

Description: The world's leading manufacturer of retread rubber tires for trucks and buses. Bandag serves over 1,000 franchised dealers in the United States and overseas.

How they're growing/Recent developments: Bandag has plans to expand its tread rubber capacity by 25% by increasing capacity at the Muscatine plant and opening a new plant in Griffin, Georgia. In addition, the company's foreign sales are expanding. Employment has grown from an estimated 2,113 in 1987 to 2,411 in 1991.

BANYAN SYSTEMS
115 Flanders Road
Westboro, Massachusetts 01581
(508) 898-1000

Founded: 1983. **No. of Employees:** 595. **Revenues (1990):** $98 million.
Revenues (1986): $10 million. **Five-Year Revenue Growth:** 880%.

Description: Company manufactures network file servers in pedestal and desktop form.

How they're growing/Recent developments: Banyan Systems is the developer of the Unix-based network operating system software which is used with the file servers and IBM ATs or IBM clones. In February, 1991, the company formalized a joint development, distribution and marketing agreement for LAN hardware and software with AT&T. The company's VINES (Virtual Networking Systems) offers unique features, although it has 7.5% share of LAN server operating systems, due to competition with larger, better known companies. Revenues have grown at an average of annually 107% since 1985, posting 17 straight profitable quarters. The company plan is to increase market share, by spending up to as much as 40% of revenues on marketing and sales. Employment has grown from an estimated 111 in 1987 to 585 in 1991.

C.R. BARD, INC.
730 Central Avenue
Murray Hill, New Jersey 07974
(908) 277-8000

Founded: 1972. **No. of Employees:** 8,750. **Revenues (1990):** $785 million.
Revenues (1986): $548 million. **Five-Year Revenue Growth:** 42%.

Description: Manufactures and markets disposable medical, surgical, diagnostic and patient care products.

How they're growing/Recent developments: The Food and Drug Administration recently gave approval to Bard's Probe III catheter. Research and development funds are being spent on a new PET balloon technology using laser technology, and on a joint project with Collegen Corporation aimed at the development of a treatment product for urinary incontinence. Employment has grown from an estimated 6,360 in 1987 to 8,550 in 1991.

BEMIS CORPORATION
625 Marquette Avenue
Minneapolis, Minnesota 55402
(612) 340-6000

Contact: Lawrence Schwanke, Vice President, Human Resources. **Founded:** 1885. **No. of Employees:** 7,950. **Revenues (1990):** $1.128 billion. **Revenues (1986):** $865 million. **Five-Year Revenue Growth:** 30%.

Description: Bemis manufactures a wide range of consumer and indstrial packaging materials, packaging machinery, and industrial products.

How they're growing/Recent developments: Bemis should continue to grow over the long-term, with management emphasizing increased production of specialty films for food packaging and also pressure-sensitive materials. In October, 1990, Bemis acquired Milprint, Inc., a Milwaukee based manufacturer of flexible packaging materials, further extending Bemis' dominance of that market. Milprint's annual sales were approximately $70 million. Bemis' sales for the six months ending June 30, 1991, rose 2.3 percent. Employment rose by about 425 jobs between 1990 and 1991.

BEN & JERRY'S HOMEMADE, INC.
Duxtown Common Plaza
N. Moretown, Vermont 05660
(802) 244-6957

Founded: 1977. **No. of Employees:** 326. **Revenues (1990):** $77 million. **Revenues (1986):** $31.8 million. **Five-Year Revenue Growth:** 142%.

Description: Producers of premium ice cream, in both traditional and unusual flavors, as well as dairy products and frozen foods.

How they're growing/Recent developments: The year 1991 began slowly for Ben & Jerry's, but things have since taken off, with stock advancing 86% over the course of the year. Their newest flavor, Chocolate Chip Cookie Dough, has become the company's number one seller; Ben & Jerry's frozen yogurt has done very well in limited markets and was expected to be released nationwide by the end of 1991. Employment has grown from an estimated 300 in 1987 to 326 in 1991.

BERKSHIRE HATHAWAY
1440 Kiewit Plaza
Omaha, Nebraska 68131
(402) 346-1400

Founded: 1889. **No. of Employees:** 3,000. **Revenues (1990):** $2.5 billion. **Revenues (1986):** $940 million. **Five-Year Revenue Growth:** 166%.

Description: A diversified Fortune 500 corporation. Operations include uniform manufacturing, encyclopedia and newspaper publishing, home cleaning systems, candy manufacturing and sale, insurance and savings and loan, and several high tech operating units involved in the subassembly and test and measurement industries.

How they're growing/Recent developments: Berkshire is headed by Warren Buffet, a renowned investor, who recently took an interim position at Salomon Bros., when that company's management team resigned under fire after a bond-dealing scandal. During the past several years, Berkshire has continued to carefully buy stakes in growing companies, and has sold its stakes in less profitable performers. In 1986, the company sold its shares in the *Boston Globe* and bought sole ownership of Scott Fetzer, publishers of *World Book* encyclopedias. The company has also assisted several companies threatened by hostile takeover, Salomon Bros. included.

BERNE GROUP
555 IH 35 West, Suite 300
New Braunfels, TX 78130
(512) 629-7924

Founded: 1985. **No. of Employees:** 1,000. **Revenues (1990):** $22 million. **Revenues (1986):** $1 million. **Five-Year Revenue Growth:** 2,100%.

Description: Owns and operates fast-food restaurants.

BERTUCCI'S
60 Cummings Park
Woburn, Massachusetts 01801
(617) 935-9700

Founded: 1981. **No. of Employees:** 1,700. **Revenues (1990):** $29 million. **Revenues (1986):** $3.7 million. **Five-Year Revenue Growth:** 684%.

Description: A chain of Italian-style gourmet pizza restaurants.

How they're growing/Recent developments: Bertucci's reported a 112% gain in revenue in the second quarter of 1991. Since the company successfully went public in July, Bertucci's has cut expenses and food costs. Expansion plans call for the company to expand by about 25% annually. During 1991, Bertucci's expanded into Connecticut, and is looking into expansion into New Jersey, Philadelphia, and possibly New York City.

BINDLEY WESTERN INDUSTRIES, INC.
4212 West 71st Street
Indianapolis, Indiana 46268
(317) 298-9900

Founded: 1968. **No. of Employees:** 406. **Revenues (1990):** $2.04 billion. **Revenues (1986):** $711 million. **Five-Year Revenue Growth:** 187%.

Description: One of the largest wholesale distributors of pharmaceuticals, health products, and beauty aids in the United States. As a full service distributor, Bindley supplies a broad customer base including chain drug companies operating their own warehouses, independent drug stores, chain drug stores, hospitals, clinics and health care providers. The company distributes products to customers in 39 states from 11 regional centers geographically positioned throughout the United States.

How they're growing/Recent developments: Bindley is now the fifth-largest wholesale drug distributor in the United States and the second largest distributor in chain warehousing volume. The company has recorded 22 straight years of record sales, with a compound growth rate above 20% since its inception in 1968. A changing customer mix is adding to profit margins and creating additional opportunities for growth. The company has long been considered one of the most efficient distributors in the industry, with sales per employee three times the industry average. A $12 million expansion program that tripled warehouse space and enhanced ordering systems will allow the company to grow to $3 billion in sales without significant additions to capital spending.

BIOMET
P.O. Box 587
Warsaw, Indiana 46581-0587
(219) 267-6639

Founded: 1977. **No. of Employees:** 773. **Revenues (1991):** $210 million. **Revenues (1986):** $44 million. **Five-Year Revenue Growth:** 377%.

Description: Biomet and its subsidiaries design, manufacture, and market products used primarily by orthopedic medical specialists in both surgical and non-surgical therapy, including reconstructive and trauma devices, electrical bone growth and neuromuscular stimulators, orthopedic support devices, operating room supplies, powered surgical instruments and arthroscopy products.

Common positions include: Accountant; Computer Programmer; Biomedical Engineer; Mechanical Engineer; Metallurgical Engineer; CVC Machinist; Orthopedic Polisher.

Principal educational backgrounds sought: Accounting; Computer Science; Engineering; Marketing.

Company benefits: Medical Insurance; Life Insurance; Disability Coverage; Savings Plan; 401K; Employee Stock Bonus Plan.

Operations at this facility include: Divisional Headquarters; Manufacturing; Research/Development; Administration; Service; Sales.

How they're growing/Recent developments: Increased revenues have come in part from the success of the company's reconstructive and electrical stimulation devices. Employment grew 39% from 1989 to 1990.

BIO-RAD LABORATORIES
1000 Alfred Nobel Drive
Hercules, California 94547
(510) 724-7000

Contact: Joseph M. Hardy, Manager, Employment Support. **Founded:** 1957. **No. of Employees:** 2,300. **Revenues (1990):** $286.7 million. **Revenues (1986):** $126.6 million. **Five-Year Revenue Growth:** 126%.

Description: Company produces life sciences products, clinical diagnostics, and analytical instruments for materials and biological research. American Stock Exchange.

Common positions include: Biochemist; Biologist; Chemist; Chemical Engineer; Electrical Engineer; Mechanical Engineer; Medical Technologist.

Principal educational backgrounds sought: Biology; Chemistry; Engineering.

Company benefits: Medical Insurance; Dental Insurance; Life Insurance; Tuition Assistance; Disability Coverage; Profit Sharing; Employee Discounts; Savings Plan; Stock Purchase Plan.

Operations at this facility: Regional Headquarters; Divisional Headquarters; Manufacturing; Research/Development; Administration; Service; Sales.

How they're growing/Recent developments: Bio-Rad established record growth in 1990. In May, 1991, the company signed a licensing agreement with Dupont, giving Bio-Rad exclusive rights to Biolistics, whose applications include production of disease-and-insect resistant crops. The company's continued commitment to new product development has fueled an average annual growth of 23% for the company's 34-year history. Employment has grown from an estimated 1,400 in 1987 to 2,300 in 1991.

BIRMINGHAM STEEL CORPORATION
P.O. Box 1208
Birmingham, Alabama 35201
(205) 985-9290

Founded: 1983. **No. of Employees:** 177. **Revenues (1990):** $433 million. **Revenues (1986):** $152 million. **Five-Year Revenue Growth:** 185%.

Description: Birmingham Steel operates mini-mills in the United States that produce steel reinforced bar -- or rebar -- used in the construction industry and merchant products that are sold to fabricators. The company also markets roof support systems for use in coal mines.

How they're growing/Recent developments: Sales are expected to rise in 1992, although that forecast relies on an upturn in the national economy as a whole. Sales will be aided by contributions from subsidiary Seattle Steel and the recovery of the company's mine roof products.

H&R BLOCK
4410 Main Street
Kansas City Missouri 64111
(816) 753-6900

Founded: 1946. **No. of Employees:** 81,000. **Revenues (1990):** $1.2 billion. **Revenues (1986):** $687 million. **Five-Year Revenue Growth:** 75%.

Description: Operators and franchisors of over 8,000 tax preparation offices in the U.S. and abroad. One of the company's subsidiaries, Personnel Pool of America, supplies supplemental clerical, medical, legal, industrial and food franchise personnel through owned and franchised offices in the United States, Canada and Puerto Rico. Another is CompuServ, which engages in information processing and provides specialized computer programs to individuals and businesses.

How they're growing/Recent developments: Ironically, the company's growth was spurred by the 1986 "tax simplification," when the company's clientele actually increased. The company's aggressive expansion into other services, including personnel and computer services has also spurred revenues. CompuServ itself has taken an aggressive acquisitions stance by buying its longtime competitor The Source, as well as MicroSolutions, a vendor of computer connectivity products.

BLOCKBUSTER ENTERTAINMENT
901 East Los Olas Boulevard
Fort Lauderdale, Florida 33301
(305) 524-8200

Founded: 1985. **No. of Employees:** 9,000. **Revenues (1990):** $633 million. **Revenues (1986):** $8 million. **Five-Year Revenue Growth:** 7,812%.

Description: Operators and franchisors of a national chain of 1,943 video stores.

How they're growing/Recent developments: Blockbuster's experienced management team is led by CEO Wayne Huizenga, who previously built the fast-growing Waste Management. Huizenga is now considered one of the most powerful figures in the entertainment industry, which shouldn't be surprising -- Blockbuster currently rents about a million tapes a day. The company is continuing to expand through acquisitions. Although video rentals fell off sharply early in 1991 because of the Gulf War, Blockbuster acquired Erol's that same year. Employment has grown from an estimated 1,500 in 1987 to 9,000 in 1991.

BMC SOFTWARE
P.O. Box 2002
Sugarland, Texas 77487
(713) 240-8800

Founded: 1980. **No. of Employees:** 640. **Revenues (1990):** $93 million. **Revenues (1986):** $42 million. **Five-Year Revenue Growth:** 121%.

Description: Manufacturers of computer software.

How they're growing/Recent developments: Revenues have been enhanced by some of BMC's new products, including Recovery Plus and LoadPlus. Enhancements of other products and extremely strong international sales growth have also boosted company fortunes.

THE BOEING COMPANY
7755 East Marginal Way South
Seattle, Washington 98108
(206) 655-2121

Founded: 1916. **No. of Employees:** 160,500. **Revenues (1990):** $27.6 billion. **Revenues (1986):** $16.3 billion. **Five-Year Revenue Growth:** 69%.

Description: A diversified aerospace company that designs and manufactures commercial and military aircraft, missiles, helicopters, spare parts, and related products.

How they're growing/Recent developments: Boeing is the nation's number one exporter, with almost 60% of revenues generated from overseas sales. The company also boasts a backlog of orders for over $100 million. The company's new 777 model plane should generate even greater revenues when it is delivered in 1995. Employment has grown from an estimated 127,294 in 1987 to 160,500 in 1991.

BOHDAN ASSOCIATES, INC.

220 Girard Street, Caller 6004
Gaithersburg, Maryland 20884
(301) 258-2965

Founded: 1984. **No. of Employees:** 155. **Revenues (1990):** $91 million. **Revenues (1986):** $9.7 million. **Five-Year Revenue Growth:** 838%.

Description: Providers of computer systems integration services and consulting services. Bohdan specializes in integrating desktop publishing and networking systems.

How they're growing/Recent developments: Employment has grown from an estimated 31 in 1987 to 155 in 1991. Employment grew about 15% between 1989 and 1990 alone.

BOLT BERANEK & NEWMAN
70 Fawcett Street
Cambridge, Massachusetts 02138
(617) 873-2000

Contact: Manager of Human Resources. **Founded:** 1948. **No. of Employees:** 2,900. **Revenues (1990):** $262 million. **Revenues (1986):** $178 million. **Five-Year Revenue Growth:** 47%.

Description: A diversified high-technology company, Bolt, Beranek & Newman, conducts its business through wholly owned products and services subsidiaries. They include: BBN Communications Corporation, which is a leading supplier of private, wide area network systems; BBN Software Products Corporation, which develops, markets, and distributes integrated statistical data analysis software products sold primarily for applications in manufacturing, engineering, and research and development; BBN Advanced Computers, Inc., which develops and markets high-performance applications in industry and research; and BBN Systems and Technology Corporation, which is a leader in acoustics and computer information, specializing in architectural acoustics and environmental technologies, physical sciences, and graphic technology.

How they're growing/Recent developments: For the quarter ending September 30, 1990, BBN's income rose to $5.2 million, after the company suffered a $3.1 million loss in 1989. The turnaround can be attributed to a major equipment sale to Delta Airlines, which netted $4.7 million, as well as to improved profit margins. The communications division was boosted by a contract with the Defense Communications Agency, and the advanced computers division sold two TC2000 parallel computer systems to aerospace and defense companies. In the short run, sales of these systems may be dampened due to the economy, and the advanced computer division has recently undergone a downsizing. Employment has grown from an estimated 2,800 in 1987 to 2,900 in 1991.

BORDEN, INC.
277 Park Avenue
New York, New York 10172
(212) 573-4000

Contact: Carl Braun, Manager of Professional Staffing. **Founded:** 1899. **No. of Employees:** 46,300. **Revenues (1990):** $7.6 billion. **Revenues (1986):** $5 billion. **Five-Year Revenue Growth:** 52%.

Description: A diversified food company, well-known as the largest producer of dairy and pasta products in the country. The company also produces specialty chemical products like Elmer's Glue and Wall-Tex wallcoverings. New York Stock Exchange.

Common positions include: Accountant; Chemist; Computer Programmer; Credit Manager; Financial Analyst; Food Technologist; Operations/Production Manager; Marketing Specialist; Personnel and Labor Relations Specialist.

Principal educational backgrounds sought: Accounting; Biology; Business Administration; Computer Science; Finance; Liberal Arts.

Company benefits: Medical Insurance; Dental Insurance; Pension Plan; Life Insurance; Disability Coverage; Employee Discounts; Savings Plans.

Operations at this facility: Regional Headquarters; Divisional Headquarters; Research/Development; Administration; Sales.

How they're growing/Recent developments: Borden is essentially a combination of a large number of regional brands, and, since 1986, the company has emphasized acquisitions of small to medium-sized companies. Borden is also growing increasingly strong in the snack market, with products like Wise and New York Deli potato chips and Cracker Jacks, and is now second in the market behind only Pepsico-owned Frito-Lay. Employment has grown from an estimated 39,400 in 1987 to 40,300 in 1991.

BORLAND INTERNATIONAL, INC.
1800 Green Hills Road
Scotts Valley, California 95066
(408) 438-8400

Founded: 1982. **No. of Employees:** 986. **Revenues (1990):** $227 million. **Revenues (1966):** $29 million. **Five-Year Revenue Growth:** 683%.

Description: Borland is the number one maker of database software in the world, and the third-largest maker of PC software.

How they're growing/Recent developments: In 1991, Borland doubled its size by buying rival Ashton-Tate. Paradox, the company's most successful software, now has 35% of that market, and is growing into the corporate world's first choice for software. Borland plans to continue to produce new products, such as Window versions of Paradox and Quatro Pro.

BOSTON ACOUSTICS INC.
70 Broadway
Lynnfield, Masshachusetts 01940
(617)592-9000

Founded: 1979. **No. of Employees:** 174. **Revenues (1990):** $26 million. **Revenues (1988):** $17 million. **Three-Year Revenue Growth:** 53%.

Description: Engineers, manufactures and markets moderately priced, high-quality loudspeaker systems for the home and automotive audio and video entertainment market.

How they're growing/Recent developments: Revenues have been enhanced by a growing product line and the increased profitability of individual products. Employment has grown from an estimated 150 in 1987 to 174 in 1991.

BRAJDAS
P.O. Box 58196
Santa Clara, California 95052
(408) 987-0350

Founded: 1979. **No. of Employees:** 240. **Revenues (1990):** $59 million. **Revenues (1986):** $19 million. **Five-Year Revenue Growth:** 211%.

Description: A wholesale distributor of electromechanical devices.

How they're growing/Recent developments: Brajdas more than tripled its revenues between 1986 and 1989, but due to the severe slump in the electronics industry, revenues have been slumping of late. In response, the company has phased out its line of semiconductors and begun to reduce its product line. In July, 1991, Brajdas reached agreement in principle to acquire three electronics procurement concerns. In return, these three concerns would be given control of 49% of Brajdas. The new combination was projected at the time to realize annual revenues of over $100 million. Employment has grown from an estimated 170 in 1987 to 240 in 1991.

BRIDGFORD FOODS
1308 North Patt Street
Anaheim, California 92801
(714) 526-5533

Founded: 1932. **No. of Employees:** 575. **Revenues (1991):** $92.9 million. **Revenues (1986):** $54 million. **Six-Year Revenue Growth:** 72%.

Description: Bridgford Foods and its subsidiaries are engaged in the manufacture and distribution of refrigerated, frozen and snack food products. Principal products include a variety of sliced luncheon meats and cheese items, weiners, bacon, fresh meats, dry sausages, biscuits, bread and roll dough items and sandwiches.

Common positions include: Accountant; Blue-Collar Worker Supervisor; Computer Programmer; Credit Manager; Customer Service Representative; Dietician; Food Technologist; Operations/Production Manager; Quality Control Supervisor; Sales Representative; Systems Analyst; Transportation and Traffic Specialist.

Principal educational backgrounds sought: Business Administration; Communications; Computer Science; Marketing.

Company benefits: Medical Insurance; Dental Insurance; Pension Plan; Life Insurance.

Operations at this facility: Regional Headquarters; Manufacturing; Research/ Development; Administration; Service; Sales.

How they're growing/Recent developments: Sales for the 12 months that ended November 1, 1991, rose 10% over the same period of 1990. Employment has grown from an estimated 450 in 1987 to 575 in 1991.

BRINKER INTERNATIONAL
6820 LBJ Freeway
Suite 200
Dallas, Texas 75240
(214) 980-9917

Founded: 1983. **No. of Employees:** 7,200. **Revenues (1990):** $347 million. **Revenues (1986):** $107 million. **Five-Year Revenue Growth:** 224%.

Description: This fast-growing restaurant chain was formerly Chili's, Inc., after the Chili's Bar and Grill restaurant chain that it operates. In May, 1991, the company was renamed (after chairman Norman Brinker). The name change reflects the company's ownership of two other smaller restaurant franchises.

How they're growing/Recent developments: In March, 1991, Brinker completed a public stock offering, with net proceeds targeted for the expanding of Romano Macaroni Grill, which was acquired in 1989, for increasing the percentage of owned versus leased restaurants; and for retiring bank debt.

BRISTOL-MEYERS SQUIBB COMPANY
345 Park Avenue
New York, New York 10154
(212) 546-4000

Founded: 1858. **No. of Employees:** 52,900. **Revenues (1990):** $10.3 billion. **Revenues (1986):** $4.8 billion. **Five-Year Revenue Growth:** 114%.

Description: The world's second-largest pharmaceuticals and consumer products firm. Well-known consumer products include Bufferin, Excedrin, Ultress hair coloring, Renuzit, and Drano, among others.

How they're growing/Recent developments: The 1989 merger between Squibb and Bristol-Meyers has created a giant, and Squibb's strength in blood pressure and cholesterol control products is a good match with Bristol-Meyers' antidepressant, anticancer, anti-AIDS, antibiotics and antiviral drugs. A new cholesterol-lowering drug is awaiting FDA approval, and should boost revenue growth even further.

BRITEVOICE SYSTEMS
7309 East 21st Street North
Wichita, Kansas 67206-1083
(316) 652-6500

Founded: 1984. **No. of Employees:** 195. **Revenues (1990):** $12 million. **Revenues (1986):** $900 thousand. **Five-Year Revenue Growth:** 1,233%.

Description: Manufactures voice response and audiotex systems that allow businesses to offer the public direct access to computer-stored data via touchtone telephones.

How they're growing/Recent developments: In May, 1991, the company acquired Feranti International's Voice Systems Group, one of Europe's leading voice messaging companies. In addition, the company completed major sales of its Gateway 5000 system to AMERICALL 900 and Bell Canada.

BROOKTREE
9950 Barnes Canyon Road
San Diego, California 92121
(619) 452-7580

Founded: 1981. **No. of Employees:** 451. **Revenues (1990):** $68 million. **Revenues (1986):** $2 million. **Five-Year Revenue Growth:** 3,300%.

Description: A manufacturer of mixed signal integrated circuits for computer graphics, automatic test equipment and imaging applications. Products include DAC (digital analog conversion) ICs and A-to-D ICs. Products are sold to the graphics, imaging, and automatic test equipment and instrumentation industries.

How they're growing/Recent developments: While almost all of Brooktree's sales have come from its graphics products, the company has begun moving into the design of new products for computer multimedia and computer imaging applications. In addition, the company believes its new automatic test equipment products will succeed by enhancing testing accuracy and speed, while also reducing system cost and power consumption. Employment has grown 37% in the last year.

BROWNING-FERRIS INDUSTRIES
P.O. Box 3151
Houston, Texas 77253
(713) 870-8100

Founded: 1969. **No. of Employees:** 25,200. **Revenues (1990):** $3 billion. **Revenues (1986):** $1.3 billion. **Five-Year Revenue Growth:** 131%.

Description: BFI is the second largest solid waste collection, transport, processing and disposal service in the nation.

How they're growing/Recent developments: BFI has recently signed several new municipal contracts and has benefitted from the continued growth in medical waste. In addition, the company is becoming more and more involved in the recovery and recycling of waste materials. In May, 1989, BFI signed an agreement with Wellman, Inc. to reprocess plastics, and is hoping to increase its waste to fuel generation capability as well. Management has spurred growth further through the acquisition of small, independent trash companies. Employment has grown from an estimated 18,200 in 1987 to 25,200 in 1991.

BRUNO'S INC.
800 Lakeshore Parkway
Birmingham, Alabama 35211
(205)940-9400

Founded: 1932. **No. of Employees:** 8,399 full-time, 11,988 part-time. **Revenues (1990):** $2.4 billion. **Revenues (1986):** $1 billion. **Five-Year Revenue Growth:** 140%.

Description: Bruno's operates supermarkets and combination food and drug stores, specializing in a high volume of brand names at competitive prices. Chains include Piggly Wiggly Stores, Food World, Food Max and Food Fair. The company is able to tailor each store's product mix and decor to each environment.

How they're growing/Recent developments: Bruno's acquired the 76 Georgia-based Piggly Wiggly stores and turned the struggling chain aground with aggressive pricing and tight cost controls. The company has also entered into a partnership agreement with K mart on an American Fare 240,000-square-foot hypermarket, which will offer general merchandise, clothing, and food. Management has set a goal of doubling sales and profits by 1995.

BUFFETS
10260 Viking Drive, Suite 100
Eden Prairie, Minnesota 55344
(612) 942-9760

Contact: Laura Zauner, Director of Human Resources. **Founded:** 1983. **No. of Employees:** 6,000. **Revenues (1990):** $145 million. **Revenues (1986):** $27 million. **Five-Year Revenue Growth:** 437%.

Description: A Minnesota-based buffet style restaurant chain.

Common positions include: General Manager; Management Trainee; Restaurant Management.

Principal educational backgrounds sought: Business Administration; Hotel and Restaurant Management.

Company benefits: Medical Insurance; Life Insurance; Tuition Assistance; Disability Coverage; Employee Discounts; Stock Option.

Operations at this facility: Divisional Headquarters; Administration; Service.

How they're growing/Recent developments: The company has boasted rapidly expanding revenues since it was founded in 1983. Price value to consumers is very high. Company plans to double in size to over 200 units within the next five years. Employment has grown from an estimated 642 in 1987 to 6,000 in 1991.

CABLETRON SYSTEMS
35 Industrial Way
Rochester, New Hampshire 03867
(603) 332-9400

Contact: Linda Pepin, Director of Human Resources. **Founded:** 1983. **No. of Employees:** 2,000. **Revenues (1990):** $180.5 million. **Revenues (1986):** $4 million. **Five-Year Revenue Growth:** 4,412%.

Description: Cabletron manufactures and markets LAN (Local Area Network) products. New York Stock Exchange.

Common positions include: Accountant; Administrator; Blue-Collar Worker Supervisor; Computer Programmer; Customer Service Representative; Electrical, Industrial and Mechanical Engineers; Department Manager; Marketing Specialist; Public Relations Specialist.

Principal educational backgrounds sought: Accounting; Computer Science; Engineering; Finance.

Company benefits: Medical, Dental, and Life Insurance; Tuition Assistance; Disability Coverage; Employee Discounts.

Operations at this facility: Regional Headquarters; Manufacturing; Research/ Development; Administration; Service; Sales.

How they're growing/Recent developments: Cabletron's direct sales force sets it apart from competitors that sell mostly through dealers. Customer service is of major importance to Cabletron's management. In June, 1991, the company agreed with Silicon Graphics to form a strategic alliance involving joint product development, marketing and distribution. Cabletron does business with about 80% of the Fortune 100 companies. International sales doubled in 1991.

CABOT MEDICAL
2021 Cabot Boulevard West
Lanhorne, Pennsylvania 19047
(215) 752-8300

Founded: 1983. **No. of Employees:** 147. **Revenues (1990):** $27.6 million. **Revenues (1986):** $10.5 million. **Five-Year Revenue Growth:** 163%.

Description: Manufacturers of female reproductive health equipment.

How they're growing/Recent developments: In May, 1990, Cabot developed a range of instruments for diversified medical procedures such as gall bladder removal and appendectomies, which utilize less-invasive techniques. In August, 1991, the company agreed to acquire property and facilities to double overall space.

CADENCE DESIGN SYSTEMS
555 River Oaks Parkway
San Jose, California 95134
(408) 943-1234

Founded: 1987. **No. of Employees:** 1,676. **Revenues (1990):** $231 million. **Revenues (1986):** $17 million. **Five-Year Revenue Growth:** 1,259%.

Description: Manufactures computer aided design and engineering systems.

How they're growing/Recent developments: Cadence acquired Tangent Systems Corporation and Gateway Design Automation Corporation in 1989, and Automated Systems Inc. in 1990, which has helped to increase the company's overall market penetration. New products include the Integrator's Toolkit.

CALIDAD ELECTRONICS
1920 SE Industrial Road
Edinburg, Texas 78539
(512) 381-0909

Founded: 1985. **No. of Employees:** 345. **Revenues (1990):** $6.6 million. **Revenues (1986):** $782 thousand. **Five-Year Revenue Growth:** 744%.

Description: Producers of printer circuit boards.

How they're growing/Recent developments: Calidad has grown through new product development and its ability to provide quick, flexible services. At any time, Calidad will have a number of different products in process. Employment has grown from an estimated 65 in 1987 to 345 in 1991.

CALIFORNIA ENERGY
10831 Old Mill Road
Omaha, Nebraska 68154
(402) 330-8900

Founded: 1971. **No. of Employees:** 150. **Revenues (1990):** $95 million. **Revenues (1986):** $3 million. **Five-Year Revenue Growth:** 3,067%.

Description: Operates a 240-megawatt geothermal plant in the Mojave desert.

How they're growing/Recent developments: California Energy has a long-term contract with Southern California Edison. In March, 1991, the company completed acquisition of geothermal properties in Utah and Nevada. Employment has grown from an estimated 31 in 1987 to 150 in 1991.

CALIFORNIA MICROWAVE
985 Almanor Avenue
Sunnyvale, California 94086
(408) 732-4000

Founded: 1968. **No. of Employees:** 1,050. **Revenues (1990):** $146 million. **Revenues (1986):** $104 million. **Five-Year Revenue Growth:** 40%.

Description: Manufacturers of communications and telecommunications equipment.

How they're growing/Recent developments: In August, 1991, Satellite Transmissions Systems awarded California Microwave a $15.4 million contract to build a major domestic telephone system satellite network. Employment has grown from an estimated 900 in 1987 to 1,050 in 1991.

CAMBEX
360 Second Avenue
Waltham, Massachusetts 02154
(617) 890-6000

Founded: 1968. **No. of Employees:** 122. **Revenues (1990):** $30 million. **Revenues (1986):** $9 million. **Five-Year Revenue Growth:** 233%.

Description: Manufacturers of computer equipment and software.

How they're growing/Recent developments: Cambex's new product line, led by the STOR/9000, is used with IBM's largest mainframe computers. The STOR/3993 is another new product used in IBM's direct access storage.

CANDELA LASER
530 Boston Post Road
Wayland, Massachusetts 01778
(508) 358-7637

Founded: 1970. **No. of Employees:** 193. **Revenues (1990):** $33 million. **Revenues (1986):** $2 million. **Five-Year Revenue Growth:** 1,550%.

Description: Candela designs and manufactures flashlamp excited tunable dye lasers for medical and scientific applications, including urology laser systems to treat kidney stones and dermatology systems to treat vascular skin lesions.

How they're growing/Recent developments: Late in 1990, Candela received FDA approval to market its pulsed dye dermatology system to treat benign vascular lesions of the skin, and is testing a laser system to be used in glaucoma treatment. The company's revenues grew rapidly well into 1991, due to the success of the skin lesion treatment system. Employment has grown from an estimated 105 in 1987 to 193 in 1991.

CANNON EXPRESS, INC.
P.O. Box 364
Springdale, Arkansas 72764
(501) 751-9209

Contact: Larry Patrick, Vice President. **Founded:** 1958. **No. of Employees:** 301. **Revenues (1991):** $27 million. **Revenues (1987):** $6.7 million. **Five-Year Revenue Growth:** 302%.

Description: An Arkansas-based carrier of general commodities between all points in the United States. NASDAQ-CANX

Common positions include: Accountant; Computer Programmer; Marketing Specialist; Sales Representative; Transportation and Traffic Specialist.

Principal educational backgrounds sought: Computer Science; Marketing.

Company benefits: Medical and Life Insurance.

How they're growing/Recent developments: Revenues soared in 1991, due to additions to the fleet which, generates more sales and income annually. In December, 1991, the company began offering Air Freight and Ocean service to customers for domestic and international shipments.

CANONIE ENVIRONMENTAL SERVICES CORPORATION

800 Canonie Drive
Porter, Indiana 46304
(219) 926-8651

Contact: Andrew Koczon, Human Resource Manager. **Founded:** 1980. **No. of Employees:** 375. **Revenues (1990):** $38 million . **Revenues (1986):** $22 million. **Five-Year Revenue Growth:** 73%.

Description: Provides comprehensive services throughout the United States for the remediation of sites contaminated by hazardous waste.

Common positions include: Accountant; Administrator; Attorney; Civil Engineer; Electrical Engineer; Industrial Engineer; Mechanical Engineer; Metallurgical Engineer; Geologist; Department Manager; Marketing Specialist; Personnel and Labor Relation Specialist; Sales Representative; Systems Analyst.

Principal educational backgrounds include: Accounting; Biology; Business Administration; Engineering; Geology; Marketing.

Company benefits include: medical insurance; dental insurance; life insurance; tuition assistance; disability coverage.

Operations at this facility include: regional headquarters; administration; sales.

How they're growing/Recent developments: In May, 1988, the company incorporated Canonie Technologies, Inc., a wholly-owned subsidiary, which in turn acquired a 50% stake in Soiltech, Inc. the following year, and a 50% stake in Nuclear Remediation Technologies Corporation during 1990. In June, 1990, Canonie also acquired a 20% stake in La Posta Recycling Center, Inc. Revenues leaped to $69 million for fiscal 1991.

CAPE FEAR INSULATION, INC.

P.O. Box 10175
Wilmington, North Carolina 28405
(919) 799-3397

Founded: 1984. **No. of Employees:** 100. **Revenues (1990):** $4 million. **Revenues (1986):** $1 million. **Five-Year Revenue Growth:** 300%.

Description: Cape Fear provides commercial and industrial insulation services.

Company benefits: Life Insurance.

Operations at this facility: Regional Headquarters.

CAPITOL TRANSAMERICA CORPORATION
4610 University Avenue
Madison, Wisconsin 53705
(608) 231-4450

Contact: Virgiline M. Scuhulte, Personnel Director. **Founded:** 1965. **No. of Employees:** 70. **Revenues (1990):** $30.7 million. **Revenues (1986):** $15.6 million. **Five-Year Revenue Growth:** 97%.

Description: A major insurance provider concentrating in specialty multi-peril insurance such as for daycare centers, camp grounds, clubs, and taverns, and fidelity and surety bonds.

Principal educational backgrounds: Bachelors Degree, CPCU, CIC, Ins. 21, 22, 23.

Company benefits: Life, health disability, 401k plan, ESOP, stock options

How they're growing/Recent developments: The company has a lower loss, loss expense and expense ratio than industry average. For the six months ending June 30, 1991, Capitol's revenues gained 19%. Employment has grown from an estimated 36 in 1987 to 70 in 1991.

CARDINAL DISTRIBUTION INC.
655 Metro Place, 9th Floor
South Dublin, Ohio 43017
(614)761-8700

Founded: 1971. **No. of Employees:** 1000. **Revenues (1990):** $874 million. **Revenues (1986):** $429 million. **Five-Year Revenue Growth:** 104%.

Description: A wholesale distributor of pharmaceuticals, medical and surgical supplies and related health products, serving customers in the Midwest and Northeast.

How they're growing/Recent developments: The company's operations have been expanding rapidly since 1986. In that year, Cardinal acquired James W. Daley, Inc. and in subsequent years have also acquired Marmac Distributors and Ohio-Valley Clarksburg. Cardinal consolidated its businesses in 1988 by selling off its food distribution services. Revenues climbed to $1.2 billion in fiscal 1991. Employment has grown from an estimated 800 in 1987 to 1,000 in 1991.

CARENETWORK INC.
111 West Pleasant Street
P.O. Box 12359
Milwaukee, Wisconsin 53212-0359
(414) 223-3300

Founded: 1985. **No. of Employees:** 173. **Revenues (1990):** $121 million. **Revenues (1986):** $23 million. **Five-Year Revenue Growth:** 426%.

Description: A major health insurance provider.

How they're growing/Recent developments: Carenetwork is the parent to WHO-Wisconsin Health Organization Insurance Corporation. Earning rose sharply in 1990, due to higher margins and revenues. Revenues for 1990 gained 42% year-to-year, over those for 1989, based on increases in premium rates and membership. Management has kept a tight rein on expenses and costs. In March, 1991, Carenetwork completed initial public offering of common shares. Proceeds are being used to expand operations and upgrade the company's data processing system.

CARGILL, INC.
P.O. Box 9300
15407 McGinty Road
Minnetonka, Minnesota 55440-9300
(612) 475-7575

Founded: 1870. **No. of Employees:** 60,000. **Revenues (1990):** $42 billion (est.). **Revenues (1986):** $32.4 billion (est.). **Five-Year Revenue Growth:** 30%.

Description: The nation's largest privately owned agricultural commodities broker.

How they're growing/Recent developments: Cargill, whose main success has been the trading of such commodities as sugar, grains and seeds, rubber, molasses, orange juice, cocoa, petroleum products, and precious and scrap metals, has recently entered the realm of selling meats and packaged foods directly to supermarkets. In 1991, the company became the world's largest maltster by acquiring Milwaukee-based Ladish Malting.

CARPENTER HEALTHCARE SYSTEMS
13723 Riverport Drive
Suite 340
Maryland Heights, Missouri 63043
(314) 291-3900

Founded: 1984. **No. of Employees:** 140. **Revenues (1990):** $10 million. **Revenues (1986):** $1 million. **Five-Year Revenue Growth:** 900%.

Description: A chain of outpatient drug rehabilitation centers.

How they're growing/Recent developments: Employment has grown from 35 in 1986 to 140 in 1991.

CARTER-WALLACE, INC.
1345 Avenue of the Americas
New York, New York 10105
(212) 339-5000

Founded: 1968. **No. of Employees:** 4,270. **Revenues (1990):** $555 million. **Revenues (1986):** $400 million. **Five-Year Revenue Growth:** 39%.

Description: Manufactures and markets ethical pharmaceuticals, personal care items and over the counter sundries. Well-known products include Carter's Little Liver Pills, Sea and Ski sun care lotion, Arrid deodorant and Trojan condoms. The company is also involved in the pet care market through products like products Chirp vitamins for birds and Femalt hairball remover.

How they're growing/Recent developments: Carter-Wallace continues to expand through new product development and acquisitions. Recent new products include First Response home pregnancy, Arrid Non-Whitening and Trojan Extra Strength. A recent acquisition was Mentor Corporation, a condom manufacturer. Revenues for fiscal 1991 reached $635 million. Continued strong performance in the health care sector should offset any weaker sales in cold and cough products. The company is committed to expanding laboratories and manufacturing facilities, which will also help long-term growth.

CASCADE INTERNATIONAL INC.,
2424 North Federal Highway
Boca Raton, Florida 33431
(407) 338-8278

Founded: 1984. **No. of Employees:** 847. **Revenues (1990):** $52.4 million. **Revenues (1987):** $15.8 million. **Four-Year Revenue Growth:** 232%.

Description: Through Jean Cosmetics, Cascade retails cosmetics, and operates fashion boutiques selling high fashion women's apparel.

How they're growing/Recent developments: For the nine months ending March 31, 1991, sales rose 20%, primarily on increased revenues at cosmetic counters and select boutiques. In August, 1990, Cascade gained control of Conston Corporation, a retailer of women's clothing and accessories. In June, 1991, Cascade signed an agreement with Oleg Cassini to establish a chain of high-end specialty stores with the Oleg Cassini name. Employment has grown from an estimated 89 in 1987 to 847 in 1991.

CASH AMERICA INVESTMENTS
306 West 7th Street
Fort Worth, Texas 76102
(817) 335-1100

Founded: 1984. **No. of Employees:** 899. **Revenues (1990):** $116 million. **Revenues (1986):** $13 million. **Five-Year Revenue Growth:** 792%.

Description: Owns and operates one of the nation's largest chains of pawnshops.

How they're growing/Recent developments: Cash America follows a strategy of acquiring existing pawnshops and opening new ones. As of May, 1991, the company had opened eight stores and closed two, which were consolidated into other existing stores.

CATALINA LIGHTING INC.
6073 North West 167th Street
Miami, Florida 33015
(305) 558-4777

Contact: Kelly A. Woodring, Director of Human Resources. **Founded:** 1974. **No. of Employees:** 163. **Revenues (1990):** $85 million. **Revenues (1986):** $12 million. **Five-Year Revenue Growth:** 608%.

Description: One of the largest and fastest growing importers and distributors of residential decorative lighting and ceiling fans in the United States.

Common positions include: Accountant; Administrator; Advertising Worker; Computer Programmer; Credit Manager; Customer Service Representative; Financial Analyst; Marketing Specialist; Personnel and Labor Relations Specialist; Sales Representative; Technical Writer/Editor; Secretary; Administrative Assistant.

Principal educational backgrounds sought: Accounting; Art/Design; Liberal Arts; Marketing.

Company benefits: Medical, Dental, and Life Insurance; Disability Coverage; Profit Sharing; Employee Discounts; Stock Options.

Operations at this facility: Research/Development; Administration; Service; Sales.

How they're growing/Recent developments: In June, 1991, Catalina entered into an exclusive contract to supply K mart with residential lighting products.

C-COR ELECTRONICS
60 Decibel Road
State College, Pennsylvania 16801
(814) 238-2461

Founded: 1953. **No. of Employees:** 460. **Revenues (1990):** $60.3 million. **Revenues (1986):** $22.1 million. **Five-Year Revenue Growth:** 173%.

Description: Manufactures electronic equipment used in cable TV products.

How they're growing/Recent developments: While there is uncertainty in the cable TV industry, C-COR has been emphasizing products in the data communications field which is expected to outpace the cable TV market. Continuing to diversity. In September, 1990, C-COR acquired COMLUX, a manufacturer of fiber optics systems.

CEM CORPORATION
Box 200
Matthews, North Carolina 28106
(704) 821-7015

Founded: 1971. **No. of Employees:** 151. **Revenues (1990):** $19 million. **Revenues (1986):** $8 million. **Five-Year Revenue Growth:** 137%.

Description: Produces microwave-based instrumentation for testing and analysis.

How they're growing/Recent Developments: CEM's revenues have been on the rise recently due to the increased volume for the company's Digestion Systems, a microwave heating system designed especially for use in the digestion of samples for laboratory analysis. Employment has grown from an estimated 86 in 1987 to 151 in 1991.

CENCOM CABLE ASSOCIATES
P.O. Box 419010
635 Maryville Center Drive, Suite 300
St. Louis, Missouri 63141
(314) 576-4446

Founded: 1982. **No. of Employees:** 1,320. **Revenues (1990):** $64 million. **Revenues (1986):** $3 million. **Five-Year Revenue Growth:** 2,033%.

Description: Company provides cable television administrative management services.

How they're growing/Recent developments: Cencom had long been searching for a long-term investor to help it sustain its fast growth when Hallmark Card's Crown Media purchased a controlling interest in during 1991, citing the company's excellent management and significant potential for growth. According to the *Wall Street Journal*, management and location will remain the same. Employment has grown from an estimated 120 in 1987 to 1,320 in 1991.

CENTEX TELEMANAGEMENT
185 Berry Street, Building 1, #5100
San Francisco, California 94107
(415) 882-2300

Founded: 1983. **No. of Employees:** 348. **Revenues (1990):** $114 million. **Revenues (1987):** $14 million. **Four-Year Revenue Growth:** 714%.

Description: Provides a range of telecommunications services to small and medium sized businesses, giving them a single point of contact for all of their telecommunications needs. The company analyzes the telecommunication needs of each client and selects the best mix of services from its various third-party providers, to be shared by its clients under Centex Telemanagement.

How they're growing/Recent developments: The company's strategy has been to rapidly expand its client base by incurring initial expenses associated with opening new branch offices, and adding switches to existing branches. Through strong market penetration and economies of scale that result from a large number of clients, Centex has been able to attract a growing number of clients by offering significant savings. Employment has grown from an estimated 190 in 1987 to 348 in 1991.

CENTURY MEDICORP
4060 Whittier Boulevard
Los Angeles, California 90023
(213) 266-1254

No. of Employees: 325. **Revenues (1990):** $60 million. **Revenues (1988):** $9 million. **Three-Year Revenue Growth:** 567%.

Description: A health maintenance organization in Southern California with three HMO insurance plans. The company also operates a 128 bed hospital in East Los Angeles.

How they're growing/Recent developments: Revenues for the fiscal year ending June, 1991, jumped to $113.7 million, reflecting increased premiums and enrollment revenues.

CHAMBERS DEVELOPMENT COMPANY, INC.
10700 Frankstown Road
Pittsburgh, Pennsylvania 15235
(412) 242-6237

Founded: 1971. **No. of Employees:** 5,350. **Revenues (1990):** $258 million. **Revenues (1986):** $31 million. **Five-Year Revenue Growth:** 732%

Description: Chambers is engaged in refuse collection and disposal as well as in personal protection services.

Common positions include: Marketing Specialists; Environmental Engineers.

How they're growing/Recent developments: Company-owned landfills are double-lined with two layers of clay, separated by special barriers that can detect leaking. This system increases protection of the environment. Chambers has added to landfill capacity, continues to acquire regional haulers and land new municipal and commercial contracts. Additions include three new landfills and two under construction. Six others planned for later years. Also operates security services business which is growing through acquisitions.

Chambers' goal is to grow by 25 to 35% annually. Between 1989 and 1990, employment rose by 2,300.

CHAMPION MORTGAGE COMPANY
20 Waterview Boulevard
Parsippany, New Jersey 07054
(201) 402-7700

Founded: 1981. **No. of Employees:** 133. **Revenues (1990):** $19 million. **Revenues (1986):** $2 million. **Five-Year Revenue Growth:** 850%

Description: A financial services company specializing in first-and-second mortgage loans.

CHARMING SHOPPES
450 Winks Lane
Bensalem, Pennsylvania 19020
(215) 245-9100

Contact: Karen Foreman, Human Resources. **Founded:** 1969. **No. of Employees:** 12,200. **Revenues (1990):** $809 million. **Revenues (1986):** $392 million. **Five-Year Revenue Growth:** 106%.

Description: A retailer operating women's specialty stores under the names Fashion Bug, and Fashion Bug Plus.

How they're growing/Recent developments: During the first quarter of the 1991-92 fiscal year, the company opened 13 new stores and has plans to construct 100 new stores. The company's main expansion strategy is to expand its base in Western United States. Revenues for 1991 rose to $886 million. Employment has grown from an estimated 8,300 in 1987 to 12,200 in 1991.

CHEMICAL FABRICS
701 Daniel Webster Highway
P.O. Box 1137
Merrimack, New Hampshire 03054
(603) 424-9000

Founded: 1983. **No. of Employees:** 270. **Revenues (1990):** $48.7 million. **Revenues (1986):** $28 million. **Five-Year Revenue Growth:** 74%.

Description: Manufacturers of specialty fabrics.

How they're growing/Recent developments: Revenues have increased due to growth in the company's architectural fabric and engineered composite group sales of proprietary and industrial goods. In February, 1991, the company acquired Flourocarbon Fabricators, Ltd. of Yorkshire, England.

CHEYENNE SOFTWARE
55 Bryant Avenue
Roslyn, New York 11576
(516) 484-5110

Founded: 1983. **No. of Employees:** 210. **Revenues (1990):** $178 million. **Revenues (1986):** $5 million. **Five-Year Revenue Growth:** 3,460%.

Description: A computer software firm.

How they're growing/Recent developments: Prior to Fiscal year 1989, Cheyenne operated by using "strategic partners" who paid Cheyenne for development and then took responsibility for marketing the software. If the product was successful, Cheyenne would receive royalties. Cheyenne now develops new products on its own and markets them through agreements with original equipment manufacturers and as stand-alone products. Employment has grown from an estimated 25 in 1987 to 210 in 1991.

CHICO'S
15550 McGregor Boulevard
Ft. Myers, FL 33908
(813) 433-5505

Founded: 1983. **No. of Employees:** 325. **Revenues (1990):** $16 million. **Revenues (1986):** $1 million. **Five-Year Revenue Growth:** 1,500%.

Description: Manufactures and retails women's apparel.

How they're growing/Recent developments: Chico's has doubled its size in the past two years and is continuing to expand in all regions of the company. Chico's has enhanced its identity with its customers by selling all natural casual clothing at affordable prices, stressing close attention to customers and encouraging each store to become involved in community activities.

CHIPCOM CORPORATION
118 Turnpike Road
Southboro, Massachusetts 01772
(508) 460-8900

Contact: Ginni Spencer, Director of Human Resources. **Founded:** 1983. **No. of Employees:** 170. **Revenues (1990):** $28.4 million. **Revenues (1986):** $2.8 million. **Five-Year Revenue Growth:** 914%.

Description: Chipcom manufactures fiber optic broadband-based fault tolerant LAN systems.

How they're growing/Recent developments: Chipcom has been on the forefront of producing smart network hubs, which facilitate advances in both inter-operability and network management. While a network links multiple computers within a building, a network hub links different networks together, as well as allowing network managers to configure and diagnose multiple networks for greater efficiency. New products include Chipcom's eight-port Token Ring hub cards, which are used in local and wide area network technology. During 1991, Chipcom announced agreement with Synoptics and Digital Equipment Corporation to release a specification for transmitting 100M-hps Fiber Distributed Data Interface (FDDI) signals over shielded twisted pair (STP) wiring. The three companies believe that mutual acceptance of the new specification means that their products will now be compatible. The companies also believe that use of shielded twisted pair, rather than the more expensive fiber optic cabling will spur FDDI sales. Employment at Chipcom grew 54% between 1989 and 1990.

CINTAS CORPORATION
6800 Cintas Boulevard, P.O. Box 625737
Cincinnati, Ohio 45262-5737
(513)489-4000

Founded: 1968. **No. of Employees:** 5,930. **Revenues (1990):** $285 million. **Revenues (1986):** $124 million. **Five-Year Revenue Growth:** 130%.

Description: Cintas is engaged in uniform rentals and sales and non-uniform rentals to customers employing almost a million uniformed employees, Cintas also serves corporate and industrial clients by providing design, planning and implementation of corporate identity programs. The company manufactures, sells, and rents uniforms.

How they're growing/Recent developments: Revenues have grown through both price increases and acquisitions. The company plans to expand through acquisition to meet its goal of having a uniform rental operation in every major city. Employment has grown from an estimated 3,800 in 1987 to 5,930 in 1991.

CIRCUIT CITY STORES, INC.
9950 Mayland Drive
Richmond, Virginia 23233
(804) 527-4000

Contact: Ann Collins, Director of Human Resources. **Founded:** 1949. **No. of Employees:** 16,000. **Revenues (1991):** $2.4 billion. **Revenues (1986):** $705 million. **Six-Year Revenue Growth:** 240%.

Description: Circuit City is the nation's largest specialty retailer of brand-name consumer electronics and major appliances.

Common positions include: Store Operations; Merchandising; Staff Support.

Principal educational backgrounds sought: Varies.

Company benefits: Medical and Dental Insurance; Education Assistance; Stock Purchase; Retirement.

How they're growing/Recent developments: Although slower consumer spending has restrained profits somewhat during the recession, Circuit City opened 27 new Superstores during fiscal 1992, and 20 new Impulse stores. Employment has grown from an estimated 5,922 in 1987 to over 16,000 in 1991.

CIRRUS LOGIC, INC.
1463 Centre Pointe Drive
Milpitas, California 95035
(408) 945-8300

Founded: 1984. **No. of Employees:** 326. **Revenues (1990):** $142 million. **Revenues (1987):** $5 million. **Four-Year Revenue Growth:** 2,740%.

Description: Manufacturers of VLSI products that perform complex peripheral control functions in high-performance personal computers, workstations and other office automation tools.

How they're growing/Recent developments: Cirrus Logic subcontracts semiconductor wafer production to Japanese firms, and focuses its energies on value-added designing. In July, 1991, Cirrus acquired control of Pixel Semiconductor from Visual Information Technologies. Pixel develops integrated circuits for advanced display systems.

CISCO SYSTEMS
1525 O'Brien Drive
Menlo Park, California 94025
(415) 326-1941

Founded: 1984. **No. of Employees:** 254. **Revenues (1990):** $70 million. **Revenues (1986):** $100 thousand. **Five-Year Revenue Growth:** 69,900%.

Description: A computer networking firm that manufactures media-to-media data conversion equipment. Begun at Stanford University in 1984. Customers include AT&T and Motorola.

How they're growing/Recent developments: Strong demand and the frequent introduction of new products keep revenues rising. Sales for the 39 weeks ending April, 1991 rose 163% year to year, and, by year's end, annual revenues had rocketed to $183.2 million. The company's principal product, a set of multiprotocol routers, support more protocols than do any competing products. International sales account for about 33% of sales.

CITIZEN'S NATIONAL UTILITIES
High Ridge Park
P.O. Box 3801
Stamford, Connecticut 06905
(203) 329-8800

Founded: 1935. **No. of Employees:** 2,294. **Revenues (1990):** $528 million. **Revenues (1986):** $268 million. **Five-Year Revenue Growth:** 97%.

Description: Provides telephone, electric, water, gas and wastewater public services in 12 states.

How they're growing/Recent developments: The company's broad geographic scope and diversified services have spurred growth. The company also recently acquired Louisiana General Services, Inc.

CLAYTON HOMES
New Topside Drive At Alcoa Highway
Knoxville, Tennessee 37901
(615) 970-7200

Founded: 1968. **No. of Employees:** 2,212. **Revenues (1990):** $260 million. **Revenues (1986):** $158 million. **Five-Year Revenue Growth:** 65%.

Description: A retailer of low-to-medium priced homes.

How they're growing/Recent developments: Revenues for the fiscal year the ended in June, 1991, were up 23% from the previous fiscal year. Employment has grown from an estimated 1,550 in 1987 to 2,212 in 1991.

THE CLOROX CORPORATION
1221 Broadway
Oakland, California 94612
(415) 271-7000

Founded: 1913. **No. of Employees:** 5,500. **Revenues (1990):** $1.5 billion. **Revenues (1986):** $1.1 billion. **Five-Year Revenue Growth:** 36%.

Description: Produces a diversified line of household cleaning agents, grocery products and a line of specialty equipment for the fast-food industry. Name-brand consumer products include Clorox, Kingsford Charcoal and Hidden Valley Ranch salad dressings.

How they're growing/Recent developments: Management expects future growth to come from both new product lines and increased market share of existing products.

CNS, INC.
1250 Park Road
Chanhassen, Minnesota 55317
(612) 474-7600

Founded: 1982. **No. of Employees:** 63. **Revenues (1990):** $6 million. **Revenues (1986):** $5 million. **Five-Year Revenue Growth:** 20%.

Description: A manufacturer of computer-aided sleep disorder diagnostic systems.

How they're growing/Recent developments: Employment has grown from an estimated 50 in 1987 to 63 in 1991.

COAST DISTRIBUTION SYSTEMS
1982 Zanker Road
San Jose, California 95112
(408) 436-8611

Founded: 1977. No. of Employees: 440. Revenues (1990): $142 million. Revenues (1986): $103 million. Five-Year Revenue Growth: 38%.

Description: A wholesaler/distributor of RV and boating marine products replacement parts.

How they're growing/Recent developments: While there is currently a softness in demand for the company's products, the company has continued to grow through acquisitions. The company has now become one of the largest distributors in its field. A new computer based order system for electronic orders should increase performance. Employment has grown from an estimated 425 in 1987 to 440 in 1991.

CODE-ALARM INC.
950 East Whitcomb
Madison Heights, Michigan 48071
(313)583-9620

Founded: 1979. No. of Employees: 464. Revenues (1990): $44.5 million. Revenues (1986): $8 million. Five-Year Revenue Growth: 456%.

Description: The nation's largest manufacturer of automobile security systems.

How they're growing/Recent developments: Code-Alarm began production of a line of home security products in 1989. In addition, in May, 1989, the company announced Intercept -- a stolen vehicle recovery system employing both cellular telephone and Loran C technology. By April, 1991, Code Alarm had signed 57 new dealers to sell the Intercept product. Employment has grown from an estimated 169 in 1987 to 464 in 1991.

COGNEX
15 Crawford Street
Needham, Massachusetts 02194
(617) 449-6030

Contact: Human Resources Manager. **Founded:** 1981. **No. of Employees:** 135. **Revenues (1990):** $20.9 million. **Revenues (1987):** $6 million. **Four-Year Revenue Growth:** 248%.

Description: Manufacturers of machine vision equipment, which is used to automatically perform gauging, guidance, identification and inspection tasks. NASDAQ

Common positions include: Electrical Engineer; Systems Analyst.

Principal educational backgrounds sought: Engineering.

Company benefits: Medical, Dental and Life Insurance; Tuition Assistance; Disability Coverage; Savings Plan.

Operations at this facility: Divisional Headquarters; Manufacturing; Research/Development; Administration; Service; Sales.

How they're growing/Recent developments: The company's revenues have climbed due to the introduction of the Cognex 4000, as well as an increased demand for existing products.

COHU
5755 Kearney Villa Road
San Diego, California 92123
(619) 277-6700

Founded: 1957. **No. of Employees:** 487. **Revenues (1990):** $44 million. **Revenues (1986):** $29 million. **Five-Year Revenue Growth:** 52%.

Description: A major electronics firm.

How they're growing/Recent developments: Cohu spent over $1 million in R&D in both 1989 and 1990, and has seen an increase in sales of electronic detection and test equipment. A new plant was due to be finished in 1991. Employment has grown from an estimated 377 in 1987 to 487 in 1991.

COLONIAL COMPANIES
1200 Colonial Life Boulevard
Columbia, South Carolina 29202
(803) 798-7000

Founded: 1939. **Revenues (1990):** $306 million. **Revenues (1986):** $198 million. **Five-Year Revenue Growth:** 55%.

Description: An insurance firm.

How they're growing/Recent developments: One of the company's fastest growing areas is in supplemental coverage of accident insurance through payroll marketing. Colonial has also benefitted from a growth in new customers and better retention of policy holders.

COLUMBIA HOSPITAL CORPORATION
777 Main Street, Suite 21000
Fort Worth, Texas 76102
(817) 870-5900

Founded: 1990 (under current management). **No. of Employees:** 5,900. **Revenues (1990):** $290 million. **Revenues (1988):** $45 million. **Three-Year Revenue Growth:** 544%.

Description: A health care provider that owns 10 acute-care and two psychiatric hospitals, as well as outpatient surgery centers, diagnostic centers, and cardiac rehabilitation and radiation therapy centers.

How they're growing/Recent developments: The company plans to spur growth through the acquisition of more health care businesses and facilities. In June, 1991, Columbia acquired Kendall Regional Medical Center, a 412-bed acute case hospital in Dade County, Florida. In October, 1991, Columbia signed a letter of intent to acquire North Gables Hospital, a 53-bed facility in Miami.

COMAIR HOLDINGS, INC.
P.O. Box 75021
Cincinnati, Ohio 45275
(606) 525-2550

Founded: 1977. **No. of Employees:** 2,213. **Revenues (1990):** $158 million. **Revenues (1986):** $62 million. **Five-Year Revenue Growth:** 155%.

Description: Passenger and air freight carrier.

How they're growing/Recent developments: Comair posted a passenger boarding record for the first quarter of fiscal year 1991-1992 and has now had seven consecutive profitable quarters. Comair acquired 12 Embraer Brasilia aircraft in fiscal year 1990-91 and three more in first quarter of 1991-92.

COMARK, INC.
471 Brighton Drive
Bloomington, Illinois 60108
(708) 351-9700

Founded: 1978. **No. of Employees:** 100. **Revenues (1990):** $110 million. **Revenues (1988):** $35 million. **Five-Year Revenue Growth:** 214%.

Description: A distributor of computer media and peripheral equipment.

COMCAST CORPORATION
1234 Market Street, 16th Floor
Philadelphia, Pennsylvania 19107-3723
(215) 665-1700

Founded: 1969. **No. of Employees:** 3,478. **Revenues (1990):** $657 million. **Revenues (1986):** $131 million. **Five-Year Revenue Growth:** 402%.

Description: A cable TV system operator, which also distributes Muzak and provides cellular phone service.

How they're growing/Recent developments: Through acquisitions in recent years, Comcast has become the third-largest Cable TV system operator in the nation. In June, 1991, Comcast announced its plans to acquire the Philadelphia-area cellular operations of Metromedia. Also in June, the company received FCC authorization to experiment with new wireless communications technology. Employment has grown from an estimated 2,000 in 1987 to 3,478 in 1991.

COMDISCO, INC.
6111 North River Road
Rosemont, Illinois 60018
(708) 698-3000

Founded: 1971. **No. of Employees:** 1,875. **Revenues (1990):** $1.9 billion. **Revenues (1986):** $902 million. **Five-Year Revenue Growth:** 111%.

Description: Comdisco buys, sells and leases new and used IBM computer equipment. Also provides computer disaster recovery services in the event of flood, power outage or fire.

How they're growing/Recent developments: Comdisco's revenues should continue to grow strongly due to the availability of IBM's new generation ES/9000 mainframe, which will benefit leasing/remarketing markets for used mainframes. Its disaster recovery segment is growing. Employment has grown from an estimated 619 in 1987 to 1,875 in 1991.

COMMUNICATION CABLE

North Second Avenue, West, Box 729
West Siler City, North Carolina 27344
(919) 663-2629

Founded: 1982. No. of Employees: 240. Revenues (1990): $25 million. Revenues (1987): $6 million. Four-Year Revenue Growth: 317%.

Description: Manufacturers of specialty electronic cable, which it markets through distributors to original equipment manufacturers.

How they're growing/Recent developments: During the past year, revenues have benefitted from the startup of the company's Texarkana Wire and Saxton divisions. Employment has grown from an estimated 52 in 1987 to 240 in 1991.

COMMUNITY PSYCHIATRIC CENTERS

24502 Pacific Park Drive
Laguna Hills, California 92656
(714) 831-1166

Founded: 1962. No. of Employees: 6,374. Revenues (1990): $374 million. Revenues (1986): $231 million. Five-Year Revenue Growth: 62%.

Description: The largest publicly owned operator of psychiatric hospitals in California and 19 other states.

How they're growing/Recent developments: The company is rapidly expanding through new acquisitions and the opening of new hospitals. Recent opening include hospitals in Arkansas and Illinois. Community also specializes in cooperative agreements with HMOs, in which the company provides psychiatric care to members. Employment has grown from an estimated 5,438 in 1987 to 6,374 in 1991.

COMPLETE BUSINESS SOLUTIONS
30500 Northwestern Highway
Suite 200
Farmington Hills, Michigan 48334
(313) 737-2088

Founded: 1985. **No. of Employees:** 320. **Revenues (1990):** $19 million. **Revenues (1986):** $2 million. **Five-Year Revenue Growth:** 850%.

Description: Provides computer-related consulting services.

How they're growing/Recent developments: Employment has grown from 40 in 1987 to 320 in 1991.

COMPREHENSIVE TECHNOLOGIES INTERNATIONAL
14500 Avion Parkway
Suite 250
Chantilly, VA
(703) 263-1000

Founded: 1980. **No. of Employees:** 325. **Revenues (1990):** $20 million. **Revenues (1986):** $1 million. **Five-Year Revenue Growth:** 1,900%.

Description: Provides military and logistics-engineering services.

How they're growing/Recent developments: Employment has grown from an estimated 47 in 1987 to 325 in 1991.

COMPRESSION LABS, INC.
2860 Junction Avenue
San Jose, California 95134
(408) 435-3000

Founded: 1973. **No. of Employees:** 271. **Revenues (1990):** $53 million. **Revenues (1986):** $16 million. **Five-Year Revenue Growth:** 231%.

Description: A leader in full-motion color video conferencing systems for use in business, government and education. Employment grew 11% between 1989 and 1990.

How they're growing/Recent developments: During 1990, the sales volume of the company's two main products -- the Rembrandt and the Rembrandt

11/06 video compression devices (or codecs) grew 68%. The company has the largest installed base of videoconferencing systems in the world. Employment has grown from an estimated 130 in 1987 to 271 in 1991.

COMPTEK RESEARCH
110 Broadway
Buffalo, New York 14203
(716) 842-2700

Founded: 1968. **No. of Employees:** 619. **Revenues (1990):** $50 million. **Revenues (1986):** $28 million. **Five-Year Revenue Growth:** 78%.

Description: Manufacturers of electronics hardware and software.

How they're growing/Recent developments: In October,1991, Comptek Research agreed to acquire a partial interest in Bison Data Corporation as a joint venture to sell software and hardware for bank teller machines. In August, 1991, the company acquired Communications Systems Consultants, Inc. and Electronic Information Ltd., companies that together own three data transmission networks enabling link up with automated teller machines in the northeast.

COMPTRONIX
P.O. Box 1800
Guntersville, Alabama 35976
(205) 582-1800

Founded: 1987. **No. of Employees:** 555. **Revenues (1990):** $70.2 million. **Revenues (1986):** $6.7 million. **Five-Year Revenue Growth:** 948%.

Description: A leading provider of contract manufacturing services to the electronics and computer industries. The company provides assembly services for approximately 60 original equipment manufacturers (OEMs) producing computers, peripherals, medical electronics, communications, industrial, and test equipment. Services include component procurement, board assembly, and testing. These services are provided on either a consignment basis, where customers procure parts, or on a turnkey basis, where Comptronix purchases the parts and performs the entire assembly process.

How they're growing/Recent developments: Comptronix has succeeded by maintaining a client base that is diversified across markets. This diversification, combined with a focus on low to mid-volume programs, has enabled the company to maintain higher margins than the industry standard. Employment grew 100% between 1989 and 1990.

COMPUCOM SYSTEMS
9333 Forest Lane
Dallas, Texas 75243
(214) 783-1252

Founded: 1981. **No. of Employees:** 580. **Revenues (1990):** $400 million. **Revenues (1987):** $43 million. **Four-Year Revenue Growth:** 830%.

Description: Markets PCs to commercial and industrial users. Also offers consulting and maintenance services.

How they're growing/Recent developments: Compucom attributes much of its growth to customer service. Compucom promises to fill 95% of all orders within 24 hours. Employment has grown from an estimated 253 in 1987 to 580 in 1991.

COMPUTER ASSOCIATES INTERNATIONAL
711 Stewart Avenue
Garden City, New York 11530
(516) 227-3300

Founded: 1974. **No. of Employees:** 6,900. **Revenues (1990):** $1.3 billion. **Revenues (1986):** $191 million. **Five-Year Revenue Growth:** 581%.

Description: Develops, markets, and supports software.

How they're growing/Recent developments: Computer Associates has grown rapidly due to over 25 acquisitions and to new product development. In fact, the company posted an average annual growth rate of 65% between 1982 and 1989. During 1991, the company announced that it would be collaborating with Hewlett-Packard to develop UNIX applications. Employment has grown from an estimated 1,700 in 1987 to 6,900 in 1991.

COMPUTER DATA SYSTEMS
One Curie Court
Rockville, Maryland 20850
(301) 921-7000

Founded: 1968. **No. of Employees:** 3,000. **Revenues (1990):** $125 million. **Revenues (1986):** $55 million. **Five-Year Revenue Growth:** 127%.

Description: A data processing company, deriving much of its revenue from U.S. government contracts.

How they're growing/Recent developments: In 1990, the company introduced a new product that allows customer optimum use of existing communications systems. Employment has grown from an estimated 2,300 in 1987 to 3,000 in 1991.

COMSYS TECHNICAL SERVICES INC.
4 Research Place, Suite 300
Rockville, Maryland 20850
(301) 921-3600

Founded: 1979. **No. of Employees:** 403. **Revenues (1990):** $27 million. **Revenues (1986):** $3 million. **Five-Year Revenue Growth:** 800%.

Description: Provider of contract programming and computer and software consulting services.

How they're growing/Recent developments: Employment has grown from 70 in 1986 to 403 in 1991.

CONAGRA, INC.
One Central Park Plaza
Omaha, Nebraska 68102
(402) 595-7300

Founded: 1919. **No. of Employees:** 74,269. **Revenues (1990):** $15 billion. **Revenues (1986):** $5 billion. **Five-Year Revenue Growth:** 200%.

Description: Con Agra is a leader in the diversified brand-name and frozen foods market, and also is a major distributor of fertilizers and pesticides. Con Agra is also the nation's largest publicly held seller and exporter of grain. Finally, the company operates about 170 rural retail stores.

How they're growing/Recent developments: Con Agra has posted record earnings every year for over a decade now. Recent growth is largely attributable to the acquisition of Beatrice Company. Con Agra also recently purchased Golden Valley Microwave Foods. The company's fastest growing product segment is now prepared foods. Employment has grown from an estimated 50,000 in 1987 to 74,269 in 1991.

CONFERTECH INTERNATIONAL
2801 Youngfield, Suite 240
Golden, Colorado 80401
(303) 237-5151

Founded: 1976. **No. of Employees:** 120. **Revenues (1990):** $16 million. **Revenues (1986):** $1 million. **Five-Year Revenue Growth:** 1,500%.

Description: Manufacturers of teleconferencing equipment and services.

How they're growing/Recent developments: Employment grew 100% between 1989 and 1990. In 1990, ConferTech introduced a new product called ConferNet Virtual Network Teleconferencing, which integrates the company's ALLEGRO bridging technology and call management expertise with a customer's own virtual network. Revenues for the first half of fiscal year 1991 rose 30% year-to-year. Employment has grown from an estimated 49 in 1987 to 120 in 1991.

CONNER PERIPHERALS
3081 Zanker Road
San Jose, California 95134
(408) 433-3340

Founded: 1985. **No. of Employees:** 9,576.   **Revenues (1990):** $1.3 billion. **Revenues (1987):** $113 million. **Four-Year Revenue Growth:** 1,050%.

Description: A manufacturer of high performance 3.5-inch and 2.5-inch hard disk drives for workstations and notebook, laptop, portable and desktop microcomputers. Employment grew 32% between 1989 and 1990.

How they're growing/Recent developments: Conner's philosophy has been to find niches in the marketplace and beat its competitors in exploiting them, and there is currently a strong demand for its products. Conner is now working on 1.8-inch drives and high-end products for workstations. Employment has grown from an estimated 1,286 in 1987 to 9,576 in 1991.

CONSECO, INC.
11825 North Pennsylvania
Carmel, Indiana 46032
(317) 573-6100

Founded: 1979. **No. of Employees:** 650. **Revenues (1990):** $753 million. **Revenues (1986):** $82 million. **Five-Year Revenue Growth:** 818%.

Description: A holding company engaged in the acquisition, ownership and operation of life and health insurance companies.

How they're growing/Recent developments: Conseco finds companies that could benefit for centralized management and economies of scale. In June, 1990, the company formed a limited partnership to acquire three life insurance companies. Growth continued into 1991, as first-quarter earnings rose sharply. Product profitability, strong investment return and operating efficiency have been the keys.

CONVERGENT SOLUTIONS INC.
100 Metro Park South
Laurence Harbor, New Jersey 08878
(908) 290-0090

Founded: 1981. **No. of Employees:** 77. **Revenues (1990):** $5.2 million. **Revenues (1986):** $2.5 million. **Five-Year Revenue Growth:** 108%.

Description: Develops and markets software for use on computers made by the convergent Technologies unit of Convergent, Inc. (a subsidiary of Unisys).

How they're growing/Recent developments: In 1989, the company completed the conversion of its major product for use on other systems, including UNIX and MS-DOS. In October of that year, the company also entered the IBM mainframe market. Employment has grown from an estimated 25 in 1987 to 77 in 1991.

COOPER TIRE & RUBBER
Lima at Western Avenue
Findlay, Ohio 45840
(419) 432-1321

Contact: Dr. Allan Pass, Vice President of Human Resources. **Founded:** 1930. **No. of Employees:** 6,225. **Revenues (1990):** $896 million. **Revenues (1986):** $578 million. **Five-Year Revenue Growth:** 55%.

Description: A manufacturer of tires, hoses, and a variety of related products.

How they're growing/Recent developments: Cooper focuses on producing tires for the replacement market, not on sales to automotive manufacturers. In this way, the company is not dependent on the sale of new automotives for its own sales. The company's management has also kept debt to a minimum. Employment has grown from an estimated 5,700 in 1987 to 6,225 in 1991.

CORNING INC.
Houghton Park
Corning, NY 14831
(607) 974-9000

Contact: Richard Marks, Vice President of Human Resources. **Founded:** 1936. **No. of Employees:** 28,600. **Revenues (1990):** $2.941 billion. **Revenues (1986):** $1.856 billion. **Five-Year Revenue Growth:** 58%.

Description: A leading manufacturer of glass, specialty optics, fine crystal, ceramics, and consumer items. The company also offers a variety of laboratory services.

How they're growing/Recent developments: Corning has grown through acquisitions and extensive research and development. Especially strong segments in 1991 were communications and laboratory services. Sales for the 40 weeks ending October 6, 1991, increased 12% year to year. Employment has been rising quickly since 1987. Between 1989 and 1990, about 1,100 new hires were made, and the company has earned itself a reputation as an especially good workplace for women and minorities. The company has been investing in new plants and distribution centers, which should promise even more new jobs in the future.

CORPORATE EXPRESS
13800 East 39th Avenue
Aurora, Colorado 80011
(303) 373-2800

Founded: 1985. **No. of Employees:** 260. **Revenues (1990):** $35 million. **Revenues (1986):** $351 thousand. **Five-Year Revenue Growth:** 9,871%.

Description: An office supply company.

How they're growing/Recent developments: Employment has grown from an estimated 23 in 1987 to 260 in 1991.

CORPORATE SOFTWARE
275 Dan Road
Canton, Massachusetts 02021
(617) 821-4500

Contact: Irene O'Donnell, Vice President of Human Resources. **Founded:** 1983. **No. of Employees:** 500. **Revenues (1990):** $197 million. **Revenues (1986):** $32 million. **Five-Year Revenue Growth:** 516%.

Description: Corporate Software wholesales and services computer software and hardware. Employment grew 103% between 1989 and 1990.

How they're growing/Recent developments: The company recently announced a partnership with Microsoft in which Corporate Software will provide services to large companies switching to Microsoft Windows. Employment has grown from an estimated 153 in 1987 to 500 in 1991.

COSMETIC & FRAGRANCE CONCEPTS, INC./ COSMETIC CENTER
8839 Greenwood Place
Savage, Maryland 20763
(301) 497-6800

Founded: 1955. **No. of Employees:** 825. **Revenues (1991):** $76 million. **Revenues (1986):** $35 million. **Six-Year Revenue Growth:** 117%.

Description: Operates The Cosmetic Center Stores carry over 20,000 brand name cosmetics, fragrances and beauty aides, as well as its own line of Courtney Brooke cosmetics. The company also operates a wholesale division. The company's 37 stores are located in metro Washington, D.C., Richmond, Virginia, and Chicago. NASDAQ.

Principal educational background sought: Retail.

Operations at this facility: Regional headquarters.

How they're growing/Recent Developments: The company's increases in retail sales is primarily attributable to the opening on new stores and an aggressive sales plan, which included advertising in the major metropolitan newspapers every week during the past fiscal year. Store expansion has been high on the company's list of priorities of late. Seven new Cosmetic Center stores were added to the chain over a period of 73 days, all opening before Thanksgiving Day, in order to take advantage of the holiday seasonal sales. Two stores, located in Bowie, Maryland, and Dale City, Virginia, opened in September, 1990; one store, located in Countryside, Illinois, opened in October, 1990; and four stores, in Waldorf, Maryland; Wheaton, Maryland; Wheaton, Illinois; and Skokie, Illinois, opened in November, 1990.

COSTCO WHOLESALE CORPORATION
10809 120th Avenue, N.E.
Kirkland, Wisconsin 98033
(206) 828-8100

Founded: 1983. **No. of Employees:** 12,400. **Revenues (1990):** $4.133 billion. **Revenues (1986):** $762 million. **Five-Year Revenue Growth:** 442%.

Description: The third-largest membership wholesale club in the United States.

How they're growing/Recent developments: Management has a policy of strict cost control and refuses to accept credit cards, helping to keep selling costs at approximately 8%. Employment has grown from an estimated 4,500 in 1987 to 12,400 in 1991.

COVENTRY CORPORATION
424 Church Street, Suite 2600
Nashville, Tennessee 37219
(615) 251-5500

Founded: 1986. **No. of Employees:** 2,475. **Revenues (1990):** $384 million. **Revenues (1987):** $10 million. **Four-Year Revenue Growth:** 3,740%

Description: Owners and operators of health maintenance organizations based in Pennsylvania and Missouri. Coventry also owns American Service, a health insurance company.

How they're growing/Recent developments: The company has experienced rapid growth in recent years due to strong enrollment at the company HMOs. Revenues advanced 26% year to year from June 30, 1991.

CPAC INC.
2364 Leicester Road
Leicester, New York 14481
(716) 382-3223

Contact: Wendy Clay, Human Resources. **Founded:** 1969. **No. of Employees:** 181. **Revenues (1990):** $28 million. **Revenues (1986):** $10 million. **Five-Year Revenue Growth:** 180%.

Description: Manufacturer of imaging chemicals and chemical recycling equipment for the imaging industry. NASDAQ.

Common positions include: Accountant; Blue-Collar Worker; Customer Service Representative; Draftsperson; Mechanical Engineer; Sales Representative.

Principal educational backgrounds sought: Accounting; Business Administration; Chemistry; Communications; Engineering; Finance; Marketing.

Company benefits: Medical, Dental, and Life Insurance; Tuition Assistance; Disability Coverage; Savings Plan; 401K; Stock Purchase.

Operations at this facility: Corporate and Divisional Headquarters; Manufacturing.

How they're growing/Recent developments: CPAC's subsidiary Allied Photo Products, acquired in 1988, supplies about 60% of the dental X-ray processor chemical market and 10% of the medical X-ray market. In December, 1989, CPAC announced the formation of CPAC Europe, which sells photographic chemicals to markets in Belgium, Germany, the United Kingdom, Scandinavia, Spain, and Portugal. The company is also just beginning to tap the East European market. Employment has grown from an estimated 164 in 1987 to 181 in 1991.

CRACKER BARREL OLD COUNTRY STORE, INC.
Hartman Drive
Box 787
Lebanon, Tennessee 37088-0787
(615) 444-5533

Founded: 1969. **No. of Employees:** 9,278. **Revenues (1990):** $226 million. **Revenues (1986):** $68 million. **Five-Year Revenue Growth:** 135%.

Description: Owners and operators of a chain of full-service country store restaurants and gift shops, located mostly in the Southeast and Midwest.

How they're growing/Recent developments: Cracker Barrel expects to open 21 new stores in 1992. Employment has grown from an estimated 2,750 in 1987 to 9,278 in 1991.

CRITICAL INDUSTRIES, INC.
5815 Gulf Freeway
Houston Texas 77023
(713) 923-1300

Founded: 1984. **No. of Employees:** 225. **Revenues (1990):** $40 million. **Revenues (1986):** $17 million. **Five-Year Revenue Growth:** 135%.

Description: Manufacturer of asbestos removing filter systems.

How they're growing/Recent developments: Employment has grown from an estimated 139 in 1987 to 225 in 1991.

CROWN CRAFTS, INC.
P.O. Box 12371
Calhoun, Georgia 30701
(404)629-7941

Founded: 1957. **No. of Employees:** 1,500. **Revenues (1990):** $102 million. **Revenues (1986):** $42 million. **Five-Year Revenue Growth:** 143%.

Description: Sells bedcovering products and accessories; supplier to retail stores.

How they're growing/Recent developments: Crown Crafts tries to respond to changing tastes and fashions by constantly identifying new products. Employment has grown from an estimated 1,070 in 1987 to 1,500 in 1991.

CSS INDUSTRIES
1401 Walnut Street
Philadelphia, Pennsylvania 19102
(215) 569-9900

Founded: 1923. **No. of Employees:** 1,557. **Revenues (1990):** $159 million. **Revenues (1986):** $34 million. **Five-Year Revenue Growth:** 368%.

Description: CSS is a holding company for companies engaged in both retail (stationery supplies) and manufacturing (metal packaging products).

How they're growing/Recent developments: Sales have continued to advance, aided by acquisitions. In 1990, CSS acquired a 75% stake in Standard Forms, as well as the Sloane Greeting Card line, and Marlenn Corporation, a maker of air fresheners.

CXR CORPORATION
521 Charcot Avenue
San Jose, California 95131
(408) 435-8520

Founded: 1984. No. of Employees: 245. Revenues (1990): $32.5 million. Revenues (1986): $5.2 million. Five-Year Revenue Growth: 525%.

Description: The parent company for CXR Telcom, a California-based manufacturer of telecommunications and monitoring equipment and modem products, and Digilog, Inc. a Pennsylvania-based manufacturer of electronic test equipment.

How they're growing/Recent developments: CXR's products are used by AT&T, the regional Bell companies and independent telecommunications companies. Employment has grown from an estimated 12 in 1987 to 245 in 1991.

CYPRESS SEMICONDUCTOR
3901 North First Street
San Jose, California 95134
(408) 943-2600

Founded: 1982. No. of Employees: 1,595. Revenues (1990): $225 million. Revenues (1986): $51 million. Five-Year Revenue Growth: 341%.

Description: Manufacturers of semiconductors.

How they're growing/Recent developments: Revenues have been climbing due to higher product yields and prices, and the success of new products. Much of the company's growth has come from the industry's hottest areas -- microcomputers, workstations, and aerospace. Over $55 million was spent on research and development in 1990. Employment has grown from an estimated 340 in 1987 to 1,595 in 1991.

DAIRY MART CONVENIENCE STORES
240 South Road
Enfield, Connecticut 06082
(203) 741-3611

Founded: 1972. No. of Employees: 5,272. Revenues (1990): $571 million. Revenues (1986): $254 million. Five-Year Revenue Growth: 125%.

Description: Convenience store chain.

How they're growing/Recent developments: Between 1990 and 1991, Dairy Mart acquired 137 Stop 'n' Go convenience stores.

DAISYTEK
500 North Central Express
Suite 500
Plano, Texas 75075
(214) 881-4700

Founded: 1977. **No. of Employees:** 240. **Revenues (1990):** $150.8 million. **Revenues (1986):** $15.9 million. **Five-Year Revenue Growth:** 848%.

Description: Distributes computer supplies and accessories.

How they're growing/Recent developments: Employment has grown from 45 in 1986 to 240 in 1991.

DALLAS SEMICONDUCTOR CORPORATION
4401 South Beltwood Parkway
Dallas, Texas 75244
(214) 450-0400

Founded: 1984. **No. of Employees:** 715. **Revenues (1990):** $100 million. **Revenues (1986):** $13 million. **Five-Year Revenue Growth:** 669%.

Description: Manufactures high-performance integrated circuits.

How they're growing/Recent development: Dallas Semiconductor has over 100 base products with more than 500 variations. The company introduced 26 new base products in 1991. Employment has grown from an estimated 224 in 1987 to 715 in 1991.

DANAHER CORPORATION
1250 24th Street North West, Suite 800
Washington, D.C. 20037
(202) 828-0850

Founded: 1969. **No. of Employees:** 8,000. **Revenues (1990):** $845 million. **Revenues (1986):** $454 million. **Five-Year Revenue Growth:** 86%.

Description: Manufacturer of automotive parts, precision components, and hand tools.

How they're growing/Recent developments: Danaher recently acquired Easco Hand Tools, a supplier of Sears Craftsman tools. Employment has grown from an estimated 7,100 in 1987 to 8,000 in 1991.

DANEK GROUP, INC.
3092 Directors Row
Memphis, Tennessee 38131
(901) 396-2695

Founded: 1983. **No. of Employees:** 230. **Revenues (1990):** $25.9 million. **Revenues (1988):** $7.5 million. **Three-Year Revenue Growth:** 245%

Description: A holding company whose subsidiaries are engaged in the development, manufacture, and marketing of spinal implant devices which are used in the surgical treatment of spinal degenerative diseases and deformities, and to increase stability during the healing of spinal trauma.

How they're growing/Recent developments: In August, 1991, the company signed licensing and development agreements for a porous patented biodegradable polymer that promotes bone and tissue growth, and could allow Danek to broaden its product line.

DART GROUP
3300 75th Avenue
Landover, Maryland 20785
(301) 731-1200

Founded: 1960. **No. of Employees:** 8,842. **Revenues (1990):** $1.1 million. **Revenues (1986):** $105 million. **Five-Year Revenue Growth:** 948%.

Description: Dart is engaged in operating retail discount auto parts stores through Trak Auto Corporation, retail book stores through Crown Books, retail discount grocery stores through Jumbo Food stores and Shoppers Foods, a real estate company through Cabot-Morgan Real Estate Company, and a financial business which purchases banker's acceptances through Dart Financial.

How they're growing/Recent developments: For the six months ended July 31, 1991, revenues rose 14% year to year, due to the opening of new Trak Auto, Crown Books and Shoppers Food Stores, as well as increased real estate revenues.

DATAFLEX CORPORATION
3920 Park Avenue
Edison, New Jersey 08820
(908) 321-1100

Contact: Diana Lombardo, Human Resources Placement Coordinator. **Founded:** 1976. **No. of Employees:** 206. **Revenues (1990):** $79.9 million. **Revenues (1986):** $9.3 million. **Five-Year Revenue Growth:** 759%.

Description: Dataflex specializes in the sale, support, and maintenance of personal computers and peripheral equipment. New York Stock Exchange.

Common positions include: Hardware/Software Computer Technicians.

Principal educational background sought: Technical School.

Company benefits: Medical and Life Insurance; Tuition Assistance; Disability Coverage.

Operations at this facility: Administration; Service; Sales.

How they're growing/Recent developments: To increase growth, Dataflex will be focusing on higher margin services, such as maintenance, network consulting and technical services; plans to broaden products and services. Recently expanded with a sales and service office in Hartford, Connecticut. Revenues for Fiscal 1991 rose to 92.4 million.

DATASCOPE CORPORATION
14 Philips Parkway
Montvale, New Jersey 07645
(201) 391-8100

Founded: 1964. **No. of Employees:** 1,200. **Revenues (1990):** $120 million. **Revenues (1986):** $67 million. **Five-Year Revenue Growth:** 79%.

Description: Manufactures products for clinical healthcare market.

How they're growing/Recent developments: In June, 1991, Datascope's product VasoSeal received approval from the FDA. The product can rapidly seal punctures associated with catheterizations. Employment has grown from an estimated 974 in 1987 to 1,200 in 1991. Employment has grown from an estimated 974 in 1987 to 1,200 in 1991.

DAVIS WATER & WASTE INDUSTRIES, INC.
1820 Metcalf Avenue
Thomasville, Georgia 31792
(912) 226-5733

Founded: 1956. **No. of Employees:** 867. **Revenues (1990):** $193 million. **Revenues (1986):** $101 million. **Five-Year Revenue Growth:** 91%.

Description: Manufactures products for the distribution of water and the treatment of water and sewage.

How they're growing/Recent developments: Davis acquired the Tolman Company in September, 1990. Employment has grown from an estimated 700 in 1987 to 867 in 1991.

DELL COMPUTER
9505 Arboretum Boulevard
Austin, Texas 78759
(512) 338-4400

Contact: Savino Ferrales, V.P. of Human Resources. **Founded:** 1984. **No. of Employees:** 1,900. **Revenues (1990):** $546 million. **Revenues (1986):** $69 million. **Five-Year Revenue Growth:** 691%.

Description: Designers and manufacturers of IBM-compatible PCs, peripherals and software.

How they're growing/Recent developments: Company founder Michael Dell started the firm from his college dorm room at age nineteen. At age twenty-six, he now heads one of the great success stories of American Business. Dell has recently introduced two computers based on Intel's 80486 microprocessor. The company has also replaced its line of 486-based machines with products which can be upgraded to use the new microprocessors. Employment has grown from an estimated 62 in 1987 to 1,900 in 1991.

DELUXE CORPORATION
1080 West County Road F
St. Paul, Minnesota 55126
(612) 483-7111

Founded: 1915. **No. of Employees:** 15,346. **Revenues (1990):** $1.4 billion. **Revenues (1986):** $867 million. **Five-Year Revenue Growth:** 61%.

Description: Deluxe is the largest check printing company in the United States. Other products include deposit slips and computer forms. The company serves the majority of the nation's banks, controlling over 50% of the market. Related operations include Deluxe Data Systems, which provides software and processing services to the electronic payment transfer market, and Business Systems, which supplies computer forms and record-keeping systems.

How they're growing/Recent developments: Since 1986 alone, Deluxe has acquired, among others, A.O. Smith Data Systems, Current Inc., SCH Systems, and most recently, Electronic Transaction Corporation, the nation's leading check authorization service. One of Deluxe's latest moves is into the point-of-sale market, having recently installed point-of-sale equipment into a St. Louis area supermarket chain. It is also now providing software for Canada's national point-of-sale network. The company's software market is also expanding into the Pacific Rim via a marketing arrangement with IBM. Deluxe's workforce increased by about 170 new jobs in 1991.

DESTEC ENERGY, INC.
2500 City West Boulevard, # 1700
Houston, Texas 77042
(713) 974-8200

Founded: 1989. **No. of Employees:** 436. **Revenues (1990):** $412 million. **Revenues (1986):** $11 million. **Five-Year Revenue Growth:** 3,645%.

Description: Company generates electric power. One of the largest non-utility producers of power.

How they're growing/Recent developments: The company has announced plans to build a $350 million gas-fired cogeneration power plant in Texas.

DEVCON INTERNATIONAL CORPORATION
1350 East Newport Center
Deerfield, Florida 33442
(305)429-1500

Founded: 1951. **No. of Employees:** 638. **Revenues (1990):** $90.1 million. **Revenues (1986):** $48.2 million. **Five-Year Revenue Growth:** 87%.

Description: Manufacturer of heavy construction and concrete products.

How they're growing/Recent developments: In April, 1991, Devcon acquired control of a marina in the Virgin Islands. The previous November, the company acquired Tortola Concrete Products LTD. In October, 1990, Devcon received $20 million in construction contracts in Florida, including two from Walt Disney World totaling $13 million. Employment has grown from an estimated 275 in 1987 to 638 in 1991.

DH TECHNOLOGY INC.
15070 Avenue of Science
San Diego, California 92128
(619) 451-3485

Founded: 1983. **No. of Employees:** 448. **Revenues (1990):** $41.1 million. **Revenues (1986):** $16.9 million. **Five-Year Revenue Growth:** 143%.

Description: Manufactures dot matrix printerheads and printer products used by specialty industries (lottery, labeling).

How they're growing/Recent developments: DH has expanded its international markets through the purchase of Datac, PLC of Manchester, England, a computer peripheral products company.

DIAGNOSTEK, INC.
4500 Alexander Boulevard NE
Albuquerque, New Mexico 87107
(505) 345-8080

Contact: Mary D'Ornellas, Director of Human Resources. **Founded:** 1983. **No. of Employees:** 775. **Revenues (1990):** $220 million. **Revenues (1986):** $14 million. **Five-Year Revenue Growth:** 1,471%.

Description: Diagnostek is engaged in mail order prescription drug operations, and well as running diagnostic-imaging centers.

Common positions include: Pharmacists; Management Information Systems Employees; Marketing Specialists; Financial Analysts; Purchasing Agents; Customer Service Representatives.

How they're growing/Recent developments: Diagnostek recently signed a $100 million deal with New Mexico's leading health maintenance organization. The company projects that it will fill nearly a million prescriptions during the contract's first year alone. Employment has grown from an estimated 175 in 1987 to 775 in 1991.

DIAGNOSTIC ENGINEERING, INC.
50 East Foothill Boulevard
Arcadia, California 91006
(818) 447-5216

Founded: 1983. **No. of Employees:** 165. **Revenues (1990):** $15 million. **Revenues (1986):** $500 thousand. **Five-Year Revenue Growth:** 2,900%.

Description: Providers of environmental consulting to businesses.

Common positions include: Architect; Chemist; Draftsperson; Civil Engineer; Geologist; Environmental Engineer; Industrial Hygienist.

Principal educational backgrounds sought: Biology; Chemistry; Engineering; Geology.

Company benefits include: medical insurance; dental insurance; life insurance; disability coverage.

Operations at this facility include: regional headquarters.

DIAGNOSTIC PRODUCTS CORPORATION
5700 West 96th Street
Los Angeles, California 90045
(213) 776-0180

Founded: 1971. **No. of Employees:** 619. **Revenues (1990):** $75.9 million. **Revenues (1986):** $29.0 million. **Five-Year Revenue Growth:** 162%.

Description: Manufactures immunodiagnostic test kits.

How they're growing/Recent developments: After increasing for seven consecutive years through 1990, earnings continued to advance in first quarter of 1991. In May, 1991, the company completed its acquisition of its German distributor, making it the largest supplier to the diagnostic market in Western Europe. Employment has grown from an estimated 345 in 1987 to 619 in 1991.

DIANON SYSTEMS
200 Watson Boulevard
Stratford, Connecticut 06497
(203) 381-4000

Founded: 1983. **No. of Employees:** 165. **Revenues (1990):** $20.8 million. **Revenues (1986):** $3.02 million. **Five-Year Revenue Growth:** 589%.

Description: Dianon is a leading provider of oncology testing services and diagnostic information to a focused audience of 12,500 cancer-treating physicians in the United States. Dianon purchases or licenses new technology from test developers which it markets directly to physicians as testing and information services rather than as products or test kits.

How they're growing/Recent developments: Dianon is expanding its business internationally by marketing its services directly to physicians in Europe and by sourcing new testing technology developed there. Dianon believes that its focus on oncology testing services provides several competitive advantages. As Dianon continues to expand its physician customer base, specimen bank and database, it is increasingly able to access new cancer testing technology from researchers and test developers. By offering early access to new testing technology and by combining it with the opportunity to participate in the company's clinical evaluation program, the company believes it is able to further expand its customer base. Revenues climbed to $27 million in fiscal 1991. Employment grew 11% from 1989 to 1990.

DIBRELL BROTHERS, INC.
512 Bridge Street
Danville, Virginia 24543
(804) 792-7511

Contact: Norma Lutz, Director of Human Resources. **Founded:** 1904. **No. of Employees:** 2,850. **Revenues (1990):** $765 million. **Revenues (1986):** $342 million. **Five-Year Revenue Growth:** 124%.

Description: Redries and packs leaf tobacco for sale to manufacturers of cigarettes and other tobacco products

Common positions include: Accountant; Administrator; Blue-Collar Worker Supervisor; Computer Programmer; Department Manager; Management Trainee; Operations/Production Manager; Quality Control Supervisor; Sales Representative.

Principal educational backgrounds sought: Accounting; Business Administration; Computer Science.

Company benefits: Medical, Dental, and Life Insurance; Pension Plan; Disability Coverage; Profit Sharing; Savings Plan.

Operations at this facility: Regional and Divisional Headquarters; Administration; Sales.

How they're growing/Recent developments: Most of the company's tobacco revenues derive from companies based outside of the United States. Revenues for fiscal 1991 rose rapidly once more, to just over a billion dollars, largely from ever increasing foreign sales. In 1988, the company entered the international flower brokerage market.

DICEON ELECTRONICS
18522 Von Karmon Avenue
Irvine, California 92715
(714) 833-0870

Contact: Robert Kollin, Director of Human Resources. **Founded:** 1980 . **No. of Employees:** 1500. **Revenues (1990):** $125 million. **Revenues (1986):** $85 million. **Five-Year Revenue Growth:** 47%.

Description: Manufacturer of printed circuit boards.

Common positions include: Accountant: Administrator; Blue-Collar Worker Supervisor; Buyer; Chemist; Electrical Engineer; Industrial Engineer; Metallurgical Engineer; Department Manager; Operations/Production Manager; Quality Control Supervisor; Sales Representative.

Principal educational backgrounds sought: Accounting; Business Administration; Chemistry; Engineering; Finance.

Company benefits: Medical, Dental, and Life Insurance; Tuition Assistance; Disability Coverage; Profit Sharing.

Operations at this facility: Manufacturing; Administration; Service; Sales.

DIGI INTERNATIONAL
6400 Flying Cloud Drive
Eden Prairie, Minnesota 55344
(612) 943-9020

Founded: 1985. **No. of Employees:** 164. **Revenues (1990):** $23.2 million. **Revenues (1987):** $3.7 million. **Four-Year Revenue Growth:** 527%.

Description: Digi International is a leading producer of data communications hardware and software products that permit microcomputers to function as multiuser computer systems in a variety of operating system environments. These multiuser systems allow one or more persons to share computing power as well as the programs and data of a single microcomputer. The company produces these communications subsystems under the names DigiBoard and Arnet.

How they're growing/Recent developments: Revenues have risen sharply since the company's founding, due to ever increasing demand for the companies products, making Digi, in the words of *Fortune* magazine, "a company to watch." Products are sold through a network of over 50 distributors in the United States, Canada, and abroad. The company completed acquisition of Arnet Corporation in March, 1991. New products include the DigiBoard ISDN NetLink and the Arnet ClusterPort/S.

DIGITAL MICROWAVE CORPORATION
170 Rose Orchard Way
San Jose, California 95134
(408) 943-0777

Founded: 1984. **No. of Employees:** 514. **Revenues (1990):** $111 million. **Revenues (1987):** $20 million. **Four-Year Revenue Growth:** 455%.

Description: One of the nation's leading manufacturers and marketers of advanced high-performance, short-haul microwave radio and fiber optic communications products.

How they're growing/Recent developments: In February, 1991, Digital formed a joint venture with Alpine Resource Sdn and Superior Communications Sdn to manufacture selected digital microwave products for the Malaysian and, eventually, the entire Asian market. Employment has grown from an estimated 154 in 1987 to 514 in 1991.

DILLARD DEPARTMENT STORES
P.O. Box 486
Little Rock, Arkansas 72203
(501) 376-5200

Founded: 1964. **No. of Employees:** 31,786. **Revenues (1990):** $3.2 billion. **Revenues (1986):** $1.6 billion. **Five-Year Revenue Growth:** 100%.

Description: Operates one of the largest regional department store chains in the nation, with over 170 stores in the Midwest and Southwest.

Common positions include: Computer Specialists; Buyer; Marketing Specialist.

How they're growing/Recent developments: The company has grown both through new store openings and the acquisition of stores from smaller regional retailers that are in trouble. Employment grew by 5,400 between 1989 and 1990 alone.

DIONEX
501 Mercury Drive
Sunnyvale, California 94088
(408) 737-0700

Founded: 1980. **No. of Employees:** 532. **Revenues (1990):** $81 million. **Revenues (1986):** $45 million. **Five-Year Revenue Growth:** 80%.

Description: Manufacturers of chemical analysis equipment.

How they're growing/Recent developments: Dionex boasts an extremely strong presence in foreign markets. In fact, international sales accounted for 52% of the total net sales for fiscal 1990. Marketing in Japan began in June, 1990. One of the latest products the company has introduced is a new system to separate proteins, carbohydrates and amino acids. Employment has grown from an estimated 370 in 1987 to 532 in 1991.

WALT DISNEY COMPANY
500 South Buena Vista Street
Burbank, California 91521
(818) 560-1000

Founded: 1938. **No. of Employees:** 52,000. **Revenues (1990):** $5.8 billion. **Revenues (1986):** $2.5 billion. **Five-Year Revenue Growth:** 132%.

Description: Perhaps the world's most famous entertainment company, Disney is engaged in a wide variety of entertainment and communication businesses, including the ownership and operation of amusement parks and hotels; film, television, and video production and syndication; audio production; book and magazine publishing; and the merchandising of Disney-related products.

How they're growing/Recent developments: Although the company's growth slowed slightly in fiscal 1991 due to the weak U.S. economy, Disney has grown remarkably since 1986 under the management of Michael Eisner. The company's new Euro Disney, located near Paris, is scheduled to open in the spring of 1992. In May, 1991, Disney unveiled its plan for "Westcot" a Disney-style world's fair. In addition, the company plans to build more hotels and a planned community in Orlando's Walt Disney World. The company also launched a full-scale book publishing division in 1990.

DIVERSIFIED TECHNOLOGY

P.O. Box 12988
Newport News, VA 23612-2988
(804)873-0725

Founded: 1982. **No. of Employees:** 137. **Revenues (1990):** $3.5 million. **Revenues (1986):** $427 thousand. **Five-Year Revenue Growth:** 720%.

Description: Provides government contracting services.

How they're growing/Recent developments: Employment has grown from 50 in 1986 to 137 in 1991.

R.R DONNELLEY & SONS CO.

2223 S. Martin Luther King Drive
Chicago, Illinois 60616
(312) 326-8000

Contact: Tom Jeswald, Manager of Human Relations. **Founded:** 1864. **No. of Employees:** 31,000. **Revenues (1990):** $3.5 billion. **Revenues (1986):** $2.2 billion. **Five-Year Revenue Growth:** 59%.

Description: The largest commercial printer in the world, specializing in a complete range of books, magazines, catalogues, directories, and tabloids. Provides financial and computer documentation, and related information services. New York Stock Exchange.

Common positions include: Accountant; Administrator; Attorney; Blue-Collar Worker; Buyer; Computer Programmer; Credit Manager; Customer Service Representative; Management Trainee; Sales Representative; Technical Writer/Editor; Transportation and Traffic Specialist.

Principal educational backgrounds sought: Accounting; Business Administration; Computer Science; Engineering; Liberal Arts.

Company benefits: Medical, Dental, and Life Insurance; Pension Plan; Tuition Assistance; Disability Coverage; Daycare Assistance; Savings Plan.

Operations at this facility: Regional and Divisional Headquarters; Manufacturing; Research/Development; Administration; Service; Sales.

How they're growing/Recent developments: Donnelley recently acquired Meredeth/Burda, a smaller commercial printer. In 1987, Donnelley purchased Metromail, a direct mail listing service. The company has added about 3,000 new staff members in the last two years.

DOW JONES & CO.
200 Liberty Street
New York, New York 10281
(212) 416-2000

Founded: 1882. **No. of Employees:** 9,000. **Revenues (1990):** $1.7 billion. **Revenues (1986):** $1.1 billion. **Five-Year Revenue Growth:** 55%.

Description: Dow Jones is a leading publisher of business news, information services and community newspapers. *The Wall Street Journal*, the company's best known publication, is the global business daily. With *The Wall Street Journal Europe*, published in Brussels, and *The Asian Wall Street Journal*, published in Hong Kong, world-wide circulation is more than two million. Dow Jones' other business publications include *Barron's* magazine, *The Far Eastern Economic Review, The National Business Employment Weekly, The Asian Wall Street Journal Weekly* and *American Demographics* magazine. The company's information services include wholly owned Telerate, Inc., a global supplier of real-time market data, decision support products, and services for the electronic trading of financial instruments; Dow Jones News/Retrieval, an interactive provider of business and financial information, Dow Jones News Services, which include the "Broadtape," the Capital Markets Report, the Professional Investor Report, the AP-Dow Jones International Newswires, Federal Filings and readio and television news services, and interactive telephone information services such as DowPhone and Journal Phone. and other newspapers, and operates newswires and information retrieval systems.

How they're growing/Recent developments: Revenues have grown recently due to increased advertising rates, a move made by management to counter an eroding ad base. In addition, Telerate, which is owned by the company, is currently marketing the Japan Business Newsline, an English-language service covering the Japanese financial markets from the Japanese point-of-view. In 1989, Telerate entered into an agreement with Intex Holdings, Ltd.

to provide fully automated trading systems for the London International Financial Futures Exchange.

THE DRESS BARN, INC.
88 Hamilton Avenue
Stamford, Connecticut 06902
(203) 327-4242

Founded: 1966. No. of Employees: 4,000. Revenues (1990): $284 million. Revenues (1986): $136 million. Five-Year Revenue Growth: 109%.

Description: Operates a chain of women's apparel stores.

How they're growing/Recent developments: In June, 1991, the Dress Barn announced a significant increase in business since the end of The Gulf War, following the opening of 54 new stores in fiscal 1990. The Dress Barn expected to open 100 new stores in 1991. Employment has grown from an estimated 1,500 in 1987 to 4,000 in 1991.

DREYER'S GRAND ICE CREAM
5929 College Avenue
Oakland, California 94618
(415) 652-8187

Founded: 1928. No. of Employees: 1,149. Revenues (1990): $308 million. Revenues (1986): $134 million. Five-Year Revenue Growth: 130%.

Description: Dreyer's manufactures and distributes premium-quality ice cream and other frozen dessert products. Also distributes frozen desserts manufactured by others.

How they're growing/Recent developments: Dreyer's strategy is based largely on careful quality control. New products are developed on the basis of blind taste tests, without regard to the expense of ingredients. The company also resists making formula changes, even when less expensive alternatives are available. Dreyer's has also moved quickly in the low-fat, low-cholesterol market through the introduction of three new products in that category in recent years. The company distributes for Ben & Jerry's Homemade, and Dove brand ice cream novelties, among others. In May, 1991, the company reached an agreement with Conagra, Inc. to manufacture and exclusively distribute Healthy Choice frozen dessert products. Dreyer's is also now an exporter to Japan. Employment has grown from an estimated 575 in 1987 to 1,149 in 1991.

DUAL & ASSOCIATES
2101 Wilson Boulevard
Arlington, VA 22201
(703) 527-3500

Founded: 1983. **No. of Employees:** 225. **Revenues (1990):** $19 million. **Revenues (1986):** $1 million. **Five-Year Revenue Growth:** 1,800%.

Description: Provides support services and contract manufacturing to the government.

How they're growing/Recent developments: Employment has grown from an estimated 50 in 1987 to 225 in 1991.

DUN & BRADSTREET CORPORATION
299 Park Avenue
New York, New York 10171
(212) 593-6800

Founded: 1930. **No. of Employees:** 71,500. **Revenues (1990):** $4.8 million. **Revenues (1986):** $3.1 million. **Five-Year Revenue Growth:** 55%.

Description: One of the nation's leading business services companies. The company publishes business, credit, financial and marketing information services, and provides business and credit information through its subsidiary McCormick & Dodge. Among the company's other operations are: Reuben H. Donnelly, publishers of yellow page telephone directories, Moody's Investors, providers of financial information, and Neodata Services, a marketing services company.

How they're growing/Recent developments: Dun & Bradstreet is an extremely strong company, and clearly dominates it market. It has expanded rapidly through aggressive marketing and acquisitions. In 1989, the company bought Sales Technologies, an automated sales systems with laptop technology. In 1991, the company published the USSR Exporters Directory for the first time, which contains information on Soviet mining and manufacturing firms. Although the eventual shape of the former Soviet Union is still unclear, other directories are planned.

DURIRON
3100 Research Boulevard
Dayton, Ohio 45420
(513) 226-4000

Founded: 1912. **No. of Employees:** 2,500. **Revenues (1990):** $297 million. **Revenues (1986):** $144 million. **Five-Year Revenue Growth:** 106%.

Description: Manufacturers of chemical processing equipment.

How they're growing/Recent developments: In 1989, Duriron acquired Automax Inc. The previous year, the company purchased the Atomac Unit of Fisher Controls, Gmbh. Employment has grown from an estimated 2,150 in 1987 to 2,500 in 1991.

DURR-FILLAUER MEDICAL, INC.
218 Commerce Street
Montgomery, Alabama 36104
(205) 241-8800

Founded: 1896. **No. of Employees:** 1,295. **Revenues (1990):** $815 million. **Revenues (1986):** $489 million. **Five-Year Revenue Growth:** 67%.

Description: One of the largest distributors of pharmaceuticals, medical products and veterinary supplies in the Southeast. The company also makes components for artificial limbs.

How they're growing/Recent developments: The company recently acquired the medical-surgical division of J.M. Keckler Medical Company, and also opened a new distribution center in Seattle, thus expanding it market coverage. Employment has grown from an estimated 1,120 in 1987 to 1,295 in 1991.

DUTY FREE INTERNATIONAL
19 Katonah Street
Ridgefield, Connecticut 06877
(203) 431-6057

Founded: 1983. **No. of Employees:** 950. **Revenues (1990):** $86 million. **Revenues (1986):** $16 million. **Five-Year Revenue Growth:** 437%.

Description: Owns and operates duty free retail stores.

How they're growing/Recent developments: The company's recent acquisition of a 16-store chain sharply increased sales. The company is also benefitting from heavier U.S.-Canadian traffic as well as increased travel through New York's John F. Kennedy International Airport by the Japanese. Fiscal 1991 revenues rose to $105 million.

DYCOM INDUSTRIES
450 Australia Road, Suite 860
West Palm Beach, Florida 33401
(407) 659-6301

Founded: 1969. **No. of Employees:** 2,325. **Revenues (1990):** $165 million. **Revenues (1986):** $46 million. **Five-Year Revenue Growth:** 259%.

Description: Provider of telecommunications and utility services.

How they're growing/Recent developments: Dycom's long-term revenue growth has been fueled by acquisitions, nine of which have been made since November, 1982. Employment has grown from an estimated 1,400 in 1987 to 2,325 in 1991.

DYNAMICS RESEARCH CORPORATION
60 Concord Street
Wilmington, Massachusetts 01887
(617) 438-3900

Founded: 1955. **No. of Employees:** 1,174. **Revenues (1990):** $90.5 million. **Revenues (1986):** $75.2 million. **Five-Year Revenue Growth:** 20%.

Description: Provider of advanced analytical engineering services and technical management services.

How they're growing/Recent developments: Despite cuts at the Department of Defense, Dynamics has successfully attracted funding for programs that have future larger market applications.

DYNATECH CORPORATION
3 New England Executive Park
Burlington, Massachusetts 01803
(617) 272-6100

Founded: 1959. **No. of Employees:** 3,150. **Revenues (1990):** $433 million. **Revenues (1986):** $257 million. **Five-Year Revenue Growth:** 68%.

Description: Manufactures and sells electronic instruments.

How they're growing/Recent developments: Following several acquisitions and divestitures recently, the company currently owns 40 manufacturing and 26 sales subsidiaries. Although earnings dropped in the first quarter of 1991 due to the recession, Dynatech has had increasing revenues each year since 1982. Employment has grown from an estimated 3,060 in 1987 to 3,150 in 1991.

EATON VANCE
24 Federal Street
Boston, Massachusetts 02110
(617) 482-8260

Founded: 1959. **No. of Employees:** 255. **Revenues (1990):** $55.1 million. **Revenues (1986):** $25.0 million. **Five-Year Revenue Growth:** 120%.

Description: A holding company whose primary business is investment management.

How they're growing/Recent developments: In May, 1990, Eaton Vance acquired the securities custody business of the now-defunct Bank of New England, effectively tripling assets and helping revenues soar. Employment has grown from an estimated 180 in 1987 to 255 in 1991.

ECOLOGY AND ENVIRONMENT
368 Pleasantview Drive
Lancaster, New York 14086
(716) 684-8060

Contact: Ms. Janet A. Steinbruckner, Personnel Director. **Founded:** 1970. **No. of Employees:** 1,200. **Revenues (1990):** $73 million. **Revenues (1986):** $27 million. **Five-Year Revenue Growth:** 170%.

Description: An environmental consulting company. American Stock Exchange.

Common positions include: Accountant; Attorney; Biochemist; Biologist; Chemist; Computer Programmer; Draftsperson; Economist; Ceramics, Civil, Electrical, Industrial, Mechanical, Metallurgical, and Petroleum Engineers; Forester; Geographer; Geologist; Geophysicist; Department Manager; Marketing Specialist; Personnel and Labor Relations Specialist; Physicist; Purchasing Agent; Quality Control Supervisor; Systems Analyst; Technical Writer/Editor.

Principal educational backgrounds sought: Accounting; Biology; Business Administration; Chemistry; Communications; Computer Science; Economics; Engineering; Finance; Geology; Physics.

Company benefits: Medical and Life Insurance; Pension Plan; Tuition Assistance; Disability Coverage; Profit Sharing.

Operations at this facility: Regional Headquarters; Research/Development; Administration; Sales.

How they're growing/Recent developments: Ecology and Environment's revenues come largely from Superfund contracts through the Environmental Protection Agency for field investigation and technical assistance teams. In 1990, the company was awarded a contract that could yield over $100 million. Employment has grown from an estimated 650 in 1987 to 1,200 in 1991.

EFI ELECTRONICS CORPORATION
2415 South 2300 West
Salt Lake City, Utah 84119
(801)977-9009

Founded: 1981. **No. of Employees:** 94. **Revenues (1990):** $9.7 million. **Revenues (1986):** $4.9 million. **Five-Year Revenue Growth:** 98%

Description: EFI Electronics Corporation is a leading American manufacturer in the power conditioning industry. The company's patented voltage surge suppression (VSS) and uninterrupted power supply (UPS) products are designed to ensure electrical power to protect computer, telecommunications and microprocessor based equipment in a wide range of industrial, medical, and consumer applications.

How they're growing/Recent developments: Management attributes much of EFI's recent growth to improved marketing and manufacturing techniques and a shifting to higher margin products. The company expanded its marketing department with the addition of new product managers with greater involvement in product development and sales promotion. Late in 1991, the company launched its 500VA UPS battery back-up product for LANs (local area networks) and stand alone applications was a direct result of the company's stated resolve to respond to the changing marketplace." Revenues rose to $11.9 million in fiscal 1991.

EG&G

45 William Street
Wellesley, Massachusetts
(617) 237-5100

Founded: 1947. **No. of Employees:** 32,000. **Revenues (1990):** $2.27 billion. **Revenues (1986):** $1.1 billion. **Five-Year Revenue Growth:** 106%.

Description: EG&G is the parent to more than 50 providers of services and products to government and industry. Government contracts include military engineering, development and management programs. The largest segment of the company is contracted with the Department of Energy to provide services related to nuclear weapons testing and other energy research. The company's private sector business provides services to the automotive and aerospace industries.

How they're growing/Recent developments: Over the years, EG&G has spurred growth through expansion and acquisitions. Acquisitions have helped to broaden the company's product line. In 1990, EG&G took over management of the troubled Rocky Flats nuclear weapons production facility near Golden, Colorado. Employment has grown from an estimated 25,000 in 1987 to 32,000 in 1991.

EGGHEAD, INC.

P. O. Box 7004
Issaquah, Washington 98027-7004
(206) 391-5160

Founded: 1984. **No. of Employees:** 1,708. **Revenues (1990):** $519 million. **Revenues (1986):** $27 million. **Five-Year Revenue Growth:** 1,822%.

Description: Egghead is the nation's largest specialty retailer of personal computer software. As of March, 1991, the company operated 187 stores and had a 322-person direct sales staff serving medium-sized and large businesses.

How they're growing/Recent developments: Since it opened its first store in 1984, Egghead has expanded extremely rapidly. When a new management team took over in early 1989, the company refocused in favor of closer management of existing operations and keeping tighter cost controls. Employment has grown from an estimated 1,439 in 1987 to 1,708 in 1991.

EHMAN

P.O. Box 2126
Evanston, Wyoming 82931-2126
(307) 789-3830

Contact: Jim Sauerbreit, Personnel. **Founded:** 1985. **No. of Employees:** 134.
Revenues (1990): $30 million. **Revenues (1986):** $341 thousand. **Five-Year Revenue Growth:** 8,698%.

Description: Manufacturers of Macintosh computer peripherals, including storage devices and video products.

Common positions include: Accountant; Buyer; Customer Service Representative; Department Manager; Operations/Production Manager; Marketing Specialist; Purchasing Agent; Sales Representative.

Principal educational background sought: Business Administration; Computer Science; Engineering; Marketing.

Company benefits: Medical, Dental, and Life Insurance; Disability Coverage.

Operations at this facility: Manufacturing, Research/Development; Administration; Service; Sales.

How they're growing/Recent developments: Ehman's products have consistently garnered good industry reviews. In the November, 1991 issue of MacUser, the company's 100 megabyte 105Q LPS hardrive was rated sixth out of 100 in overall performance. Employment has grown from an estimated 20 in 1987 to 134 in 1991.

ELECTRONIC ARTS

1450 Fashion Island Boulevard
San Mateo, California 94404
(415) 571-7171

Founded: 1982. **No. of Employees:** 300. **Revenues (1990):** $72 million. **Revenues (1986):** $17 million. **Five-Year Revenue Growth:** 324%.

Description: Manufacturers of consumer computer games.

How they're growing/Recent developments: The company's claim to fame is designing games for Nintendo Entertainment System Gameboy products. Electronic Arts has also benefitted from strong sales of Sega Genesis games. In July, 1991, the company acquired Distinctive Software, Inc.

EMCON
400 South El Camino Real, Suite 1200
San Mateo, California 94402
(415) 375-1522

Contact: Barry A. Langford, Vice President. **Founded:** 1971. **No. of Employees:** 850. **Revenues (1990):** $56 million. **Revenues (1986):** $15 million. **Five-Year Revenue Growth:** 273%.

Description: Emcon provides comprehensive environmental engineering and consulting services to generators, handlers, and disposers of solid and hazardous wastes. The company conducts operations from 30 locations in Alaska, Washington, Oregon, California, Arizona, Massachusetts, Georgia, and Florida. NASDAQ.

How they're growing/Recent developments: During the summer of 1991, Emcon acquired Golden State Analytical Services and E&A Environmental Consultants. The former is a small, Southern California-based lab, and E&A is a Massachusetts-based company specializing in composting and recycling. The Georgia-based Special Environmental Services (now EMCON Southeast) was acquired in October, 1991. EMCON attributes its growth to a combination of internal growth and a highly successful acquisition program.

EMERSON ELECTRIC COMPANY
8000 West Florissant Avenue
St. Louis, Missouri 63136
(314) 553-2000

Founded: 1890. **No. of Employees:** 73,700. **Revenues (1990):** $7.6 billion. **Revenues (1986):** $5 billion. **Five-Year Revenue Growth:** 52%.

Description: The seventh largest producer of electrical and electronic products in the United states. Products range from electric motors, switches, valves, and uninterruptible power supplies for computers, to consumer products like saws and drills.

How they're growing/Recent developments: Emerson has posted over 30 consecutive years of annual growth. Management strategy has been to constantly acquire new companies, while carefully selling off any unprofitable operations. During 1990, Emerson acquired the French motor manufacturer Levoy-Somer and the Italian motor manufacturer CESET, as well as a 47% stake in the Hong Kong-based Astec, a maker of power supply equipment. International sales have expanded to 30% of the company's total. Employment has grown from an estimated 68,000 in 1987 to 73,700 in 1991.

EMPI
1275 Grey Fox Road
St. Paul, Minnesota 55112
(612) 636-6600

Founded: 1977. **No. of Employees:** 162. **Revenues (1990):** $16 million. **Revenues (1986):** $10 million. **Five-Year Revenue Growth:** 60%.

Description: Empi manufactures non-invasive biomedical devices and accessories for electrotherapeutic applications in physical medicine, orthopedic, rehabilitation and neurology markets.

How they're growing/Recent developments: Sales reached record levels during the first half of 1991, based on rising sales of the company's pain control and rehabilitation business. Employment has grown from an estimated 110 in 1987 to 162 in 1991.

ENCLEAN INC.
1600 East Highway 6
Alvin, Texas 77511
(713) 331-5406

Founded: 1984. **No. of Employees:** 500. **Revenues (1990):** $53 million. **Revenues (1988):** $31 million. **Three-Year Revenue Growth:** 71%.

Description: Provides industrial and environmental cleaning services to major companies in the refining, gas processing, petrochemical, chemical, utility, pulp and paper, steel, food and other process industries.

How they're growing/Recent developments: EnClean's management has pursued an extremely aggressive growth strategy through acquisitions. Revenues for the fiscal year that ended June 30, 1991, climbed to $100 million -- almost doubling 1990's total.

ENCORE COMPUTER
6901 West Sunrise Boulevard
Fort Lauderdale, Florida 33313-4499
(305) 587-2900

Founded: 1983. **No. of Employees:** 1,679. **Revenues (1990):** $215 million. **Revenues (1986):** $5 million. **Five-Year Revenue Growth:** 4,200%.

Description: Manufactures and markets computer systems.

How they're growing/Recent developments: Although Encore suffered a setback recently when it was outbid by IBM on a NASA contract, revenues had climbed sharply each year previous to 1991. In April, 1989, Encore acquired the computer systems business of Gould, Inc. Employment has grown from an estimated 265 in 1987 to 1,679 in 1991.

ENERGY VENTURES
5 Post Oak Park, Suite 1760
Houston, Texas 77027
(713) 297-8400

Founded: 1972. **No. of Employees:** 1,800. **Revenues (1990):** $153.1 million. **Revenues (1987):** $2.5 million. **Four-Year Revenue Growth:** 6,024%.

Description: Energy Ventures is an oilfield service and equipment company. The company provides drilling and workover services and manufactures specialty tubular products and artificial life equipment.

How they're growing/Recent developments: For the year ending December 31, 1990, the company's revenues were $153.1 million, and increase of 42% over revenues for 1989. The company made four major acquisitions during 1990, and will continue to grow through further acquisitions and internal development within the oilfield service and equipment industry.

ENNIS BUSINESS FORMS, INC.
107 North Sherman Street
Ennis, Texas, 75119
(214) 875-6581

Founded: 1909. **No. of Employees:** 1,270. **Revenues (1990):** $130 million. **Revenues (1986):** $111 million. **Five-Year Revenue Growth:** 17%.

Description: A major producer of custom and semi-custom business forms for international distribution.

How they're growing/Recent developments: In 1991, Ennis purchased Ardmore, Inc., a specialty printing company with annual sales of about $15 million.

ENTERTAINMENT MARKETING
10310 Harwin
Houston, Texas 77036
(713) 995-4433

Founded: 1983. **No. of Employees:** 133. **Revenues (1990):** $232 million. **Revenues (1986):** $21 million. **Five-Year Revenue Growth:** 1,004%.

Description: Wholesaler of home electronics appliances.

ESQUIRE RADIO & ELECTRONICS
4116 1st Avenue
Brooklyn, New York 11220
(718) 499-0020

Founded: 1960. **No. of Employees:** 180. **Revenues (1990):** $74 million. **Revenues (1986):** $16.1 million. **Five-Year Revenue Growth:** 360%.

Description: A distributor of consumer telecommunications products, mainly telephones.

How they're growing/Recent developments: Revenues have climbed since 1988 as a result of an agreement with Southwestern Bell Telecommunications. The agreement was recently extended through the end of 1994.

ETHYL CORPORATION
330 South Fourth Street
Richmond, Virginia 23217
(804) 788-5000

Founded: 1877. **No. of Employees:** 5,700. **Revenues (1990):** $2.4 billion. **Revenues (1986):** $1.6 billion. **Five-Year Revenue Growth:** 50%.

Description: Produces specialty industrial and petroleum chemicals. The company also is the parent of First Colony Life Insurance.

How they're growing/Recent developments: Ethyl Corporation has benefitted from a strong worldwide demand for both industrial and petroleum chemicals. First Colony has been particularly strong in annuity sales. In 1989, the company acquired Russ Pharmaceuticals, a manufacturer of ethical analgesics.

BOB EVANS FARMS, INC.
Box 07863, Station G
Columbus, Ohio 43207-9947
(614) 491-2225

Founded: 1957. **No. of Employees:** 17,300. **Revenues (1990):** $454 million. **Revenues (1986):** $263 million. **Five-Year Revenue Growth:** 73%.

Description: Bob Evans Farms operates over 250 family restaurants, as well as manufacturing sausages.

How they're growing/Recent developments: The company has expanded both through acquisitions and new concepts, like a combination restaurant and general store. Even as the consumption of red meat has declined and despite rising labor costs, the company has increased its earnings through expansion. In 1987, the company acquired the Texas-based Owens Family Restaurant chain and Owens Country sausages. The company's plans also include the expansion of the company's Cantina del Rio chain of Mexican restaurants.

EVEREX SYSTEMS
48431 Milmont Drive
Fremont, California 94538
(415) 498-1111

Founded: 1983. **No. of Employees:** 2,150. **Revenues (1990):** $437 million. **Revenues (1986):** $63 million. **Five-Year Revenue Growth:** 594%.

Description: Manufacturers of personal computers, as well as over 100 peripheral and enhancement products.

How they're growing/Recent developments: Although total revenues declined slightly for the nine-month period ending April 30, 1991, due to the national recession, new products should increase demand. The company currently has under development a laser printer, a flatbed scanner and hard disk and graphics controllers, among other new products.

EXECU*SYSTEMS
4427 North 36th Street
Suite 200
Phoenix, Arizona 85018
(602) 957-0444

Founded: 1965. **No. of Employees:** 120. **Revenues (1990):** $1.8 million. **Revenues (1986):** $194 thousand. **Five-Year Revenue Growth:** 828%.

Description: Provides real estate brokerage services.

How they're growing/Recent developments: Employment has grown from an estimated 2 in 1987 to 120 in 1991.

EXCEL INDUSTRIES
P.O. Box 3118
Elkhart, Indiana 46515-3118
(219) 264-2131

Founded: 1935. **No. of Employees:** 2,649. **Revenues (1990):** $281 million. **Revenues (1986):** $148 million. **Five-Year Revenue Growth:** 90%.

Description: Supplier of window systems to trucks, vans and bus sellers, mainly Ford, General Motors, and Chrysler.

How they're growing/Recent developments: In late 1990, Excel acquired the Door Systems Division of Johnson Controls. Employment has grown from an estimated 2,500 in 1987 to 2,649 in 1991.

EXPEDITORS INTERNATIONAL
19119 16th Avenue South
Seattle, Washington 98118
(206) 246-3711

Founded: 1979. **No. of Employees:** 744. **Revenues (1990):** $207 million. **Revenues (1986):** $109 million. **Five-Year Revenue Growth:** 90%.

Description: This Seattle-based company is an air freight forwarder, customhouse broker, and ocean freight forwarder.

How they're growing/Recent developments: Most revenues have come from freight forwarding of imports from the Far East to the United States. Expeditors International is currently attempting to diversify into export shipments from the United States to the Far East and Europe. Employment has grown from an estimated 350 in 1987 to 744 in 1991.

FASTENAL COMPANY
2001 Theurer Boulevard
Winona, Minnesota 55987
(507)454-5374

Founded: 1967. **No. of Employees:** 199. **Revenues (1990):** $53 million. **Revenues (1987):** $20 million. **Five-Year Revenue Growth:** 169%.

Description: Operates through 125 outlets located in 11 Midwestern states as well as Pennsylvania, New York, West Virginia, and Kentucky. This company sells 24,000 types of threaded fasteners and other industrial and construction supplies.

FEDDERS CORPORATION
158 Highway 206
Peapack, New Jersey 07977
(908) 234-2100

Founded: 1984. **No. of Employees:** 2,200. **Revenues (1990):** $241 million. **Revenues (1986):** $94 million. **Five-Year Revenue Growth:** 156%.

Description: An air conditioner manufacturer.

How they're growing/Recent developments: Fedders has increased market share from 8% in 1982 to 24% in 1990. It latest product is the Microsonic, which is 40% smaller and one-third lighter and quieter than conventional models. fiscal 1991 was a difficult year, however, as orders fell sharply following a cooler than normal summer of 1990. Excess inventory has now been used up, and retailers should be placing normal reorders for 1992. The company will also begin to see increased revenues as a result of the company's acquisition of Emerson Quiet Cool. Employment has grown from an estimated 1,000 in 1987 to 2,200 in 1991.

FEDERAL EXPRESS CORPORATION
P.O. Box 727
Memphis, Tennessee 38194
(901) 369-3600

Founded: 1971. **No. of Employees:** 91,550. **Revenues (1990):** $7.7 billion. **Revenues (1986):** $2.6 billion. **Five-Year Revenue Growth:** 196%.

Description: The nation's largest private overnight delivery service.

How they're growing/Recent developments: FEDEX has been trying to expand into overseas, though it has been costly. As of February, 1992, the company was considering ways to stem overseas losses. During 1991, FEDEX began to explore diversifying into aviation services and pilot training through its new FEDEX Aeronautics Corporation.

FIRST FINANCIAL MANAGEMENT
3 Corporate Square, Suite 700
Atlanta, Georgia 30329
(404) 321-0120

Founded: 1971. **No. of Employees:** 2,700. **Revenues (1990):** $925 million. **Revenues (1986):** $74.4 million. **Five-Year Revenue Growth:** 1,143%.

Description: First Financial Management Corporation is a leader in information services, offering a vertically integrated set of data processing, storage and management products for the capture, manipulation and distribution of data. Services include merchant credit card authorization, processing and settlement; debt collection and accounts receivable management; data imaging, micrographics and electronic database management; financial institutions processing; health and pharmaceutical claims processing; and the development and marketing of data communications and information and information processing systems. In addition, the company owns one of the nation's largest savings institutions. The company serves a large and diverse institutional customer base that serves the consumer: merchants, restaurants, hotels, manufacturers, wholesalers, banks, thrifts, mortgage loan services, credit unions, insurance companies, hospitals and physicians, various national, state and local government agencies, and the consumer as well. The company provides services to 120,000 commercial and governmental customers and a 470,000 customers through a distribution network of 200,000 on-line devices and 379 business units throughout the United States.

How they're growing/Recent developments: Acquisitions play a major role in the company's growth, providing geographic expansion and greater market penetration of existing businesses, entry into new business lines and additional management depth and expertise. During 1990 alone, the company completed seven acquisitions: Electro Data Corporation, OnLine Financial Communications Systems, Nationwide Credit, Zytron Corporation, the assets of Finance South and Post-Tron Systems Corporation, and part of the assets of Chilton Data Services. The company also signed a major systems contract with Ryder Truck Rental, Inc. Revenues increased 39% from the previous fiscal year. The company's largest and fastest growing segment is Merchant Services, which handled $24 billion in credit card sales in 1990 alone.

FOOD LION, INC.
P.O. Box 1330
Salisbury, North Carolina 28145-1350
(704) 633-8250

Founded: 1957. **No. of Employees:** 60,000. **Revenues (1990):** $5.6 billion. **Revenues (1986):** $2.4 billion. **Five-Year Revenue Growth:** 132%.

Description: A supermarket chain based in North Carolina.

How they're growing/Recent developments: Management has placed a focus on volume to keep prices down. When Food Lion expands into an area, it opens stores and a distribution warehouse nearby, thus cutting down on warehouse and transportation costs. Fiscal 1991 revenues rose to $6.4 billion. The company goal is to have 2,000 stores opened across the nation by the year 2000. Employment reached about 60,000 in 1990, up an astounding 10,000 jobs from the previous year alone.

FOREST LABORATORIES
150 East 58th Street
New York, New York 10155
(212) 421-7850

Founded: 1956. **No. of Employees:** 1,005. **Revenues (1990):** $176 million. **Revenues (1986):** $64 million. **Five-Year Revenue Growth:** 175%.

Description: Sells pharmaceutical and related products.

How they're growing/Recent developments: Earnings have been in long-term uptrend. In August, 1991, the company completed an interim analysis of clinical studies of Synapton, a drug being investigated for use in treating Alzheimer's disease.

FOUNDATION HEALTH CORPORATION
3400 Data Drive
Rancha Cordova, California 95670
(916) 631-5000

Founded: 1986. **No. of Employees:** 1,100. **Revenues (1990):** $889 million. **Revenues (1987):** $99 million. **Four-Year Revenue Growth:** 798%.

Description: A provider of medical and health service plans.

Common positions include: Accountant; Actuary; Buyer; Computer Programmer; Customer Service Representative; Department Manager; Personnel and Labor Relations Manager; Public Relations Manager; Purchasing Agent; Reporter/Editor; Systems Analyst; Technical Writer/Editor.

Principal educational backgrounds sought: Accounting; Business Administration; Communications; Computer Science; Economics; Finance; Marketing.

Company benefits: Medical, Dental, and Life Insurance; Pension Plan; Tuition Assistance.

Operations at this facility: Regional Headquarters; Administration; Sales.

How they're growing/Recent developments: Earnings rose strongly in fiscal 91, assisted by cost control efforts. In August, 1991, Foundation Health acquired National Health Care Systems, Inc. Earlier in the year, Foundation Health received a five-year contract from the Department of Defense to provide health care services for military families in the New Orleans area.

FRANKLIN INTERNATIONAL INSTITUTE
2640 Decker Lake Boulevard
Salt Lake City, Utah 84119
(801) 975-1776

Founded: 1984. **No. of Employees:** 513. **Revenues (1990):** $51.6 million. **Revenues (1986):** $3 million. **Five-Year Revenue Growth:** 1,620%.

Description: Produces time management seminars and products.

How they're growing/Recent developments: The company's growth strategy has been to develop business through "seeding," or giving away products to a selective group of CEO's and corporate managers, and then letting them market the product if they like it. This strategy has built sales up to more than $52 million in sales in six years. The company stresses customer service, which it sees as providing the competitive advantage of the 1990s. The company's time management seminars are now delivered to over 20,000 participants a month. Employment has grown from 48 in 1986 to 513 in 1991.

FRANKLIN RESOURCES
777 Mariner's Island Boulevard
San Mateo, California 94404
(415) 570-3000

Founded: 1969. **No. of Employees:** 2,054. **Revenues (1990):** $479 million. **Revenues (1986):** $88 million. **Five-Year Revenue Growth:** 444%.

Description: The holding company for The Ben Franklin Group of mutual funds.

How they're growing/Recent developments: Franklin is the largest mutual fund group in the nation and has gained a solid reputation for consistent performance and a high customer retention rate. Assets have increased year to year since 1989. Employment has grown from an estimated 1,700 in 1987 to 2,054 in 1991.

FREDERICK'S OF HOLLYWOOD
6608 Hollywood Boulevard
Los Angeles, California 90028
(213) 466-5151

Founded: 1962. **No. of Employees:** 1,400. **Revenues (1990):** $99 million. **Revenues (1986):** $49 million. **Five-Year Revenue Growth:** 102%.

Description: A retail and mail-order marketer of intimate apparel.

How they're growing/Recent developments: In July, 1991, Frederick's opened five new stores. The company backs its stores with aggressive promotional campaigns that include ads in newspapers and in national television. Both catalog and retail sales are up. Employment has grown from an estimated 1,000 in 1987 to 1,400 in 1991.

FREEPORT McMORAN RESOURCES
1615 Poydras Street
New Orleans, Louisiana 70112
(504) 582-4000

Founded: 1986. **No. of Employees:** 5,730. **Revenues (1990):** $864 million. **Revenues (1986):** $217 million. **Five-Year Revenue Growth:** 298%.

Description: Freeport McMoran mines sulfur and manufactures phosphated fertilizers.

How they're growing/Recent developments: In early 1991, Freeport completed a restructuring program which was initiated to fund development of a major sulfur and oil discovery in the Gulf of Mexico. The company's earnings have improved in light of strong demand and higher prices for fertilizers.

FRONTIER INSURANCE GROUP
196 Broadway, P.O. Box 5016
Monticello, New York 12701
(914) 796-2100

Founded: 1986. **No. of Employees:** 190. **Revenues (1990):** $72 million.
Revenues (1986): $26 million. **Five-Year Revenue Growth:** 177%.

Description: A specialty property and casualty insurance company.

How they're growing/Recent developments: In October, 1991, Frontier acquired Contractor's Surety Co. in order to expand sureties in California. Employment has grown from an estimated 53 in 1987 to 190 in 1991.

FROZEN FOOD EXPRESS INDUSTRIES
P.O. Box 655888
Dallas, Texas 75265
(214) 428-7661

Founded: 1969. **No. of Employees:** 1,044. **Revenues (1990):** $160 million.
Revenues (1986): $91 million. **Five-Year Revenue Growth:** 76%.

Description: The largest publicly owned motor carrier of frozen perishables in the United States.

How they're growing/Recent developments: The company has recently expanded its fleet of company-owned tractor trailers to help boost profits. Company owned trucks save money that would otherwise be spent on contracting from independents. Employment has grown from an estimated 600 in 1987 to 1,044 in 1991.

FRS, INC.
1101 National Drive
Sacramento, California 95834
(916) 928-1107

Founded: 1984. **No. of Employees:** 280. **Revenues (1990):** $14 million.
Revenues (1986): $3 million. **Five-Year Revenue Growth:** 367%.

Description: The company provides inventory management and repair services for computer products.

Common positions include: Customer Service Representative; Electrical Engineer; Operations/Production Manager; Marketing Specialist; Purchasing Agent; Quality Control Supervisor.

Principal educational backgrounds sought: Business Administration; Engineering; Marketing.

Company benefits: Medical, Dental, and Life Insurance; Tuition Assistance; Disability Coverage.

Operations at this facility: Manufacturing; Research/Development; Administration; Service; Sales.

How they're growing/Recent developments: The company attributes its growth to expansions, recent acquisitions, and its overall growth strategy.

FURON COMPANY
29982 Ivy Glenn Drive
Laguna Nigul, California 92677
(714) 831-5350

Founded: 1957. **No. of Employees:** 2,846. **Revenues (1990):** $327 million. **Revenues (1986):** $97.8 million. **Five-Year Revenue Growth:** 234%.

Description: Furon is a major supplier of highly engineered components made primarily from specially formulated high-performance polymers and elastomeric compounds.

How they're growing/Recent developments: Most orders are custom designed and engineered to meet customers specifications. This is especially true for the company's European customers.

FUTURE NOW
2722 East Kemper Road
Cincinnati, Ohio 45241
(513) 771-7110

Founded: 1988. **No. of Employees:** 180. **Revenues (1990):** $83.2 million. **Revenues (1986):** $8.5 million. **Five-Year Revenue Growth:** 897%

Description: Future Now sells installs and services microcomputers, micro-computer software products and turnkey microcomputer systems for business, professional, educational and governmental customers. The company offers a wide range of related customer support services, including network analysis and design, systems configuration, custom installation, training, maintenance and repair. Future Now has six sales offices located in Cincinnati, Columbus and Dayton, Ohio; Fort Wayne and Indianapolis, Indiana; and Louisville, Kentucky.

How they're growing/Recent developments: Approximately 48% of the company's product purchases were made through franchise agreements with Intelligent Electronics, a leading reseller of microcomputer products. Future Now believes that it receives the lowest mark-ups offered by Intelligent Electronics. The company's growth strategy is to increase it market share in existing markets and to expand into new geographic areas. Growth and increased penetration in its existing markets will come with the identification of new customers, the addition of marketing and support personnel, local acquisitions and further implementation of the company's Solution Center concept. Solution Centers are sales office facilities featuring interconnected and fully operational product demonstration and evaluation areas, conference rooms, classrooms and technical facilities. The company's principal method for expanding into new geographic areas will continue to be the acquisition and subsequent enhancement of existing businesses.

GAINEY TRANSPORTATION SERVICES
P.O. Box 8487
Grand Rapids, Michigan 49518
(616) 530-8551

Founded: 1984. **No. of Employees:** 305. **Revenues (1990):** $28 million. **Revenues (1986):** $3 million. **Five-Year Revenue Growth:** 833%.

Description: Operates a long-distance trucking service.

How they're growing/Recent developments: Employment has grown from an estimated 42 in 1987 to 305 in 1991.

GAINSCO
500 Commerce
Fort Worth, Texas 76102
(817) 336-2500

Founded: 1978. **No. of Employees:** 124. **Revenues (1990):** $42.7 million. **Revenues (1986):** $8.3 million. **Five-Year Revenue Growth:** 414%.

Description: A property and casualty insurer.

How they're growing/Recent developments: MGA Insurance Co., a unit of Gainsco, was appointed by Pennsylvania to service insurance policies in the state assigned-risk plan for car insurance. Gainsco also recently signed a joint venture agreement with Shared Resource Management of Minnesota, Inc. to develop software for general agents. Employment has grown from an estimated 62 in 1987 to 124 in 1991.

GALE GROUP
111 North Orlando Avenue
Winter Park, Florida 32789
(407) 621-4253

Founded: 1981. **No. of Employees:** 395. **Revenues (1990):** $36.7 million. **Revenues (1986):** $2.6 million. **Five-Year Revenue Growth:** 1,311%.

Description: Manufacturers of plastic products and coated fabrics.

How they're growing/Recent developments: Employment has grown from an estimated 39 in 1987 to 395 in 1991.

ARTHUR J. GALLAGHER
2 Pierce Place
Itasca, Illinois 60143-3141
(708) 773-3800

Contact: William J. Hornig, Director of Human Resources. **Founded:** 1927. **No. of Employees:** 2,044. **Revenues (1990):** $198 million. **Revenues (1986):** $119 million. **Five-Year Revenue Growth:** 66%.

Description: An insurance brokerage and risk management business. New York Stock Exchange.

Common positions include: Accountant; Administrator; Claim Representative; Computer Programmer; Insurance Agent/Broker; Department Manager; Personnel and Labor Relations Specialist; Sales Representative.

Principal educational backgrounds sought: Accounting; Business Administration; Finance; Liberal Arts.

Company benefits: Medical, Dental, and Life Insurance; Pension Plan; Tuition Assistance; Disability Coverage; Employee Discounts; Savings Plan.

Operations at this facility: Regional Headquarters; Divisional Headquarters; Administration.

How they're growing/Recent developments: Operations have expanded under an ongoing acquisitions program begun in 1986. In May, 1991, Gallagher acquired three separate insurance brokerage concerns. Employment has grown from an estimated 1,200 in 1987 to 2,044 in 1991.

GANNETT COMPANY, INC.
1000 Wilson Boulevard
Arlington, VA 22229
(703) 284-6054

Founded: 1923. **No. of Employees:** 36,000. **Revenues (1990):** $3.4 billion. **Revenues (1986):** $2.8 billion. **Five-Year Revenue Growth:** 21%.

Description: One of the nation's largest newspaper publishers. Papers include *USA Today*, the second-largest national paper, 87 daily papers and 35 non-dailies. Gannett also owns 16 radio stations and 10 television stations -- nine of which are network affiliated. It also operates Louis Harris & Associates, the public polling company, and Gannett Outdoor, the largest U.S. billboard advertising company.

How they're growing/Recent developments: Despite extremely tough times in the newspaper industry, Gannett remains very strong financially. The company was burdened in 1991 by the enormous expense of covering the Gulf War, an expense it won't have in 1992. In addition, Gannett has sold the Arkansas Gazette, which had been losing money.

THE GAP
One Harrison Street
San Francisco, California 94105
(415)952-4400

Founded: 1969. **No. of Employees:** 26,000. **Revenues (1990):** $1.9 billion. **Revenues (1986):** $647 million. **Five-Year Revenue Growth:** 194%.

Description: Operates a chain of clothing stores, focusing on casual apparel.

How they're growing/Recent developments: In May, 1991, Gap management announced plans to open between 150 and 160 new stores. In addition, 40 of most productive will be enlarged. There has been improved merchandising at the Banana Republic stores and for the Baby Gap line. Employment has grown from an estimated 12,000 in 1987 to 26,000 in 1991.

GATEWAY 2000
610 Gateway Drive
North Sioux City, South Dakota 57049-2000
(605) 232-2000

Founded: 1985. **No. of Employees:** 600. **Revenues (1990):** $276 million. **Revenues (1986):** $1 million. **Five-Year Revenue Growth:** 27,500%.

Description: A retailer of computers, software and peripherals.

How they're growing/Recent developments: According to Inc. magazine, Gateway is the nation's fastest growing private company. It got to the top through strict adherence to low-overhead and consistantly undercutting competitors by at least 10%. Employment has grown from an estimated 4 in 1987 to 600 in 1991.

GENENTECH INC.
460 Point San Bruno Boulevard
South San Francisco, California 94080
(415) 266-1000

Founded: 1976. **No. of Employees:** 1,923. **Revenues (1990):** $435 million. **Revenues (1986):** $127 million. **Five-Year Revenue Growth:** 243%.

Description: One of the world's leading biotechnology companies. The company is 60% owned by Roche, the Swiss pharmaceutical company.

How they're growing/Recent developments: Genentech spends 40% of sales on research and development, which has allowed the company to proceed on projects such as relaxin, a drug that facilitates childbirth, and gp120, an possible AIDS treatment vaccine. One of the company's recent successes has been Activase, a blood clot dissolving agent.

GENERAL CINEMA
27 Boylston Street
Chestnut Hill, Massachusetts 02167
(617) 232-8200

Contact: Carl D. Angel, Corporate Director of Human Resources. **Founded:** 1950. **No. of Employees:** 25,500. **Revenues (1990):** $2.2 billion. **Revenues (1986):** $998 million. **Five-Year Revenue Growth:** 120%.

Description: General Cinema, the fourth largest movie theater chain in the nation, also owns a majority interest in the Neiman Marcus Group (Neiman Marcus, Contempo Casuals, and Bergdorf Goodman department stores), and recently acquired, the Harcourt Brace Jovanovich publishing company.

How they're growing/Recent developments: In August, 1991, reached agreements concerning the acquisition of publisher Harcourt Brace Jovanovich, which eventually could bring in as much as $1 billion a year. A stronger economy is expected to increase profit growth of 61% owned Neiman Marcus Group. General Cinemas employs about 100 on its corporate staff, 10,000 full-time and over 7,000 part-time in its movie theaters, and about 21,000 in the Neiman Marcus Group.

GENERAL ELECTRIC COMPANY
3135 Easton Turnpike
Fairfield, Connecticut 06431
(203) 373-2211

Founded: 1892. **No. of Employees:** 298,000. **Revenues (1990):** $57.7 billion. **Revenues (1986):** $35.2 billion. **Five-Year Revenue Growth:** 64%.

Description: GE consists of 14 businesses in three major groupings: manufacturing, technology, and financial services. Manufacturing operations include electrical equipment, lighting, power systems and electrical motors. Technology operations include aircraft engines, aerospace, plastics, medical systems and factory automation. Financial services include: GE Financial Services, GE Credit Corporation, and Kidder Peabody, among others.

How they're growing/Recent developments: GE maintains a leadership position in all of its areas of operation, and the company continues to grow through strategic acquisitions and divestitures. In 1986, the company acquired RCA, and its subsidiary, the National Broadcasting Corporation. In 1988, it acquired the plastics operations of Borg Warner. The company's fastest growing segments are now financial services, plastics, and medical systems.

GENERAL MILLS, INC.
1 General Mills Boulevard, P.O. Box 1113
Minneapolis, Minnesota 55440
(612) 540-2311

Founded: 1925. **No. of Employees:** 108,077. **Revenues (1990):** $7.153 billion. **Revenues (1986):** $5.189 billion. **Five-Year Revenue Growth:** 38%.

Description: The nation's second-largest producer of breakfast cereals and a leading producer of various food products.

How they're growing/Recent developments: In 1989, General Mills formed the CPW (Cereal Partners Worldwide) with Nestle, in an attempt to challenge Kellogg's dominance in the European cereal market. General Mills' Cheerios are the nation's best selling cereal. The company's highly successful Red Lobster and Olive Garden chains are operating in the United States and Canada, making the restaurant division General Mills' fastest area of growth. Forty-six Red Lobsters have opened in Japan, making overseas expansion look promising. Employment has grown from an estimated 74.453 in 1987 to 108,077 in 1991.

GENERAL SCIENCES CORPORATION
6100 Chevy Chase Drive
Laurel, Maryland 20707
(301) 953-2700

Founded: 1977. **No. of Employees:** 240. **Revenues (1990):** $14.1 million. **Revenues (1987):** $9 million. **Four-Year Revenue Growth:** 57%.

Description: General Sciences Corporation provides technical development and support services, primarily to U.S. government agencies and its prime contractors. Services include meteorological and oceanographic scientific research and information processing, remote sensing applications; environmental modeling, data systems modeling and simulation, astronomical research, information resources management, and systems engineering and integration.

How they're growing/Recent development: General Sciences' revenues increased 9% in Fiscal 1990, over 1989, largely due to the several new orders received from Saudi Arabia, Pakistan, Mexico and Brazil for the commercial Meteorological product line. Revenues grew to $15.4 million for Fiscal 1991.

GENERAL TRANSPORTATION SERVICES
4 Lumbar Way
Liverpool, New York 13090
(315) 451-8840

Founded: 1983. **No. of Employees:** 221. **Revenues (1990):** $7.7 million. **Revenues (1986):** $877 thousand. **Five-Year Revenue Growth:** 778%.

Description: Provides transportation and delivery services.

How they're growing/Recent developments: Employment has grown from an estimated 47 in 1987 to 221 in 1991.

GENUINE PARTS CORPORATION
2999 Circle 75 Parkway
Atlanta, Georgia 30339
(404) 953-1700

Founded: 1928. **No. of Employees:** 16,200. **Revenues (1990):** $3.3 billion. **Revenues (1986):** $2.4 billion. **Five-Year Revenue Growth:** 37%.

Description: A national distributor of automotive replacement parts through its subsidiary, Motion Industries.

How they're growing/Recent developments: In 1989, Genuine Parts formed a partnership with UAP, one of the largest auto parts distributors in Canada. Demand is expected to pick up in the automotive aftermarket during 1992, and high margin, more non-discretionary types of parts are likely to increase in sales and boost the company's profits. Genuine Parts has a broad product line, and because of its strong NAPA retail network, it is well positioned to prosper from improved industry fortunes. Increased competition from the major chains such as Pep Boys will be a long-term challenge.

GERAGHTY AND MILLER INC.
125 East Bethpage Road
Plainview, New York 11803
(516) 249-7600

Founded: 1957. **No. of Employees:** 977. **Revenues (1990):** $110.2 million. **Revenues (1986):** $23.9 million. **Five-Year Revenue Growth:** 361%.

Description: A full-service environmental company that provides a wide spectrum of consulting, engineering, hydrocarbon and remediation services. The company specializes in the development, management and protection of ground water resources and the correction of ground water contamination.

Common positions include: Hydrogeologist; Civil Engineer; Geochemist; Environmental Scientist; Environmental Engineer; Toxicologist; Chemical Engineer; Hydrologic Modelers; Geophyisicist; Hydrologist; Geologist.

Educational backgrounds sought: The company's 977 employees include over 675 professionals, approximately 325 of whom have advanced degrees.

How they're growing/Recent developments: The company's net revenues increased 32% in 1990. In December, 1990, the company formed a joint venture with Dutch-based Heidemij to sell a soil washing system in the U.S. Employment has grown from an estimated 411 in 1987 to 977 in 1991.

GERBER ALLEY & ASSOCIATES
6575 The Corners Parkway
Norcross, Georgia 30092
(404) 441-7793

Contact Jenny Burnett, Recruiter. **Founded:** 1982. **No. of Employees:** 700. **Revenues (1990):** $67.9 million. **Revenues (1986):** $12.3 million. **Five-Year Revenue Growth:** 452%

Description: Developer of The Precision Alternative, an integrated health care information system which contains a full range of patient care, financial and clinical applicators.

Common positions include: Computer Programmer; Marketing Specialist; Quality Control Supervisor; Sales Representative; Systems Analyst; Technical Writer/Editor.

Principal educational backgrounds sought: Business Administration; Computer Science; Marketing.

Company benefits include: medical insurance; dental insurance; pension plan; life insurance; disability coverage; employee discounts; savings plan.

Operations at this facility include: regional headquarters location; divisional headquarters; administration; service; sales.

GERBER PRODUCTS
455 State Street
Fremont, Michigan 49412
(616) 928-2000

Contact: E. Curtis Mairs, Vice President, Human Resources. **Founded:** 1901. **No. of Employees:** 12,025. **Revenues (1990):** $1.136 billion. **Revenues (1987):** $917 million. **Four-Year Revenue Growth:** 24%.

Description: The largest producer of baby foods in the world. Also engaged in children's apparel and accessories, and the life insurance business.

How they're growing/Recent developments: During the past few years, Gerber's new management team has sold off unprofitable businesses, improved the baby food business and introduced several new products. In 1989, the company reentered the baby formula business, and it is placing more emphasis on a line of foods for toddlers.

GIANT FOODS
6300 Sheriff Road
Landover, Maryland 20785
(301) 341-4100

Founded: 1935. **No. of Employees:** 25,700. **Revenues (1990):** $3.350 billion. **Revenues (1986):** $2.529 billion. **Five-Year Revenue Growth:** 32%.

Description: Based in Landover, Maryland, Giant Foods operates 152 stores in the Baltimore/Washington area. They are the number one grocer in the D.C. market.

How they're growing/Recent developments: Giant Foods opened four new stores in 1990, and expected to open six more in 1991. In June, 1991, the company announced it is considering entering the deep-discount drug business; its merchandising program, SUPERdeals, which offers large-size and multi-pack items at big discounts, has been successful. Employment has grown from an estimated 22,700 in 1987 to 25,700 in 1991.

GISH BIOMEDICAL INC.
2350 South Pullman Avenue
Santa Ana, California 92705
(714) 261-1330

Founded: 1976. **No. of Employees:** 224. **Revenues (1990):** $18 million. **Revenues (1986):** $7 million. **Five-Year Revenue Growth:** 157%.

Description: Manufacturers of specialty devices used in open heart surgery, oncology, emergency care, obstetrics and other specialized hospital applications.

How they're growing/Recent developments: For the fiscal year that ended June 30, 1991, revenues climbed to $20 million. Economic conditions have slowed growth since that time, due in part to a a decline in expensive cardiovascular procedures. Long-term growth is expected to continue as the national economy picks up. Employment has grown from an estimated 160 in 1987 to 224 in 1991.

P.H. GLATFELTER COMPANY
228 South Main Street
Spring Grove, Pennsylvania 17362
(717) 225-4711

Founded: 1864. **No. of Employees:** 3,500. **Revenues (1990):** $625.4 million. **Revenues (1986):** $284.8 million. **Five-Year Revenue Growth:** 120%.

Description: A manufacturer of printing papers, and tobacco and other specialty papers. The company's paper mills are located in Spring, Grove, Pennsylvania, Pisgah Forest, North Carolina, and Neenah, Wisconsin. The Spring Grove facility is an integrated paper manufacturing plant, producing a substantial part of its fiber requirements from wood. The Pisgah Forest mill produces flax fiber pulp used to manufacture some of its tobacco industry products and uses purchased virgin wood pulp to manufacture nearly all other Ecusta Division papers. The Neenah mill recycles high grade wastepapers to provide its principal fiber raw material. All these mills recycle internally generated waste to supply part of the fiber required for operations. The Glatfeler Pulp Wood Company, a wholly-owned subsidiary, is responsible for woodlands management and procurement of pulpwood from company-owned land and from independent sources for use by the Spring Grove mill. Ecusta Fibres, Ltd., a wholly-owned subsidiary operating in Canada, buys and processes flax straw, the basic raw material required by the Pigsah Forest pulp mill. American Stock Exchange.

Common positions include: Accountant; Buyer; Chemist; Computer Programmer; Customer Service Representative; Draftsperson; Electrical Engineer; Mechanical Engineer; Personnel and Labor Relations Specialist; Public Relations Specialist; Sales Representative; Systems Analyst.

Principal educational backgrounds sought: Accounting; Business Administration; Chemistry; Computer Science; Engineering; Liberal Arts; Marketing; Mathematics.

Company benefits include: Medical insurance; dental insurance; pension plan; life insurance; tuition assistance; disability coverage; profit sharing; savings plan.

Operations at this facility include: Divisional headquarters; manufacturing; research and development; service; sales.

How they're growing/ Recent developments: During 1990, the company achieved all-time record sales levels. Increased sales from the tobacco and other specialty papers sales group were responsible for about 60% of the increase, with sales from the printing papers sales group accounting for the rest.

GOVERNMENT TECHNOLOGY SERVICES
4100 Lafayette Center Drive
Chantilly, Virginia 22021
(703) 631-3333

Contact: Cathy Skahan, Human Resources Manager. **Founded:** 1983. **No. of Employees:** 500. **Revenues (1990):** $300 million. **Revenues (1986):** $51 million. **Five-Year Revenue Growth:** 488%.

Description: Company integrates and resells computer equipment. NASDAQ/NMS.

Common positions: Accountant; Administrator; Advertising Worker; Attorney; Blue-Collar Worker; Buyer; Commercial Artist; Computer Programmer; Credit Manager; Electrical Engineer; Financial Analyst; Marketing Specialist; Personnel and Labor Relations Specialist; Public Relations Specialist; Purchasing Agent; Sales Representative; Systems Analyst; Technical Writer/Editor.

Principal educational backgrounds sought: Accounting; Art/Design; Business Administration; Communications; Computer Science; Finance; Liberal Arts; Marketing.

Company benefits: Medical, Dental, and Life Insurance; Pension Plan; Tuition Assistance; Disability Coverage; Daycare Assistance; Employee Discounts; Savings Plan; Stock Purchase Plan.

Operations at this facility: Regional Headquarters; Administration; Service; Sales.

GRAPHIC INDUSTRIES, INC.
2155 Monroe Drive NE
Atlanta, Georgia 30324
(404)874-3327

Founded: 1970. **No. of Employees:** 2,900. **Revenues (1990):** $329 million. **Revenues (1986):** $130 million. **Five-Year Revenue Growth:** 153%.

Description: A graphics communications firm.

How they're growing/Recent developments: Graphic Industries has expanded its printing and graphic arts services through acquisitions and internal growth and development. Between 1970 and 1991, the company made 19 acquisitions. Employment has grown from an estimated 2,600 in 1987 to 2,900 in 1991.

GREAT LAKES CHEMICAL CORPORATION
P.O. Box 2200
Highway 52 N.W.
West Lafayette, Indiana 47906
(317) 497-6100

Founded: 1933. **No. of Employees:** 5,500. **Revenues (1990):** $1 billion. **Revenues (1986):** $300 million. **Five-Year Revenue Growth:** 233%.

Description: Manufacturer of specialty and brominated chemicals.

How they're growing/Recent developments: Great Lakes has interests in a number of diverse businesses, including a 51% interest in Octel Associates and 40% interest in Huntsman Chemical. Gains are expected in most businesses. In August, 1991, Great Lakes stated that second-quarter performances for 1991 were solid: Octel saw its best results ever. Employment has grown from an estimated 1,800 in 1987 to 5,500 in 1991.

GREEN THUMB ENTERPRISES, INC.
Route 1, Box 200
Chantilly, Virginia 22021
(703) 471-5033

Founded: 1982. **No. of Employees:** 230. **Revenues (1990):** $13 million. **Revenues (1986):** $1.6 million. **Five-Year Revenue Growth:** 712%.

Description: A full service landscape maintenance firm.

How they're growing/Recent developments: Management has an increasing need for experienced mid- and upper-level managers, and recruits from across the nation. The company has expanded by opening several new offices over the past few years. The company opened a Newark, Delaware branch several years ago to serve the Delaware and Philadelphia area. Long-range goals call for the company to reach $40 million to $50 million in annual sales by the mid-1990s. Employment has grown from 95 in 1986 to 230 in 1991.

GRIST MILL COMPANY
21340 Hayes Avenue
Lakeville, Minnesota 55044
(612) 469-4981

Founded: 1917. **No. of Employees:** 386. **Revenues (1990):** $60 million. **Revenues (1986):** $23 million. **Five-Year Revenue Growth:** 161%.

Description: A manufacturer of snack and confectionery products sold to supermarket chains under private labels.

How they're growing/Recent developments: Over the past several years, Grist Mill has increased the number of products sold under its own name. Employment has grown from an estimated 200 in 1987 to 386 in 1991.

GROUP 1 SOFTWARE INC.
6404 Ivy Lane, Suite 500
Greenbelt, Maryland 20770-1400
(301)982-2000

Contact: Trent Lutz, Human Resources Manager. **Founded:** 1981. **No. of Employees:** 160. **Revenues (1990):** $20 million. **Revenues (1986):** $6 million. **Five-Year Revenue Growth:** 233%.

Description: Manufacturers of direct-mail computer software. NASDAQ

Common positions include: Administrator; Computer Programmer; Customer Service Representative; Financial Analyst; Marketing Specialist; Sales Representative; Systems Analyst; Technical Writer/Editor

Principal educational backgrounds sought: Accounting; Business Administration; Computer Science; Finance; Marketing.

Company benefits: Medical, Dental, and Life Insurance; Pension Plan; Tuition Assistance; Disability Coverage.

Operations at this facility: Regional Headquarters; Research/Development; Administration; Sales.

How they're growing/Recent developments: With demand continuing to increase, revenues for fiscal 1991 advanced to over $26 million, and then again by another 35% year-to-year for the first quarter period that ended June 30, 1991. Group 1's revenue and earnings continue to be high. The company is growing due to the recent and pending release of such products as desktop Group 1 and CODE-1 Plus. The company's growth strategy includes continued development of new products and enhancements of existing products. Employment has grown from an estimated 100 in 1987 to 160 in 1991.

GUNDLE ENVIRONMENTAL SYSTEMS
19103 Gundle Road
Houston, Texas 77073
(713) 443-8564

Founded: 1986. **No. of Employees:** 826. **Revenues (1990):** $120 million. **Revenues (1986):** $31 million. **Five-Year Revenue Growth:** 287%.

Description: Produces liners for hazardous waste control.

How they're growing/Recent developments: Backlog had a backlog of orders worth $75 million as of March, 1990. Demand is continuing to increase for services in the United States, Canada and 40 other countries. Employment has grown from an estimated 200 in 1987 to 826 in 1991.

HACH
5600 Lindbergh Drive
P.O. Box 389
Loveland, Colorado 80539
(303) 669-3050

Founded: 1947. **No. of Employees:** 600. **Revenues (1990):** $63.1 million. **Revenues (1986):** $37.4 million. **Five-Year Revenue Growth:** 69%.

Description: Hach Company operates primarily in a single industry segment encompassing laboratory instruments, process analyzers and test kits which analyze the chemical content and other properties of water and aqueous solution. This segment also encompasses the chemicals manufactured and sold by Hach for use with many of the instruments and test kits that it manufactures. Hach also manufactures and sells a small amount of chemicals for uses not associated with its analytical systems. The company's analytical systems are sold to industrial groups, municipalities and government and educational institutions.

How they're growing/Recent developments: Sales reached a record $72.3 million in 1991, an increase of 14.6% over 1990's sales. Increases were due primarily to unit volume increases in most of the company's major product lines, as well as a small price increase instituted on certain products in January, 1990.

HAEMONETICS
400 Wood Road
Braintree, Massachusetts 02184
(617) 848-7100

Founded: 1985. **No. of Employees:** 923. **Revenues (1990):** $124 million. **Revenues (1987):** $53 million. **Five-Year Revenue Growth:** 134%.

Description: Produces blood reinfusion equipment.

How they're growing/Recent developments: Haemonetics benefits from a strong demand for single use disposable products. Pioneering systems and technologies improving safety and quality of blood related procedures and reducing the risk of disease transmission. Employment has grown from an estimated 800 in 1987 to 923 in 1991.

HALLMARK CARDS, INC.
2501 McGee, P.O. Box 419580
Kansas City, Missouri 64141-6580
(816) 274-5111

Founded: 1911. **No. of Employees:** 34,000. **Revenues (1990):** $2.7 billion. **Revenues (1986):** $1.68 billion. **Five-Year Revenue Growth:** 61%.

Description: The number one producer of greeting cards and a leading manufacturer of ribbons, bow, giftwrap, crayons, candles, jigsaw puzzles, Christmas ornaments, wedding products, party goods and gift items.

How they're growing/Recent developments: Hallmark's domestic employment rose from 17,495 to 23,880 between 1986 and 1990, a sign of the company's continued growth. Hallmark ventured into cable in 1991 by purchasing a controlling interest in St. Louis-based Cencom Cable, and acquired collectibles company Willitts Designs in 1990. Employment has grown from an estimated 25,900 in 1987 to 34,000 in 1991.

HANDEX ENVIRON RECOVERY
500 Campus Drive
Morganville, New Jersey 07751
(908) 536-8500

Founded: 1968. **No. of Employees:** 407. **Revenues (1990):** $39 million. **Revenues (1988):** $16.2 million. **Five-Year Revenue Growth:** 141%.

Description: Engaged in oil tank pollution control services.

How they're growing/Recent developments: New locations have opened in Florida, Pennsylvania, and Virginia. Expansion is expected to continue with more offices in the Midwest and Carolinas.

HANDLEMAN COMPANY
500 Kirts Boulevard
Troy, Michigan 48084
(313) 362-4400

Founded: 1936. **No. of Employees:** 3,000. **Revenues (1990):** $703 million. **Revenues (1986):** $460.3 million. **Five-Year Revenue Growth:** 53%.

Description: Distributors of recorded music, tapes, videocasettes and paperback books.

How they're growing/Recent developments: K mart currently accounts for 43% of Handleman's sales. The company is expanding sales through leased departments at Sears and Montgomery Ward stores. The fastest growing segment of the company's business is video cassettes and compact discs.

M.A. HANNA COMPANY
1301 East 9th Street, Suite 3600
Cleveland, Ohio 44114-1860
(216) 589-4000

Contact: Thomas A. Wilson, Vice-President of Human Resources and Industrial Relations. **Founded:** 1927. **No. of Employees:** 5,960. **Revenues (1990):** $1.1 billion. **Revenues (1986):** $130.3 million. **Five-Year Revenue Growth:** 744%.

Description: Hanna is a leading international specialty chemicals company -- a compounder of rubber and plastic, manufacturer of colorants for plastics, and distributor of plastic shapes and resins.

How they're growing/Recent developments: In June, 1991, Hanna acquired Fiberchem, Inc., a leading West Coast distributor of plastic resins and additives. In December, 1990, Hanna acquired Synthecolor S.A., a producer of formulated colorants for the French plastics industry, giving it a foundation for European expansion. Employment has grown from an estimated 3,636 in 1987 to 5,960 in 1991.

HANNAFORD BROTHERS COMPANY
P.O. Box 1000
Portland, Maine 04104
(207) 883-2911

Founded: 1902. **No. of Employees:** 9,000. **Revenues (1990):** $1.7 billion. **Revenues (1986):** $899 million. **Five-Year Revenue Growth:** 89%.

Description: Northern New England's foremost supermarket company. Chains include Shop 'N Save, Sun Foods, and Martin's.

How they're growing/Recent developments: Hannaford has expanded rapidly in New Hampshire and, more recently, in upper New York State. The New York stores have done even better than the company's own projections, and the company now controls 9% of the Albany market.

HARDING ASSOCIATES INC.
7655 Redwood Boulevard
Novato, California 94945
(415) 892-0821

Founded: 1957. **No. of Employees:** 940. **Revenues (1990):** $69 million. **Revenues (1986):** $22 million. **Five-Year Revenue Growth:** 214%.

Description: Through its wholly owned, Anchorage-based subsidiary, Harding Lawson & Associates, the company's network of 21 offices in 11 states and the District of Columbia provides a wide range of environmental, engineering and consulting services.

How they're growing/Recent developments: In May, 1991, Harding acquired Yates & Auberle, Ltd., an engineering consulting firm specializing in issues of air quality and hazardous materials. Employment has grown from an estimated 488 in 1987 to 940 in 1991.

JOHN H. HARLAND COMPANY
2939 Miller Road
Decatur, Georgia 30035
(404) 981-9460

Contact: Carol King, Director of Recruiting. **Founded:** 1923. **No. of Employees:** 5,600. **Revenues (1990):** $371 million. **Revenues (1986):** $293 million. **Five-Year Revenue Growth:** 27%.

Description: Atlanta-based Harland is one of the nation's largest check printer, and also serves the financial community with a variety of related products and services. In addition, Harland is a national participant in the data service industry, serving educational and commercial markets. The company has production facilities for its business units across the United States and in Puerto Rico and Switzerland.

Common positions include: Accountant; Commercial Artist; Computer Programmer; Mechanical Engineer; Operations/Production Manager; Sales Representative.

Principal educational backgrounds sought: Accounting; Art/Design; Business Administration; Computer Science; Engineering; Finance.

Company benefits: Medical, Dental, and Life Insurance; Pension Plan; Tuition Assistance; Disability Coverage; Profit Sharing.

How they're growing/Recent developments: Harland has been converting its plants to offset technology in an effort to increase productivity. In 1988, the company acquired Scantron, which produces optical mark reading equipment and supplies. Scantron is used to read educational test answers, but the company intends to expand its use commercially. Harland introduced the first nationally distributed documents on recycled paper (also released a recycled paper content box). The company also completed 100% conversion to offset printing technology and installed a new computer system to create ordering, production, and billing efficiencies. Harland is a low-cost producer in a competitive market. Employment has grown from an estimated 5,200 in 1987 to 5,600 in 1991.

HARLEY-DAVIDSON, INC.
3700 West Juneau Avenue, P.O. Box 653
Milwaukee, Wisconsin 53208
(414) 342-4680

Founded: 1903. **No. of Employees:** 5,000. **Revenues (1990):** $865 million. **Revenues (1986):** $295 million. **Five-Year Revenue Growth:** 193%.

Description: One of the world's leading manufacturers of motorcycles.

How they're growing/Recent developments: As the only U.S.-based manufacturer of bikes with engines of 850cc or larger, Harley controls over 60% of its market. Harley's management keeps careful controls on production levels in order to keep demand strong. Overseas, the company is especially successful in the United Kingdom, Germany and Japan. The company also recently opened its first retail outlet. Employment has grown from an estimated 4,700 in 1987 to 5,000 in 1991.

THE HARMONY SCHOOL
Princeton Forrestal Village
139 Village Boulevard
Princeton, New Jersey 08540
(609) 799-4411

Founded: 1980. **No. of Employees:** 105. **Revenues (1990):** $2.4 million. **Revenues (1986):** $291 thousand. **Five-Year Revenue Growth:** 725%.

Description: Operates daycare centers.

How they're growing/Recent developments: Harmony Schools have grown by offering a flexible array of options for working parents, including its Stay & Play Drop-in Care Program, its Mend-a-Friend Mildly Ill Center, and its variety of enrichment programs. Employment has grown from 20 in 1986 to 105 in 1991.

HARNISCHFEGER INDUSTRIES, INC.
13400 Bishop's Lane, P.O. Box 310
Milwaukee, Wisconsin 53201
(414) 671-4400

Founded: 1910. **No. of Employees:** 12,200. **Revenues (1990):** $1.7 billion. **Revenues (1986):** $727 million. **Five-Year Revenue Growth:** 134%.

Description: Manufactures overhead cranes and hoists and excavating equipment.

How they're growing/Recent developments: Although the economy has hurt the company's revenues of late, overall earnings for 1991 were expected to increase, due in part to a better product mix and less subcontracting. Employment has grown from an estimated 11,400 in 1987 to 12,200 in 1991.

HEALTHCARE COMPARE
3200 Highland Avenue
Downers Grove, Illinois 60515-1223
(708) 719-9000

Founded: 1982. **No. of Employees:** 631. **Revenues (1990):** $42 million. **Revenues (1986):** $5 million. **Five-Year Revenue Growth:** 740%.

Description: A leading independent provider of health care utilization review and cost management services. The services control a client's health care costs by reducing unnecessary hospital admissions and lengths of stay and by monitoring medical necessity and appropriateness of other health care services.

How they're growing/Recent developments: For the six month period to June 30, 1991, revenues rose 71% year to year, largely because of the company's expansion of its preferred provider organization (PPOs) system. Employment has grown from an estimated 168 in 1987 to 631 in 1991.

HEALTHSOUTH REHABILITATION CORPORATION
2 Perimeter Park South
Suite 224 West
Birmingham, Alabama 35243
(205) 967-7116

Founded: 1984. **No. of Employees:** 3,567. **Revenues (1990):** $180 million. **Revenues (1986):** $19 million. **Five-Year Revenue Growth:** 847%.

Description: Providers of outpatient physical rehabilitation services.

How they're growing/Recent developments: During the summer of 1991, the company opened four new facilities. The company's ability to provide interdisciplinary care in one location is a strong marketing advantage. Employment has grown from an estimated 854 in 1987 to 3,567 in 1991.

HEALTHSTAFFERS, INC.
5636 North Broadway
Chicago, Illinois 60660
(312) 561-5400

Founded: 1977. **No. of Employees:** 362. **Revenues (1990):** $14 million. **Revenues (1986):** $1 million. **Five-Year Revenue Growth:** 1,300%.

Description: HealthStaffers, Inc. is a medical travel services company, which provides three-month assignments for travelling nurses.

How they're growing/Recent developments: Employment has grown from 95 in 1986 to 362 in 1991.

HEARTLAND EXPRESS INC.
2777 Heartland Drive
Coralville, Iowa 52241
(319) 645-2728

Founded: 1986. **No. of Employees:** 109. **Revenues (1990):** $62.9 million. **Revenues (1986):** $21.6 million. **Five-Year Revenue Growth:** 191%.

Description: Heartland Express is an irregular route carrier authorized to transport general commodities in interstate commerce throughout the 48 contiguous states.

How they're growing/Recent developments: During 1990, Heartland completed its fleet conversion from 48-foot trailers to 53-foot units, and added to the fleet by converting to cabover tractors while upsizing the number of tractors from 205 units at the end of 1989 to 299 by the end of 1990.

HECHINGER COMPANY
1616 McCormick Drive
Landover, Maryland 20785
(301) 341-1000

Founded: 1959. **No. of Employees:** 8,000. **Revenues (1990):** $1.2 billion. **Revenues (1986):** $479 million. **Five-Year Revenue Growth:** 150%.

Description: Retails do-it-yourself home improvement products.

How they're growing/Recent developments: The company has grown through an aggressive acquisitions strategy. Recent acquisitions have included 11 Home Quarters stores in 1988, and 13 Bradlees stores in 1989.

HEILIG-MYERS COMPANY
2235 Staples Mill Road
Richmond, Virginia 23230
(804)359-9171

Founded: 1913. **No. of Employees:** 5,910. **Revenues (1990):** $393 million. **Revenues (1986):** $182 million. **Five-Year Revenue Growth:** 116%.

Description: Retailer of home furnishing in eastern Sunbelt.

How they're growing/Recent developments: Profits have risen for five consecutive years in part because of an expanding store base. In January, 1991, the company acquired nine stores from Furniture Center and announced in May, 1991, plans to open 30-35 stores. Despite the generally sluggish retail economy, company revenues for the three months ending May, 1991, were up 10.5% from the previous year. Employment has grown from an estimated 4.300 in 1987 to 5,910 in 1991.

H.J. HEINZ COMPANY
P.O. Box 57
Pittsburgh. Pennsylvania 15230
(412) 237-5757

Contact: Ross Craig, Manager of Personnel. **Founded:** 1869. **No. of Employees:** 34,100. **Revenues (1990):** $6.6 billion. **Revenues (1986):** $4.6 billion. **Five-Year Revenue Growth:** 43%.

Description: One of the foremost processed-food companies in the United States. The company manufactures soup, ketchup, baked beans, pickles, vinegar, baby foods, tuna, cat food, frozen potatoes, Chico San rice cakes, and Weight Watchers and Alba Diet products.

How they're growing/Recent developments: Heinz's fastest growing division is Weight Watchers, which now controls half of the weight loss services market in the United States. The company initiated its Quick Success Program in 1988 and has seen a 15% increase in attendance. The Weight Watchers at Work program is now subscribed to by over 2,500 companies. Heinz has also engaged in an active acquisitions campaign in recent years. Between 1979 and 1989, the firm gained control of over 35 companies.

HELEN OF TROY
6827 Market Avenue
El Paso, Texas 79915
(915) 779-6363

Founded: 1968. **No. of Employees:** 365. **Revenues (1990):** $119 million. **Revenues (1986):** $41 million. **Five-Year Revenue Growth:** 190%.

Description: Sells electrical hair care appliances.

How they're growing/Recent developments: As of January, 1990, the company became licensed to market products under the Vidal Sassoon name in nine West European countries. Employment has grown from an estimated 100 in 1987 to 365 in 1991.

HERSHEY FOODS CORPORATION
P.O. Box 810
Hershey, Pennsylvania 17033-0810
(717) 534-4000

Founded: 1893. **No. of Employees:** 12,700. **Revenues (1990):** $2.7 billion. **Revenues (1986):** $2.2 billion. **Five-Year Revenue Growth:** 23%.

Description: Hershey is the largest confectionery and chocolate manufacturer and second-largest pasta maker in the country.

How they're growing/Recent developments: Hershey has expanded largely by means of acquisitions and divestitures. Some of the most recent acquisitions have included Luden's, the Canadian operations of Nabisco, Cadbury, and Peter Paul candies. In 1988, the company sold the Friendly Ice Cream shop chain. Overall, Hershey revenues should continue to be boosted by lower world cocoa prices and a growing wheat supply.

HEWLETT-PACKARD COMPANY
3000 Hanover Street
Palo Alto, California 94304-1181
(415) 857-1501

Founded: 1939. **No. of Employees:** 92,000. **Revenues (1990):** $13.2 billion. **Revenues (1986):** $7.1 billion. **Five-Year Revenue Growth:** 86%.

Description: A multi-billion dollar electronics giant, whose products include laser printers, electronic measurement instruments and increasingly, personal computers.

How they're growing/Recent developments: HP's 1989 acquisition of Massachusetts-based Apollo Computer has moved the company strongly into the workstation market. The company introduced its new Model 700 line and the product was a major success.

HEXCEL CORPORATION
11555 Dublin Boulevard
Dublin, California 94568-0705
(415) 828-4200

Founded: 1946. **No. of Employees:** 3,000. **Revenues (1990):** $383 million. **Revenues (1986):** $290 million. **Five-Year Revenue Growth:** 32%.

Description: Producer of technologically advanced structural products and resins used in the aerospace industry.

How they're growing/Recent developments: The commercial aerospace business remains strong despite the recession. Hexcel is negotiating for a sale of its fine chemical business.

HILLENBRAND INDUSTRIES, INC.
Highway 46
Batesville, Indiana 47006
(812) 934-7000

Founded: 1891. **No. of Employees:** 5,900. **Revenues (1990):** $1.1 billion. **Revenues (1986):** $641 million. **Five-Year Revenue Growth:** 72%.

Description: Parent company of a group of diversified companies, ranging from Batesville Casket Company, a maker of funeral caskets, to American Tourister, the well-known luggage maker.

How they're growing/Recent developments: Growth has been spurred by further and further acquisition. In 1986, for example, the company purchased SSI Medical Services, now the market leader in supplying beds and related equipment for the bedridden patient.

HITOX CORPORATION OF AMERICA
P.O. Box 2544
Corpus Christi, Texas 78403
(512)882-5175

Founded: 1980. **No. of Employees:** 234. **Revenues (1990):** $15 million. **Revenues (1986):** $10 million. **Five-Year Revenue Growth:** 50%.

Description: Manufactures and sells mineral products for use as pigments and pigment extenders, primarily in paints, coatings and plastics.

How they're growing/Recent developments: Hitox has recently finished refurbishing its Malaysia plant. The plant has an annual capacity of 50,000 tons, and Hitox received the plant's first shipment of synthetic rutile in August, 1991.

HOLIDAY RV SUPERSTORES, INC.

7851 Greenbriar Parkway
Orlando, Florida 32819
(407)363-9211

Contact: Paul Oulette, Personnel Director. **Founded:** 1978. **No. of Employees:** 147. **Revenues (1990):** $41 million. **Revenues (1986):** $19.8 million. **Five-Year Revenue Growth:** 107%.

Description: Holiday RV Superstores is one of the largest companies in the United States engaged in the retail sales and service of recreational vehicles. The company operates six retail sales and service dealerships, one in the heart of the Walt Disney World tourist area in Orlando, Florida; two in the Gulf Coast tourist area of Tampa and Fort Myers, Florida; one in the port city of Jacksonville, Florida; and a sixth in Greer, South Carolina. The company offers for sale and service various product lines of towable and motorized recreational vehicles, principally manufactured by Fleetwood Enterprises, Thor Industries, Winnebago Industries, Mallard Coach Company, and Gulf Stream Coach.

Common positions include: Accountant; Blue-Collar Worker Supervisor; Branch, Department, and General Managers; Management Trainee; Purchasing Agent; Sales Representative.

Principal educational backgrounds sought: Business Administration; Finance; Liberal Arts; Marketing.

Company benefits: Medical, Dental, and Life Insurance; Pension Plan; Tuition Assistance; Disability Coverage; Profit Sharing; Employee Discounts; Savings Plan; Stock Options and Bonuses.

Operations at this facility: Administration; Sales.

How they're growing/Recent developments: Although sales fell slightly during 1991 due to the national economic slowdown and the uncertainty brought on by the Persian Gulf War, management expects that overall sales of RVs will increase greatly during the next few years. According to management, recent demographic studies have shown that the prime RV buying age group, 45 to 54, will substantially increase through to the year 2000. Nearly 30% of all Americans will be 50 years old or older.

THE HOME DEPOT INC.
2727 Paces Ferry Road, Suite 700
Atlanta, Georgia 30339
(404) 433-8211

Founded: 1978. **No. of Employees:** 21,500. **Revenues (1990):** $3.8 billion.
Revenues (1986): $701 million. **Five-Year Revenue Growth:** 442%.

Description: Supplier of building materials and home improvement products.

How they're growing/Recent developments: Home Depot's fortunes have
been rising sharply -- and are expected to continue to do so -- as more and
more consumers seek savings by doing home improvement and repair work
themselves. The company has a goal of 365 stores by the mid-1990's, and 22
stores were opened in the first quarter of 1991 alone. Employment grew by
4,000 jobs in 1991.

HOME INTENSIVE CARE INC.
150 North West 168th Street
North Miami Beach, Florida 33169
(305)653-0000

Founded: 1973. **No. of Employees:** 580. **Revenues (1990):** $32 million.
Revenues (1986): $3 million. **Five-Year Revenue Growth:** 967%.

Description: Provides a full line of home health care infusion therapy services
in 23 states, including home dialysis, and, in seven states, dialysis clinics.

How they're growing/Recent developments: Revenues climbed 74% for the
nine months ending June 30, 1991, reflecting a shift away from Medicare related businesses and into other areas of the home infusion market.

HOME NUTRITIONAL SERVICES, INC.
1850 Parkway Place
Marietta, Georgia 30067
(404) 423-4500

Contact: Marty Le Maserier, Vice President of Human Resources; **Founded:**
1980; **No. of Employees:** 750; **Revenues (1990):** $81.4 million; **Revenues
(1986):** $28.4 million. **Five-Year Revenue Growth:** 187%

Description: HNS is a national health care service company engaged in providing infusion therapies to patients outside the hospital setting through 30
regional centers and 44 other service sites. Infusion therapy is the delivery of

medications or nutrients intravenously into specific organs or other sites of administration. HNS provides service using a team approach, combining nurse clinician, pharmacist, and patient service representatives to consistently provide high quality of care and quality of life for the patient.

How they're growing/Recent developments: During 1990, the company expanded its market base with an increase of eight facilities, bringing the current total to 74 sites in 27 states. For 1991, the company planned to open 10 new service locations, and 19 new infusion clinics. During 1990, the company began installation of a new management information system that it hopes will further enhance efficiency in functions ranging from managing accounts to standardizing product usage, and monitoring clinical productivity. Since 1990, the company's growth strategy has included the creation of new positions and personnel.

HOME OFFICE REFERENCE LABORATORY
10310 West 84th Terrace
Lenexa, Kansas 66214
(913) 888-8397

Contact: Sue McMorrough, Employment Office Coordinator. **Founded:** 1972. **No. of Employees:** 640. **Revenues (1990):** $81 million. **Revenues (1986):** $16.5 million. **Five-Year Revenue Growth:** 391%.

Description: Home Office Reference Laboratory is one of the nation's leading providers of laboratory testing services to the insurance industry, serving over 800 insurance companies in the United States and Canada. The company's tests are specifically designed to provide a standardized format to assist an insurance company in objectively evaluating mortality or morbidity risk posed by a policy applicant.

Common positions include: Biologist; Chemist; Computer Programmer; Customer Service Representative; Laboratory technician; medical technician; data entry operator.

Principal educational backgrounds sought: Biology; Chemistry; Liberal Arts.

Company benefits include: Medical insurance; dental insurance; pension plan; life insurance; tuition assistance; disability coverage.

Operations at this facility include: Research and development; administration; service; sales.

How they're growing/Recent developments: During 1990, the company obtained the exclusive right to distribute a saliva-based collection device, Ora-Sure, from Epitope, Inc. which allowed the company to begin saliva-based testing in 1991. Employment has grown from an estimated 155 in 1987 to 640 in 1991.

HOOPER HOLMES
170 Mount Airy Road
Basking Ridge, New Jersey 07920
(908) 766-5000

Founded: 1906. **No. of Employees:** 4,000. **Revenues (1990):** $108 million. **Revenues (1986):** $62 million. **Five-Year Revenue Growth:** 74%.

Description: Provides health information and healthcare services.

How they're growing/Recent developments: During 1990, Hooper Holmes acquired Talent Tree Health Care Services of Massachusetts, Iven Laboratories of Ohio, and Care-At-Home of Illinois and Iowa. The company also boosts revenues by selling computerized customer lists to direct mail companies.

HUBBELL, INC.
584 Derby Milford Road
P.O. Box
Orange, Connecticut 06477
(203) 799-4100

Founded: 1888. **No. of Employees:** 5,800. **Revenues (1990):** $720 million. **Revenues (1986):** $559 million. **Five-Year Revenue Growth:** 59%.

Description: One of the oldest electrical equipment companies in the nation. Manufactures electric and electronic products for telecommunications, utility, commercial and industrial markets.

How they're growing/Recent developments: Hubbell's diversified product line -- from lighting and wiring to refrigeration -- has helped it remain one of the most consistently profitable companies in America. The company has increased earnings for three consecutive decades. Employment has grown from an estimated 5,211 in 1987 to 5,800 in 1991.

J.B. HUNT TRANSPORT SERVICES, INC.
P.O. Box 130
Lowell, Arkansas 72745
(501) 820-0000

Founded: 1961. **No. of Employees:** 9,018. **Revenues (1990):** $580 million. **Revenues (1986):** $204 million. **Five-Year Revenue Growth:** 184%.

Description: An interstate trucking firm.

How they're growing/Recent developments: Hunt benefits from its wide geographical reach as well as from the diverse industries it serves. Hunt has been expanding throughout North America. In 1988, the company received authority to operate in both Quebec and Mexico. In attracting customers, Hunt targets service-sensitive portions of the marketplace, as opposed to those that simply rely on price. Employment has grown from an estimated 3,665 in 1987 to 9,018 in 1991.

ICF INTERNATIONAL
9300 Lee Highway
Fairfax, Virginia 22031
(703) 934-3000

Founded: 1969. **No. of Employees:** 4,850. **Revenues (1990):** $355 million. **Revenues (1986):** $34 million. **Five Year Annual Revenue Growth:** 944%.

Description: A major provider of comprehensive environmental engineering and other professional services through its many subsidiaries.

How they're growing/Recent developments: For the six months ending August, 31, 1991, revenues rose 22% year-to-year.

IDB COMMUNICATIONS GROUP
10525 W. Washington Boulevard
Culver City, California 90232
(213) 870-9000

Founded: 1984. **No. of Employees:** 185. **Revenues (1990):** $86.5 million. **Revenues (1986):** $6.3 million. **Five-Year Revenue Growth:** 1,273%.

Description: IDB Communications Group is a leading provider of advanced telecommunications services for radio, television, and digital communications. Each day, the company distributes hundreds of hours of radio and television programming domestically and internationally for networks, producers and syndicators. The company also provides digital communications services to multinational corporations and government agencies for their worldwide voice and data networks. The company also provides mobile satellite communications services to transportation industries such as shipping and aviation.

How they're growing/Recent developments: In 1989, IDB acquired Hughes Television Network and CICI, Inc. Revenues for 1990 grew over 40% from the year before. The biggest revenue increase in 1990 came from the digital communications market. The company also expects continued growth in international program transmission services for customers in the United States and abroad. In 1990, IDB initiated such services as "Sputnik Express" in conjunction with the then-Soviet telecommunications authority, for program transmission from that country. Despite the break-up of the Soviet Union, "Sputnik Express" has expanded as of January, 1992, in conjunction with authorities of the Russian republic. Employment has grown from an estimated 70 in 1987 to 185 in 1991.

ILC TECHNOLOGY
399 Java Drive
Sunnyvale, California 94089
(408) 745-7900

Founded: 1967. **No. of Employees:** 400. **Revenues (1990):** $25.6 million. **Revenues (1987):** $15.1 million. **Four-Year Revenue Growth:** 70%

Description: ILC designs, develops, manufactures, markets and distributes replaceable high performance light source products, for the medical, aerospace, industrial, entertainment and military industries.

How they're growing/Recent developments: Sales for the fiscal year ending September 28, 1991, rose to $40.2 million, a gain of 57% over fiscal 1991. The company announced in July, 1991 that it had signed a letter of intent to acquire Q-Arc, Ltd. of Cambridge, England. Q-Arc is a supplier of specialty lamps for laser and non-laser applications. Some of the new products that ILC has in the works are: a short arc lamp to compete with lower-end tungsten halogen based lamps which are of lower quality, provide less light and have a shorter life; a lamp for video projection and other applications; and a xenon-mercury-based lamp for the wafer stepper process used in semiconductor microlithography. Analysts believe that all of these new products should have major impacts on sales by 1993 or 1994.

ILLINOIS TOOL WORKS INC.
3600 West Lake Avenue
Glenview, Illinois 60025
(708) 724-7500

Contact: Ileana Perez, Personnel Manager. **Founded:** 1912. **No. of Employees:** 18,400. **Revenues (1990):** $2.5 billion. **Revenues (1986):** $961 million. **Five-Year Revenue Growth:** 160%.

Description: ITW is a multinational of highly engineered components and systems. American Stock Exchange. New York Stock Exchange.

Common positions include: Accountant; Attorney; Chemist; Financial Analyst; Personnel and Labor Relations Specialist.

Principal educational backgrounds sought: Accounting; Business Administration; Communications; Computer Science; Finance; Marketing.

Operations at this facility: Administration.

How they're growing/Recent developments: In April, 1990, the company acquired DeVilbiss Industrial Commercial Division from Eagle Industries.

INFORMATION RESOURCES
150 North Clinton Street
Chicago, Illinois 60606
(312) 726-1221

Contact: Mrs. Nancy Weinger, Employment Manager. **Founded:** 1982. **No. of Employees:** 2,982. **Revenues (1990):** $167 million. **Revenues (1986):** $94 million. **Five-Year Revenue Growth:** 78%.

Description: A marketing research and software organization.

Common positions include: Accountant; Attorney; Computer Programmer; Financial Analyst; Department Manager; General manager; Operations/Production manager; Marketing Specialist; Public Relations Specialist; Public Relations Specialist; Purchasing Agent; Reporter/Editor; Sales Representative; Statistician; Systems Analyst.

Principal educational backgrounds sought: Accounting; Business Administration; Communications; Finance; Marketing.

Company benefits include: Medical insurance; dental insurance; life insurance; tuition assistance; disability coverage; daycare assistance.

How they're growing/Recent developments: The company's InfoScan tracks weekly purchases of each UPC coded product sold. Plans call for the expansion of this service to drug store chains and mass merchandisers, as well as for overseas expansion. Employment has grown from an estimated 2,500 in 1987 to 2.982 in 1991.

INFRASONICS, INC.
9944 Barnes Canyon Road
San Diego, California 92121
(619) 450-9898

Founded: 1982. **No. of Employees:** 160. **Revenues (1990):** $7.4 million. **Revenues (1987):** $2.9 million. **Four-Year Revenue Growth:** 155%.

Description: Infrasonics develops, manufactures and markets a product line of microprocessor based ventilators and other equipment to assist or control breathing for patients who have limited or no respiratory function, such as premature infants with immature lungs, children and adults with respiratory diseases, and accident victims. Ventilators connect to a patient's airway through a series of tubes supplying a mixture of oxygen and/or air pumped under controlled pressure to the patient's lungs. The company markets and sells its products in approximately 40 countries through a sales force of approximately 400 independent dealer-representatives who are responsible for installation, training and service of Infrasonics' products.

How they're growing/Recent developments: For the fiscal year ending December 31, 1991, revenues climbed to $13.3 million. The company plans to increase its research and development activities, expand sales and marketing efforts and grow by searching for appropriate product of company acquisitions. The company has identified a number of new products in the respiratory care field that it believes will contribute to the company's growth. Management expects that these new products, as well as the company's current projects that are nearing completion, will expand the company into a multi-faceted, broad-ranged respiratory care manufacturer and distributor. Increasing sales and marketing efforts simultaneously with new product introductions, the company feels, will facilitate continued rapid growth. Employment has grown from an estimated 60 in 1987 to 160 in 1991.

INSITUFORM MID-AMERICA
17988 Edison Avenue
Chesterfield, Missouri 63005
(314) 532-6137

Founded: 1983. **No. of Employees:** 244. **Revenues (1990):** $36.3 million. **Revenues (1986):** $15.9 million. **Five-Year Revenue Growth:** 128%.

Description: Engages in pipe, sewer, and conduit repair.

How they're growing/Recent Developments: In March, 1991, the company acquired the operating assets of United Pipeline Systems USA, Inc. in order to access the "Tite Liner Process," a method of installing corrosion resistant linings. Employment has grown from an estimated 140 in 1987 to 244 in 1991.

INSTRUMENT SYSTEMS
100 Jericho Quadrangle
Jericho, New York 11753
(516) 938-5544

Founded: 1970. **No. of Employees:** 5,700. **Revenues (1990):** $459 million. **Revenues (1986):** $237 million. **Five-Year Revenue Growth:** 937%.

Description: A manufacturer of industrial and consumer electronics products.

How they're growing/Recent developments: A diversified product line is the key behind this company's success. Improvements in the company's garage doors, plastic films, and electronics operations have increased revenues. Employment has grown from an estimated 4,000 in 1987 to 5,700 in 1991.

INTEGRATED DEVICE TECHNOLOGY, INC.
2972 Stender Way
Santa Clara, California 95054
(408) 727-6116

Founded: 1980. **No. of Employees:** 2,052. **Revenues (1990):** $209 million. **Revenues (1986):** $58 million. **Five-Year Revenue Growth:** 260%.

Description: A leader in the design and manufacture of complex proprietary and industry-standard integrated circuits used in high-performance, complimentary metal oxide silicon (CMOS) process technology.

How they're growing/Recent developments: Although sales fell between 1990 and 1991, the introduction of new products has helped restore solid revenue growth. Employment has grown from an estimated 1,300 in 1987 to 2,052 in 1991.

INTEL CORPORATION
3065 Bowers Avenue
Santa Clara, California 95052
(408) 765-8080

Founded: 1968. No. of Employees: 23,000. Revenues (1990): $3.9 billion. Revenues (1986): $1.2 billion. Five-Year Revenue Growth: 225%.

Description: Intel is one of the nation's largest manufacturers of semiconductors.

How they're growing/Recent developments: Intel's new 80468 chip, released in 1989, has the power to boost PC capabilities to that of mainframes. During 1991, the company demonstrated its new 100 MHz microprocessor. As the company moved into 1992, it faced increasingly fierce competition from longtime rival Advanced Micro Devices. According to a *Wall Street Journal* article on January 31, 1992, Advanced Micro plans to begin selling clones of the 80486, after having begun selling 386 clones in March, 1991. Intel should be able to maintain its advantage since Advanced Micro won't begin shipping its 486 product until the 4th quarter of 1992. Employment at Intel has grown from an estimated 19,200 in 1987 to 23,000 in 1991.

INTELLIGENT ELECTRONICS
411 Eagleview Boulevard
Exton, Pennsylvania 19341
(215) 458-5500

Founded: 1982. No. of Employees: 745. Revenues (1990): $1.5 billion. Revenues (1986): $81 million. Five-Year Revenue Growth: 1,752%.

Description: A franchisor of retail PC stores. Customers are primarily small businesses, outside of large cities.

How they're growing/Recent developments: Most of the company's growth has been fueled by acquisitions. In 1989, the company purchased Entre Computer Centers.One of the company's latest strategic moves is into computer and office supply superstores, supported by its purchase of BizMart office products stores. By mid-September 1991, the company had opened 60 BizMart stores.

INTER VOICE INC.

17811 Waterview Parkway
Dallas, Texas 75252
(214)669-3988

Founded: 1984. **No. of Employees:** 150. **Revenues (1990):** $24 million. **Revenues (1986):** $6 million. **Five-Year Revenue Growth:** 300%.

Description: The company specializes in voice automated voice messaging and response services, allowing customers and database access using telephone keys.

How they're growing/Recent developments: In January, 1991, the company expanded to include an outbound call processing system, which is used primarily by telemarketing and collections companies. Inter Voice also boasts a strong presence in foreign markets. Employment has grown from an estimated 54 in 1987 to 150 in 1991.

INTERFACE, INC.

Orchard Hill Road
Box 1503
La Grange, Georgia 30241
(404) 882-1891

Founded: 1973. **No. of Employees:** 3,000. **Revenues (1990):** $623 million. **Revenues (1986):** $137 million. **Five-Year Revenue Growth:** 355%.

Description: A holding company whose subsidiaries are engaged in the manufacture and sale of carpet tiles.

How they're growing/Recent developments: In 1988, Interface acquired Huega Holding, B.V., the largest carpet tile manufacturer outside of the United States.

INTERGRAPH CORPORATION

One Madison Industrial Park
Huntsville, Alabama 35894-0001
(205) 730-2000

Founded: 1969. **No. of Employees:** 9,600. **Revenues (1990):** $1 billion. **Revenues (1986):** $606 million. **Five-Year Revenue Growth:** 65%.

Description: The second-largest producer of computer aided design, manufacturing, and engineering systems in the world.

How they're growing/Recent developments: Intergraph is supplying contractors now at work on the rebuilding of Kuwait with the Kuwaiti Municipal Database, an information systems that contacts detailed plans of Kuwait City's infrastructure. Intergraph is consistently named tops in customer satisfaction by annual surveys of computer vendors. Employment has grown from an estimated 5,600 in 1987 to 9,600 in 1991.

INTERNATIONAL BROADCASTING
5101 IDS Center
Minneapolis, Minnesota 55402
(612) 333-5100

Founded: 1972. **No. of Employees:** 872. **Revenues (1990):** $97.1 million. **Revenues (1986):** $2.1 million. **Four-Year Revenue Growth:** 4,524%.

Description: International Broadcasting Corporation and its subsidiaries own and operate the Harlem Globetrotters and Ice Capades touring shows as well as the Bob-Lo Island, Great Escape, and Fantasy Island amusement parks. The company also operates 10 Ice Capades Chalets ice skating recreational facilities and manages six other Chalets under management contracts. In addition, the company owns and operates the Chanhassen Dinner Theater, and owns approximately 65% of Century Park Pictures Corporation, which develops and packages motion picture concepts for sale to production studios.

How they're growing/Recent developments: The company's growth was fueled by the acquisition of the Globetrotters, Ice Capades, and Ice Chalets from Metromedia. During 1990, the company enhanced its operations through improved marketing methods, including closer attention to targeted demographic groups. Globetrotter and Ice Capade tours are now scheduled much more tightly in order to select only the most profitable tour dates. Employment has grown from an estimated 200 in 1987 to 872 in 1991.

INTERNATIONAL DAIRY QUEEN
5701 Green Valley Drive
Minneapolis, Minnesota 55437
(612) 830-0200

Founded: 1962. **No. of Employees:** 429. **Revenues (1990):** $283 million. **Revenues (1986):** $183 million. **Five-Year Revenue Growth:** 55%.

Description: International Dairy Queen, Inc is engaged in the business of developing, licensing and servicing a system of over 5,200 Dairy Queen stores in the United States, Canada and other countries. The stores feature hamburgers, hot dogs, various dairy desserts, and beverages. The company also franchises more than 600 Orange Julius stores in the United States, Canada, and elsewhere. These stores feature blended drinks made from oranges and other fruit flavors, as well as various snack items. The company also franchises more than 130 KarmelKorn Shoppes, featuring popcorn and other treat items, and over 70 Golden Skillet stores featuring fried chicken.

How they're growing/Recent developments: The main source of the company's success is that virtually all stores are franchises, and therefore capital expenses are minimal. The Dairy Queen menu is unique, with limited direct competition. The abundance of small town locations for individual stores further insulates the company from competition.

INTERNATIONAL FLAVORS AND FRAGRANCES
521 West 57th Street
New York, New York 10019
(212) 765-5500

Founded: 1909. **No. of Employees:** 4,180. **Revenues (1990):** $963 million. **Revenues (1986):** $621 million. **Five-Year Revenue Growth:** 55%.

Description: The world's leading independent producer of synthetic tastes and smells. Their products are sold to producers of perfumes, cosmetics, and cleaners, such as Procter and Gamble, Calvin Klein, and Estee Lauder.

How they're growing/Recent developments: International holds an estimated 13% of the world's market. The company is in a very good position to take advantage of the increasingly globalized economy, as 70% of its sales come from overseas. International continues to grow, with new facilities in China, Korea, Spain, Argentina and Turkey. There is great room for growth in the Pacific Rim. Employment has grown from an estimated 3,590 in 1987 to 4,180 in 1991.

INTERNATIONAL GAME TECHNOLOGY
520 South Rock Boulevard
Reno, Nevada 89502
(702) 688-0100

Founded: 1980. **No. of Employees:** 2,150. **Revenues (1990):** $210 million. **Revenues (1986):** $42 million. **Five-Year Revenue Growth:** 400%.

Description: Manufactures and sells slot machines and other gaming devices used primarily in casinos located in Nevada and the Caribbean.

How they're growing/Recent developments: The company's products are reaching expanding foreign and domestic markets, a reflection of the increase in legalized gaming. New systems additions link slot machines to central computers in order to build prizes more quickly. Employment has grown from an estimated 900 in 1987 to 2,150 in 1991.

INTERNATIONAL PAPER COMPANY
2 Manhattanville Road
Purchase, New York 10577
(914) 397-1500

Founded: 1898. **No. of Employees:** 69,000. **Revenues (1990):** $13 billion. **Revenues (1986):** $5 billion. **Five-Year Revenue Growth:** 160%.

Description: The world's leading manufacturer of paper products.

How they're growing/Recent developments: One of International Paper's main goals is to increase production through recycling used juice and milk cartons. In recent years, the company has modernized plants in order to broaden its mix of products. Starting in 1986, the company has done that primarily through acquisitions. Among the company's purchases have been Hammermill Paper (1986), Arvey (1987), Masonite (1989), and Leslie Paper (1991). The company has also made some important acquisitions in Europe. Employment has grown from an estimated 44,000 in 1987 to 69,000 in 1991.

INTERNATIONAL RECOVERY CORPORATION
700 S. Royal Poinciana Boulevard, #800
Miami Springs, Florida 33166
(305) 884-2001

Contact: Howard Goldman, Director of Personnel. **Founded:** 1984. **No. of Employees:** 289. **Revenues (1990):** $234 million. **Revenues (1986):** $7 million. **Five-Year Revenue Growth:** 3,243%.

Description: International Recovery Corporation (IRC) is a world leader in aviation fuel services air carriers and the leading used oil recycler in the southeastern United States.

Common positions include: Accountant; Biochemist; Chemist; Credit Manager; Petroleum Engineer; Geologist; Sales Representative.

Principal educational backgrounds sought: Accounting; Business Administration; Chemistry.

Company benefits include: Medical insurance; dental insurance; life insurance.

How they're growing/Recent developments: Employment has grown from an estimated 144 in 1987 to 289 in 1991.

INTERNATIONAL TECHNOLOGY CORPORATION
23456 Hawthorne Boulevard, Suite 300
Torrance, California 90505
(213) 378-9933

Founded: 1983. **No. of Employees:** 3,905. **Revenues (1990):** $307 million. **Revenues (1986):** $208 million. **Five-Year Revenue Growth:** 48%.

Description: Engaged in environmental management services for decontamination situations.

How they're growing/Recent developments: In June, 1991, the company signed a $110 million contract with the U.S. Army Corps of Engineers for remediation of Superfund site in Slidell, Louisiana. Another major contract was signed in July, 1990, when the company was awarded a seven-year contract with the New York City Department of Sanitation.

INTUIT, INC.
P.O. Box 3014
Menlo Park, California 94026
(415) 322-0573

Founded: 1983. **No. of Employees:** 172. **Revenues (1990):** $33 million. **Revenues (1986):** $786 thousand. **Five-Year Revenue Growth:** 4,108%.

Description: Company provides and develops customized and prepackaged computer software.

How they're growing/Recent developments: Employment has grown from 6 in 1986 to 172 in 1991.

IPL SYSTEMS INC.
60 Hickory Drive
Waltham, Massachusetts 02154
(617)890-6620

Founded: 1973. **No. of Employees:** 82. **Revenues (1990):** $28.7 million.
Revenues (1986): $2.5 million. **Five-Year Revenue Growth:** 1,048%.

Description: IPL Systems, Inc. designs, manufactures, markets and services a
broad range of high-quality, cost-effective data storage subsystems for IBM
midrange and mainframe computer systems, and add-inn memory products
for IBM midrange computer systems. IPL supplies its products to customers
worldwide through a network of distributors in the Americas, Europe, and
the Pacific Rim.

How they're growing: In 1990, IPL experienced solid revenue gains resulting
from continued penetration of the AS/400 market with new products, coupled with a significant expansion of the company's worldwide sales and service network. Sales grew to $28.7 million, an increase of 95% over 1989. New
products in the storage subsystems market include the 6890 and 6850 tape
drives, while the 7636 Disk Array is IPL's initial entry in the promising
DASD (Direct Access Storage Device) market. Much of the growth in 1990
came from the company's overseas market, where the company has made
significant investments. In January, 1990, IPL opened its first overseas office
in Brussels, Belgium to provide direct support to European distributors. Distribution agreements were reached with leading systems vendors, including
one of Europe's largest suppliers of IBM peripherals. Key distributors were
also signed up in Germany, Belgium, The Netherlands, Denmark, and Nor-
way. In America, IPL broadened its North American marketing reach
through service contracts signed with Richard Besner & Associates Ltd. in
Canada, and Bull HN in the U.S. Among leading distributors and OEMs who
joined IPL's growing network were Decision Data, XL/Datacomp, and Sun
Data. Employment has grown from an estimated 30 in 1987 to 82 in 1991.

ISCO
P.O. Box 5347
Lincoln, Nebraska 68505
(402) 464-0231

Founded: 1959. **No. of Employees:** 532. **Revenues (1990):** $31.6 million.
Revenues (1986): $22.2 million. **Five-Year Revenue Growth:** 42%.

Description: Isco designs and manufactures instruments and equipment used
in scientific research and environmental protection control.

How they're growing/Recent developments: End of the year revenues for 1991 climbed to $37.1 million. Isco's environmental division sales between 1990 and 1991 increased 24%, driven by new environmental regulations and new products. The storm water runoff regulations implemented in December, 1990 increased demand for both waste water sampleters and flow meters. In addition, the company's successful 3200 series flow meters continued to gain market share. The market for the company's environmental products will continue to grow due to increasing awareness of water quality

ITEL CORPORATION
Two North Riverside Plaza, Suite 1950
Chicago, Illinois 60606
(312) 902-1515

Founded: 1967. **No. of Employee:** 8,000. **Revenues (1990):** $2 billion. **Revenues (1986):** $195.5 million. **Five-Year Revenue Growth:** 923%.

Description: Itel has operations in rail transportation, logistics, communications and marine dredging. Itel Rail is the largest independent lessor of rail cars in the United States, as well as the owner of short-line railroads and a rail car maintenance business; Itel Distribution Systems is a third-party logistics and distribution services company; Anixter is a leading supply specialist for wiring systems products to the cable TV, data and voice communications and industrial electrical cable markets; and Great Lakes Dredge & Dock is the largest marine dredging and construction company in the nation.

How they're growing/Recent developments: Itel acquired Anixter Brothers, a distributor of wiring systems products, in 1986. Anixter is now one of the company's most promising holdings. The company should benefit in the long term from sales to cable television operators when they begin updating their systems to new technologies like fiber optics. Employment has grown from an estimated 4,133 in 1987 to 8,000 in 1991.

IVAX CORPORATION
8800 NW 36th Street
Miami, Florida 33178-2404
(305) 590-2200

Founded: 1972. **No. of Employees:** 770. **Revenues (1990):** $142 million. **Revenues (1986):** $5 million. **Five-Year Revenue Growth:** 2,740%.

Description: Company is engaged in the research and development of pharmaceuticals, and the production of specialty chemicals, generic drugs, and medical diagnostics.

How they're growing/Recent developments: Ivax recently won worldwide license for a new Alzheimer's drug. The company has taken an aggressive acquisitions stance by acquiring Medical Market Specialties in March, 1991, and Delta Biologicals in August, 1991. In September, Ivax signed a letter of intent to purchase Noven Pharmaceuticals. Employment has grown from an estimated 60 in 1987 to 770 in 1991.

J&J SNACK FOODS
6000 Central Highway
Pennsauken, New Jersey 08109
(609) 665-9533

Founded: 1971. **No. of Employees:** 950. **Revenues (1990):** $96 million. **Revenues (1986):** $25 million. **Five-Year Revenue Growth:** 284%.

Description: Produces snack foods and beverages.

Common positions include: Accountant; Administrator; Blue-Collar Worker Supervisor; Commercial Artist; Customer Service Representative; Financial Analyst; Food Technologist; Operations/Production Manager; Marketing Specialist; Quality Control Supervisor; Reporter/Editor; Sales Representative.

Educational backgrounds sought include: Accounting; Art/Design; Business Administration; Communications; Finance; Marketing.

Company benefits include: Medical insurance; life insurance; tuition assistance; disability coverage; profit sharing; savings plan.

How they're growing/Recent developments: In March, 1990, J&J acquired Michigan Carbonic Company, a distributor of frozen carbonated drinks. Employment has grown from an estimated 600 in 1987 to 950 in 1991.

JACO ELECTRONICS
145 Oser Avenue
Hauppauge, New York 11788
(516) 273-5500

Founded: 1961. **No. of Employees:** 260. **Revenues (1990):** $79.9 million. **Revenues (1986):** $29.3 million. **Five-Year Revenue Growth:** 173%.

Description: Distributor of electronic components.

How they're growing/Recent developments: Due to soft market conditions, Jaco has been implementing cost reductions. Prior to the recession, the company acquired Quality Components, Inc., a distributor of semiconductors. Jaco's strategy has been to maintain extensive inventories of products so that it can respond quickly to customer requirements. Employment has grown from an estimated 205 in 1987 to 260 in 1991.

JACOBS ENGINEERING GROUP INC.
251 South Lake Avenue
Pasadena, California 91101
(818) 449-2171

Contact: William Gebhardt, Director of Human Resources. **Founded:** 1957. **No. of Employees:** 4,420. **Revenues (1990):** $882 million. **Revenues (1986):** $208 million. **Five-Year Revenue Growth:** 324%.

Description: An engineering services and construction company with clients ranging from the federal government to private industry. New York Stock Exchange.

Common positions include: Architect; Biochemist; Biologist; Buyer; Computer Programmer; Draftsperson; Economist; Aerospace, Agricultural, Biomedical, Ceramics, Civil, Electrical, Industrial, Mechanical, Metallurgical, Mining and Petroleum Engineers; Geologist; Geophysicist; Physicist; Statistician; Technical Writer/Editor.

Principal educational backgrounds sought: Accounting; Art/Design; Biology; Business Administration; Chemistry; Communications; Computer Science; Economics; Engineering; Finance; Geology; Marketing.

Company benefits: Medical, Dental, and Life Insurance; Tuition Assistance; Disability Coverage; Savings Plan.

Operations at this facility: Regional and Divisional Headquarters; Administration; Sales.

How they're growing/Recent developments: Earnings have been growing since 1986. In July, 1991, Jacobs signed a letter of intent to acquire Trial Technologies Inc. The previous month, the company received a contract from Exxon to provide engineering and construction services. Employment has grown from an estimated 2,600 in 1987 to 4,420 in 1991.

JAK CONSTRUCTION
102 West Jefferson Street
Falls Church, Virginia 22046
(703) 241-0341

Founded: 1982. **No. of Employees:** 95. **Revenues (1990):** $21 million. **Revenues (1986):** $2 million. **Five-Year Revenue Growth:** 950%.

Description: Company renovates and repairs commercial and office buildings.

How they're growing/Recent developments: Employment has grown from 12 in 1986 to 95 in 1991.

JJW CONSTRUCTION
P.O. Box 16298
Plantation, Florida 33317
(305) 587-5597

Founded: 1984. **No. of Employees:** 305. **Revenues (1990):** $46.8 million. **Revenues (1986):** $3 million. **Five-Year Revenue Growth:** 1,460%.

Description: A major South Florida commercial and office building construction company.

How they're growing/Recent developments: Employment has grown from 41 1986 to 305 in 1991.

JOHNSON & JOHNSON
One Johnson & Johnson Plaza
New Brunswick, New Jersey 08933
(908) 524-0400

Founded: 1885. **No. of Employees:** 82,200. **Revenues (1990):** $11.2 billion. **Revenues (1986):** $7 billion. **Five-Year Revenue Growth:** 60%

Description: A leading manufacturer in the consumer and pharmaceutical industries.

How they're growing/Recent developments: Johnson & Johnson spends 7.4% of sales on research and development, which has paid off in the release of new drugs. The company entered the European market in 1990, opening facilities in Hungary, Poland, and Yugoslavia, as well as an administrative office in Moscow. J&J cultivates business relationships with several companies which often have profitable outcomes, such as the development of the first screening test for hepatitis C, done in partnership with the biotech firm Chiron. Employment has grown from an estimated 78,200 in 1987 to 82,200 in 1991.

JOHNSON CONTROLS
5757 North Green Bay Avenue
P.O. Box 591
Milwaukee, Wisconsin 53201
(414) 228-1200

Founded: 1900. **No. of Employees:** 43,500. **Revenues (1990):** $4 billion. **Revenues (1986):** $2 billion. **Five-Year Revenue Growth:** 100%.

Description: Manufacturer of automated building controls, batteries, and automotive seating.

How they're growing/Recent developments: Johnson is evaluating the future of its battery and plastics businesses. Analysts believe that sales for fiscal 1992 should continue to advance as the economy improves. Employment has grown from an estimated 26,500 in 1987 to 43,500 in 1991.

JOSTENS, INC.
5501 Norman Center Drive
Minneapolis, Minnesota 55437
(612) 830-3300

Founded: 1897. **No. of Employees:** 7,000. **Revenues (1990):** $788 million. **Revenues (1986):** $582 million. **Five-Year Revenue Growth:** 35%.

Description: A producer of class rings, yearbooks, computer software, diplomas, caps and gowns.

How they're growing/Recent developments: In 1988, the company acquired School Pictures, Inc. and World Pictures, Inc., and in 1989, Educational Systems Corporation, which has helped position the company as a leader in programmed learning. The company has also introduced video yearbooks and has begun to pursue markets outside of education by offering rings related to special occasions, such as the Olympics, the World Series and other sporting events.

JUNO LIGHTING ONE
2001 South Mount Prospect Road
Des Plaines, Illinois 60018
(708) 827-9880

Founded: 1976. **No. of Employees:** 590. **Revenues (1990):** $85.5 million. **Revenues (1987):** $42.8 million. **Four-Year Revenue Growth:** 100%

Description: Manufactures and sells recessed and track lighting fixtures.

How they're growing/Recent developments: Fiscal 1990 was Juno's 14th consecutive year of record sales. The company's continued growth is the result of new product introductions, new catalogs, and increased merchandising activities. New products include the Real Nail Bar Hanger System, and installation system for recessed fixtures, the "Strap" Series, which features a die cast lamp mounting plate with and exposed lamp style and die formed yoke, and "Coil Cord Clamp-Ons" that are designed for high-tech display and exhibition lighting situations. For the year ending November 30, 1990, sales increased 12% year to year. Employment has grown from an estimated 400 in 1987 to 590 in 1991.

JWP
2975 Westchester Avenue
Purchase, New York 10577
(914) 935-4000

Founded: 1986. **No. of Employees:** 16,000. **Revenues (1990):** $2.8 billion. **Revenues (1986):** $379 million. **Five-Year Revenue Growth:** 639%.

Description: Produces integrated solutions for complex facility, information, and energy environmental systems.

How they're growing/Recent developments: In September, 1991, JWP completed an offer to acquire Businessland, Inc. The acquisition was expected to be completed by the end of 1991, with Businessland accounting for 40-50% of sales. Revenues for first six months of 1991 rose 14% year to year. Employment has grown from an estimated 7,000 in 1987 to 16,000 in 1991.

KAMAN CORPORATION
Blue Hills Avenue
Bloomfield, Connecticut 06002
(203) 243-8311

Founded: 1945. **No. of Employees:** 6,333. **Revenues (1990):** $825 million.
Revenues (1986): $588 million. **Five-Year Revenue Growth:** 40%.

Description: Manufacturer of parts for the aerospace and defense industries.
Its primary product is the SH-2 Seasprite helicopter.

How they're growing/Recent developments: Kaman has a long history of annual earnings increases. The Seasprite is standard equipment on U.S. warships and a newer model, the Seasprite SH-2, which can carry up to nine passengers and two crew members has also been active in antimissile defense.

KASLER CORPORATION
27400 East 5th Street
Highland, California 92346
(714) 884-4811

Founded: 1961. **No. of Employees:** 606. **Revenues (1990):** 153 million.
Revenues (1987): $107 million. **Four-Year Revenue Growth:** 43%.

Description: A general contractor specializing in the construction of concrete
roadways, bridges and other public works projects.

How they're growing/Recent developments: Kasler has ten projects with the
Century Freeway in Los Angeles, which is the largest highway project underway in the nation.

KAYDON CORPORATION
19329 US 19 North, Suite 101
Clearwater, Florida 34624
(813) 531-1101

Founded: 1983. **No. of Employees:** 1,638. **Revenues (1990):** 169 million.
Revenues (1987): $113 million. **Four-Year Revenue Growth:** 50%.

Description: Manufacture bearings and filtration products.

How they're growing/Recent developments: Management has adopted a
steady acquisitions policy. In 1989, the company acquired KDI Electro-Tech

Corporation and IDM Electronics. In 1987, the company purchased the Spirolex retaining ring business from TRW.

KAUFMAN AND BROAD HOME CORP.
10877 Wilshire Boulevard
Los Angeles, California 90024

Founded: 1957. **No. of Employees:** 815. **Revenues (1990):** $1.36 billion. **Revenues (1986):** $491 million. **Five-Year Revenue Growth:** 177%.

Description: A regional builder of single-family homes, usually in medium-sized developments, primarily for use in Southern California and Paris, France.

How they're growing/Recent developments: Employment has grown from an estimated 600 in 1987 to 815 in 1991.

KEANE, INC.
10 City Square
Boston, Massachusetts 02129
(617) 241-9200

Founded: 1965. **No. of Employees:** 1,358. **Revenues (1990):** $93 million. **Revenues (1986):** $40 million. **Five-Year Revenue Growth:** 132%.

Description: Company offers software services for large corporations and applications software for hospitals.

How they're growing/Recent developments: Keane management favors the development of long-term relationships with client companies. Keane acquired a regional office of Broadway Seymour, Inc. in 1991. Employment has grown from an estimated 700 in 1987 to 1,358 in 1991.

KELLOGG COMPANY
One Kellogg Square
P.O. Box 3599
Battle Creek, Michigan 49016
(616) 961-2000

Founded: 1922. **No. of Employees:** 17,239. **Revenues (1990):** $5.2 billion. **Revenues (1987):** $3.3 billion. **Four-Year Revenue Growth:** 58%.

Description: The leading producer of dry cereals in the United States and Europe.

How they're growing/Recent developments: Kellogg's European sales are increasing much faster that its sales in the United States. Product expansion in recent years has led the company outside of the cereal market, and the company now sells such diversified food items as frozen pies, waffles and dessert mixes. Management is currently placing a great deal of the company's resources into advertising in order to compete with their major competitor, General Mills, for a share of the oat bran products market. The company also spends a great deal of its resources on plant modernization and expansion. One of the newest plants is located in Memphis, Tennessee.

KENT ELECTRONICS
5600 Bonhomme Road
Houston, Texas 77036
(713) 780-7770

Founded: 1983. **No. of Employees:** 368. **Revenues (1990):** 47.5 million. **Revenues (1987):** $14.7 million. **Four-Year Revenue Growth:** 223%.

Description: A specialty electronics distributor and custom contract manufacturer.

How they're growing/Recent developments: In August, 1991, Kent opened an operation in Maryland, after opening one earlier in Connecticut. In January, 1990, the company acquired Pyramid Electronics Supply. Continued expansion is planned. Revenues jumped to over $71.1 million in fiscal 1991.

KILLEARN PROPERTIES, INC.
P.O. Box 12789
Tallahassee, Florida 32317
(904) 893-2111

Founded: 1964. **No. of Employees:** 138. **Revenues (1990):** $20.2 million. **Revenues (1986):** $5.2 million. **Five-Year Revenue Growth:** 288%.

Description: Killearn Properties sells fully developed homesites in Leon County, Florida and Henry County, Georgia, to builders and individuals under contracts, which generally provide for small down payments and monthly installments.

How they're growing/Recent developments: During 1991, the company began development of its last golf course unit in Killearn Estates and began sales of this unit in May, 1991. During 1992, the company anticipates developing the last single-family unit in this community. Employment has grown from an estimated 52 in 1987 to 138 in 1991.

KIMBERLY-CLARK CORPORATION
P.O. Box 619100, DFW Airport Station
Dallas, Texas 75261-9100
(214) 830-1200

Founded: 1872. **No. of Employees:** 39,954. **Revenues (1990):** $6.407 billion. **Revenues (1986):** $4.303 billion. **Five-Year Revenue Growth:** 49%.

Description: Makers of paper and fiber products for personal, health care and industrial use. Some of their more well known products include Kleenex, Kotex, and Huggies.

How they're growing/Recent developments: Kimberly-Clark controls 45% of the tissue market, 33% of the feminine napkin market, 49% of the incontinence care market, and 32% of the disposable diapers market. The company is dedicated to increasing business in foreign markets during the 1990s. Employment has grown from an estimated 36,648 in 1987 to 39,954 in 1991.

KIMMINS ENVIRONMENTAL SERVICE CORPORATION
1501 2nd Avenue
Tampa, Florida 33605
(813) 248-3878

Founded: 1985. **No. of Employees:** 580. **Revenues (1990):** $107 million. **Revenues (1986):** $10 million. **Five-Year Revenue Growth:** 970%.

Description: A provider of hazardous and non-hazardous waste remediation services.

How they're growing/Recent developments: Much of the company's recent growth can be attributed to services related to incinerator, recycling and solid waste management.

KING WORLD PRODUCTIONS, INC.
830 Morris Turnpike
Short Hills, New Jersey 07078
(201) 376-1313

Founded: 1964. **No. of Employees:** 124. **Revenues (1990):** $454 million. **Revenues (1986):** $146 million. **Five-Year Revenue Growth:** 211%.

Description: King World is a leading worldwide distributor of first-run programming, including "Wheel of Fortune," "Jeopardy!" and "The Oprah Winfrey Show," the three highest rated shows in syndication, and "Inside Edition," a first-run syndicated newsmagazine strip, which is produced by the company. King World is also the producer of "Candid Camera," a half hour comedy strip and "Arts & Entertainment Revue," an hour-long weekly magazine the company produces in association with the Arts & Entertainment Network. King World distributes its own library of 68 feature films and 210 television programs, and through its barter subsidiary, Camelot Entertainment Sales, Inc., sells national advertising time in King World and other television programming.

How they're growing/Recent developments: King World is expecting its new version of "Candid Camera," hosted by actor Dom DeLuise, to boost profits. In 1988, King World acquired WIVB-TV, a Buffalo, New York, affiliate of CBS. Employment has grown from an estimated 107 in 1987 to 124 in 1991.

KIRBY CORPORATION
1775 St. James Place, Box 1745
Houston, Texas 77251
(713) 629-9370

Founded: 1969. **No. of Employees:** 953. **Revenues (1990):** $174 million. **Revenues (1986):** $61 million. **Five-Year Revenue Growth:** 185%.

Description: Kirby is a diversified corporation engaged, through its subsidiaries, in marine transportation, diesel repair and property and casualty insurance. Kirby's marine transportation subsidiary is engaged in the inland transportation of petrochemicals, other petroleum products and liquid fertilizer by tank barge along the Gulf Intracoastal Waterway and Mississippi River Systems and the offshore transportation of dry bulk and liquid caro by barge primarily in the Gulf of Mexico, the Caribbean Basin and the U.S. East Coast. The diesel repair subsidiary is engaged in the repair and overhaul of large diesel engines and related parts sales, primarily for customers in the inland and offshore marine industry. Kirby's property and casualty insurance subsidiary is engaged in the writing of property and casualty insurance in the Commonwealth of Puerto Rico.

How they're growing/Recent developments: In January, 1992, Kirby announced its intent to acquire all of the assets of Ole Man River Towing, Inc. Ole Man River, located in Vicksburg, Mississippi, is engaged in inland barge transportation, with recorded revenues of approximately $14.6 million in fiscal 1990 and $11.5 million for the nine months ending September 30, 1991. Kirby is planning to continue expansion of its marine fleet by new construction of inland tank barges and acquisitions of used barges and boats.

KNIGHT-RIDDER, INC.
One Herald Plaza
Miami, Florida 33132
(305) 376-3800

Founded: 1941. **No. of Employees:** 21,000. **Revenues (1990):** $2.3 billion. **Revenues (1986):** $1.9 billion. **Five-Year Revenue Growth:** 21%.

Description: One of the nation's largest newspaper chains. The company also has interests in cable television, and in the transfer of electronic information.

How they're growing/Recent developments: When Knight-Ridder acquired Dialog Information Services, it took over the largest computer databank in the world. Although the company's newspaper businesses are hampered by declining advertising revenues, the company's electronic information business is expanding rapidly.

KOLL MANAGEMENT SERVICES
4343 Von Karman Avenue
Newport Beach, California 92660
(714) 833-9360

Founded: 1961. **No. of Employees:** 365. **Revenues (1990):** $17.5 million. **Revenues (1987):** $8.5 million. **Four-Year Revenue Growth:** 106%.

Description: Koll Management Services is one of the nation's largest real estate management firms. Founded by The Koll Company, a nationally recognized real estate company in its 30th year of operations, Koll Management Services provides property and asset management services for over 400 properties containing over 40 million square feet under lease to nearly 7,200 tenants. Koll manages properties in major metropolitan areas primarily located in the western United States for numerous property owners including, among others, Aetna Realty Investors, Cigna Capital Advisors, Copley Real Estate Advisors, The Irvine Company, John Hancock Properties, Northwestern

Mutual Life Insurance Company, the Resolution Trust Corporation, Teachers Insurance & Annuity Association and Travelers Insurance.

How they're growing/Recent developments: The key elements to Koll's growth strategy include acquisitions of property management companies, new business development efforts focused in metropolitan areas where the company has existing operation, securing of additional asset management agreements, and continued cultivation of business from existing property and asset management clients, including affiliates of The Koll Company. The company has targeted three additional markets from which it has begun to obtain new property or asset management agreements: corporations which own and manage their own properties and which may benefit from management services provided by the company; financial institution with properties acquired through foreclosure proceedings or otherwise; and The Resolution Trust Corporation. Koll recruits "highly qualified personnel who have requisite education, training and experience to render superior levels of service to clients and their tenants." To provide employee training, Koll established a specialized educational program in August, 1990 known as "Koll College" which offers to the employees of the company and its service providers over 20 different courses related to property and asset management and customer service. Twenty-one of the company's managers have earned the Real Property Administrator (RPA) or Certified Property Manager (CPM) professional designations awarded by the Building Owners and Managers Association and the Institute of Real Estate management, respectively.

KOMAG, INC.
275 South Hillview Drive
Milpitas, California 95035
(408) 946-2300

Founded: 1979. **No. of Employees:** 1,542. **Revenues (1990):** $150 million. **Revenues (1986):** $20 million. **Five-Year Revenue Growth:** 650%.

Description: The largest U.S. supplier of thin metallic disks used in Winchester computer disk drives.

How they're growing/Recent developments: In 1987, the company broke into the Japanese market through a joint venture with Asaki Komag Company, Ltd. Employment has grown from an estimated 260 in 1987 to 1,400 in 1991. Employment has grown from an estimated 830 in 1987 to 1.542 in 1991.

L.A. GEAR
4221 Redwood Avenue
Los Angeles, California 90066
(213) 822-1995

Founded: 1979. **No. of Employees:** 1,502. **Revenues (1990):** $902.2 million. **Revenues (1986):** $36.3 million. **Five-Year Revenue Growth:** 2,385%.

Description: Designers, importers and distributors of athletic footwear.

How they're growing/Recent developments: During 1990, L.A. Gear's sales grew significantly, spurred in part by international business, which tripled in volume. New products include the Street Hiker collection, and the Catapult shoe, which is made with a lightweight fiber composite that "absorbs and diffuses impact while offering additional resilience, stability and comfort." Employment has grown from an estimated 196 in 1987 to 1,502 in 1991.

LANCE, INC.
8600 South Boulevard, P.O. Box 32368
Charlotte, North Carolina 28232
(704) 554-1421

Founded: 1912. **No. of Employees:** 4,500. **Revenues (1990):** $446 million. **Revenues (1986):** $367 million **Five-Year Revenue Growth:** 22%.

Description: Maker and distributor of packaged snacks, such as potato chips, peanuts, and popcorn.

How they're growing/Recent developments: Spotting the health and nutrition trend ahead of many of its competitors, Lance was one of the first snack food makers to convert to vegetable oils from animal fats.

LANDAUER
2 Science Road
Glenwood, Illinois 60425
(708) 755-7000

Founded: 1988 (in current form). **No. of Employees:** 260. **Revenues (1990):** 24.7 million. **Revenues (1986):** 14.4 million. **Five-Year Revenue Growth:** 72%

Description: Provides services that help determine exposure to occupational and environmental hazards, especially radiation.

How they're growing/Recent developments: Landauer is now the largest supplier of personnel radiation monitoring services and has a growing position in radon gas detection.

LANDMARK GRAPHICS
16001 Park Ten Place, Suite 350
Houston, Texas 77084
(713) 578-4200

Founded: 1982. **No. of Employees:** 327. **Revenues (1990):** $56.7 million. **Revenues (1986):** $24.2 million. **Five-Year Revenue Growth:** 132%.

Description: Manufactures computerized oil exploration equipment.

How they're growing/Recent developments: In November, 1990, Landmark acquired Inverse Theory & Applications, Inc., a geophysical software developer. Landmark has spent over $7 million on research and development for new applications and products.

LA PETITE ACADEMY, INC.
P.O. Box 26610
Kansas City, Missouri 64196
(816) 474-4750

Founded: 1981. **No. of Employees:** 11,000. **Revenues (1990):** $201 million. **Revenues (1986):** $105 million . **Five-Year Revenue Growth:** 91%.

Description: Providers of day care and pre-school services.

How they're growing/Recent developments: La Petite Academy continues to expand with on-worksite academies for employee children.

LASER PRECISION CORPORATION
32242 Paseo Adelanto, Suite A
San Juan Capistrano, California 92675
(714) 489-2991

Founded: 1969. **No. of Employees:** 234. **Revenues (1990):** $22.5 million. **Revenues (1986):** $16 million. **Five-Year Revenue Growth:** 40%.

Description: Manufactures precision instruments.

How they're growing/Recent developments: The company has benefitted from strong demand and its innovative product development in fiber optics and radiometry instruments. In March, 1990, Laser Precision acquired Lightwave Communications, Inc. Employment has grown from an estimated 220 in 1987 to 234 in 1991.

ESTEE LAUDER
767 5th Avenue
New York, New York 10153
(212) 572-4600

Founded: 1944. **No of Employees:** 10,000. **Revenues (1990):** $2.093 billion (est.). **Revenues (1986):** $1.2 billion (est.). **Five-Year Revenue Growth:** 74%.

Description: Estee Lauder is the leading brand of cosmetics sold in department stores. Some of its well known companies include Aramis, Clinique Laboratories, and Estee Lauder.

How they're growing/Recent developments: Opened the first shop for its environmentally safe skin care line, Origins, in 1991. That same year, ex-Calvin Klein executive Robin Burns joined the team, revamping the company's usually conservative advertising.

LAWTER INTERNATIONAL
990 Skokie Boulevard
Northbrook, Illinois 60062
(708) 498-4700

Founded: 1958. **No. of Employees:** 467. **Revenues (1990):** $150 million. **Revenues (1986):** $104 million. **Five-Year Revenue Growth:** 44%.

Description: Produces printing inks and resins.

How they're growing/Recent developments: Lawter plans considerable expansion both in the United States and in China to take advantage of growing demand for the company's products. Employment has grown from an estimated 389 in 1987 to 467 in 1991.

LDDS COMMUNICATIONS
4780 Interstate 55 N, Suite 500
Jackson, Mississippi 39211
(601) 987-4900

Founded: 1983. **No. of Employees:** 800. **Revenues (1990):** $154 million. **Revenues (1986):** $6 million. **Five-Year Revenue Growth:** 2,467%.

Description: One of the nation's largest regional telecommunications companies in the United States, serving the South and Midwest.

How they're growing/Recent developments: In July, 1991, LDDS acquired Mid-American Technologies, Inc. of Omaha, Nebraska. In 1990, the company acquired Mercury, Inc. and Telemarketing Corporation. Other 1991 acquisitions include Tri-J Enterprises, National Teleservices Co., and Phone America of Carolina, Inc.

LDI
30033 Clemens Road
Westlake, Ohio 44145
(216) 687-0100

Founded: 1972. **No. of Employees:** 531. **Revenues (1990):** $334 million. **Revenues (1987):** $74 million. **Four-Year Revenue Growth:** 351%.

Description: The company leases and sells a complete range of new and used data processing and other high-tech computer and computer-peripheral equipment. The company also offers computer disaster recovery services.

How they're growing/Recent developments: In June, 1991, the company acquired Ergonomic Systems Corporation, an information services company that serves retail businesses. The company is also expanding into telecommunications equipment sales and leasing. Revenues rose to $383 million in 1991. Employment has grown from an estimated 310 in 1987 to 531 in 1991.

LECHTER'S
One Cape May Street
Harrison, New Jersey 07029
(201) 481-1100

Founded: 1975. **No. of Employees:** 2,928. **Revenues (1990):** $157 million. **Revenues (1986):** $40 million. **Five-Year Revenue Growth:** 293%.

Description: A specialty retailer.

How they're growing/Recent developments: In May, 1990, the company introduced a new store format under the name Famous Brands Housewares Outlet. The new stores represent a cooperative effort with manufacturers to provide competitive prices. In the past two years, Lechter's has opened 130 new stores. Approximately 300 of the company's employees work at the headquarters office and main distribution center.

LEGENT CORPORATION
8615 Westwood Center Drive
Vienna, Virginia 22182-2218
(703) 734-9494

Founded: 1970. **No. of Employees:** 1,051. **Revenues. (1990):** $170 million. **Revenues (1986):** $24 million. **Five-Year Revenue Growth:** 608%.

Description: Company supplies productivity enhancement system software for IBM and compatibles worldwide.

How they're growing/Recent developments: In November, 1989, LEGENT acquired Business Software Technology, Inc.

P. LEINER NUTRITIONAL PRODUCTS
1845 West 205th Street
Torrance, California 90501
(213) 328-9610

Founded: 1977. **No. of Employees:** 1,000. **Revenues (1990):** $148.2. **Revenues (1987):** $73.3. **Four-Year Revenue Growth:** 102%.

Description: P. Leiner Nutritional Products Corporation is a leading national marketer and manufacturer of vitamins and other health and beauty aid products with distribution through a majority of the major mass-market retail chains in America. The company is the largest full-line supplier of vitamins and nutritional supplements in the United States and the largest manufacturer of private label vitamins. Its own brands include Your Life, Pharmaceutical Formula, and Natural Life. Your Life is one of the two largest broadline vitamin brands. The company's products are sold in more than 52,000 retail outlets in all 50 states.

How they're growing/Recent developments: The company's growth strategy is based on the following components: increasing its share of the vitamin and nutritional supplement market through product and service enhancements; expanding sales of over-the-counter drugs by extending the product line and gaining distribution of the line to more of the company's customers; and building on an established customer base with the addition of other lines of self-care products. In 1992, the company expects to introduce its Proven Release feature for the company's private label vitamin programs. The company expects to increase the number of items in the OTC drug line, and to test market a new range of natural body care products under the Bodycology label, the rights to which the company acquired in May, 1991. Employment has grown from an estimated 205 in 1987 to 1,000 in 1991.

LIFETIME CORPORATION
75 State Street
Boston, Massachusetts 02109-1807
(617) 330-5080

Founded: 1976. **No. of Employees:** 5,750. **Revenues (1990):** $708 million. **Revenues (1986):** $24 million. **Five-Year Revenue Growth:** 2,850%.

Description: A provider of home health care services.

How they're growing/Recent developments: Revenues have increased for past several years. For the period ending March, 1991, revenues rose 28% year to year with a 50% increase in the home healthcare segment. Its Kimberly Quality Care division has recently entered into several "preferred provider agreements" with HMO's and insurance companies whereby a discount is given in exchange for a large volume of business. Employment grew by approximately 1,600 jobs between 1989 and 1990.

ELI LILLY AND COMPANY
Lilly Corporate Center
Indianapolis, Indiana 46285
(317) 276-2000

Founded: 1901. **No. of Employees:** 29,900. **Revenues (1990):** $5.2 billion. **Revenues (1986):** $3.7 billion. **Five-Year Revenue Growth:** 41%.

Description: One of the nation's leading medical products and pharmaceutical companies.

How they're growing/Recent developments: Lilly's best known, though controversial success story of recent years has been Prozac, a new antidepressant drug. Most of Lilly's major markets are growing, and new products should continue to expand the company's revenues. Lilly's R&D program is one of the best financed in the industry. Employment has grown from an estimated 25,700 in 1987 to 29,900 in 1991.

THE LIMITED, INC.
P.O. Box 182199
Columbus, Ohio 43216
(614) 479-7000

Founded: 1982. **No. of Employees:** 72,500. **Revenues (1990):** $4.8 billion. **Revenues (1986):** $2.4 billion. **Five-Year Revenue Growth:** 100%.

Description: Women's apparel chain which includes Victoria's Secret and Lane Bryant stores.

How they're growing/Recent developments: The company recently acquired Abercrombie & Fich, and launched Express Man, a new store catering to men's apparel. Revenues rose to almost $5.4 billion in 1991.

LIUSKI INTERNATIONAL
10 Hub Drive
Melville, New York 11747
(516) 454-8220

Founded: 1984. **No. of Employees:** 270. **Revenues (1990):** $129.6 million. **Revenues (1986):** $12 million. **Five-Year Revenue Growth:** 980%.

Description: Distributes PCs and components.

How they're growing/Recent developments: Liuski's products have consistently garnered favorable reviews from the industry press. Employment has grown from 50 in 1986 to 3,000 in 1991.

LIZ CLAIBORNE
1441 Broadway
New York, New York 10018
(212) 354-4900

Founded: 1976. **No. of Employees:** 6,000. **Revenues (1990):** $1.7 billion. **Revenues (1986):** $813 million. **Five-Year Revenue Growth:** 109%.

Description: A renowned apparel company that designs and manufactures men's and women's clothes, accessories, and cosmetics.

How they're growing/Recent developments: Despite the sluggish retail economy, company revenues have grown substantially due to demand for the brand name products. New divisions developed since 1989 specialize in large sizes, cosmetics, and jewelry, have contributed to growth. The company is also expanding into British markets. First Issue store chain opened in 1988 with its own label. Employment has grown from an estimated 3,000 in 1987 to 6,000 in 1991.

LONGS DRUG STORES CORPORATION
141 N. Civic Drive
Walnut Creek, California 94596
(415) 937-1170

Founded: 1938. **No. of Employees:** 15,100. **Revenues (1990):** $2.334 billion. **Revenues (1986):** $1.635 billion. **Five-Year Revenue Growth:** 43%.

Description: Longs operates 261 drugstores in six Western states.

How they're growing/Recent developments: By the end of 1991, Longs hopes to have completed upgrading its checkout, inventory, and ordering systems, which will improve efficiency. Store managers are given a great deal of independence and responsibility, which allows them to better tailor their area stores to consumer needs. The company is consistently adding new stores and keeping high levels of profitability. Employment has grown from an estimated 11,000 in 1987 to 15,100 in 1991.

LOREDAN BIOMEDICAL INC.
3650 Industrial Boulevard
West Sacramento, California 95691
(916) 374-8009

Founded: 1980. **No. of Employees:** 75. **Revenues (1990):** $21 million. **Revenues (1987):** $9 million. **Four-Year Revenue Growth:** 133%.

Description: Manufactures and markets computerized equipment software for a variety of physical therapy testing and rehabilitation. The company's LIDO family of equipment is sold to clinics, hospitals and physicians.

How they're growing/Recent developments: Management fully expects Loredan to be a $100 million company by 1995 or 1996. Loredan's largest foreign market is Japan, and the company is planning an even greater marketing push for the rest of the Far East. Loredan also sells to Italy, Switzerland, Germany, France, Saudi Arabia, and Sweden, among others.

LOREN INDUSTRIES, INC.
2801 Greene Street
Hollywood, Florida 33020
(305)920-6622

Founded: 1972. **No. of Employees:** 185. **Revenues (1990):** $589.8 million. **Revenues (1986):** $359 million. **Five-Year Revenue Growth:** 64%.

Description: Manufacturers of jewelry.

How they're growing/Recent developments: Employment has grown from an estimated 175 in 1987 to 185 in 1991.

LSI LOGIC CORPORATION
1551 McCarthy Boulevard
Milpitas, California 95035
(408)433-8000

Founded: 1981. **No. of Employees:** 4,000. **Revenues (1990):** $655 million. **Revenues (1986):** $194 million. **Five-Year Revenue Growth:** 238%.

Description: A leading designer, manufacturer and supplier of high-performance application specific integrated circuits, standard microprocessors, and digital signal processing circuits, as well as chip sets for IBM compatible PCs.

How they're growing/Recent developments: Although LSI's revenue expansion was dimmed in 1990, losses were mainly due to restructuring charges. The company is expected to grow due to acceleration of industry growth, aggressive new product introduction program, and higher selling prices. Concentrated in a high-growth market and spends on research and development aggressively. Employment has grown from an estimated 2,322 in 1987 to 4,000 in 1991.

LUBY'S CAFETERIAS, INC.
2211 Northeast Loop 410
P.O. Box 33069
San Antonio, Texas 78265

Founded: 1946. **No. of Employees:** 6,300. **Revenues (1990):** $311 million. **Revenues (1986):** $215 million. **Five-Year Revenue Growth:** 45%.

Description: Chain of cafeterias mainly located in Texas malls.

How they're growing/Recent developments: Luby's is expanding take-out and cafeteria size-eateries serving children and family dining.

LYNCH CORPORATION
8 Sound Shore Drive, Suite 290
Greenwich, Connecticut 06830
(203) 629-3333

Founded: 1928. **No. of Employees:** 551. **Revenues (1990):** $98.4 million. **Revenues (1986):** $11.3 million. **Five-Year Revenue Growth:** 770%.

Description: Lynch Corporation is a diversified company with subsidiaries in communications, services and manufacturing. Subsidiaries include: Lynch Telecommunications Corporation, which was formed in 1989 for the purpose of acquiring independent telephone and other telecommunications businesses; Lynch Entertainment Corporation, which holds a 20% interest in Coronet Communications; Lynch Services Corporation, which owns 100% of Morgan Drive Away, Inc., a domestic common and contract carrier of mobile homes; Lynch Asset Management, formed in 1987 to acquire and operate investment management firms; Lynch Capital Corporation, which executes securities transactions for the parent company; Lynch Machinery-Miller Hydro, Inc., which manufactures glass-forming machines and automated case-packing machines; M-tron Industries, a manufacturer and importer of quartz crystal products and clock oscillator modules used for clocking digital circuits, precision time base references and frequency and time related circuits; and Safety Railway Service Corporation, which, through a subsidiary, produces industrial processing and air-pollution control equipment.

How they're growing/Recent developments: During 1990, Lynch Machinery invested in state-of-the-art computer controlled production equipment, the result being that the company was able to extend the warranty on major portions of its product line from one to five years. M-tron's quality goal is to have zero defects in its quartz crystal and clock oscillator products. Western New Mexico Telephone Company, which was recently acquired by Lynch Telecommunications, is building a new fiber optic cable to its long distance meet point at Lordsburg in southwestern New Mexico to assure its customers the best possible service, as demands on its system increase during the next several years. Employment has grown from an estimated 260 in 1987 to 551 in 1991.

MACNEAL-SCHWENDLER CORPORATION
815 Colorado Boulevard
Los Angeles, California 90041
(213) 258-9111

Founded: 1963. **No. of Employees:** 319. **Revenues (1990):** $57 million. **Revenues (1986):** $27 million. **Five-Year Revenue Growth:** 111%.

Description: Company provides applications software. Products are used in CAD engineering.

How they're growing/Recent developments: Although revenue growth has slowed due to the recession, growth is expected to continue. The company leases its products, which results in continuing revenues while the company attracts of new customers. Devotes large portion of capital to research and development. Employment has grown from an estimated 92 in 1987 to 319 in 1991.

MAGIC YEARS CHILD CARE & LEARNING CENTERS
532 East Main Street
Plains, Pennsylvania 18702
(717) 825-5437

Founded: 1984. **No. of Employees:** 450. **Revenues (1990):** $6.3 million. **Revenues (1986):** $586 thousand. **Five-Year Revenue Growth:** 975%.

Description: Operates daycare centers.

MAIL BOXES ETC.
5555 Oberlin Drive
San Diego, California 92121
(619) 452-1553

Founded: 1983. **No. of Employees:** 100. **Revenues (1990):** 25.7 million. **Revenues (1987):** 14.6 million. **Four-Year Revenue Growth:** 76%.

Description: Mail Boxes provides private postal and business services.

How they're growing/Recent developments: In July, 1991, the company signed a service agreement with Xerox to pack and ship Xerox copiers, fax machines and other small business products to Xerox service centers from customers around the country. During 1990 and 1991, the company opened

287 Mail Boxes, Etc Service Centers. Foreign franchises are also on the rise. Revenues rose to $30.3 million in 1991.

MARINE SHALE PROCESSORS
110 James Drive West, Suite 120
St. Rose, Louisiana 70087
(504) 465-3300

Founded: 1984. **No. of Employees:** 320. **Revenues (1990):** $46 million. **Revenues (1986):** $5 million. **Five-Year Revenue Growth:** 820%.

Description: A major a recycler of hazardous waste, MSP uses hazardous materials as ingredients in its patented verification process to manufacture aggregates and recover grade one steel.

How they're growing/Recent developments: MSP was named as one of only four Louisiana companies to receive the Blue Chip Enterprise Initiative Award. Since 1986, employment has grown from 92 to 320.

MARK IV INDUSTRIES
501 John James Audobon Parkway
Box 450
Amherst, New York 14226
(716) 689-4972

Founded: 1970. **No. of Employees:** 11,400. **Revenues (1990):** $937 million. **Revenues (1986):** $83 million. **Five-Year Revenue Growth:** 1,029%.

Description: Manufacturer of a variety of specialized products including consumer audio and visual equipment, industrial plastic hoses and belting, motor vehicle parts, and accessories.

How they're growing/Recent developments: The company reduced its long term debt by 137 million during the first half of fiscal year 1991-92 and is committed to continuing to reduce debt. Earnings should continue to rise due to recent acquisitions. Employment has grown from an estimated 5,100 in 1987 to 11,400 in 1991.

MARRIOTT CORPORATION
Marriott Drive
Washington, DC 20058
(301)380-9000

Founded: 1929. **No. of Employees:** 209,000. **Revenues (1990):** $7.6 billion. **Revenues (1986):** $5.3 billion. **Five-Year Revenue Growth:** 43%.

Description: One of the nation's largest hotel chains in the world, Marriott also provides catering for restaurants and airlines.

How they're growing/Recent developments: Sales for the nine months ending September, 1991 increased 9.7% year to year. Marriott should fare even better in 1992 if the economy can rebound.

MARS, INC.
6885 Elm Street
McLean, Virginia 22101
(703) 821-4900

Founded: 1920. **No. of Employees:** 22,000. **Revenues (1990):** $8.450 billion (est.). **Revenues (1986):** $7 billion (est.). **Five-Year Revenue Growth:** 21% (est.)

Description: Mars is the second-largest candy maker in the world, producing such well known favorites as M&Ms, Milky Way, Snickers, and 3 Musketeers.

How they're growing/Recent developments: Mars is continuing to offer new products or new versions of old products, such as mint and almond M&Ms and Milky Way Dark, in an effort to compete with Hershey. In 1991, the company introduced the Dove division, which produces dark chocolate and ice cream bars. Mars has also refined its policy of remaining aloof by entering the realm of joint promotions, something it had previously shied away from.

MARSH & MCLENNAN COMPANIES, INC.
1166 Avenue of the Americas
New York, New York 10036
(212) 345-3000

Founded: 1904. **No. of Employees:** 24,400. **Revenues (1990):** $2.723 billion. **Revenues (1986):** $1.804 billion. **Five-Year Revenue Growth:** 51%.

Description: The world's largest insurance broker.

How they're growing/Recent developments: Marsh & McLennan is dedicated to continued growth; currently that growth is in its consulting division, which accounts for 33% of its revenues. The company desires to move into the European market in anticipation of EC unification in 1992; in 1991, it sold off interests in a Dutch consulting firm to open its own in the Netherlands. Employment has grown from an estimated 22,700 in 1987 to 24,400 in 1991.

MARSHALL INDUSTRIES
9674 Telstar Avenue
El Monte, California 91731
(818) 459-5500/not in serv.

Founded: 1954. **No. of Employees:** 1,600. **Revenues (1990):** $544 million. **Revenues (1986):** $245 million. **Five-Year Revenue Growth:** 122%.

Description: National distributors of electronic components.

How they're growing/Recent developments: In April, 1991, Marshall became the exclusive distributor for Hitachi Ltd.'s fax machines. Revenues for 1991 rose to 583 million.

MASCO CORPORATION
21001 Van Born Road
Taylor, Michigan 48180
(313) 274-7400

Founded: 1929. **No. of Employees:** 41,300. **Revenues (1990):** $3.2 billion. **Revenues (1986):** $1.4 billion. **Five-Year Revenue Growth:** 128%.

Description: A leading manufacturer of building and home improvement products.

How they're growing/Recent developments: Masco has built itself up through acquisitions and is now the largest U.S. manufacturer of furniture, with brand names such as Henredon, Drexel Heritage and Universal.

MAXIM INTERGRATED PRODUCTS
120 San Gabriel Drive
Sunnyvale, California 94086
(408) 737-7600

Founded: 1983. **Employees:** 505. **Revenues (1990):** $56 million. **Revenues (1987):** $16 million. **Four-Year Revenue Growth:** 250%.

Description: Maxim designs, develops, manufactures and markets a broad range of linear and mixed signal integrated circuits for use in a variety of electronic products. The company's products include data converters, interface circuits, amplifiers, power control circuits, timers and counters, display circuits, multiplexers and switches, voltage detectors and filers. These circuits are marketed worldwide, principally through distributors and independent sales representatives, and are available in a number of different packages to meet varying requirements.

How they're growing/Recent developments: Revenues for fiscal 1991 jumped to $73.8 million. During the fiscal year, the company announced 62 new products, bringing the company's total to 433, the most introduced by any anolog company during the past 8 years.

MAXXAM
P.O. Box 572887
Houston, Texas 77257-2887
(713) 975-7600

Founded: 1955. **No. of Employees:** 12,741. **Revenues (1990):** $2.3 billion. **Revenues (1986):** $108 million. **Five-Year Revenue Growth:** 2,030%.

Description: A major holding company with operations in forest products, real estate, and metals fabrication.

How they're growing/Recent developments: Most of Maxxam's growth in the past few years has come from its 1988 takeover of Kaiser Aluminum, which now accounts for almost 90% of the company's total sales. The company is also an aggressive harvester of redwoods.

THE MAY DEPARTMENT STORES COMPANY
611 Olive Street, Suite 1250
St. Louis, Missouri 63101
(314) 342-6300

Contact: Keith Gross, Manager of Corporate Human Resources. **Founded:** 1910. **No. of Employees:** 116,000. **Revenues (1990):** $10 billion. **Revenues (1986):** $5.1 billion. **Five-Year Revenue Growth:** 96%.

Description: The corporate headquarters office of a retail organization with 13 department store companies and a shoe discount division. These department store companies are located in various areas scattered across the United States and operate under various names.

Common positions include: Accountant; Architect; Attorney; Claim Representative; Computer Programmer; Draftsperson; Civil Engineer; Electrical Engineer; Mechanical Engineer; Financial Analyst; Systems Analyst.

Principal educational backgrounds sought: Accounting; Computer Science; Engineering; Finance; Mathematics.

Company benefits include: Medical and life insurance; pension plan; tuition assistance; disability coverage; profit sharing; employee discounts.

How they're growing/Recent developments: The company's growth has been fueled by rising individual stores sales, new store openings and May's recent acquisition of the Thalhimers chain.

MBIA
113 King Street
Armonk, New York 10504
(914) 273-4545

Founded: 1986. **No. of Employees:** 259. **Revenues (1990):** $107 million. **Revenues (1986):** $60 million. **Five-Year Revenue Growth:** 78%.

Description: Municipal bond insurer.

How they're growing/Recent developments: In 1989, MBIA acquired Bond Investors Corporation. In addition, the company is expanding services to the European Economic Community through an agreement with a French financial institution.

McDATA CORPORATION
310 Interlocken Parkway
Broomfield, Colorado 80021
(303) 460-9200

Contact: Betty Mackenzie, Manager of Human Resources. **Founded:** 1983. **No. of Employees:** 350. **Revenues (1991):** $58.7 million. **Revenues (1986):** $28.7 million. **Six Year Revenue Growth:** 76%

Description: Manufactures and markets network communication systems.

Common positions include: Software Engineers.

Principal educational background sought: Engineering.

Company benefits: Medical, Dental, and Life Insurance; Tuition Assistance; Disability Coverage; Employee Discounts Savings Plan.

Operations at this facility: Manufacturing; Research/Development; Administration; Service; Sales.

McDONALD'S CORPORATION
One McDonald's Plaza
Oak Brook, Illinois 60521
(708) 575-7428

Founded: 1955. **No. of Employees:** 137,000. **Revenues (1990):** $6.6 billion. **Revenues (1986):** $4.1 billion. **Five-Year Revenue Growth:** 61%.

Description: McDonald's is the largest chain of fast-food restaurants in the world.

How they're growing/Recent developments: Much of McDonald's recent expansion has come in virtually untapped international markets. The company is also now experimenting with pizza in some areas.

MCI COMMUNICATIONS CORPORATION
1133 19th Street NW
Washington DC 20036
(202) 872-1600

Contact: Carlton A. Stockton, Vice-President, Employee Relations. **Founded:** 1968. **No. of Employees:** 24,509. **Revenues (1990):** $7.7 billion. **Revenues (1986):** 3.6 billion. **Five-Year Revenue Growth:** 114%.

Description: Offers long distance intercity telephone service, and other telecommunications services to businesses, government, and private customers throughout the United States.

Principal educational backgrounds sought: Accounting; Business Administration; Communications; Computer Science; Engineering; Finance; Liberal Arts; Marketing; Mathematics; Physics; Internships offered.

Company benefits include: Medical, dental, and life insurance. pension plan; tuition assistance; disability coverage.

How they're growing/Recent developments: MCI, currently the second-largest long distance company in the nation acquired Telecom, USA, the nation's fourth-largest, in August, 1990. Revenues in 1992 are expected to grow by about 10%, due to increasing market share and overall industry performance.

McGRATH INDUSTRIES
100 Sitterly Road
Clifton Park, New York 12065
(518) 371-5671

Founded: 1985. **No. of Employees:** 150. **Revenues (1990):** $33 million. **Revenues (1986):** $2.6 million. **Five-Year Revenue Growth:** 1,170%.

Description: A commercial and office building construction company.

How they're growing/Recent developments: Employment has grown from 25 1986 to 150 in 1991.

McKINSEY & CO.
55 East 52nd Street
New York, New York 10022
(212) 446-7000

Founded: 1926. **No. of Employees:** 4,500. **Revenues (1990):** $900 million. **Revenues (1986):** $400 million. **Five-Year Revenue Growth:** 125%.

Description: The world's largest independent management consulting firm.

How they're growing/Recent developments: In response to the changing demands of the company's clients in the face of the recession, McKinsey has been concentrating on the technical side of its business. A recent acquisition was Washington D.C.'s Information Consulting Group.

MDT CORPORATION
2300 205th Street
Torrance, California 90501
(213) 618-9269

Founded: 1971. **No. of Employees:** 1,051. **Revenues (1990):** $103 million. **Revenues (1986):** $70.39 million. **Five-Year Revenue Growth:** 46%.

Description: MDT Corporation develops, manufactures, markets and services sterility assurance systems, including sterilizers, ultrasonic cleaners, washers, dryers, scrub sinks and related equipment, accessories and consumable. These products and services are used by health care professionals to prevent cross-infection of communicable diseases caused by the use of contaminated instruments. MDT also develops, manufactures, markets and services examining and operatory equipment, including electrosurgery devices, examination and surgical lights, dental X-ray machines, power systems, sedation systems and other products, including related accessories and consumables. The company derives about 36% of its revenues from parts, service and consumables provided for MDT's installed base of approximately 10,000 large sterilizers, 70,000 table-top sterilizers and other equipment, as well as for the installed base of equipment of other manufacturers. The company employs 512 people in manufacturing and quality assurance; 140 in marketing and sales; 275 in product support; 71 in administration; and 53 in research and development.

How they're growing/Recent development: In June, 1991, MDT acquired the Equipment Division of Smith & Nephew, Inc. Sales for the fiscal year ending March 31, 1991, were $108.3 million. The largest sales increases were for hospital and dental equipment, as well as for parts, services and consumables.

MEDCHEM PRODUCTS, INC.
232 West Cummings Park
Woburn, Massachusetts 01801
(617) 938-9328

Founded: 1970. **No. of Employees:** 56. **Revenues (1990):** $16.4 million. **Revenues (1986):** $5.9 million. **Five-Year Revenue Growth:** 233%.

Description: Manufacturer of biomedical products for surgical and veterinary use.

How they're growing/Recent developments: Revenues have benefitted from increased sales to the U.S. government. In addition, the company also purchased Japanese distribution rights of the Avatene product line. Avatene is the most effective product of its kind used in surgical procedures. Revenues rose to $18.4 million in fiscal 1991.

MEDCO CONTAINMENT SERVICES
100 Summit Avenue
Montvale, New Jersey 07645
(201) 358-5400

Founded: 1983. **No. of Employees:** 2300. **Revenues (1990):** $ 1 billion. **Revenues (1987):** $ 300.5 million. **Four-Year Revenue Growth:** 232%.

Description: Medco Containment Services provides prescription drug services for some 1,100 benefit plans, covering 25 million active employees, retirees and dependants. Medco designs prescription benefit plans to meet the individual needs of its client companies through its National Rx family of mail service pharmacies and through PAID Prescription's retail programs. The National Rx family of mail order pharmacies consists of 10 pharmacies that dispense over 21 million prescriptions annually. PAID Prescriptions, Inc., which developed the first prescription drug benefit card program and started processing drug benefit claims in 1964, now processes over 44 million retail claims a year. Medco's subsidiary companies include Medical Marketing Group, Inc., a company that creates and develops marketing services and information products for pharmaceutical manufacturers, and Synetic, Inc., a holding company for subsidiaries that include Porex Technologies Corporation, a manufacturer of porous plastic components used in health care industrial and consumer applications, and Dunnington Drug, Inc., a provider of pharmacy services to nursing homes in eastern Massachusetts and Rhode Island.

How they're growing/Recent developments: Some analysts believe that Medco's revenues may triple again by 1995. Sales for the year ending June 30, 1991, increased 33.8% over sales for the previous fiscal year due largely to increased sales to existing clients and the addition of new clients in the company's mail service prescription drug program. During 1991, the company opened its 10th mail-order service pharmacy near Spokane, Washington. Employment has grown from an estimated 1,500 in 1987 to 2,300 in 1991.

MEDEX, INC.
3637 Grand Avenue
Long Beach, California 90815
(213) 426-1368

Founded: 1959. **No. of Employees:** 600.**Revenues (1990):** $37 million. **Revenues (1987):** $23.2 million. **Four-Year Revenue Growth:** 59%.

Description: Medex designs, manufactures and markets a range of disposable products for life support systems used in hospitals and home health care.

How they're growing/Recent developments: Medex recently acquired Ivion Corporation, manufacturers of IV infusion equipment for hospital and home use. Employment has grown from an estimated 400 in 1987 to 600 in 1991.

MEDICAL IMAGING CENTERS OF AMERICA
9444 Farnham Street, Suite 100
San Diego, California 92123
(619)560-0110

Founded: 1981. **No. of Employees:** 388. **Revenues (1990):** $78.3 million. **Revenues (1986):** $2 million. **Five-Year Revenue Growth:** 3,815%.

Description: Medical Imaging Centers of America provides high technology medical services to the hospital and physician communities. MICA has become a full spectrum company able to provide medical services in the following three key segments: Mobile Fee-for-Service; Fixed Site Fee-for-Service; and the High Technology Medical Service Center. The company also expects to participate in the following emerging high technology service markets: Imaging Services; Cardiac Catheterization; Positron Emission Tomography; Nuclear Medicine; Ultrasound; and other emerging technologies. In each instance, MICA can provide the technology, personnel, service, training, billing and collection, marketing and management as required.

How they're growing/Recent developments: Employment has grown from an estimated 60 in 1987 to 388 in 1991.

MEDICINE SHOPPE INTERNATIONAL
1100 North Lindbergh Boulevard
St. Louis, Missouri 63132
(314) 993-6000

Founded: 1970. **No. of Employees:** 195. **Revenues (1990):** $32.3 million. **Revenues (1986):** $17 million. **Five-Year Revenue Growth:** 90%.

Description: Medicine Shoppe International is a franchisor of 858 retail pharmacies coast to coast. All of the company's pharmacies are independently owned and operated.

How they're growing/Recent developments: During 1990, Medicine Shoppe experienced record sales, as the 19% total sales growth for the company's stores were well above industry norms. Unlike independent drug stores that struggle to compete with chains, have trouble obtaining third party contracts with HMOs and others and have problems maintaining profits in the face of declining sales and eroding margins, Medicine Shoppe pharmacists are able to take advantage of the best aspects of both chain and independent businesses. While both chains and independents rely on "front-end" merchandise, Medicine Shoppe stores derive over 90% of their sales from prescriptions, which are not a cyclical demand item. Medicine Shoppe's management expects to maintain double-digit same-store sales growth rates, and will be placing greater emphasis on systemwide marketing programs to support that goal. The company also expects to increase the rate of new store openings through a combination of new marketing programs aimed at both potential new unit franchisees and conversion and acquisition prospects.

MEDISENSE INC.
12 Emily Street
Cambridge, Massachusetts 02139
(617) 547-8007

Founded: 1981. **Revenues (1989):** $30 million. **Revenues (1987):** $2 million. **Four-Year Revenue Growth:** 1,400%.

Description: MediSense manufactures home health equipment for cholesterol testing.

How they're growing/Recent developments: Its desk-calculator-size cholesterol measuring device has been distributed to pharmacies, where customers can now have their cholesterol level checked while waiting for a prescription. Revenues went from $2 million in 1987 to $30 million in 1989.

MEDSTAT SYSTEMS, INC.
777 East Eisenhower Parkway, Suite 500
Ann Arbor, Michigan 48108
(313) 996-1180

Contact: Katy Pek, Human Resources Manager. **Founded:** 1981. **No. of Employees:** 205. **Revenues (1990):** $12.9 million. **Revenues (1986):** $3.8 million. **Five-Year Revenue Growth:** 239%.

Description: A healthcare information company and leading supplier of specialized databases and software systems and services for controlling medical costs and measuring healthcare markets.

Common positions include: Accountant. Administrator. Computer Programmer. Financial Analyst. Marketing Specialist. Systems Analyst. Technical Writer/Editor.

Principal educational backgrounds sought: Accounting; Business Administration; Communications; Computer Science; Finance; Marketing; Public Health Administrator.

Company benefits: Medical, Dental, and Life Insurance; Disability Coverage; Profit Sharing; Savings Plan.

Operations at this facility: Divisional Headquarters; Administration; Service; Sales.

How they're growing/Recent developments: During 1991, MEDSTAT continued the expansion of its large employer customerbase with the addition of 13 clients including 3 public employers, bringing the total number of large employers covered under long-term service agreements to 75. In turn, the company's proprietary MarketScan database grew over 51% from 167 million to 252 million medical claims. Also during 1991, MEDSTAT was named as a Business Partner and "Industry Applications Specialist" by IBM. Five years ago, MEDSTAT was one-fifth the size it is today. Revenues rose from $12.9 million in 1990, to $17.9 million in fiscal 1991. Management has set a target of sustained revenue growth between 30 and 40 percent. Employment has grown from an estimated 40 in 1987 to 205 in 1991.

MELVILLE CORPORATION
1 Theall Road
Rye, New York 10580
(914) 925-4000

Founded: 1914. **No. of Employees:** 119,590. **Revenues (1990):** $8.7 billion. **Revenues (1986):** $5.3 billion. **Five-Year Revenue Growth:** 64%.

Description: Melville is one of the nation's largest retail companies. The company owns a number of chains, including Tom McAn shoe stores, Marshalls department stores, CVS drug stores, and Kay-Bee Toy and Hobby Centers, among others.

How they're growing/Recent developments: The company's aggressive acquisitions stance allows it to build about 200 new stores each year.

MENTOR GRAPHICS
8005 Southwest Boeckman
Wilsonville, Oregon 97070-7777
(503) 685-7000

Founded: 1981. **No. of Employees:** 2,400. **Revenues (1990):** $380 million. **Revenues (1987):** $221.82 million. **Four-Year Revenue Growth:** 71%.

Description: A worldwide leader in electronic design automation systems.

How they're growing/Recent developments: Mentor Graphics recently began releasing its new concurrent Design Environment -- a new plan which will support all of the company's EDA tools and increase the availability of the company's software. Employment has grown from an estimated 950 in 1987 to 2,400 in 1991.

MERCANTILE STORES COMPANY, INC.
1100 North Market Street
Wilmington, Delaware 19801
(302) 575-1816

Founded: 1919. **No. of Employees:** 18,000. **Revenues (1990):** $2.4 billion. **Revenues (1986):** $1.9 billion. **Five-Year Revenue Growth:** 26%.

Description: Operates 83 department stores and one specialty store in the South and Midwest.

How they're growing/Recent developments: The company has been adding two or three stores per year, remodeling present stores, and integrating computer processing systems to aid efficiency.

MERCHANTS GROUP
250 Main Street
Buffalo, New York 14202
(716) 849-3333

Founded: 1946. **No. of Employees:** 1910. **Revenues (1990):** $133 million. **Revenues (1986):** $96 million. **Five-Year Revenue Growth:** 39%.

Description: An insurance company.

How they're growing/Recent developments: The company has developed EDGE, an exclusive automation system geared to improving customer service.

MERCK & CO., INC.
P.O. Box 2000
Rahway, New Jersey 07065
(908) 574-4000

Founded: 1934. **No. of Employees:** 30,700. **Revenues (1990):** $7.7 billion. **Revenues (1986):** $4.1 billion. **Five-Year Revenue Growth:** 88%.

Description: Merck is the world's largest pharmaceutical manufacturer. Makes anti-hypertensives, cholesterol-lowering treatments, and animal health products. The Calgon division is involved in water purification.

How they're growing/Recent developments: Merck boasts extensive research and development, and is currently enjoying the benefits of several joint ventures with Johnson & Johnson and Dupont. Sales are expected to rise strongly again in 1992.

MERCURY GENERAL CORPORATION
4484 Wilshire Boulevard
Los Angeles, California 90010
(213) 937-1060

Founded: 1961. **No. of Employees:** 1,070. **Revenues (1990):** $529.3 million. **Revenues (1986):** $266.1 million. **Five-Year Revenue Growth:** 99%.

Description: A major specialty writer of all-risk classifications of passenger automobile insurance.

How they're growing/Recent developments: Since Mercury's inception in 1961, the company has been able to offer rates for most coverages which, based on California Department of Insurance surveys, have been among the most competitive available in the state. The company has been able to offer these low rates through careful underwriting and strict cost controls. Premium growth averaging 25% a year since 1985 has been supported by consistent above-industry average profitability as measured by both underwriting results and return on equity. Employment has grown from an estimated 850 in 1987 to 1,070 in 1991.

MERRY-GO-ROUND ENTERPRISES
3300 Fashion Way
Joppa, Maryland 21085
(301) 538-1000

Founded: 1971. **No. of Employees:** 9,895. **Revenues (1990):** $628 million. **Revenues (1986):** $207 million. **Five-Year Revenue Growth:** 203%.

Description: Specialty retailer of men's and women's clothing.

How they're growing/Recent developments: The number of stores has grown rapidly through internal expansion and acquisitions. Sales are expected to continue to advance, although more slowly, in the face of the recession. Further acquisitions are a possibility. Current plans call for the company to open 29 new stores and remodel another 22. Employment has grown from an estimated 4,460 in 1987 to 9,895 in 1991.

MESTEK, INC.
260 North Elm Street
Westfield, Massachusetts 01085
(413) 568-9571

Founded: 1898. **No. of Employees:** 2,347. **Revenues (1990):** $204 million. **Revenues (1986):** $87 million. **Five-Year Revenue Growth:** 134%.

Description: Manufacturer of HVAC equipment.

How they're growing/Recent developments: In February, 1991, the company acquired NEA, Inc., which was engaged in consulting and analytic services related to air quality. In March, 1990, the company acquired a 48.6% stake in H.B. Smith Co., a maker of boiler systems.

METHODE ELECTRONICS
7444 West Wilson Avenue
Chicago, Illinois 60656
(708) 867-9600

Founded: 1960. **No. of Employees:** 1,910. **Revenues (1990):** $133 million. **Revenues (1986):** $96 million. **Five-Year Revenue Growth:** 39%.

Description: Manufactures electronic equipment.

How they're growing/Recent developments: Revenues have been boosted by new products, including Ultra Couprofile chip carrier sockets and components for airbags. New projects have met with increased acceptance by the market.

METRO MOBILE CTS
110 East 59th Street
New York, New York 10022
(212) 319-7444

Founded: 1983. **No. of Employees:** 1,101. **Revenues (1990):** $224 million. **Revenues (1986):** $8 million. **Five-Year Revenue Growth:** 2,700%.

Description: Company is engaged in the operation of a cellular telephone service. Also sells propane.

How they're growing/Recent developments: Although telephone communications and propane sales may seem to have nothing to do with each other, CEO George Lindemann sees them as "consistent with our long-standing preference to operate utilitylike businesses." Employment has grown from an estimated 88 in 1987 to 1,101 in 1991.

METTERS INDUSTRIES
8200 Greensborough Drive
Suite 500
McLean, Virginia 22102
(703) 821-3300

Founded: 1981. **No. of Employees:** 320. **Revenues (1990):** $19.6 million. **Revenues (1986):** $2 million. **Five-Year Revenue Growth:** 880%.

Description: Provides engineering and technical supports services.

How they're growing/Recent developments: In response to continuing cutbacks in military spending, Metters plans to rely less on defense contracts. To do this, it has been using consultants, hiring managers from the private sector, and acquiring small arms companies and divisions to enhance product line. Employment has grown from 37 in 1986 to 320 in 1991. Employment has grown from an estimated 37 in 1987 to 320 in 1991.

MEYERS INDUSTRIES, INC.
P.O. Box 160
Adrian, Michigan 49221
(517)423-2151

Founded: 1937. **No. of Employees:** 100. **Revenues (1990):** $4 million. **Revenues (1986):** $3 million. **Five-Year Revenue Growth:** 33%.

Description: Produces sporting and recreational goods, including aluminum boats and canoes..

How they're growing/Recent developments: Employment has grown from an estimated 50 in 1987 to 100 in 1991.

MICRO HEALTHSYSTEMS
414 Eagle Rock Avenue
West Orange, New Jersey 07052
(201) 731-9252

Founded: 1971. **No. of Employees:** 50. **Revenues (1990):** $7.4 million. **Revenues (1987):** $3.2 million. **Four-Year Revenue Growth:** 131%.

Description: Micro Healthsystems is a provider of computerized financial and patient information systems to the health care industry. It is engaged in the design, development and marketing of a broad range of software management systems and its MedTake computerized bedside nurse charting system. The company's products are marketed exclusively to hospitals and other health care facilities. Each may be used individually in a specific area of such facilities or integrated with any other of the company's products or other vendor products, to share patient information between various departments.

How they're growing/Recent developments: During the fiscal year ending March 31, 1991, the company once again established new operating records, with revenues rising to $10.2 million. In addition, the company entered into an exclusive marketing agreement with Baxter Healthcare Corporation and expanded it software development program to include a series of interfaces which will permit the company's MedTake unit to be used in many on-line activities at hospitals and medical institutions.

MICRO TECHNOLOGY, INC.
5065 E. Hunter Avenue
Anaheim, California 92807
(714) 970-0300

Contact: Barbara Tedford. Manager of Human Resources. **Founded:** 1979. **No. of Employees:** 360. **Revenues (1990):** $83 million. **Revenues (1986):** $3 million. **Five-Year Revenue Growth:** 2,667%.

Description: Manufactures disk and tape drives for mainframe computers.

How they're growing/Recent developments: When Steven Hamerslag and Raymond Noorda bought 80% of this company in 1987 it was "dying"; today it has customers like the Christian Science Monitor Publishing society, which chose Micro Tech's Lance network management software package. Hamerslag received honorable mention for "Emerging Enterprise" in *Inc.*, January, 1991. Micro Technology offers strong customer service, and regularly gets product development from "roundtable sessions" from an advisory board of customers. Employment has grown from 25 in 1986 to 360 in 1991. Employment has grown from an estimated 25 in 1987 to 360 in 1991.

MICROCOM, INC.
500 River Ridge Drive
Norwood, Massachusetts 02062
(617) 551-1000

Founded: 1980. **No. of Employees:** 423. **Revenues (1990):** $71 million. **Revenues (1986):** $25 million. **Five-Year Revenue Growth:** 184%.

Description: Microcom produces hardware and software necessary for connecting computer workstations, regardless of geographic location.

How they're growing/Recent developments: In August, 1991, the company introduced Citadel, a data security file for Macintosh. The emphasis in new product development is on products geared to Windows and LAN markets. Employment has grown from an estimated 225 in 1987 to 423 in 1991.

MICROENERGY, INC.
350 Randy Road
Carol Stream, Illinois 60188
(708) 653-5900

Founded: 1982. **No. of Employees:** 136. **Revenues (1990):** $5.6 million. **Revenues (1987):** $2.5 million. **Four-Year Revenue Growth:** 124%.

Description: Manufacturer of switching power supplies.

How they're growing/Recent developments: Employment has grown from an estimated 50 in 1987 to 136 in 1991.

MICRON TECHNOLOGY, INC.
2805 East Columbia Road
Boise, Idaho 83706-9698
(208)368-4000

Contact: Susan Metzger, Personnel Director. **Founded:** 1978. **No. of Employees:** 3606. **Revenues (1990):** $333 million. **Revenues (1986):** $48 million. **Five-Year Revenue Growth:** 594%.

Description: Manufacturers of semiconductor memory components. New York Stock Exchange.

Common positions include: Accountant; Administrator; Buyer; Chemist; Computer Programmer; Draftsperson; Ceramics, Chemical, Civil, Electrical, Industrial and Metallurgical Engineers; Financial Analyst; Physicist; Purchasing Agent; Statistician; Systems Analyst; Electronics Technician.

Principal educational backgrounds sought: Accounting; Business Administration; Chemistry; Computer Science; Engineering; Finance; Marketing; Mathematics; Physics.

Company benefits: Medical, Dental, and Life Insurance; Tuition Assistance; Disability Coverage; Profit Sharing; Savings Plan; Employee Stock Plan.

Operations at this facility: Manufacturing; Research/Development; Administration; Service; Sales.

How they're growing/Recent developments: Despite sluggish semiconductor industry performance, Micron's sales for the nine months that ended in May, 1991 were up 32% over the same period of the previous year. Revenues should increase more rapidly in 1992 with the introduction of new advanced semiconductors. Micron has used its high-volume, low-cost manufacturing expertise to gain market shares and will continue to exploit this expertise to its fullest potential. The company is continually making improvements in its ability to compete in a global market and now enjoys a leading edge position in shrink technology and mask-layer reduction. Employment has grown from an estimated 1,430 in 1987 to 1,978 in 1991.

MICRONICS COMPUTERS
232 E. Warren Avenue
Fremont, California 94539
(415) 651-2300

Founded: 1986. **No. of Employees:** 260. **Revenues (1990):** $81 million. **Revenues (1986):** $4 million. **Five-Year Revenue Growth:** 1,925%.

Description: Produces systems boards for IBM compatible personal computers.

How they're growing/Recent developments: New products include two portable computers and 3X Windows models. The company prides itself on its ability to respond quickly to market demands. Much of the company's R&D is now focused on developing an applications specific integrated circuit (ASIC).

MICROPOLIS
21211 Nordhoff Street
Chatsworth, California 91311
(818)709-3300

Founded: 1976. **No. of Employees:** 3,020. **Revenues (1990):** $381 million. **Revenues (1986):** $213 million. **Five-Year Revenue Growth:** 79%.

Description: Micropolis produces high-performance Winchester disk drives used to record store and retrieve digital information.

How they're growing/Recent developments: Micropolis has implemented a cost-reduction program and anticipates strong sales of high capacity products. Employment has grown from an estimated 2,385 in 1987 to 3,020 in 1991.

MICROS SYSTEMS
12000 Baltimore Avenue
Beltsville, Maryland 20705
(301) 490-2000

Founded: 1977. **No. of Employees:** 300. **Revenues (1990):** $35.23 million. **Revenues (1987):** $18.27 million. **Four-Year Revenue Growth:** 93%.

Description: Micros Systems, 66% owned by Westinghouse Electric, is a manufacturer of point-of-sale and property management systems. Products include terminals, display devices, printers and computers, all software-tailored to the needs of retailers. Customers include hotels, restaurants and fast-food establishments.

How they're growing/Recent developments: Profits were up for the fifth year in a row in 1991, spurred in part by a 39% increase in sales of the MICROS 2700 Hospitality Management System. The company is also planning to expand overseas sales, most notably to Russia and the other former Soviet republics. Employment has grown from an estimated 285 in 1987 to 300 in 1991.

MICROSOFT CORPORATION
One Microsoft Way
Redmond, Washington 98052
(206) 882-8080

Founded: 1975. **No. of Employees:** 5,635. **Revenues (1990):** $1.2 billion. **Revenues (1986):** $198 million. **Five-Year Revenue Growth:** 506%.

Description: Microsoft designs, develops and supports a line of systems and applications for IBM and compatibles, including MS/DOS, IBM's most widely used operating system.

How they're growing/Recent developments: Microsoft draws much of its strength from its broad product line, which boasts leadership positions in all areas, especially in international markets. Windows 3.0 and related applications are the current focus in R&D.

MICROWARE, INC.
9400 SW Gemini Drive
Beaverton, Oregon 97005
(503) 644-4800

Founded: 1979. **No. of Employees:** 393. **Revenues (1990):** $203.9 million. **Revenues (1986):** $18 million. **Five-Year Revenue Growth:** 1,032%.

Description: A computer company.

How they're growing/Recent developments: Employment has grown from 56 in 1986 to 393 in 1991.

MID-AMERICA WASTE SYSTEMS

P.O. Box 156
Canal Winchester, Ohio 43110
(614) 833-9155

Founded: 1985. **No. of Employees:** 925. **Revenues (1990):** $78.7 million. **Revenues (1986):** $3.8 million. **Five-Year Revenue Growth:** 1,971%.

Description: Non-hazardous solid waste management business.

How they're growing/Recent developments: Mid-America has acquired independent solid waste collection operations and landfills. Revenues have also benefitted from price increases. Revenues for the three months ending March, 1991 rose 48% year to year. In July, 1991, Mid-America acquired the assets of two hauling companies in Ohio. In some markets, the company offers waste reduction programs like recycling and composting

MINNESOTA MINING & MANUFACTURING COMPANY (3M)

3M Center
St. Paul, Minnesota 55144-1000
(612) 733-1110

Founded: 1902. **No. of Employees:** 89,601. **Revenues (1990):** $13 billion. **Revenues (1986):** $8.6 billion. **Five-Year Revenue Growth:** 51%.

Description: 3M is a leading manufacturer of thousands of consumer and industrial products, including magnetic storage disks, adhesive tape, highway signs, and many others.

How they're growing/Recent developments: 3M is known for the tough production goals and standards that it sets for itself. Currently management hopes to cut manufacturing costs by 10%, waste by 35%, and energy by 20% - - all by 1995. In addition, the company hopes to continue its overseas expansion. Exports accounted for approximately 50% of 1990 sales. Employment has grown from an estimated 82,405 in 1987 to 89,601 in 1991.

MMI MEDICAL, INC.

11155 Jersey Boulevard, Unit D
Rancho Cucamonga, California 91730
(714) 466-9884

Founded: 1938. **No. of Employees:** 6700. **Revenues (1990):** $38 million. **Revenues (1986):** $22.2 million. **Five-Year Revenue Growth:** 71%.

Description: MMI Medical, Inc. and its subsidiaries provide specialized services to hospital radiology and cardiology departments and other health care providers. R-Squared Scan Systems is the leading national third party provider of competitively priced, high quality maintenance and repair service programs for diagnostic imaging equipment, including computerized tomography (CT) scanners, cardiac catheterization labs and general X-ray equipment. Additionally, R-Squared reloads and distributes X-ray tubes, spare parts and accessories used with CT scanners and other diagnostic imaging equipment and supplies used and refurbished imaging equipment to both domestic and foreign end users. MMI Medical is a provider of shared diagnostic imaging services. Operating a fleet of mobile CT scanners, the company makes this capital intensive technology available to smaller health care providers on a shared service basis. The company also rents CT scanners and cardiac catheterization labs to hospitals for interim use during in-house construction, repair or upgrade programs of existing facilities. Advanced Imaging Technologies distributes X-ray film, processor chemicals, radiology accessories and X-ray capital equipment. Also, the company provides maintenance services for X-ray equipment and film processors.

Why they're growing/Recent developments: In July, 1990, the company acquired Advanced Imaging Technologies, in order to increase its service to the radiology market. In order to keep up with the rapidly changing diagnostic, maintenance and distribution services market, MMI Medical is beginning to develop additional MRI diagnostic software. New research and development activities in both MRI diagnostics and cardiac cath diagnostics are planned for 1992. In a recent development, MMI Medical was chosen by NASA to provide mobile cath lab equipment for the Spacelab life sciences/shuttle mission.

MOBILE AMERICA CORPORATION
2118 Gulf Life Tower
Jacksonville, Florida 32207
(904) 396-0571

Founded: 1968. **No. of Employees:** 60. **Revenues (1990):** $27.6 million. **Revenues (1986):** $11.7 million. **Five-Year Revenue Growth:** 136%.

Description: Mobile America Corporation, and its subsidiaries, Mobile America Insurance Group, Fortune Insurance Company and Fortune Life Insurance Company, engage in a variety of activities, primarily relating to the insurance industry. Fortune Insurance Company, which generates the largest share of the company's revenues, is a property and casualty insurance company. Fortune is engaged in the writing of several specialized lines of insurance coverage that are marketed in Florida through a network of independent agents. Fortune Life Insurance Company, a wholly-owned subsidiary of Fortune Insurance, is engaged in the business of writing a variety of life and accident and health insurance coverages which are also marketed through independent agents in Florida, Louisiana and Arizona. Mobile America Insurance Group is a wholly-owned subsidiary of Mobile America and serves as a managing general agent for certain lines written by the other subsidiaries.

Company benefits include: Each new professional and associate receives at least 50 hours of in-house training, and the company's new orientation program includes providing each new employee with computer, telephone, and communication training. Almost all management and supervisory employees attend outside seminars averaging 100 hours of specialized advanced management and technical skill seminars. In addition, the company offers to pay complete tuition and reimbursement for books required for college courses or approved insurance courses leading to a BA or BS, or an advanced degree.

How they're growing/Recent developments: Mobile America's record revenues in 1990 were a culmination of a strategy developed in 1988 to take advantage of a new minimum requirement automotive insurance law enacted in Florida in 1989. The company's strategy anticipated a much broader market for minimum required insurance and which was fully realized when the company's direct written premiums from minimum requirement automotive insurance increased from $16 million in 1988 to $47 million in the year ending December 31, 1990. To meet the demands of this new business, the company hired and trained 60 new employees.

MOBILE TECHNOLOGIES CORPORATION
9841 Airport Boulevard, 12th Floor
Los Angeles, California 90045
(213) 641-8614

Founded: 1983. **No. of Employees:** 465. **Revenues (1990):** $87.9 million. **Revenues (1986):** $10.1 million. **Five-Year Revenue Growth:** 770%.

Description: Provides nationwide paging services, telephone answering services, and air-to-ground and marine telecommunications systems.

How they're growing/Recent developments: The company is developing an international paging system and voice messaging network. Employment has grown from 68 1986 to 465 in 1991.

MOCON
(MODERN CONTROLS)
7500 Boone Avenue North
Minneapolis, Minnesota 55428
(612) 493-6370

Founded: 1966. **No. of Employees:** 71. **Revenues (1990):** $11.5 million. **Revenues (1986):** $5.9 million. **Five-Year Revenue Growth:** 98%.

Description: A leading manufacturer of high tech instrumentation used for testing packages and packaging material for permeation of gases and water vapor, weighing and sorting instruments for the pharmaceutical industry.

How they're growing/Recent developments: During 1990, the company's sales rose 18% from the previous year. MOCON will benefit from the continued strength of the plastic packaging industry. Analysts Dain Bosworth have predicted that revenues for 1992 will rise to over $16 million. Successful new products include the Aromatran, a measurement test system able to detect small changes in the loss or gain of flavors, fragrances and aromas in packaging materials, and the Veritab, a system to test pharmaceutical products.

MODERN TECHNOLOGIES CORPORATION
4032 Linden Avenue
Dayton, Ohio 45432
(513) 252-9199

Contact: Ken Simon, Human Resources Manager. **Founded:** 1984. **No. of Employees:** 385. **Revenues (1990):** $19 million. **Revenues (1986):** $1 million. **Five-Year Revenue Growth:** 1,800%.

Description: Modern Technologies provides engineering and technical services, and manufacturing.

Common positions include: Accountant; Blue-Collar Worker Supervisor; Buyer; Chemist; Computer Programmer; Draftsperson; Aerospace, Biomedical, Civil, Electrical, Industrial and Mechanical Engineers; Financial Analyst; Industrial Manager; Department Manager; General Manager; Operations/Production Manager; Personnel and Labor Relations Specialist; Purchasing Agent; Quality Control Supervisor; Systems Analyst; Technical Writer/Editor; Logistic Configuration Management.

Principal educational backgrounds sought: Computer Science; Engineering.

Company benefits: Medical, Dental, and Life Insurance; Pension Plan; Tuition Assistance; Disability Coverage; Flexible Account.

How they're growing/Recent developments: Employment has grown from 50 in 1986 to 385 in 1991.

MOLECULAR BIOSYSTEMS
10030 Barnes Canyon Road
San Diego, California 92121
(619) 452-0681

Contact: Cynthia Mendez, Director of Human Resources. **Founded:** 1981. **No. of Employees:** 114. **Revenues (1990):** $16.7 million. **Revenues (1986):** 1.2 million. **Five-Year Revenue Growth:** 1,292%.

Description: Manufacturers of ultrasound imaging agents. New York Stock Exchange.

Common positions include: Accountant; Administrator; Advertising Worker; Attorney; Biochemist; Buyer; Chemist; Biomedical Engineer; Financial Analyst; Department and General Managers; Operations/Production Manager; Marketing Specialist; Personnel and Labor Relations Specialist; Public Relations Specialist; Purchasing Agent; Quality Control Supervisor; Research Scientist.

Principal educational backgrounds sought: Accounting; Biology; Chemistry; Communications; Finance; Liberal Arts; Marketing; Mathematics; Physics.

Company benefits: Medical, Dental, and Life Insurance; Employee Discounts; Savings Plan.

Operations at this facility: Regional and Divisional Headquarters; Manufacturing; Research/Development; Administration.

How they're growing/Recent developments: The company is expanding operation and funding further development of new agents for medical imaging. Employment has grown from an estimated 63 in 1987 to 114 in 1991.

MOLEX
2222 Wellington Court
Lisle, Illinois 60532
(708)969-4550

Founded: 1938. **No. of Employees:** 6900. **Revenues (1990):** $594 million. **Revenues (1986):** $253 million. **Five-Year Revenue Growth:** 135%.

Description: Molex Incorporated is a Fortune 500 company that designs a broad line of electrical/electronic fiber optic connectors, flat cables, switches, and associated application tooling.

Common positions include: Accountant; Administrator; Advertising Worker; Computer Programmer; Electrical Engineer; Industrial Engineer; Mechanical Engineer; General Manager; Operations/Production Manager; Marketing Specialist; Personnel and Labor Relations Specialist; Purchasing Agent; Quality Control Supervisor; Systems Analyst.

Principal educational backgrounds sought: Accounting; Business Administration; Computer Science; Engineering; Finance; Liberal Arts; Marketing; Mathematics; Physics.

Company benefits include: Medical insurance; dental insurance; pension plan; life insurance; tuition assistance; disability coverage; profit sharing.

Operations at this facility include: Manufacturing; research and development; administration; service; sales.

How they're growing/Recent developments: Molex acquired Winchester Electronics/Germany, which produces components and high-density systems used in telecommunications, computers and office equipment. For the fiscal year ending June 30, 1991, revenues rose to $708 million. Employment has grown from an estimated 4,962 in 1987 to 6,700 in 1991.

MYERS INDUSTRIES INC.
1293 South Main Street
Akron, Ohio 44301
(216) 253-5592

Founded: 1955. **No. of Employees:** 1,481. **Revenues (1990):** $202 million. **Revenues (1986):** $90 million. **Five-Year Revenue Growth:** 124%.

Description: Myers Industries makes and markets tire service equipment and plastic and metal storage containers.

How they're growing/Recent developments: In order to widen product range Myers bought Buckhorn, Inc., a reusable plastic storage producer in 1987. In 1988, it bought Plastic Parts, Inc., a custom-engineered foam components company. Employment has grown from an estimated 740 in 1987 to 1,481 in 1991.

MYLEX CORPORATION
P.O. Box 5035
Fremont, California 94537-5035
(510) 796-6100

Founded: 1983. **No. of Employees:** 150. **Revenues (1990):** $47.9 million. **Revenues (1987):** $2.4 million. **Four-Year Revenue Growth:** 1,896%.

Description: Mylex is a technology based company engaged in the design, development, production, and marketing of 80386 and EISA-based microprocessor-based boards for single and multiprocessing systems, as well as EISA-based graphic, LAN and disk controllers. These increasingly powerful and sophisticated hardware products are used in applications such as LANs, multi-user systems, real-time environments, CAD/CAM, desktop publishing, and engineering scientific workstations. Mylex has also developed BIOS and device drivers, the necessary software to support all of its products. The company's products are purchased by original equipment manufacturers (OEMs), system integrators, value-added resellers (VARs), and computer distributors and dealers. In addition to a broad base of domestic customers, Mylex has over 100 customers and dealers in Europe and Asia.

How they're growing/Recent developments: Fiscal 1990 sales increased 19% over the previous year, largely because of the success of the company's EISA-based products, which were developed in 1989. Mylex is attempting to expand its customer base so that no one customer exceeds 25% of total net sales.

NAC RE
One Greenwich Plaza
P.O. Box 2568
Greenwich, Connecticut 06836
(203) 622-5200

Founded: 1929. **No. of Employees:** 171. **Revenues (1990):** $266 million. **Revenues (1986):** $102 million. **Five-Year Revenue Growth:** 161%.

Description: Property and casualty reinsurance.

How they're growing/Recent developments: In December, 1990, the company acquired Harbor Insurance Company. Employment has grown from an estimated 87 in 1987 to 171 in 1991.

NATIONAL DATA PRODUCTS, INC.
P.O. Box 7280
Clearwater, Florida 34618
(813)442-8400

Founded: 1982. **No. of Employees:** 92. **Revenues (1990):** $50 million. **Revenues (1986):** $1.5 million. **Five-Year Revenue Growth:** 3,233%.

Description: Company distributes computers, equipment, and supplies.

How they're growing/Recent developments: Employment has grown from 7 in 1986 to 92 in 1991.

NATIONAL EDUCATION CORPORATION
18400 Von Karmen Avenue
Irvine, California 92715
(714) 474-9400

Founded: 1972. **No. of Employees:** 4,200. **Revenues (1990):** $371 million. **Revenues (1986):** $247 million. **Five-Year Revenue Growth:** 50%.

Description: The world's largest training company, the company providers of educational publishing services and vocational industry training.

How they're growing/Recent developments: The company has expanded in recent years with the acquisition of Advanced Systems, Inc., and Spectrum Interactive, Inc. The company's Applied Learning unit announced a joint venture with James T. Martin, an information systems expert, to develop training products to help organizations learn new technologies.

NATIONAL PATENT DEVELOPMENT CORPORATION
9 West 57th Street
New York, New York 10019
(212) 826-8500

Founded: 1959. **No. of Employee:** 3,200. **Revenues (1990):** $293 million. **Revenues (1986):** $191 million. **Five-Year Sales Growth:** 53%.

Description: Manufacturers of surgical appliances and supplies.

How they're growing/Recent developments: Product demand. One company segment is developing products for removing low-level radioactive contaminants from waste-water systems in nuclear plants, the other is developing pharmaceutical products for treatment of viral diseases, cancers and AIDS and other diseases of the immune system. Employment has grown from an estimated 2,400 in 1987 to 3,200 in 1991.

NATIONAL PIZZA COMPANY
720 West 20th Street, Box 62643
Pittsburg, Kansas 66762
(316) 231-3390

Founded: 1962. **No. of Employees:** 7,000. **Revenues (1990):** $198 million. **Revenues (1987):** $96.48 million. **Four-Year Revenue Growth:** 105%.

Description: The largest franchisee of Pizza Hut restaurants. The company also franchises 212 Skipper's seafood restaurants.

How they're growing/Recent developments: The company has recently purchased the Long John Silver restaurants located in Denver and Colorado Springs, Colorado. Employment has grown from an estimated 3,200 in 1987 to 7,000 in 1991.

NATIONAL SAFETY ASSOCIATES
P.O. Box 18603
Memphis, Tennessee 38181
(901) 366-9288

Founded: 1970. **No. of Employees:** 600. **Revenues (1990):** $255 million. **Revenues (1986):** $4 million. **Five-Year Revenue Growth:** 6,275%.

Description: A Memphis-based manufacturer and distributor of water and air filtration systems.

How they're growing/Recent developments: Employment has grown from 100 in 1986 to 600 in 1991.

NATIONAL SERVICE INDUSTRIES, INC.
1180 Peachtree Street NE
Atlanta, Georgia 30309
(404) 892-2400

Founded: 1928. **No. of Employees:** 18,270. **Revenues (1990):** $1.6 billion. **Revenues (1986):** $1.3 billion. **Five-Year Revenue Growth:** 23%.

Description: Seven divisions provide diversified interests in textiles, lighting equipment, chemicals and insulation.

How they're growing/Recent developments: The company has acquired Hunter Specialty Chemicals, Inc., and intends to purchase Rental Towel & Uniform Service, Inc.. More acquisitions are planned.

NATURE'S SUNSHINE PRODUCTS, INC.
1655 North Main
Spanish Fork, Utah 84660
(801) 798-9861

Founded: 1978. **No. of Employees:** 281. **Revenues (1990):** $60.1 million. **Revenues (1986):** $31.1 million. **Five-Year Revenue Growth:** 93%.

Description: The largest U.S. maker of encapsulated, concentrated herbal products. The company also has a natural vitamin line and water treatment items.

How they're growing/Recent developments: The company's sales force is expanding constantly, boosted by new product development and solid growth in overseas operations. In 1990, the company acquired Earth Science Products, Inc., a producer of all-natural liquid food supplements. Employment has grown from an estimated 195 in 1987 to 281 in 1991.

NELLCOR
25495 Whitesell Street
Hayward, California 94545
(510) 887-5858

Founded: 1986. **No. of Employees:** 634. **Revenues (1990):** $143 million.**Revenues (1986):** $46 million. **Five-Year Revenue Growth:** 211%.

Description: Manufacturers of patient monitoring instruments.

How they're growing/Recent developments: In March, 1990, Nellcor acquired Radiant Systems, a systems development and software company. In October, 1991, the company acquired Fenem, Inc. and in September, 1991, EdenTec Corporation, both of which are detection and patient monitoring systems companies.

NETWORK EQUIPMENT TECHNOLOGIES
800 Saginaw Drive
Redwood City, California 94063
(415) 366-4400

Founded: 1983. **No. of Employees:** 963. **Revenues (1990):** $135 million. **Revenues (1986):** $9 million. **Five-Year Revenue Growth:** 1,400%.

Description: Manufacturers of advanced building-wide office network communications products.

How they're growing/Recent developments: Revenues continued to climb well into 1991. Revenues climbed another 48% between June, 1990 and June, 1991 due to a strong European market and new sales accounts. Employment has grown from an estimated 429 in 1987 to 963 in 1991.

NEUTROGENA CORPORATION
5760 West 96th Street
Los Angeles, California 90045
(213) 642-1150

Founded: 1962. **No. of Employees:** 729. **Revenues (1990):** $210 million. **Revenues (1986):** $96 million. **Five-Year Revenue Growth:** 118%.

Description: Makes and markets skin and hair care products and is market leader in sales of specialty soaps.

How they're growing/Recent developments: Revenues are increasing due to price increases, favorable European exchange rate fluctuations, new products and strictly controlled operating costs. Emphasis on new product development specializing in normal, sensitive and problem skin and hair. Employment has grown from an estimated 529 in 1987 to 729 in 1991.

NEW ENGLAND BUSINESS SERVICE, INC.
500 Main Street
Groton, Massachusetts 01471
(508) 448-6111

Founded: 1951. **No. of Employees:** 2,000. **Revenues (1990):** $233 million. **Revenues (1986):** $176 million. **Five-Year Revenue Growth:** 32%.

Description: A leading mail order supplier of standardized business forms and other products to over 1 million businesses in the United States, United Kingdom and Canada.

How they're growing/Recent developments: The company places great emphasis on extensive market research and new product development. Revenues were boosted by the opening of NEBS Stationary in the United Kingdom in 1988.

NEW LINE CINEMA
575 Eighth Avenue
New York, New York 10018
(212) 329-8880

Founded: 1967. **No. of Employees:** 160. **Revenues (1990):** $133 million. **Revenues (1986):** $26 million. **Five-Year Revenue Growth:** 412%.

Description: An independent producer and distributor of motion pictures geared toward the youth market. The company is also involved in the home video and television markets.

How they're growing/Recent developments: In 1990, the company released the film "Teenage Mutant Ninja Turtles," which became the biggest grossing independent film of all time. The following year, the company followed its standard practice of releasing sequels with the release of "Teenage Mutant Ninja Turtles 2: The Secret of the Ooze." New Line also owns 52% of RHI, a television production company that specializes in made-for-television movie and mini-series productions for both cable and television. In March, 1991, New Line signed an exclusive three-year home video agreement with RCA/Columbia. Employment has grown from an estimated 100 in 1987 to 160 in 1991.

NEW YORK STYLE BAGEL CHIP

P.O. Box 3562
Princeton, New Jersey 08543
(609) 683-5400

Founded: 1985. **No. of Employees:** 200. **Revenues (1990):** $16 million.
Revenues (1986): $1 million. **Five-Year Revenue Growth:** 1,500%.

Description: A producer of bagel chips and other snack foods.

How they're growing/Recent developments: Employment has grown from 3
1986 to 200 in 1991.

NEWELL COMPANY

29 East Stephenson Street
Freeport, Illinois 61032
(815) 235-4171

Founded: 1905. **No. of Employees:** 11,500. **Revenues (1990):** $1.1 billion.
Revenues (1986): $401 million. **Five-Year Revenue Growth:** 174%.

Description: Manufactures hardware, cookware, tableware, packaging products, and a variety of other consumer products.

How they're growing/Recent developments: Newell has grown through a series of acquisitions. As of June, 1991, the company was seeking Justice Department approval of a plan to acquire $15 million worth of common stock from Stanley Works, the hardware products company. Newell recently acquires W.T. Rogers Company.

NICHOLS INSTITUTE

33608 Ortega Highway
San Juan Capistrano, California 92690-6130
(714) 661-8000

Founded: 1971. **No. of Employees:** 2,400. **Revenues (1990):** $175 million.
Revenues (1986): $35 million. **Five-Year Revenue Growth:** 400%.

Description: Provider of specific, complex clinical testing services to physicians, and hospitals. Nichols manufactures diagnostic kits, as well.

How they're growing/Recent developments: In 1991, the company acquired
Immuno Technology Service Productions and MPC Laboratories. In addi-

tion, the company was certified in 1989 by the National Institute on Drug Abuse to test federal employees of government agencies.

NICHOLS RESEARCH CORPORATION
4040 Memorial Parkway
Huntsville, Alabama 35802
(205) 883-1140

Founded: 1976. **No. of Employees:** 763. **Revenues (1990):** $54 million. **Revenues (1987):** $38.26 million. **Four-Year Revenue Growth:** 41%.

Description: Provides software systems and related services to the military.

How they're growing/Recent developments: Employment has grown from an estimated 430 in 1987 to 763 in 1991.

NIKE, INC.
3700 Southwest Murray Boulevard
Beaverton, Oregon 97005
(503) 641-6453

Founded: 1968. **No. of Employees:** 4,515. **Revenues (1990):** $2.2 billion. **Revenues (1986):** $1 billion. **Five-Year Revenue Growth:** 120%.

Description: Nike develops, designs and markets footwear and clothing for a wide range of sports and leisure activities.

How they're growing/Recent developments: Nike's sales to international markets have been advancing especially strongly. The women's footwear market is also generating stronger demand. Employment has grown from an estimated 3,000 in 1987 to 4,515 in 1991.

NMR OF AMERICA, INC.
355 Madison Avenue
Morristown, New Jersey 07960
(201) 539-1082

Contact: Keith E. Andreotta, Human Resources Manager. **Founded:** 1982. **No. of Employees:** 120. **Revenues (1990):** $15.6 million. **Revenues (1987):** $13 million. **Four-Year Revenue Growth:** 20%.

Description: Installs and maintains medical imaging systems. NASDAQ.

Common positions include: Sales Representative; Technologist-Almodalities; Transcriptionists and Secretaries.

Principal educational backgrounds sought: Biology; Marketing; X-Ray Registration.

Company benefits: Medical, Dental and Life Insurance; Disability Coverage; 401K.

Operations at this facility: Regional Headquarters; Service.

How they're growing/Recent developments: The company plans on adding centers. Employment has grown from an estimated 86 in 1987 to 120 in 1991.

NORDSTROM
1501 5th Avenue
Seattle, Washington 98101
(206) 628-2111

Founded: 1946. **No. of Employees:** 37,000. **Revenues (1990):** $2.7 billion. **Revenues (1986):** $1.3 billion. **Five Year Revenue Growth:** 107%.

Description: Specialty retailer of apparel and accessories.

How they're growing/Recent developments: The company's expansion plans call for the opening of a number of new stores on the East Coast, as well as new stores openings in West and Midwest. Organized Nordstrom National Credit Bank to provide credit to its customers. Employment has grown from an estimated 14,0000 in 1987 to 37,000 in 1991.

NOVACARE
P.O. Box 928
Valley Forge, Pennsylvania 19482
(215) 631-9300

Founded: 1985. **No. of Employees:** 1,800. **Revenues (1990):** $102.1 million. **Revenues (1987):** $26.8 million. **Four-Year Revenue Growth:** 281%.

Description: NovaCare is a provider of comprehensive medical rehabilitation services. The company contracts with over 1,700 health care institutions -- principally nursing homes -- in 34 states to provide physical therapy, occupational therapy and speech-language pathology to patients. NovaCare is the only provider of such services on a national basis.

How they're growing/Recent developments: With the recent acquisition of Rehab Systems Company, NovaCare now also operates seven free-standing rehabilitation hospitals, one acute care rehabilitation hospital and six transitional care units. The acquisition provides NovaCare and its clients with integrated patient services, diversified revenue sources, and long-term career opportunities for care-givers. Fiscal 1991 marked the third consecutive year of record performance.

NOVELL, INC.
122 East 1700 South
Provo, Utah 84601
(801) 379-3900

Founded: 1983. **No. of Employees:** 2,557. **Revenues (1990):** $498 million. **Revenues (1986):** $82 million. **Five-Year Revenue Growth:** 507%.

Description: Manufacturer of software operating systems. Novell's NetWare, a network operating systems, is an industry standard. NASDAQ.

Common positions include: Software Engineers.

Principal educational background sought: Computer Science.

Company benefits: Medical, Dental, and Life Insurance; Pension Plan; Tuition Assistance; Disability Coverage; Daycare Assistance; Savings Plan.

How they're growing/Recent developments: Novell is currently undertaking a major upgrade of the NetWare system software. Through a licensing and distribution agreement with IBM, IBM's sales force will now be offering NetWare. Employment has grown from an estimated 950 in 1987 to 2,557 in 1991.

NUTMEG INDUSTRIES
4408 West Linebaugh Avenue
Tampa, Florida 33624
(813) 963-6153

Founded: 1985. **No. of Employees:** 700. **Revenues (1990):** $51 million. **Revenues (1986):** $12 million. **Five-Year Revenue Growth:** 325%.

Description: Designer of customized apparel bearing cartoon, college and sports team logos.

How they're growing/Recent developments: Nutmeg's order backlog was up 41% for the first quarter of 1991-1992. The company announced a licensing agreement with ABC Sports, Inc. to use trademarks for "ABC Monday Night Football" and "ABC Wide World of Sports" worldwide. McBrier Sportswear was acquired in May, 1990. Employment has grown from an estimated 650 in 1987 to 700 in 1991.

NWA, INC.
Minneapolis-St. Paul International Airport
St. Paul, Minnesota 55111
(612) 726-2111

Founded: 1926. **No. of Employees:** 45,000. **Revenues (1990):** $8 billion. **Revenues (1986):** $145.8 million. **Five-Year Revenue Growth:** 5,386%.

Description: The holding company for Northwest Airlines.

Common positions include: Accountant; Computer Programmer; Customer Service Representative; Aerospace Engineer; Financial Analyst; Marketing Specialist; Personnel and Labor Relations Specialist; Sales Representative; Systems Analyst; Transportation and Traffic Specialist.

Principal educational backgrounds sought: Accounting; Business Administration; Computer Science; Economics; Engineering; Finance; Marketing.

Company benefits: Medical, Dental, and Life Insurance; Pension Plan; Tuition Assistance; Disability Coverage; Employee Discounts; Savings Plan; Free and Reduced Travel.

Operations at this facility: Regional and Divisional Headquarters; Administration; Service; Sales.

How they're growing/Recent developments: Employment has grown from an estimated 37,000 in 1987 to 45,000 in 1991.

NYMA, INC.
7501 Greenway Center Drive, Suite 1200
Greenbelt, Maryland 20770
(301) 345-0832

Founded: 1978. **No. of Employees:** 400. **Revenues (1990):** $34 million. **Revenues (1986):** $3.9 million. **Five-Year Revenue Growth:** 772%.

Description: NYMA is a computer services company specializing in custom software development and systems integration. The company operates in four business areas: Air Traffic Systems, Aerospace Systems, Information Systems, and Computer Products.

How they're grown/Recent developments: The company recently introduced a NYMA product line which includes 386 and 486 IBM-compatible microcomputers. Management expects that systems integration product lines, and the services opportunities associated with these business areas will provide the revenue and technology base for continuing success. The company has enjoyed increased revenues and strategically important developments in each of the company's four business areas. Support from the company's long-standing clients, the Federal Aviation Administration and the National Aeronautics and Space Administration (NASA) has grown dramatically. Between 1985 and 1990, NYMA has grown from just 10 employees to over 400. The large majority of NYMA's staff have earned professional and advanced degrees, primarily in physical sciences, math, engineering and computer sciences. In addition, the company has grown from one location to over 16 separate offices. Employment has grown from 100 in 1986 to 400 in 1991.

OCCUPATIONAL-URGENT CARE HEALTH SYSTEMS, INC.
750 Riverpoint Drive
West Sacramento, California 95605
(916) 924-5200

Founded: 1982. **No. of Employees:** 311. **Revenues (1990):** $21 million. **Revenues (1986):** $1 million. **Five-Year Revenue Growth:** 2,000%.

Description: Provider of medical cost containment programs.

How they're growing/Recent developments: In 1990, the company announced it had developed a new claims systems with GM's Electronic Data Systems. In April, 1991, the company signed a letter of intent to acquire Beech St. of California, another cost management services company. Employment has grown from an estimated 130 in 1987 to 311 in 1991.

OCTEL COMMUNICATIONS CORPORATION
890 Tasman Drive
Milpitas, California 95035
(408) 942-6500

Founded: 1984. **No. of Employees:** 793. **Revenues (1990):** $87.2 million. **Revenues (1986):** $4 million. **Five-Year Revenue Growth:** 2,080%.

Description: Manufacturers of voice processing systems for the radio and television industries.

How they're growing/Recent developments: In May, 1991, the company signed a three-year distribution agreement with Wiltel Communications Systems to market the Voice Information Processing Server and Power Call.

OCTOCOM SYSTEM
One Executive Drive
Chelmsford, Massachusetts 01824
(508) 658-6050

Founded: 1984. **No. of Employees:** 144. **Revenues (1990):** $26.6 million. **Revenues (1986):** $1.8 million. **Five-Year Revenue Growth:** 1,378%.

Description: Producers of modems and other data communications equipment.

How they're growing/Recent developments: Employment has grown from an estimated 100 in 1987 to 144 in 1991.

OEA
P.O. Box 10488
Denver, Colorado 80210
(303) 693-1248

Founded: 1969. **No. of Employees:** 750. **Revenues (1990):** $76.6 million. **Revenues (1986):** $41 million. **Five-Year Revenue Growth:** 87%.

Description: Manufactures airbag propellants and equipment.

How they're growing/Recent developments: OEA has a backlog of orders valued at $92 million. The company controls 70% of the market for airbag initiators in the country. The federal government is a major customer. Employment has grown from an estimated 540 in 1987 to 750 in 1991.

OFFICE DEPOT
851 Broken Sound Parkway
Boca Raton, Florida 33487
(407)994-2131

Contact: Dave Pile, Vice President, Human Resources. **Founded:** 1986. **No. of Employees:** 7,427. **Revenues (1990):** $626 million. **Revenues (1986):** $2 million. **Five-Year Revenue Growth:** 31,200%.

Description: The nation's largest chain of office products warehouse stores, operating primarily in the Southern, Midwestern and Western U.S.

How they're growing/Recent developments: The company has more than 210 stores in operation, over 60 of which were added with the 1991 acquisition of The Office Club, Inc. The company's strategy is to offer a wide selection of brand name office products at discount prices. The company buys almost all of its merchandise directly from manufacturers in high volume. Office Depot employs about 45 people per store.

OFFSHORE PIPELINES, INC.
5718 Westheimer Road, Suite 600
Houston, Texas 77057
(713) 952-1000

Founded: 1984. **No. of Employees:** 500. **Revenues (1990):** $126 million. **Revenues (1986):** $11 million. **Five-Year Revenue Growth:** 1,045%.

Description: An offshore oil and gas field services company specializing in oil rig construction.

How they're growing/Recent developments: The company has recently signed a letter of intent to provide marine construction services for a $90 million project in West Africa.

OGDEN PROJECTS
P.O. Box 2615, 40 Lane Road
Fairfield, New Jersey 07007-615
(201) 882-9000

Founded: 1984. **No. of Employees:** 276. **Revenues (1990):** $369 million. **Revenues (1986):** $49 million. **Five-Year Sales Growth:** 653%.

Description: Company constructs and operates municipal waste-to-energy facilities, as well as hazardous waste treatment facilities, and solid waste incinerators.

How they're growing/Recent developments: Growth is being fueled by the increasing need for cities to dispose of solid wastes in an environmentally acceptable manner other than landfill disposal. Ogden has recently won eight additional projects, with all new work to commence by 1992.

OHM CORPORATION
P.O. Box 551
Findlay, Ohio 45839
(419) 423-3526

Founded: 1981. **No. of Employees:** 2,390. **Revenues (1990):** $187 million. **Revenues (1986):** $101 million. **Five-Year Revenue Growth:** 85%.

Description: A nationwide environmental services company providing hazardous waste and asbestos abatement to industry and government.

How they're growing/Recent developments: In August, 1989, the company established a joint venture with Conrail to design and develop a network of recovery, disposal and treatment facilities for hazardous waste.

O.I. CORPORATION
Graham Road at Wellborn, P.O. Box 2980
College Station, Texas 77841
(409) 690-1711

Founded: 1963. **No. of Employees:** 114. **Revenues (1990):** $15.1 million. **Revenues (1987):** $3.6 million. **Four-Year Revenue Growth:** 319%

Description: O.I. designs, manufactures, markets and services analytical instruments and systems that aid in sample handling, analyzing, detecting, and reporting of compounds that contaminate air, water, and soil. The company's products are sold worldwide by a direct sales force and independent sales representatives.

How they're growing/Recent developments: The company's strategy for growth is the development of new products to serve the environmental analysis market. Spending for the development of new products has been increasing consistently over the past few years --from about $295 thousand in 1988 to over $737 thousand in 1990. The company's gas chromatography product line was expanded during 1990 by introducing additional sample concentrator accessories and broadening the selective detection product line through the development of pesticides analysis applications. As a measure of O.I.'s product development success, over 50% of sales for 1990 were generated by the sale of products introduced during the past 5 years. The number of employees at O.I. has grown from 42 in 1986 to 114 in 1990. The company employs scientists and engineers who perform research and development on possible new products and handle matters relating to on-going business.

OLSTEN CORPORATION
One Merrick Avenue
Westbury, New York 11590
(516) 832-8200

Founded: 1950. **No. of Employees:** 3,000. **Revenues (1990):** $623 million. **Revenues (1986):** $313 million. **Five-Year Revenue Growth:** 99%.

Description: One of the nation's leading providers of temporary personnel.

How they're growing/Recent developments: Due to the growing need for home health care and supplemental hospital and nursing home staffing, Olsten is putting more emphasis on its health care division, recently acquiring Upjohn Healthcare Services. The new division is now called Olsten Health-Care, and now represents 40% of the company's revenues. Employment has grown from an estimated 1,200 in 1987 to 3,000 in 1991.

ONE PRICE CLOTHING STORES INC.
Highway 290, Commerce Park
Duncan, South Carolina 29334
(803) 439-6666

Founded: 1984. **No. of Employees:** 2,300. **Revenues (1990):** $111 million. **Revenues (1986):** $25 million. **Five-Year Revenue Growth:** 344%.

Description: Operates a chain of about 300 off-price women's clothing stores in the Southeastern United States.

How they're growing/Recent developments: The company announced in July, 1991 that it had recently opened 74 new stores, and that more expansion is planned. Employment has grown from an estimated 518 in 1987 to 2,300 in 1991.

ORACLE SYSTEMS CORPORATION
500 Oracle Parkway
Redwood Shores, California 94065
(415) 506-7000

Founded: 1982. **No. of Employees:** 6,811. **Revenues (1990):** $971 million. **Revenues (1986):** $55 million. **Five-Year Revenue Growth:** 1,765%.

Description: Provider of computer software products used for applications development and database management.

How they're growing/Recent developments: The company has reported strong demand for its products, tools and applications. Revenues have also been boosted by the introduction of new products. In June, 1991, the company announced a joint venture with Nippon Steel to market and sell in Japan. Employment has grown from an estimated 2,000 in 1987 to 6,811 in 1991.

ORBITAL SCIENCES CORPORATION
12500 Fair Lakes Circle
Suite 350
Fairfax, Virginia 22033
(703) 631-3600

Founded: 1982. **No. of Employees:** 700. **Revenues (1990):** $100.4 million. **Revenues (1986):** $4 million. **Five-Year Revenue Growth:** 2,410%.

Description: Orbital Sciences designs, manufactures, operates and markets a broad range of space transportation systems, satellite systems and services, and space support products.

How they're growing/Recent developments: During 1990, the company continued its rapid revenue growth and expanded its engineering and manufacturing capabilities. The company introduced advanced technologies to the space market, extended its product and service lines, and unified its strategic focus on the development and application of affordable small space systems. The company's staff grew to 706 in 1990, up 520 just one year earlier, and just 25 in 1986.

OREGON METALLURGICAL CORPORATION
P.O. Box 580
Albany, Oregon 97321
(503) 926-4281

Founded: 1955. **No. of Employees:** 427. **Revenues (1990):** $93 million. **Revenues (1986):** $42 million. **Five-Year Revenue Growth:** 121%.

Description: Manufactures titanium sponges and magnesium products.

How they're growing/Recent developments: This company is one of three integrated producers of titanium in the country. Plans call for an increase in production capacity. Employment has grown from an estimated 375 in 1987 to 427 in 1991.

OSMONICS
5951 Clearwater Drive
Minnetonka, Minnesota 55343
(612) 933-2277

Founded: 1969. **No. of Employees:** 453. **Revenues (1990):** $36 million. **Revenues (1987):** $20.47 million. **Four-Year Revenue Growth:** 76%.

Description: Manufacturer of fluid processing systems.

How they're growing/Recent developments: Recent acquisitions include American Pump Company, which makes non-metallic pumps, and Vaponics, Inc., a maker of water purification equipment. Employment has grown from an estimated 210 in 1987 to 453 in 1991.

OWENS & MINOR, INC.
P.O. Box 27626
Richmond, Virginia 23261
(804) 747-9794

Founded: 1926. **No. of Employees:** 1,580. **Revenues (1990):** $1.2 billion. **Revenues (1986):** $468 million. **Five-Year Revenue Growth:** 156%.

Description: Manufacturers of medical and surgical equipment and pharmaceuticals.

How they're growing/Recent developments: Owens & Minor experienced rapid growth through the 1980's, and is currently placing a major focus on profitability. Management strategy appears clear --- concentrating on hospital customers, and keeping tight internal cost controls. In May, 1991, the company was chosen by the University Hospital Consortium, an organization representing 55 academic medical centers and their affiliates, under a five-year agreement to service medical and surgery supply and distribution needs. Employment has grown from an estimated 1,100 in 1987 to 1,580 in 1991.

OXFORD ENERGY
330 Town Center Drive, Suite 900
Dearborn, Michigan 48126
(707) 575-3939

Founded: 1984. **No. of Employees:** 230. **Revenues (1990):** $29 million. **Revenues (1986):** $1 million. **Five-Year Revenue Growth:** 2,800%

Description: Operates alternative power generation facilities, specializing in recycling of used tires for use as alternative energy sources.

How they're growing/Recent developments: Oxford Energy is part of one of America's fastest growing industries. The company has engaged an investment banking firm to help explore possible acquisitions in order to improve liquidity. Employment has grown from an estimated 16 in 1987 to 230 in 1991.

PACIFICARE HEALTH SYSTEMS, INC.
5995 Plaza Drive
Cypress, California 90630
(714)952-1121

Contact: Patricia C. Jacobson, Director. **Founded:**1975. **No. of Employees:** 1560. **Revenues (1990):** $970 million. **Revenues (1986):** $167 million. **Five-Year Revenue Growth:** 481%.

Description: Owners and operators of federally-qualified health maintenance organizations in California, Oregon, Washington, Oklahoma, and Texas. New York Stock Exchange.

Common positions include: Actuary; Computer Programmer; Systems Analyst.

Principal educational backgrounds sought: Computer Science; Mathematics.

Company benefits: Medical, Dental, and Life Insurance; Pension Plan; Tuition Assistance; Disability Coverage; Daycare Assistance; Profit Sharing; Employee Discounts; Savings Plan.

Operations at this facility: Regional Headquarters.

How they're growing/Recent developments: The company is expanding quickly into Northern California and has recently added its own chain of pharmacies. The company also boasts annual contracts with the federal government to provide Medicare health services. Employment has grown from an estimated 582 in 1987 to 1,560 in 1991.

PALL CORPORATION
2200 Northern Boulevard
East Hills, New York 11548
(516) 671-4000

Contact: Pat Lowy, Director of Human Resources. **Founded:** 1946. **No. of Employees:** 6,500. **Revenues (1990):** $564 million. **Revenues (1986):** $332 million. **Five-Year Revenue Growth:** 70%.

Description: Manufactures fine filters and fluid clarification and purification products to remove solid, liquid, and gas contaminants from fluids and gases used in the health care, fluid process, and aeropower industries.

Common positions include: Accountant; Advertising Worker; Attorney; Biochemist; Blue-Collar Worker Supervisor; Chemist; Computer Programmer; Customer Service Representative; Draftsperson; Aerospace Engineer; Biomedical Engineer; Industrial Engineer; Mechanical Engineer; Financial Analyst; Industrial Manager; Department Manager; Marketing Specialist; Personnel and Labor Relations Specialist; Public Relations Specialist; Purchasing Agent; Quality Control Supervisor; Sales Representative; Systems Analyst.

Principal educational backgrounds: Accounting; Art/Design; Biology; Chemistry; Computer Science; Engineering; Finance.

Company benefits include: Medical insurance; dental insurance; pension plan; life insurance; disability coverage; profit sharing; savings plan.

Operations at this facility include: Regional headquarters; manufacturing; research/ development; administration; service; sales.

How they're growing/Recent developments: The company has been placing more and more emphasis on new health care products like blood filters. Revenues rose to $657 million in fiscal 1991. Employment has grown from an estimated 5,300 in 1987 to 6,500 in 1991.

PAR PHARMACEUTICAL, INC.
One Ram Ridge Road
Spring Valley, New York 10977
(914) 425-7100

Founded: 1978. **No. of Employees:** 600. **Revenues (1990):** $102 million. **Revenues (1987):**$78.7 million. **Four-Year Revenue Growth:** 30%.

Description: Manufactures prescription generic pharmaceutical drugs in tablet and capsule form; also through its Indianapolis subsidiary Quad Pharmaceuticals in injectable form.

PAXAR CORPORATION
275 N. Middletown Road
Pearl River, NY 10965
(914) 735-9200

Founded: 1949. **No. of Employees:** 887. **Revenues (1990):** $73 million. **Revenues (1986):** $31 million. **Five-Year Revenue Growth:** 136%.

Description: Paxar manufactures product identification systems for the apparel and textile industry.

How they're growing/Recent developments: Paxar has established industry wide name recognition with the FASCO brand name. The company is also making gains in both international operations and in the domestic bar code business. Employment has grown from an estimated 600 in 1987 to 887 in 1991.

PAYCHEX, INC.
911 Panorama Trail South
Rochester, New York 14625
(716) 383-3430

Contact: Richard Girard, Director of Human Resources. **Founded:** 1971. **No. of Employees:** 2,200. **Revenues (1990):** $120 million. **Revenues (1986):** $50 million. **Five-Year Revenue Growth:** 140%

Description: Paychex, Inc. is a national payroll processing and payroll tax preparation company for small businesses with under two hundred employees. While payroll is the core business, the company also provides human resource products and services, including a Section 125 Cafeteria Plan, benefits products, employee handbooks and an employee development and testing series. Paychex, Inc. is based in Rochester, New York, and operates in over 86 locations nationwide. Founded in 1971, the company currently has over 2,400 employees and services over 140,000 clients nationwide.

Common positions include: Administrator; Advertising Worker; Customer Service Representative; Branch Manager; Department Manager; Marketing Specialist; Public Relations Specialist; Sales Representative; Systems Analyst; Technical Writer/Editor; Payroll Specialist; Trainer.

Principal educational backgrounds include: Accounting; Communications; Marketing; Mathematics.

Company benefits include: Medical insurance; dental insurance; life insurance; disability coverage.

Operations at this facility include: Regional headquarters; administration; service; sales.

How they're growing/Recent developments: The company has revenues have grown through an increased client list and expansion of services. A human resource services division was organized in 1990, including employee handbook service; insurance services; section 125 Cafeteria Plan, and an employee development and testing series. Employment has grown from an estimated 1,560 in 1987 to 2,200 in 1991.

PDA ENGINEERING
2975 Redhill Avenue
Costa Mesa, California 92626
(714) 540-8900

Founded: 1972. **No. of Employees:** 222. **Revenues (1990):** $31.4 million. **Revenues (1986):** $17.4 million. **Five-Year Revenue Growth:** 80%.

Description: Producers of mechanical engineering software.

How they're growing/Recent developments: The company's new product line, an analysis system for computer-aided engineering, has boosted revenues. Employment has grown from an estimated 160 in 1987 to 222 in 1991.

J.C. PENNEY
14841 North Dallas Parkway
Dallas, Texas 75240
(214) 591-1000

Contact: Richard T. Erickson, Executive Vice President/Director of Corporate Personnel and Administration. **Founded:** 1924. **No. of Employees:** 196,000. **Revenues (1990):** $17.410 billion. **Revenues (1986):** $14.418 billion. **Five-Year Revenue Growth:** 20%.

Description: One of the largest retailers of family apparel, home furnishings and leisure lines, operating through more than 2,000 stores in the United States and Puerto Rico.

How they're growing/Recent developments: During the past decade, Penney's has completely revamped its image. The company discontinued its hardware, appliance and automotive departments and began to emphasize its women's apparel departments. Soft consumer spending has left sales essentially flat in recent months, and, in response, the company plans to push value by lowering prices on many items of private label merchandise.

PENRIL DATACOMM NETWORKS
1300 Quince Orchard Boulevard
Gaithersburg, Maryland 20878
(301) 417-0552

No. of Employees: 750. **Revenues (1990):** $46.6 million. **Revenues (1987):** $38 million. **Four-Year Revenue Growth:** 23%.

Description: Penril DataComm Networks designs, develops, manufactures and markets through its divisions and subsidiaries data communications networking systems and specialized electronic instrumentation equipment. The company's operating entities are its data communications division and wholly-owned subsidiaries, Electro-Metrics, Inc. and Technipower, Inc.

How they're growing/Recent developments: Penril's sales and profits have set records every quarter for four straight years. The company's growth plans include substantial increases in marketing and engineering. During 1991, Renril launched a record number of new products, many of them serving the fast-growing internetworking segment of the data communications market. Prospects for these new products have been enhanced because the company has been able to add multiport intelligent wiring hub capability to the high-speed RISC platform, which forms the basis for Penril's new bridge, router and fiber optic technologies.

PEP BOYS-MANNY, MOE, AND JACK
3111 West Allegheny Avenue
Philadelphia, Pennsylvania 19132
(215) 229-9000

Founded: 1921. **No. of Employees:** 3,700. **Revenues (1990):** $799 million. **Revenues (1986):** $389 million. **Five-Year Revenue Growth:** 105%.

Description: Retails automotive parts and accessories. Service, installation, and maintenance of parts.

How they're growing/Recent developments: Over 300 stores span the Mid-Atlantic, Southeast, West, and Southwest, with the same basic product line in each. The company has announced that 32 new units are planned.

PFIZER, INC.
235 East 42nd Street
New York, New York 10017

Founded: 1849. **No. of Employees:** 42,500. **Revenues (1990):** $6.4 billion. **Revenues (1986):** $4.5 billion. **Five-Year Revenue Growth:** 42%.

Description: Pfizer is a diversified research based health care corporation. A Fortune 100 company, Pfizer employs more than 42,000 people and operations extend to more than 140 countries around the world. The company's businesses include pharmaceuticals, hospital products, animal health, speciality chemicals, consumer products and specialty minerals.

Common positions include: Accountant; Biochemist; Biologist; Chemist; Computer Programmer; Biomedical Engineer; Industrial Engineer; Mechanical Engineer; Metallurgical Engineer; Financial Analyst; Food Technologist; Operations/Production Manager; Marketing Specialist; Personnel and Labor Relations Specialist; Sales Representative.

Principal educational backgrounds sought: Accounting; Biology; Business Administration; Chemistry; Communications; Computer Science; Economics; Engineering; Finance; Liberal Arts; Marketing.

Company benefits include: Medical insurance; dental insurance; pension plan; life insurance; tuition assistance; disability coverage; employee discounts; savings plan.

Operations at this facility include: World headquarters.

How they're growing/Recent developments: Two of Pfizer's fastest growing segments have been medical devices and consumer goods. Over the past five years, Pfizer's spending on R&D has doubled. Employment has grown from an estimated 40,000 in 1987 to 42,500 in 1991.

PHARMACY MANAGEMENT SERVICES
3611 Queen Palm Drive
Tampa, Florida 33619
(813) 626-7788

Founded: 1972. **No. of Employees:** 1,000. **Revenues (1990):** $55.7 million. **Revenues (1986):** $4.9 million. **Five-Year Revenue Growth:** 1,037%.

Description: Provides health cost containment services to worker's compensation claimants.

How they're growing/Recent developments: In 1991, the company acquired Med View, Inc., a managed health care services provider. That acquisition was just the latest of four since 1990 -- part of an overall growth strategy aimed at broadening services.

PHELPS DODGE CORPORATION
2600 North Central Avenue
Phoenix, Arizona 85004
(602) 234-8100

Founded: 1885. **No. of Employees:** 14,066. **Revenues (1990):** $2.6 billion. **Revenues (1986):** $846 million. **Five-Year Revenue Growth:** 207%.

Description: One of the world's leading producers of copper.

How they're growing/Recent developments: Following rapid growth between 1987 and 1990, Phelps Dodge's revenues slowed their rate of increase during 1991 as the national economy turned sour. Analysts believe that the company is well positioned for the economy's turnaround, as economic vitality spurs demand for the company's products. In December, 1990, the company discovered a new large copper mineral pit. In June, 1991, the company announced that the Japanese firms Sumitomo Corporation and its subsidiary Sumitomo Metal Mining have agreed to subscribe for 20% of the Chile project, or $40 million plus their share of equity needed to finance the project. The project is expected to yield over 200 million pounds of copper.

PHILIP MORRIS, INC.
120 Park Avenue
New York, New York 10017-5592
(212) 880-5000

Founded: 1919. **No. of Employees:** 168,000. **Revenues (1990):** $44 billion. **Revenues (1986):** $21 billion. **Five-Year Revenue Growth:** 109%.

Description: A leading company operating in the manufacture and sales of consumer products. Wholly owned subsidiaries include Philip Morris Incorporated, Philip Morris International, Kraft General Foods, Inc., and Miller Brewing Company. Philip Morris Capital Corporation engages in various financing and investment activities and owns a real estate subsidiary, the Mission Viejo Company, which is headquartered in Mission Viejo, California.

Common positions include: Finance; Marketing; Planning; Human Resources; Corporate Affairs; Headquarters Services; Information Services.

Company benefits include: Comprehensive benefits package.

How they're growing/Recent developments: Philip Morris made headlines during the 1980s with their acquisitions of General Foods in 1985 and Kraft in 1988. The company controls 42% of the U.S. cigarette market and 22% percent of the domestic beer market through Miller. Employment has grown from an estimated 113,000 in 1987 to 168,000 in 1991.

PITNEY BOWES, INC.
World Headquarters
Stamford, Connecticut 06926-0700
(203) 356-5000

No. of Employees: 29,460. **Revenues (1990):** $3.2 billion. **Revenues (1986):** $2 billion. **Five-Year Revenue Growth:** 60%.

Description: World's biggest manufacturer of postage meters and mailing equipment. Sells copiers, fax machines and labeling machines.

How they're growing/Recent developments: Pitney Bowes has been strengthened by strong demand for new mailroom equipment and its continued improvement in foreign markets, especially Germany.

PLAINS PETROLEUM COMPANY
P.O. Box 281306
Lakewood, Colorado 80228
(303) 969-9325

Founded: 1983. **No. of Employees:** 84. **Revenues (1990):** $49 million. **Revenues (1986):** $13 million. **Five-Year Revenue Growth:** 277%.

Description: An oil and gas exploration, development, and production company.

How they're growing/Recent developments: As of August, 1990, acquisitions had more than doubled the company's oil production rate. Employment has grown from an estimated 60 in 1987 to 84 in 1991.

PLY-GEM INDUSTRIES, INC.
777 3rd Avenue
New York, New York 10017
(212) 832-1550

Founded: 1943. **No. of Employees:** 3,200. **Revenues (1990):** $546 million. **Revenues (1986):** $226 million. **Five-Year Revenue Growth:** 142%.

Description: Manufacturers of home improvement and filtration products.

How they're growing/Recent developments: PlyGem is looking to international markets to spur future growth. In June, 1991, the company launched the U.S.-based Russian Wood Express, Inc., a joint venture with a Russian forest products trading house. Employment has grown from an estimated 1,700 in 1987 to 3,200 in 1991.

POLICY MANAGEMENT SYSTEMS
P.O. Box 10
Columbia, South Carolina 29202
(803) 735-4000

Founded: 1980. **No. of Employees:** 4,204. **Revenues (1990):** $346 million. **Revenues (1986):** $151 million. **Five-Year Revenue Growth:** 129%.

Description: Providers of insurance-related software systems.

How they're growing/Recent developments: Recent acquisitions -- like Management Data Communications -- and contributions from new products will keep profits rising. Management is focusing on the sale of longer-term products and service contracts to avoid industry cycle down periods.

PORTER MCLEOD

5895 East Evans Avenue
Denver, Colorado 80222
(303) 756-2227

Founded: 1985. **No. of Employees:** 200. **Revenues (1990):** $29 million. **Revenues (1986):** $1.7 million. **Five-Year Revenue Growth:** 1,606%.

Description: Provides general contracting services.

How they're growing/Recent developments: Employment has grown from 15 in 1986 to 200 in 1991.

PRECISION CASTPARTS CORPORATION

4600 S.E. Harney Drive
Portland, Oregon 97026
(503) 777-3881

Founded: 1956. **No. of Employees:** 7,339. **Revenues (1990):** $539 million. **Revenues (1986):** $192 million. **Five-Year Revenue Growth:** 181%.

Description: Company supplies complex structural investment castings to the aerospace and other industries.

How they're growing/Recent developments: The company is benefitting from a huge demand for its products -- in July, 1991, the order backlog was up 23%. In addition, in June, 1991, the company acquired Advanced Forming Technology, Inc. Employment has grown from an estimated 5,590 in 1987 to 7,339 in 1991.

PREFERRED HEALTH CARE LTD.

15 River Road
Wilton, Connecticut 06897
(203) 762-0993

Founded: 1983. **No. of Employees:** 315. **Revenues (1990):** $34.4 million. **Revenues (1986):** $4.9 million. **Five-Year Revenue Growth:** 602%.

Description: Preferred Health Care is a leading provider of programs that manage the delivery by independent professional providers of mental health and substance abuse care. The objective of the company's programs is to increase the efficacy and manage the cost of such care under health benefit plans sponsored by the company's clients. The company also provides financial management and other nonclinical services to Four Winds, Inc. and its affiliates, which operate two tertiary care facilities in New York and one in Illinois. In addition, a subsidiary of Preferred Health Care is the general partner in CareSys Partners, L.P., which provides quality assurance and cost containment services in the area of worker's-compensation relating to orthopedic injuries.

How they're growing/Recent developments: In April, 1990, the company formed a wholly-owned subsidiary, Preferred Systems, Inc. to market software for local area networks that had been developed by the company as practical applications in information processing networks. Also during 1990, the company expanded its line of traditional mental health and substance abuse managed care services to offer a national employee assistance program, which has been fully integrated into the company's managed health care services. The company also opened offices in Tampa and Dallas. Employment has grown from an estimated 160 in 1987 to 315 in 1991.

PRESTIGE LEATHER
P.O. Box 58800
Vernon, California 90058
(213) 588-8146

Founded: 1974. **No. of Employees:** 274. **Revenues (1990):** $20 million. **Revenues (1986):** $1,8 million. **Five-Year Revenue Growth:** 1,011%.

Description: Manufactures fashion belts.

How they're growing/Recent developments: Employment has grown from 75 in 1986 to 274 in 1991.

PRICE COMPANY
2647 Ariane Drive
San Diego, California 92117
(619) 581-4600

Contact: John Matthews, Human Resources Manager. **Founded:** 1976. **No. of Employees:** 13,000. **Revenues (1990):** $5.4 billion. **Revenues (1986):** $2.6 billion. **Five-Year Revenue Growth:** 108%.

Description: Operates The Price Club cash and carry membership wholesale outlets.

How they're growing/Recent developments: The company has expanded with the acquisition of Price Club Canada and new U.S. store openings, and has benefitted from rising consumer price consciousness. The company is planning to expand into Pennsylvania. Employment has grown from an estimated 9,000 in 1987 to 13,000 in 1991.

PRINCE STREET TECHNOLOGIES
36 Enterprise Boulevard
Atlanta, Georgia 30336
(404) 691-0507

Contact: John S. Upham, Director of Human Resources. **Founded:** 1984. **No. of Employees:** 200. **Revenues (1990):** $22 million (est.). **Revenues (1986):** $3.8 million. **Five-Year Revenue Growth:** 479%.

Description: A manufacturer of commercial carpets.

Common positions include: Accountant; Blue-Collar Worker Supervisor; Computer Programmer; Customer Service Representative; Department Manager; Personnel and Labor Relations Specialist.

Principal educational backgrounds sought: Medical insurance; dental insurance; life insurance; disability coverage.

PROGRAMMING & SYSTEMS
100 Melrose Square
Greenwich, Connecticut 06830
(203) 944-9200

Founded: 1959. **No. of Employees:** 676. **Revenues (1990):** $30.5 million. **Revenues (1987):** $12 million. **Four-Year Revenue Growth:** 154%.

Description: Programming & Systems operates proprietary career vocational schools offering courses in computer programming, computer technology, computer operations, electronics, executive secretarial, administrative word processing and data entry.

How they're growing/Recent developments: Despite new federal regulations governing financial aid which are hurting the vocational school industry, PSI's revenues increased to a record $31.6 million in fiscal 1991. Some of the company's competitors are expected to close their doors when the Department of Education withholds Title IV Funds from those with default rates in excess of

35% for three consecutive years. PSI's default rate in 1991 was under 11%. In the long run, as the nation becomes an increasingly technical and service-oriented society, business will experience an increasing need for employees with specialized skills. PSI is positioning itself to prepare vocationally-oriented and economically disadvantaged persons for the workplaces of the 1990s. Employment has grown from an estimated 175 in 1987 to 676 in 1991.

PROGRESS SOFTWARE CORPORATION
14 Oak Park
Bedford, Massachusetts 01730
(617) 275-4500

Founded: 1981. **No. of Employees:** 260. **Revenues (1990):** $40.3 million. **Revenues (1986):** $4.6 million. **Five-Year Revenue Growth:** 771%.

Description: Progress Software supplies application development software to businesses, governments and industries worldwide. The company's principal product is PROGRESS, an integrated application development system which consists of the PROGRESS relational database management system, and associated tools for application development and end-user query and reporting.

How they're growing/Recent developments: Growing demand for the company's products and services led to strong increases in revenues in the fourth fiscal quarter of 1991, ending November 30, 1991. In November, 1991, the company announced and shipped the PROGRESS NLM Server, which provides enhanced performance to PROGRESS users deploying applications on Novell networks. PSC also announced and shipped support for Windows 3.0, which combines PROGRESS' applications with the Microsoft Windows environment. The company's long-term goal continues to be gaining market share in the application development software market, while maintaining operating margins of approximately 15% on an annual basis, a strong balance sheet, and conservative policies with regard to revenue recognition and R&D capitalization. During 1992, the company plans to increase expenditures in development and marketing in order to introduce PROGRESS for the AS/$)), extend PROGRESS' capabilities to create and maintain large scale applications using graphical user interfaces, and continue developing new approaches to application development. In fiscal 1991, revenues rose to $58.3 million, a 45% increase over 1990.

PROGRESSIVE CORPORATION
6000 Parkland Boulevard
Mayfield Heights, Ohio 44124
(216) 464-8000

Founded: 1965. **No. of Employees:** 6,370. **Revenues (1990):** $1.4 billion. **Revenues (1986):** $732 million. **Five-Year Revenue Growth:** 91%.

Description: One of the nation's leading insurance underwriters.

How they're growing/Recent developments: Progressive's operating expenses are rising, but this is primarily due to costs related to the development of a more efficient claim service operation. There is a strong demand for Progressive's principal personal line products, including non-standard auto insurance for customers rejected or cancelled by other companies. Employment has grown from an estimated 4,700 in 1987 to 6,370 in 1991.

PSICOR
16818 Via Del Campo Court
San Diego, California 92127
(619) 485-5599

Founded: 1968. **No. of Employees:** 496. **Revenues (1990):** $61.8 million. **Revenues (1986):** $21.2 million. **Five-Year Revenue Growth:** 192%.

Description: Provides and services supplies and equipment to hospitals for the performance of open-heart surgery and related procedures.

How they're growing/Recent developments: The company's growth strategy has been to focus on the company's core business and to strengthen systems to support it. Revenues have benefitted from an increase in hospital served and improved services at client hospitals.

PUBLIX SUPER MARKETS, INC.
P.O. Box 407
1936 George Jenkins Boulevard
Lakeland, Florida 33802-0407
(813) 688-1188

Founded: 1930. **No. of Employees:** 66,756. **Revenues (1990):** $5.758 billion. **Revenues (1986):** $3.760 billion. **Five-Year Revenue Growth:** 53%.

Description: The largest grocery store chain in Florida, and the eighth-largest in the United States.

How they're growing/Recent developments: Employment at Publix rose from 44,813 in 1986 to 66,756 in 1990. The company's low level of debt at the present puts it in a good position to expand. The chairman, Howard Jenkins, expects Publix to become a major player across the Southeast. As part of this plan, Publix continually adopts new strategies to tempt people into stores, such as a new set-up that makes a variety of food available in an outdoor marketplace atmosphere, distinguishing it from a more traditional supermarket. Employment has grown from an estimated 40,000 in 1987 to 66,756 in 1991.

PYRAMID TECHNOLOGY CORPORATION
3860 North First Street
San Jose, California 95134
(415) 965-7200

Founded: 1981. **No. of Employees:** 1,126. **Revenues (1990):** $180 million. **Revenues (1986):** $44 million; **Five-Year Revenue Growth:** 309%.

Description: Company makes 32-bit supermini and mini-mainframe computer systems.

How they're growing/Recent developments: The company recently announced that its had been signed by AT&T as a subcontractor on AT&T's $1.4 billion contract with the U.S. Treasury Department.

THE QUAKER OATS COMPANY
Quaker Tower
321 North Clark Street
P.O.Box 9001
Chicago, Illinois 60604-9001

Founded: 1891. **No. of Employees:** 30,000. **Revenues (1990):** $5 billion. **Revenues (1986):** $3.7 billion. **Five-Year Revenue Growth:** 35%.

Description: A worldwide provider of brand name packaged foods.

How they're growing/Recent developments: Sales volumes have been rising, led by Gatorade. Management is planning to improve the company's product mix.

QUANTUM CORPORATION
500 McCarthy Boulevard
Milpitas, California 95035
(408) 894-4000

Founded: 1980. **No. of Employees:** 763. **Revenues (1990):** $446 million. **Revenues (1987):** $120.76 million. **Four-Year Revenue Growth:** 269%.

Description: Supplies hard disk drives for use in personal computers and desktop workstations.

How they're growing/Recent developments: Quantum has seen strong demand for its Pro Drive series, a recent addition to the product line. Employment has grown from an estimated 665 in 1987 to 763 in 1991.

QUICKSILVER, INC.
1740 Monrovia Avenue
Costa Mesa, California 92627
(714) 645-1395

Founded: 1976. **No. of Employees:** 258. **Revenues (1990):** $91 million. **Revenues (1986):** $19 million. **Five-Year Revenue Growth:** 379%.

Description: Manufacturer of shirts and shorts for men and boys.

How they're growing/Recent developments: In February, 1991, Quicksilver acquired NaPali, S.A., which will open the company's products up to the European marketplace. All manufacturing will still be done in the U.S. Employment has grown from an estimated 75 in 1987 to 258 in 1991.

RAINBOW TECHNOLOGIES INC.
9292 Jeronimo Road
Irvine, California 92718
(714) 454-2100

Founded: 1983. **No. of Employees:** 57. **Revenues (1990):** $13.7 million. **Revenues (1988):** $5.9 million. **Three-Year Revenue Growth:** 132%.

Description: Manufacturer of software security devices that protect against unlicensed use of computer software programs and use encryption technology intended to secure the confidentiality of data stored in computers or being transmitted over telephone lines and LANS.

How they're growing/Recent developments: Since 1988, Rainbow has moved into international markets by opening subsidiary operations in the United Kingdom, Barbados, and Germany. In November, 1990, the company announced its intention to acquire Pyramid Development Corporation. Employment has grown from an estimated 15 in 1987 to 57 in 1991.

RALLY'S
10002 Shelbyville Road, Suite 150
Louisville, Kentucky 40223
(502) 245-8900

Founded: 1982. **No. of Employees:** 1,428. **Revenues (1990):** $56.2 million. **Revenues (1986):** $15.9 million. **Five-Year Revenue Growth:** 253%.

Description: Operates a chain of drive-through hamburger restaurants.

How they're growing/Recent developments: Rally's has recently acquired Maxie's of America and Snapp Drive-Thru, and in March, 1991, signed an agreement to acquire six restaurants from RT Fast Food Enterprises.

RAMSEY HMO
2850 Douglas Road
Coral Gables, Florida 33134
(305) 447-3200

Founded: 1987. **No. of Employees:** 635. **Revenues (1990):** $108.3 million. **Revenues (1988):** $15.8 million. **Three-Year Revenue Growth:** 585%.

Description: A health maintenance and insurance organization.

How they're growing/Recent developments: In August, 1990, the company acquired Comprehensive Benefits Administrators, Inc. and CBAI Administrators, Inc.

RANPAC ENGINEERING
27447 Enterprise Circle West
Temecula, California 92590
(714) 676-7000

Founded: 1979. **No. of Employees:** 175. **Revenues (1990):** $14 million. **Revenues (1986):** $870,000. **Five-Year Revenue Growth:** 1,509%.

Description: Provides civil engineering and architectural services.

How they're growing/Recent developments: Employment has grown from 10 in 1986 to 175 in 1991.

RAVEN INDUSTRIES
P.O. Box 1007
Sioux Falls, South Dakota 57117
(605) 336-2750

Founded: 1956. **No. of Employees:** 1150. **Revenues (1990):** $91 million. **Revenues (1986):** $41.9 million. **Five-Year Revenue Growth:** 117%.

Description: Manufacturer of electronic, plastic, and sewn products.

How they're growing/recent developments: Company fortunes have been boosted by higher electronics segment profits, which have recently scored record backlogs over $73 million. Employment has grown from an estimated 800 in 1987 to 1,150 in 1991.

RAYMOND JAMES FINANCIAL
880 Carrillon Parkway
St. Petersburg, Florida 33716
(813) 573-3800

Founded: 1974. **No. of Employees:** 3,000. **Revenues (1990):** $257 million. **Revenues (1986):** $121 million. **Five-Year Revenue Growth:** 112%.

Description: A financial services organization engaged in securities brokerage, investment banking and financial planning services.

How they're growing/Recent developments: The company's main subsidiary, Raymond James & Associates, is the largest brokerage and investment firm in Florida. The company posted record earnings during the first nine months of 1991. Employment has grown from an estimated 2,000 in 1987 to 3,000 in 1991.

THE READER'S DIGEST ASSOCIATION
Pleasantville, New York 10570
(914) 238-1000

Founded: 1922. **No. of Employees:** 7,400. **Revenues (1990):** $2 billion. **Revenues (1986):** $1.3 billion. **Five-Year Revenue Growth:** 54%

Description: A publisher of books, magazines, recorded music, and videocassettes. The company is best known for its flagship publication, *Reader's Digest* magazine

How they're growing/Recent developments: Since 1984, Reader's Digest has cut costs selling off unprofitable subsidiaries, adding several successful new magazines, including *Holiday-Travel*, *Family Handyman*, and *American Health*. The company also purchased 50% of the British publisher Dorling-Kindersley in 1987. Employment has grown from an estimated 2,300 in 1987 to 7,400 in 1991.

REEBOK INTERNATIONAL
100 Technology Center Drive
Stoughton, Massachusetts 02172
(617) 341-5000

Founded: 1979. No. of Employees: 3,800. Revenues (1990): $2.16 billion. Revenues (1986): $919 million. Five-Year Revenue Growth: 135%.

Description: A leading manufacturer of athletic footwear.

How they're growing/Recent developments: Reebok has been diversifying its product line through acquisitions since 1987. Sales for the first nine months of 1991 increased 29% year to year and analysts predict that sales in 1992 will rise at least by another 15%. The increased sales are due to greater international sales, the success of new products using "The Pump" technology and the use of Hexalite, a new super-light material. Employment has grown from an estimated 2,200 in 1987 to 3,800 in 1991.

REGAL-BELOIT CORPORATION
200 State Street
Beloit, Wisconsin 53511
(608) 364-8800

Founded: 1955. No. of Employees: 2,100. Revenues (1990): $168 million. Revenues (1986): $78 million. Five-Year Revenue Growth: 115%.

Description: Manufacturers of power transmission systems and expendable cutting tools.

How they're growing/Recent developments: Although the recession hurt the company early in 1991, Regal Beloit acquired Opperman Mastergear in July from GBE International, whose products serve specialized niche markets.

REGENCY CRUISES INC.

260 Madison Avenue
New York, New York 10016
(212) 972-4774

Founded: 1981. **No. of Employees:** 85. **Revenues (1990):** $120 million. **Revenues (1985):** $5 million. **Six-Year Revenue Growth:** 2,300%.

Description: Operators of a passenger cruise line.

How they're growing/Recent developments: Employment has grown from an estimated 39 in 1987 to 85 in 1991.

RESEARCH INDUSTRIES

6864 South 300 West
Midvale, Utah 84047
(801) 562-0200

Founded: 1968. **No. of Employees:** 85. **Revenues (1990):** $10.58 million. **Revenues (1986):** $3.74 million. **Five-Year Revenue Growth:** 183%.

Description: Manufacture disposable cardiovascular products as well as specialty pharmaceuticals.

How they're growing/Recent developments: In June, 1991, the company was awarded a patent on heart muscle balloon catheters. The company has also recently signed an agreement with a European firm to guarantee the supply of open-heart surgery procedure components. Revenues for the nine months ending March, 31, 1991, grew 35% year to year, due to continuing strong demand for the company's cardiovascular products.

RESPIRONICS

1001 Murry Ridge Drive
Murrysville, Pennsylvania 15668
(412) 733-0200

Founded: 1976. **No. of Employees:** 336. **Revenues (1990):** $23 million. **Revenues (1987):** $10.2 million. **Four-Year Revenue Growth:** 125%.

Description: Manufacture respiratory medical products.

How they're growing/Recent developments: Increased demand for company products and extensive investment in research and development have fueled this firm's growth. In 1989, Respironics introduced a new product to assist patients not dependent on a ventilator but who nonetheless have difficulty breathing. Revenues grew to $36 million for fiscal 1991.

REXON
1334 Park View Avenue
Suite 200
Manhattan Beach, California 90266
(213) 545-4441

No. of Employees: 325. **Revenues (1990):** $158.2 million. **Revenues (1986):** $43.9 million. **Five-Year Revenue Growth:** 260%.

Description: Rexon is the parent company of four independent subsidiaries, including Wangtek Puerto Rico, all engaged in the manufacture and marketing of computer-related products worldwide. The Wangtek subsidiary manufactures and markets 1/4-inch cartridge and digital audio tape (DAT) tape drives and tape drive subsystems, primarily for the OEM market, through operations in both Simi Valley, California, and Ponce, Puerto Rico. Rexar's Tecmar operation produces tape back-up products, memory and multimedia boards for personal computers, software for secondary storage applications and add-on products for scientific and industrial automation markets, through facilities in Solon, Ohio. Sytron Corporation, acquired by the company in 1989, develops and markets software for file back-up and archival applications for personal computers, PC networking and computer workstations through operations in Westboro, Massachusetts.

How they're growing/Recent developments: During 1990, Rexon completed acquisition of Sytron Corporation, whose clients include Compaq, IBM, and Microsoft. One of the company's most exciting new products is Multi-Media, which enables computers to present live video, stereophonic sound and voice synchronization in connection with the display of information on computer screens. Increased revenues during 1990 were due in large part to the company's 525MB tape drive products, which began shipping late in 1990.

RHONE-POULENC RORER
500 Virginia Drive
Fort Washington, Pennsylvania 19034
(215)628-6000

Founded: 1968. **No. of Employees:** 23,500. **Revenues (1990):** $2.9 billion. **Revenues (1986):** $845 million. **Five-Year Revenue Growth:** 243%.

Description: Company produces over-the-counter and prescription drugs. Operates in all major world pharmaceutical markets.

How they're growing/Recent developments: The Rorer Group merged with Rhone-Pouleac, the largest chemicals producer in France, in July 1990, becoming Rhone-Poulenc Rorer. The merger more than tripled the company's sales base.

RIGHT MANAGEMENT CONSULTANTS
1818 Market Street
Philadelphia, Pennsylvania 19103
(215) 988-1588

Founded: 1980. **No. of Employees:** 259. **Revenues (1990):** $34.3 million. **Revenues (1986):** $11.9 million. **Five-Year Revenue Growth:** 188%.

Description: A human resources consulting firm with a growing international network of offices in the United States, Canada, and Europe.

How they're growing/Recent developments: Revenues for the first three quarters of 1991 grew 49% year to year, as the company continued to open offices. In August, 1991, the company signed a contract with the U.S. Army to provide career transition services for the Army Career and Alumni program.

RIVERSIDE GROUP, INC.
P.O. Box 44044
Jacksonville, Florida 32231-4044
(904) 359-3076

Founded: 1965. **No. of Employees:** 173. **Revenues (1990):** $209.8 million. **Revenues (1986):** $9.08 million. **Five-Year Revenue Growth:** 2,210%.

Description: An insurance and real estate company.

RJO ENTERPRISES, INC.
4500 Forbes Boulevard
Lanham, Maryland 20706
(301) 731-3600

Contact: Robert Boehm, Vice-President of Human Resources and Administration. **Founded:** 1979. **No. of Employees:** 600. **Revenues (1990):** $62 million. **Revenues (1986):** $15 million. **Five-Year Revenue Growth:** 313%.

Description: RJO is a developer and integrator of information and telecommunications systems solutions.

Common positions include: Accountant; Computer Programmer; Electrical Engineer; Department Manager; Marketing Specialist; Personnel and Labor Relations Specialist; Sales Representative; Systems Analyst; Technical Writer/Editor.

Principal educational backgrounds sought: Accounting; Business Administration; Computer Science; Engineering; Finance; Marketing; Mathematics.

Company benefits include: Medical insurance; dental insurance; pension plan; life insurance; tuition assistance; disability coverage; profit sharing; employee discounts; savings plan.

Operations at this facility include: Divisional headquarters; research and development; administration; service; sales.

ROCKFORD CORPORATION
613 South Rockford Drive
Tempe, Arizona 85281
(602) 967-3565

Founded: 1980. **No. of Employees:** 550. **Revenues (1990):** $60 million. **Revenues (1986):** $7 million. **Five-Year Revenue Growth:** 757%.

Description: Manufactures and markets car and home audio products.

How they're growing/Recent developments: Employment has grown from 117 in 1986 to 550 in 1991.

ROUSE CO.
10275 Little Patuxent Parkway
Columbia, Maryland 21044
(301)992-6000

Founded: 1956. **No. of Employees:** 5,612. **Revenues (1990):** $530 million. **Revenues (1986):** $331 million. **Five-Year Revenue Growth:** 60%.

Description: Company develops income-producing real estate in the United States and Canada through subsidiaries. Also develops suburban and downtown retail and mixed-use projects.

How they're growing/Recent developments: In a joint venture with Teachers Insurance and Annuity Association, Rouse acquired McCormick Properties Inc., a major development company. Employment has grown from an estimated 3,290 in 1987 to 5,612 in 1991.

ROYAL APPLIANCE MANUFACTURING CO.
650 Alpha Drive
Cleveland, Ohio 44143
(216) 449-6150

Founded: 1905. **No. of Employees:** 140. **Revenues (1990):** $120 million. **Revenues (1986):** $18 million. **Five-Year Revenue Growth:** 567%.

Description: Makes and markets the Dirt Devil and Royal vacuum cleaners for home and commercial use.

How they're growing/Recent developments: Royal Appliance products are the nation's best-selling line of hand-held vacuums. The company has also recently introduced a new upright cleaner for home use. Net sales for the six month period ending June 30, 1991, grew to $93.4 million, up from $37.8 million for the same period of 1990.

RPM, INC.
2628 Pearl Road
P.O. Box 777
Medina, Ohio 44258
(216) 273-5090

Founded: 1947. **No. of Employees:** 3,000. **Revenues (1990):** $500.3 million. **Revenues (1986):** $268.6 million. **Five-Year Revenue Growth:** 86%.

Description: Makes coatings and products for structural waterproofing, corrosion control, and consumer markets; also hobby and craft materials.

Common positions include: Accountant; Attorney; General Manager.

Principal educational backgrounds sought: Accounting; Chemistry; Finance; Marketing.

Company benefits include: Medical insurance; dental insurance; pension plan; life insurance; disability coverage.

Operations at this facility include: Corporate headquarters.

How they're growing/Recent developments: RPM has just had its 44th straight year of record sales and earnings. Growth has been fueled by aggressive acquisitions, including the Day-Glo Color Corporation in August, 1991 and Rust-Oleum in June, 1991. Revenues grew to $500 million in fiscal year 1991. Employment has grown from an estimated 1,600 in 1987 to 3,000 in 1991.

RUBBERMAID, INC.
1147 Akron Road
Wooster, Ohio 44691
(216) 264-6464

Founded: 1920; **No. of Employees:** 8,409; **Revenues (1990):** $1.5 billion; **Revenues (1986):** $795 million; **Five-Year Revenue Growth:** 89%.

Description: Products for commercial and consumer use.

How they're growing/Recent developments: Rubbermaid has always benefitted from the strong demand for household and office products. The company's expansion to overseas markets and the acquisition of Eldon Industries, a major maker of office products have also boosted revenues.

RYAN'S FAMILY STEAK HOUSES, INC.
405 Lancaster Avenue
Greer, South Carolina 29651
(803) 879-1000

Founded: 1977. **No. of Employees:** 8,000. **Revenues (1990):** $273 million. **Revenues (1987):** $104 million. **Four-Year Revenue Growth:** 162%.

Description: A major regional restaurant operator.

How they're growing/Recent developments: Ryan's is one of the most rapidly expanding restaurant companies in the United States Openings are expected to continue at a double-digit pace. Employment has grown from an estimated 6,000 in 1987 to 8,000 in 1991.

THE RYLAND GROUP
P.O. Box 4000
Columbia, Maryland 21044
(301)730-7222

Founded: 1967. **No. of Employees:** 2,653. **Revenues (1990):** $1.3 billion. **Revenues (1986):** $666 million. **Five-Year Revenue Growth:** 95%.

Description: A construction company that builds and sells single family homes in Florida and, the Central, Middle Atlantic, and Southwest.

How they're growing/Recent developments: Although the construction industry has been hurt by the recession, Ryland boasts a strong balance sheet and conservative accounting practices. The company has a substantial backlog of outstanding contracts (4,374 units as of July, 1991) and new contracts are also on the rise. In January, 1991, Ryland acquired Stokes-Collins, a Jacksonville, Florida, builder. Employment has grown from an estimated 2,300 in 1987 to 2,653 in 1991.

SAFEGUARD SCIENTIFICS, INC.
800 The Safeguard Building
Wayne, Pennsylvania 19087-1945
(215)293-0600

Founded: 1953. **No. of Employees:** 1,800. **Revenues (1990):** $449 million. **Revenues (1986):** $68 million. **Five-Year Revenue Growth:** 560%.

Description: A diversified entrepreneurial technology firm that acquires interests in young and growing businesses in high-growth markets.

How they're growing/Recent developments: Microcomputer systems currently account for 78% of sales. In May, 1991, the company acquired The Computer Factory, a microcomputer dealer chain. Involved in distribution of computers, office workstation systems, and data communications products. Employment has grown from an estimated 1,500 in 1987 to 1,800 in 1991.

SAFETY-KLEEN
777 Big Timber Road
Elgin, Illinois 60123
(708) 697-8460

Founded: 1963. **No. of Employees:** 5,800. **Revenues (1990):** $589 million. **Revenues (1986):** $255 million. **Five-Year Revenue Growth:** 131%.

Description: Provides recovery services to businesses generating small quantities of hazardous waste.

How they're growing/Recent developments: Given the national recession, Safety-Kleen has done exceptionally well. Revenues for the 36-week period that ended September 7, 1991, rose 20% over the same period the previous year. The longer-term prospects are enhanced by the likelihood of more stringent regulations and the need for generators of hazardous waste to properly dispose of waste materials. Employment has grown from an estimated 260 in 2,996 to 5,800 in 1991.

ST. IVES LABORATORIES, INC.
8944 Mason Avenue
Chatsworth, California 91311
(818) 709-5500

Founded: 1987. **No. of Employees:** 415. **Revenues (1990):** $105 million. **Revenues (1987):** $77 million. **Four-Year Revenue Growth:** 36%.

Description: Manufactures and distributes health and beauty aids.

ST. JUDE MEDICAL
3900 Northwoods Drive
Suite 151
St. Paul, Minnesota 55112
(612) 483-2000

Founded: 1976. **No. of Employees:** 544. **Revenues (1990):** $175 million. **Revenues (1986):** $60.5. **Five-Year Revenue Growth:** 189%

Description: The world's leading producer of mechanical heart valves.

How they're growing/Recent developments: Revenues have been boosted by a strong demand for the company's products. Net sales for the six months ending June 30, 1990, gained 18% year to year. The company has spurred growth by diversifying its product line. Employment has grown from an estimated 300 in 1987 to 544 in 1991.

SALEM SCREEN PRINTERS, INC.
1 Delaware Drive
Salem, New Hamsphire 03079
(603) 893-8808

Founded: 1980. **No. of Employees:** 317. **Revenues (1990):** $48 million. **Revenues (1986):** $3 million. **Five-Year Revenue Growth:** 1,500%.

Description: A New Hampshire based silk screen printer.

How they're growing/Recent developments: Employment has grown from an estimated 120 in 1987 to 317 in 1991.

SANFORD CORPORATION
2711 Washington Boulevard
Bellwood, Illinois 60104
(708) 547-6650

Founded: 1957. **No. of Employees:** 725. **Revenues (1990):** $139 million. **Revenues (1986):** $75 million. **Five-Year Revenue Growth:** 85%.

Description: A maker of felt tip pens and other writing equipment.

How they're growing/Recent developments: In 1990, Sanford introduced a complete line of upscale plastic desk accessories and other organizer products. The company gains a competitive advantage from the established ability of its sales force and its extensive network of distribution channels. Employment has grown from an estimated 400 in 1987 to 725 in 1991.

SARA LEE
3 First National Plaza
70 West Madison Street
Chicago, Illinois 60602
(312) 726-2600

No. of Employees: 87,000. **Revenues (1990):** $11 billion. **Revenues (1986):** $7.9 billion. **Five-Year Revenue Growth:** 39%.

Description: Manufactures quality packaged foods and a maker of household and personal care items.

Company benefits include: Daycare Assistance. Flex-time.

How they're growing/Recent developments: Sara Lee's expanding non-food sales has boosted sales volume. The company recently acquired Linter Textiles Corporation, the largest apparel and textile company in Australia. Revenues for fiscal 1991 climbed to $12.4 billion.

SBARRO, INC.
763 Larkfield Road
Commack, New York 11725
(516) 864-0200

Founded: 1959. **No. of Employees:** 5,800. **Revenues (1990):** $190 million. **Revenues (1986):** $58 million. **Five-Year Revenue Growth:** 228%.

Description: Owns and franchises a chain of Italian family style restaurants.

How they're growing/Recent developments: The company has recently added two new units in midtown Manhattan, as well as units in Philadelphia and Connecticut. More expansion -- including some international units -- are planned. An overall recovery of consumer confidence will also help, as many of the company's units are located in malls. Employment has grown from an estimated 3,800 in 1987 to 5,800 in 1991.

SBE, INC.
2400 Bisso Lane
Concord, California 94520
(415) 680-7722

Founded: 1961. **No. of Employees:** 126. **Revenues (1990):** $19 million. **Revenues (1986):** $7 million. **Five-Year Revenue Growth:** 171%.

Description: A designer and marketer of microcomputer boards and systems, processor boards and communications controllers.

How they're growing/Recent developments: The company's management puts a major emphasis on direct sales and research and development. Employment has grown from an estimated 50 in 1987 to 126 in 1991.

SCHERING-PLOUGH
One Giralda Farms
Madison, New Jersey 07940
(201) 822-7000

Founded: 1864. **No. of Employees:** 19,700. **Revenues (1990):** $3.323 billion. **Revenues (1986):** $2.399 billion. **Five-Year Revenue Growth:** 39%.

Description: A leading pharmaceutical and consumer health products manufacturer.

How they're growing/Recent developments: During 1990, the company received FDA approval to sell Gyne-Lotrimin, a yeast infection treatment, as an over-the-counter product.

SCIENTECH
1690 International Way
Idaho Falls, Idaho 83402
(208) 523-2077

Founded: 1983. **No. of Employees:** 139. **Revenues (1990):** $17 million. **Revenues (1986):** $1.3 million. **Five-Year Revenue Growth:** 1,208%.

Description: Designs computer systems and provides consulting engineer services.

How they're growing/Recent developments: Employment has grown from an estimated 33 in 1987 to 139 in 1991.

SCI-MED LIFE SYSTEMS, INC.
6655 Wedgewood Road
Maple Grove, Minnesota 55369
(612)420-0700

Founded: 1972. **No. of Employees:** 1,100. **Revenues (1990):** $67 million. **Revenues (1987):** $9 million. **Four-Year Revenue Growth:** 644%.

Description: The company designs and makes cathethers and other disposable medical products used in treating cardiovascular and vascular disease.

How they're growing/Recent developments: Sci-Med's products support the trend toward less invasive and less traumatic medical intervention. For the six-month period ending August 31, 1991, sales rose 72% year to year. Revenues for 1991 soared to $112 million. Employment has grown from an estimated 150 in 1987 to 1,100 in 1991.

THE SCORE BOARD, INC.
1951 Old Cuthbert Road
Cherry Hill, New Jersey 08034
(609) 354-9000

Founded: 1986; **No. of Employees:** 118; **Revenues (1990)** $20.3 million. **Revenues (1987):** $800 thousand. **Four-Year Revenue Growth:** 2,437%.

Description: Score Board designs, assembles, markets and distributes sports and entertainment related products for sale to television shopping networks, local retailers, national and regional toy stores, retail chains, convenience stores and the hobby market. The company sorts and repackages baseball trading cards and markets card collecting kits. Cards are purchased in sets from manufacturers such as Topps Chewing Gum, Fleer Corporation, and The Upper Deck Company.

How they're growing/Recent developments: In September, 1991, the company was granted a three-year licence by the National Football League to produce and market football trivia board games featuring NFL player cards. The company's new NFL, NBA and Major League Baseball draft cards, introduced in 1991, sold out their initial printing due to overwhelming demand.

SEAGATE TECHNOLOGY, INC.
920 Disc Drive
Scotts Valley, California 95067
(408)438-6550

Founded: 1978. **No. of Employees:** 38,000. **Revenues (1990):** $2.4 billion. **Revenues (1986):** $460 million. **Five-Year Revenue Growth:** 422%.

Description: Company is a leading maker of rigid magnetic disc drives for computer systems.

How they're growing/Recent developments: Seagate acquired Imprimis Technology in October, 1989. Imprimis was a data storage products subsidiary of Control Data. Net sales rose 11% for the fiscal year ending June 30, 1991, partly because of the Imprimis acquisition and partly due to increased volume shipments of smaller drives and a shift toward higher priced products. Employment has grown from an estimated 14,000 in 1987 to 38,000 in 1991.

SEAGULL ENERGY
10001 Fannin Street, Suite 1700
Houston, Texas 77002
(713)951-4700

Founded: 1973. **No. of Employees:** 507. **Revenues (1990):** $220 million. **Revenues (1986):** $186 million. **Five-Year Revenue Growth:** 18%.

Description: Company is engaged in oil and natural gas exploration, and the transmission and distribution of natural gas.

How they're growing/Recent developments: In March, 1991, Seagull purchased natural gas and oil producing properties, reserves and undeveloped acreage from Mesa Limited Partnership. Back in June, 1990, the company acquired Wacker Oil, Inc. The value of the company's estimated reserves has increased every year. Employment has grown from an estimated 350 in 1987 to 507 in 1991.

SEALRIGHT
7101 College Boulevard, Suite 1400
Overland Park, Kansas 66210
(913) 344-9000

Founded: 1964. **No. of Employees:** 1,502. **Revenues (1990):** $206 million. **Revenues (1986):** $121 million. **Five-Year Revenue Growth:** 70%.

Description: A producer of food and dairy product packaging.

How they're growing/Recent developments: The company has recently expanded into plastic packaging for snack foods, candies, and other grocery items. In December, 1990, the company acquired an Ohio-based packaging supplier for the food and beverage industry. Employment has grown from an estimated 1,200 in 1987 to 1,502 in 1991.

SEI
680 East Swedesford Road
Wayne, Pennsylvania 19087
(215) 254-1000

Founded: 1968. **No. of Employees:** 1,337. **Revenues (1990):** $172 million. **Revenues (1986):** $119 million. **Five-Year Revenue Growth:** 45%.

Description: Provide information services for money managers.

How they're growing/Recent developments: In 1989, SEI acquired National FSI, Inc., a provider of computer and software services relating to employee benefits plans. Revenues have grown, in part, due to higher management fees and to new and existing clients. Employment has grown from an estimated 1,000 in 1987 to 1,337 in 1991.

SENSORMATIC ELECTRONICS
500 Northwest 12th Avenue
Deerfield Beach, Florida 33442
(305) 427-9700

Founded: 1966. **No. of Employees:** 2,700. **Revenues (1990):** $239 million. **Revenues (1986):** $89 million. **Five-Year Revenue Growth:** 169%.

Description: Produces in-store electronic surveillance equipment.

Common positions include: Accountant; Computer Programmer; Customer Service Representative; Draftsperson; Electrical Engineer; Industrial Engineer; Financial Analyst; Operations/Production Manager; Marketing Specialist; Purchasing Agent; Quality control Supervisor; Sales Representative; Systems Analyst; Technical Writer/Editor; Software Engineer.

Principal educational backgrounds: Accounting; Business Administration; Computer Science; Economics; Engineering: Finance; Liberal Arts; Marketing.

Company benefits include: Medical insurance; dental insurance; pension plan; life insurance; tuition assistance; disability coverage; profit sharing; savings plan; stock purchase plan.

Operations at this facility include: Manufacturing; research and development; administration.

How they're growing/Recent developments: In April, 1991, the company announced orders of close to $10 million from Macy's, Wal-Mart and Marshall's. In 1988, the company branched out services to include the manufacture of bar code scanners. Revenues for 1991 rose to $239 million. Employment has grown from an estimated 1,157 in 1987 to over 2,700 in 1991.

SEQUA CORPORATION
200 Park Avenue
New York, New York 10166
(212) 986-5500

Contact: Human Resources Department. **Founded:** 1929. **No. of Employees:** 17,700. **Revenues (1990):** $2.2 billion. **Revenues (1986):** $371 million. **Five-Year Revenue Growth:** 493%.

Description: A diversified corporation, offering a wide range of industrial products, including pigments and printing inks; fine chemicals for the paper-making industry; aircraft instrumentation; and automotive products.

How they're growing/Recent developments: Employment has grown from an estimated 16,000 in 1987 to 17,700 in 1991.

SEQUENT COMPUTER SYSTEMS INC.
15450 South West Cole Parkway
Beaverton, Oregon 97006
(503) 626-5700

Founded: 1983. **No. of Employees:** 1.1 billion. **Revenues (1990):** $248.8 million. **Revenues (1986):** $20 million. **Five-Year Revenue Growth:** 1,144%.

Description: Manufactures and designs high-performance general purpose computer systems.

How they're growing/Recent developments: Sequent has been expanding its international business. In addition, the company recently introduced its Symmetry product line, which is based on both the Intel 80386 and 80486 microprocessors. Employment has grown from an estimated 212 in 1987 to 1,100 in 1991.

SERV-TECH
P.O. Box 4334
Houston, Texas 77210
(713) 644-9974

Founded: 1978. **No. of Employees:** 154. **Revenues (1990):** $42.4 million. **Revenues (1986):** $5.2 million. **Five-Year Revenue Growth:** 715%.

Description: Maintains oil and chemical plants.

How they're growing/Recent developments: In September, 1991, the company acquired SECO Industries, Inc. Nine out of 10 of the country's largest integrated oil companies are customers. Revenues for the first six months of 1991 more than doubled year to year because of a huge increase in projects for refining and petrochemical customers.

SERVICE CORPORATION INTERNATIONAL
1929 Allen Parkway
Houston, Texas 77019
(713) 522-5141

Founded: 1962. **No. of Employees:** 9,583. **Revenues (1990):** $563 million. **Revenues (1986):** $387 million. **Five-Year Revenue Growth:** 45%.

Description: Company provides funeral services, cemetery plots, and crematories. The largest publicly held funeral services company in the United States and Canada.

How they're growing/Recent developments: Service International has grown considerably recently, and made a number of significant acquisitions during the summer of 1991. These include the Sentinel Group, Inc., Pierce Brothers, and the Arlington Corporation. Revenues for the first three quarters of 1991 rose 10% year to year. Employment has grown from an estimated 5,500 in 1987 to 9,583 in 1991.

SERVICEMASTER LIMITED PARTNERSHIP
One ServiceMaster Way
Downers Grove, Illinois 60515
(708) 964-1300

Founded: 1956. **No. of Employees:** 6,454. **Revenues (1990):** $1.8 billion. **Revenues (1986):** $1.1 billion. **Five-Year Revenue Growth:** 64%.

Description: A housekeeping, maintenance and management company providing services to residential, commercial, educational, industrial, and health care facilities.

How they're growing/Recent developments: Profitability is expected to increase during 1992 due to growth in health care and education markets. Revenues rose 16% year to year for the first six months of 1991.

SHAW INDUSTRIES INC.
P.O. Drawer 2128
Dalton, Georgia 30722
(404)278-3812

Founded: 1967. **No. of Employees:** 14,700. **Revenues (1990):** $1.5 billion. **Revenues (1986):** $550 million. **Five-Year Revenue Growth:** 172%.

Description: The country's largest domestic carpet manufacturer, specializing in tufted carpet for residential and commercial use.

How they're growing/Recent developments: Recently there has been a decreased demand for the company's products, but as the recession lifts, earnings should gain in 1992. As part of the company's continuing efforts to increase market share, Shaw acquired Armstrong World Industries rug and carpet operations in December, 1989. Revenues climbed to $1.6 million in 1991. Employment has grown from an estimated 10,300 in 1987 to 14,700 in 1991.

SHERWIN-WILLIAMS CO.
101 Prospect Avenue N.W.
Cleveland, Ohio 44115
(216) 566-2000

Founded: 1884. **No. of Employees:** 15,906. **Revenues (1990):** $2.3 billion. **Revenues (1986):** $1.6 billion. **Five-Year Revenue Growth:** 44%.

Description: The country's largest producer of paints and varnishes, Sherwin-Williams also makes floor coverings and window treatments.

How they're growing/Recent developments: New stores and new products have combined to give Sherwin-Williams an increasing share of the market. Sales for the first three quarters of 1991 increased 14% year to year, on the strength of gains in the coatings segment and slightly higher store sales. Analysts believe that the company should profit in 1992 from still higher sales and increased strength in markets served by the company's direct sales staff.

SHOREWOOD PACKAGING CORPORATION
55 Engineers Lane
Farmingdale, New York 11735
(516) 694-2900

Founded: 1966. **No. of Employees:** 1,000. **Revenues (1990):** $139 million. **Revenues (1986):** $49 million. **Five-Year Revenue Growth:** 184%.

Description: The nation's largest manufacturer of paperboard packaging products for the music industry.

How they're growing/Recent developments: In October, 1990, Shorewood acquired Toronto Carton, Ltd., a company with $10 million in annual sales. Employment has grown from an estimated 650 in 1987 to 1,000 in 1991.

SHOWBOAT INC.
2800 Fremont Street
Las Vegas, Nevada 89104
(702) 385-9123

Founded: 1960. **No. of Employees:** 4,750. **Revenues (1990):** $334 million. **Revenues (1986):** $50 million. **Five-Year Revenue Growth:** 568%.

Description: Company operates hotels, casinos, and bowling centers.

How they're growing/Recent developments: A more favorable regulatory environment in Atlantic City has allowed more room for slot machines and the possible introduction of new games. Operating profits increased 42% during the first nine months of 1991. In October, 1990, a $28 million renovation of the company's Las Vegas casino was completed. Employment has grown from an estimated 1,200 in 1987 to 4,750 in 1991.

SIERRA TUSCON COMPANIES
16500 North Lago Del Oro Parkway
Tucson, Arizona 85737
(602)) 792-5800

No. of Employees: 422. **Revenues (1990):** $29.3 million. **Revenues (1986):** $5.3 million. **Five-Year Revenue Growth:** 453%.

Description: Sierra Tuscon provides residential treatment for persons suffering from chemical dependency and mental, psychological, emotional, behavioral and eating disorders. Sierra Tuscon has developed its own treatment programs, the Sierra Model. Unlike traditional approaches, the Sierra Model is an integrated psychological, biological, "whole person" approach to the treatment of addictions and mental health disorders that combines principles and practices from the medical, psychiatric, psychological, family systems and self-help communities. Sierra Tuscon operates a Master Treatment Center in Tuscon, Arizona, and a treatment center in Germany. Patients are referred to Sierra Tuscon by therapists, psychiatrists, and increasingly, Sierra Tuscon's growing number of alumni.

How they're growing/Recent developments: Revenues reached a seven-year high in 1990, a 59% increase over the previous year. The company has increased its capacity to treat more patients, intensified work in the area of chemical and nonchemical dependencies and extended its treatment to other disorders. Another 1990 milestone: bed capacity at the domestic facility increased over 150%. The company treated an average of 151 patients per days per day in 1990 compared to 101 in 1989.

SIGMA-ALDRICH CORPORATION
3050 Spruce Street
St. Louis, Missouri 63103
(314) 771-5765

Founded: 1975. **No. of Employees:** 4,107. **Revenues (1990):** $529 million. **Revenues (1986):** $253 million. **Five-Year Revenue Growth:** 109%.

Description: Makes and markets a line of biochemical and organic products for research and diagnosis of disease. A subsidiary company makes metal struts.

How they're growing/Recent developments: Sigma-Aldrich has benefitted from higher worldwide chemical sales. In 1989, the company acquired Fluka Chemical A.G., a Swiss biochemical company. Sales grew 14% year to year for the first six months of 1991, due to greater worldwide chemical sales, subsidiary B-Line Systems' acquisition of Kin-Line, a manufacturer of metal struts, and the release of new metal products. Employment has grown from an estimated 2,919 in 1987 to 4,107 in 1991.

SIGMA DESIGNS, INC.
46501 Landing Parkway
Fremont, California 94538
(415) 770-0100

Founded: 1982. **No. of Employees:** 220. **Revenues (1990):** $76.2 million. **Revenues (1986):** $28 million. **Five Year Growth Rate:** 172%.

Description: Sigma Designs designs, manufactures and markets color, greyscale and monochrome display systems, monitors, and controller boards for IBM, Apple Macintosh and compatible personal computers. Sigma distributes its products worldwide through original equipment manufacturers (OEMs), distributors, retail chains and value-added resellers.

How they're growing/Recent developments: In developing its products, Sigma has concentrated on the segments of the PC market that offer high-growth potential, including business graphics, desktop publishing, CAD/CAD and imaging applications. The company's marketing strategy is focused on expanding sales of both its OEM and Channels divisions. Management says that the OEM division will "continue to build upon its relationships with manufacturing representative firms to increase sales." The Channels division is developing national, as well as international, agreements with distributors and retail chains. Unfortunately, the loss of a government contract by one of the company's major OEM customers, and a general slowdown in the economy led to a major revenue decline in 1991, with sales falling to about $36 million for fiscal 1991. The setback appears only temporary, as Sigma hired a significant number of new staff members in 1991. In total, employment rose from 176 employees to 220. An experienced new senior executive was added to oversee marketing and sales operations, and many new positions were filled in customer service, quality control, and software engineering. In addition, the company spend 21% more on research and development in 1991 than in 1990. Employment has grown from 82 in 1987 to 220 in 1991.

SILICON GRAPHICS
P.O. Box 7311
Mountain View, California 94039-7311
(415) 960-1980

Founded: 1981. **No. of Employees:** 2,099. **Revenues (1990):** $420 million. **Revenues (1986):** $42 million. **Five-Year Revenue Growth:** 900%.

Description: Manufactures and services computers and software for 3-Dimensional graphics.

How they're growing/Recent developments: The company has benefitted greatly from new product introductions. Alliances with Compaq Computer and Microsoft will help bring Silicon's visualization technology into PC market. In November, 1991, Silicon signed an agreement with a German firm to distribute Silicon Graphics computers in Europe. During 1991, the company opened seven technical support centers (four of them overseas). Employment grew by 450 jobs between 1990 and 1991.

SILICON VALLEY GROUP
541 E. Trimble Road
San Jose, California 95131
(408) 432-9300

Founded: 1977. **No. of Employees:** 932. **Revenues (1990):** $184 million. **Revenues (1986):** $28 million. **Five-Year Revenue Growth:** 557%.

Description: Company manufactures advanced processing equipment for the semiconductor industry.

How they're growing/Recent developments: The company acquired Thermco Systems in 1988 and SVG Lithography Systems in 1990. Net sales for 1990 rose 49%, largely due to the latter acquisition. Employment has grown from an estimated 385 in 1987 to 932 in 1991.

THE J.M. SMUCKER COMPANY
Strawberry Lane
Orrville, Ohio 44667
(216) 682-0015

Founded: 1921. **No. of Employees:** 1,900. **Revenues (1990):** $422 million. **Revenues (1986):** $263 million. **Five-Year Revenue Growth:** 60%.

Description: Leading maker of preserves and jellies.

How they're growing/Recent developments: Revenues have grown thanks to continued growth in domestic and international consumer markets and increased sales through warehouse club stores. Employment has grown from an estimated 1,200 in 1987 to 1,900 in 1991.

SNAP-ON TOOLS CORPORATION
2801 80th Street
Kenosha, Wisconsin 53141
(414) 656-5200

Founded: 1919. **No. of Employees:** 7,600. **Revenues (1990):** $985 million. **Revenues (1986):** $696 million. **Five-Year Revenue Growth:** 41%.

Description: Snap-On manufactures and distributes tools and related products. Area dealers sell the products out of a van they drive directly to mechanic's shops.

How they're growing/Recent developments: Though sales were down in 1990 due to problems in the auto industry and the recession, Snap-On signed on more dealers in 1991 as franchisees. Employment has grown from an estimated 6,045 in 1987 to 7,600 in 1991.

SOFTWARE PUBLISHING
3165 Kifer Road
Santa Clara, California 95051
(408) 986-8000

Founded: 1980. **No. of Employees:** 476. **Revenues (1990):** $141 million. **Revenues (1986):** $24 million. **Four-Year Revenue Growth:** 487%.

Description: Company develops prepackaged software.

How they're growing/Recent developments: The company has agreed to acquire Precision Software Ltd., a maker of database packages for the Windows environment. Since 1985, much of the company's strength has come as a result of the acquisition in that year of Harvard Graphics, a leading PC graphics software package. Employment has grown from an estimated 200 in 1987 to 476 in 1991.

SOFTWARE SPECTRUM
2140 Merritt Drive
Garland, Texas 75041
(214) 840-6600

Founded: 1983. **No. of Employees:** 200. **Revenues (1990):** $118.5 million. **Revenues (1986):** $11.4 million. **Five-Year Revenue Growth:** 839%.

Description: Software Spectrum produces computer software and printers.

How they're growing/Recent developments: Employment has grown from 20 in 1986 to 200 in 1991.

SOFTWARE TOOLWORKS, INC.
60 Leveroni Court
Novato, California 94949
(415) 883-3000

Founded: 1983. **No. of Employees:** 200. **Revenues (1990):** $68 million. **Revenues (1986):** $634 thousand. **Five-Year Revenue Growth:** 10,525%.

Description: Develops, produces, and licenses software to use with Nintendo Systems and personal computers.

How they're growing/Recent developments: In March, 1990, the company acquired Mindscape, Inc., a game developer for Nintendo. Although the recession has hurt the Nintendo market in 1991 and Software Toolworks revenues have fallen slightly, the company has become more active in international markets, especially England, Germany, Japan, and Australia.

SOFTWARE 2000 INC.
1 Park Center, Drawer 6000
Hyannis, Massachusetts 02601
(508) 771-0900

Founded: 1981. **No. of Employees:** 305. **Revenues (1990):** $29 million. **Revenues (1986):** $2 million. **Five-Year Revenue Growth:** 1,350%.

Description: Developers of computer software.

How they're growing/Recent developments: As of October, 1989, the company had achieved growth rates in revenues of at least 100% for five years in a row. Software 2000 has begun providing software for companies needing to keep databases of their hazardous waste materials in order to comply with tightening regulations.

SOLECTRON
2001 Fortune Drive
San Jose, California 95131
(408) 942-1943

Founded: 1977. **No. of Employees:** 2,000. **Revenues (1990):** $205 million. **Revenues (1986):** $42 million. **Five-Year Revenue Growth:** 388%.

Description: Manufacturers of printed circuit boards.

How they're growing/Recent developments: Major customers include Sun Microsystems, IBM and Exabyte. The company emphasizes turnkey services, materials procurement, manufacturing and warehousing. Revenues rose to $265 million in 1991, up 30%. The increase reflect growth in turnkey manufacturing.

SONOCO PRODUCTS CO.
North 2nd Street
Hartsville, South Carolina 29550
(803)383-7000

Founded: 1899. **No. of Employees:** 14,556. **Revenues (1990):** $1.7 billion. **Revenues (1986):** $964 million. **Five-Year Revenue Growth:** 76%.

Description: International manufacturer of paper and plastic packaging products.

How they're growing/Recent developments: Recent acquisitions include the Consumer Packaging Division of Boise Cascade, a maker of composite cans and plastic bottles, and Gunter, S.A., which uses recycled materials for packaging products. Employment has grown from an estimated 14,000 in 1987 to 14,556 in 1991.

SOUND ADVICE, INC.
1901 Tigertail Boulevard
Dania, Florida 33004
(305) 922-4434

Founded: 1974. **No. of Employees:** 522. **Revenues (1990):** $91.5 million. **Revenues (1988):** $54.7 million. **Three-Year Revenue Growth:** 67%.

Description: Engaged in retailing and servicing home and auto audio equipment and video equipment.

How they're growing/Recent Developments: Income rose to $2.5 million in 1990, up from $2.2 million two years earlier. Employment has grown from an estimated 175 in 1987 to 522 in 1991.

SOUTHEASTERN MICHIGAN GAS ENTERPRISES, INC.
P.O. Box 5026
Port Huron, Michigan 48061-5026
(313)987-2200

Founded: 1977. **No. of Employees:** 550. **Revenues (1990):** $228 million. **Revenues (1986):** $116 million. **Five-Year Revenue Growth:** 97%.

Description: Distributes natural gas in 20 counties in Michigan and provides professional and technical service.

How they're growing/Recent developments: Increases in volume sold have boosted revenues as have a variety of exploration and distribution joint ventures and partnerships. The company is also developing commercial and residential real estate in the Port Huron area.

SPAGHETTI WAREHOUSE, INC.
6120 Aldwick Drive
Garland, Texas 75043
(214) 226-6000

Founded: 1972. **No. of Employees:** 816 full-time, 1,300 part-time. **Revenues (1990):** $37.2 million. **Revenues (1986):** $15.2 million. **Five-Year Revenue Growth:** 145%.

Description: Spaghetti Warehouse is a chain of full-service, family-style restaurants serving moderately priced Italian food in 11 states.

Common positions include: Of the company's 816 full-time employees, 38 are corporate management and staff personnel and 778 are restaurant personnel.

How they're growing/Recent Developments: The company announced in December, 1991 that it planned to open four new restaurants in 1992, followed by another six in 1993. Construction is under way on new restaurants in San Antonio, Texas, and Columbia, South Carolina. Historically, the company has sought restaurant sites in metropolitan area with populations in excess of 500,000, but is planning for future penetration of metropolitan areas with populations as low as 200,000. New restaurants in these smaller markets will seat approximately 300, as opposed to the current company average of 450. Management believes that this will position Spaghetti Warehouse for more rapid and extensive expansion.

SPAN AMERICA MEDICAL SYSTEMS, INC.
P.O. Box 5231
Commerce Center
Greenville, South Carolina 29606
(803) 288-8877

Founded: 1970. **No. of Employees:** 232. **Revenues (1990):** $25.2 million. **Revenues (1987):** $15.3 million. **Four-Year Revenue Growth:** 65%.

Description: Span America Medical Systems is a manufacturer and marketer of foam products for the health care, industrial and consumer industries. The company's patented Geo-Matt mattress and Span-Aid patient positioners are industry leaders in the care and prevention of pressure ulcers. The company also provides contract packaging services for health care and consumer products.

How they're growing/Recent developments: Income has risen from $629,000 in 1988 to $1.3 million in 1990 and then to $1.6 million in 1991. A promotion with a large retail chain contributed to a particularly strong showing in the consumer foam segment, where quarterly revenues more than doubled from the previous year. Employment has grown from an estimated 200 in 1987 to 232 in 1991.

SPARTAN MOTORS, INC.
1000 Reynolds Road
Charlotte, Michigan 48813
(517) 543-6400

Founded: 1974. **No. of Employees:** 172. **Revenues (1990):** $50.7 million. **Revenues (1987):** $14.7 million. **Four-Year Revenue Growth:** 245%.

Description: Manufacturer of custom designed heavy-duty truck chassis.

How they're growing/Recent developments: In 1990, Spartan released a new front-wheel drive ambulance that will allow for a greater vehicle weight while also providing a new low load height. The company is also developing chassis for the motor home industry in order to expand its markets. Employment has grown from an estimated 55 in 1987 to 172 in 1991.

SPEC'S MUSIC INC.
1666 N.W. 82nd Avenue
Miami, Florida 33126
(305) 592-7288

Founded: 1948. **No. of Employees:** 550. **Revenues (1990):** $49.4 million. **Revenues (1987):** $26.6 million. **Three-Year Revenue Growth:** 86%.

Description: The largest specialty retailer of prerecorded music and video products in Florida. As of July 31, 1991, the company operated 57 stores, which sell compact discs, casettes, video movies, music videos, blank audio and video tapes, and a variety of audio and vision accessories. Thirty-eight stores also rent video movies. The company's stores are located in enclosed malls, strip centers and free-standard locations throughout Florida.

How they're growing/Recent developments: During 1991, revenues rose 20% from fiscal 1990. Approximately 17% of that increase was the result of opening new stores in 1990 and 1991. Same store revenues increased 3% as a result of increased demand for compact discs and video-sell though. Revenues rose to $59.4 million in 1991.

SPI PHARMACEUTICALS
3300 Hyland Avenue
Costa Mesa, California 92626
(714) 545-0100

Founded: 1981. **No. of Employees:** 500. **Revenues (1990):** $140.7 million. **Revenues (1987):** $61.4 million. **Four-Year Revenue Growth:** 129%

Description: A subsidiary of ICN Pharmaceuticals, Inc., SPI makes, markets and distributes over 1,000 pharmaceutical and nutritional products in over 60 countries throughout the world, serving the U.S., Canada, Mexico, Europe, and the Far East. Major product lines include a variety of prescription and over-the-counter products, including antivirals, antibiotics, dermatologicals, central nervous system compounds and vision care lines. SPI products are marketed under the ICN tradename.

How they're growing/Recent developments: Sales rose a dramatic 88% for the first three quarters of 1991, boosted by the news that Hungary's national health authorities had authorized ICN to market the product Virazole in a joint venture with Galenika Pharmaceuticals of Yugoslavia. Virazole will be used to treat Hungarian AIDS patients. In early December, Virazole was approved in India for acute hepatitis.

SRA INTERNATIONAL
2000 North 15th Street
Arlington, Virginia 22201
(703)558-7800

No. of Employees: 575. **Revenues (1990):** $47 million. **Revenues (1986):** $19.3 million. **Five-Year Revenue Growth:** 147%.

Description: SRA specializes in computer and telecommunications professional services.

How they're growing/Recent developments: During 1990, SRA received almost $70 million in new contract awards, won important recompetitions in command and control programs, and expanded its Ada software activities supporting U.S. Army development centers. Also in 1991, the company increased its government and commercial telecommunications network analysis business, added to its systems integration business with the installation of a major network for the Federal Emergency Management Agency, helped the U.S. Department of Defense improve the use of its resources through analytical studies, business case analysis, prototypes, and modeling programs, and began a new commercial program providing system re-engineering and CASE tool support to large companies with extensive COBOL applications. Since the end of the fiscal year, SRA has won two major Defense Department contracts -- the first to support the corporate information management program and the second to develop and integrate the joint operation planning and execution system. These awards increased SRA's total business backlog to almost $250 million. SRA has grown from 182 employees in 1985 to 575 employees in 1991. Revenues for fiscal year 1991 rose to $48.9 million.

STAPLES
100 Pennsylvania
P.O. Box 9328
Framingham, Massachusetts 01701-9328
(508) 370-8500

Founded: 1985. **No. of Employees:** 1,749. **Revenues (1990):** $182 million. **Revenues (1986):** $9 million. **Five-Year Revenue Growth:** 1,922%.

Description: Operates high-volume office superstores that provide small and mid-sized companies with brand name supplies at discount prices.

How they're growing/Recent developments: Staples has grown with the help of an innovative free membership card-based marketing system, which gives cardholders preferential pricing. About 75% of all sales are generated in this manner. Staples opened the nation's first office superstore in 1986. The company is expanding nationwide, opening its first California stores in 1990.

STATE-O-MAINE
10 West 33rd Street, 8th Floor
New York, New York 10001
(212)244-1111

Founded: 1966. **No. of Employees:** 400. **Revenues (1990):** $95.3 million. **Revenues (1986):** $36 million. **Five-Year Revenue Growth:** 165%.

Description: Manufacturers of men's and women's activewear, robes, outerwear and casual sportswear.

How they're growing/Recent developments: Income rose between 1988 and 1990, from $4.06 million to $5.75 million.

STATE OF THE ART
56 Technology South
Irvine, California 92718
(714) 753-1222

Founded: 1981. **No. of Employees:** 106. **Revenues (1990):** $16.2 million. **Revenues (1986):** $2.5 million. **Five-Year Revenue Growth:** 548%.

Description: Produces high-end PC accounting software.

How they're growing/Recent developments: In 1990, 71% of revenues were realized through sales of software modules. Revenues for the nine months ending September 30, 1991, grew 18% year to year, thanks to expanded distribution and new product introductions. Employment has grown from an estimated 100 in 1987 to 106 in 1991.

STATISTICA
30 West Gude Drive
Suite 300
Rockville, Maryland 20850
(301) 621-5543

Founded: 1977. **No. of Employees:** 256. **Revenues (1990):** $24.2 million. **Revenues (1986):** $1.8 million. **Five-Year Revenue Growth:** 1,244%.

Description: STATISTICA provides professional and computer systems engineering consulting services.

How they're growing/Recent developments: Employment has grown from an estimated 55 in 1987 to 256 in 1991.

STEP AHEAD INVESTMENTS, INC.
1760 Enterprise Boulevard
West Sacramento, California 95691
(916) 372-8872

Founded: 1983. **No. of Employees:** 246. **Revenues (1990):** $17.8 million. **Revenues (1986):** $1.7 million. **Five-Year Revenue Growth:** 947%.

Description: Owns and operates a chain of thrift stores.

How they're growing/Recent developments: Everything in these stores sells for 98 cents or less. The company negotiates on everything from leasing costs to trucking and advertising and, of course, its goods, to operate an efficient business, as it can't raise prices to cover expenses. Employment has grown from 23 in 1986 to 246 in 1991.

STEPHAN COMPANY
1850 West McNab Road
Ft. Lauderdale, Florida 33309
(305) 971-0600

Founded: 1897. **No. of Employees:** 85. **Revenues (1990):** $5.5 million. **Revenues (1986):** $1.8 million. **Five-Year Revenue Growth:** 206%.

Description: The Stephan Company manufactures and markets hair care, skin care and fragrance products under the Stephan's brand, and manufactures custom label products for other companies. The company also manufactures and distributes a line of ethnic products under the brand name Magic Wave. Old 97 Company, a wholly owned subsidiary, manufactures and distributes over 100 different products, including hair and skin care products, fragrances, personal grooming aids and household items on a direct to the consumer basis with over 500 representatives selling in the Southeastern United States.

How they're growing/Recent developments: Continuing with its plans for expansion, the Stephan Company has increased private label sales through the steady growth of new product lines as well as the securing of new custom label clients. In 1990, a major drug chain began carrying the Stephan brand, which represents a major step in the company's ongoing search for mass retail distribution. Revenues for 1991 jumped to over $10 million. Employment has grown from an estimated 15 in 1987 to 70 in 1991.

STONE CONTAINER CORPORATION
150 North Michigan Avenue
Chicago Illinois 60601
(312) 346-6600

Contact: Jeanne Seufert, Recruiting Specialist. **Founded:** 1945. **No. of Employees:** 32,300. **Revenues (1990):** $5.8 billion. **Revenues (1986):** $2 billion. **Five-Year Revenue Growth:** 190%.

Description: A major multinational paper company, operating principally in the production and sale of commodity pulp, paper, and packaging products. More than 100 locations nationwide.

Common positions include: Accountant; Computer Programmer; Credit Manager; Customer Service Representative; Financial Analyst; Systems Analyst; Transportation and Traffic Specialist.

Principal educational backgrounds sought: Accounting; Business Administration; Computer Science; Finance.

Company benefits include: Medical, dental and life insurance; pension plan; tuition assistance; disability coverage; employee discounts; savings plan.

How they're growing/Recent developments: The company has greatly expanded operations through acquisitions, most recently ConsolidatedBathurst, a Canadian newsprint producer. Stone expects prices to increase and a recovery in newsprint market. Excellent European operations. Employment has grown from an estimated 15,500 in 1987 to 32,300 in 1991.

STONERIDGE RESOURCES, INC.
2000 North Woodward Avenue, Suite 300
Bloomfield Hills, Michigan 48304
(313) 540-9040

Founded: 1968. **No. of Employees:** 520. **Revenues (1990):** $160 million. **Revenues (1986):** $59 million. **Five-Year Revenue Growth:** 171%.

Description: A diversified holding company operating through Acceptance Insurance Holdings Inc., and Orange Company, Inc. The company acquires businesses and interests in real estate development management, citrus fruit growing, as well as land ownership in Winter Haven, Florida.

How they're growing/Recent developments: In July, 1991, Stoneridge agreed to acquire the remainder of 51%-owned Major Group, a real estate developer. Employment has grown from an estimated 30 in 1987 to 520 in 1991.

STRATUS COMPUTER INC.
55 Fairbanks Boulevard
Marlboro, Massachusetts 01752
(508) 460-2000

Founded: 1980. **No. of Employees:** 2,381. **Revenues (1990):** $340 million. **Revenues (1986):** $125 million. **Five-Year Revenue Growth:** 172

Description: Engaged in manufacturing, marketing, and servicing computer systems.

How they're growing/Recent developments: Stratus systems indentify and isolate their own failures; they automatically dial a customer assistance center to report interruptions and order replacement parts. IBM accounted for 27% of business. Employment has grown from an estimated 1,069 in 1987 to 2,381 in 1991.

STRUCTURAL DYNAMICS RESEARCH
2000 Eastman Drive
Milford, Ohio 45150
(513) 576-2400

Founded: 1967. **No. of Employees:** 1,000. **Revenues (1990):** $119 million. **Revenues (1986):** $52 million. **Five-Year Revenue Growth:** 129%.

Description: A leading supplier of mechanical design automation software and engineering services. Clients include the automotive and aerospace industries.

How they're growing/Recent developments: In August, 1991, the company signed a contract to supply GE Aerospace Group with software. In 1990, the company signed a contract with Lockheed. The company's software division has led the way to success.

STRYKER CORPORATION
2725 Fairfield Road
Kalamazoo, Michigan 49002
(616) 385-2600

Founded: 1946. **No. of Employees:** 1,913. **Revenues (1990):** $281 million. **Revenues (1986):** $121 million. **Five-Year Revenue Growth:** 132%.

Description: A developer, manufacturer, and marketer of surgical and medical products including orthopedic implants and artificial ligaments.

How they're growing/Recent developments: New products include new implants, advanced instruments and video equipment. Surgical instrument sales have been strong. Stryker is committed to an extensive research and development program. Employment has grown from an estimated 1,180 in 1987 to 1,913 in 1991.

STUART HALL COMPANY, INC.
Box 419381
Kansas City, Missouri 64141
(816) 221-8480

Contact: Gail Hamey, Personnel Manager. **Founded:** 1946. **No. of Employees:** 525. **Revenues (1990):** $111 million. **Revenues (1986):** $47 million. **Five-Year Revenue Growth:** 136%.

Description: A manufacturer of school supplies, home and office products and social stationery.

Common positions include: General Laborer; Administrative Assistant; Machine Adjuster.

Principal educational backgrounds sought: Accounting; Business Administration; Computer Science.

Company benefits include: Medical insurance; dental insurance; pension plan; life insurance; employee discounts; savings plan; 401K plan.

Operations at this facility: Corporate headquarters; manufacturing; administration; service.

How they're growing/Recent developments: In 1990, the company introduced a full line of recycled paper products. Recycled products are expected to be one of the company's fastest growing segments. A new plant opened in 1990 near Sacramento, California. Employment has grown from an estimated 1,194 in 1987 to 2,084 in 1991.

STUDENT LOAN MARKETING ASSOCIATION (SALLIE MAE)
1050 Thomas Jefferson Street NW
Washington, D.C. 20007
(202) 333-8000

Founded: 1972. **No. of Employees:** 2084. **Revenues (1990):** $3.6 billion. **Revenues (1986):** $1.3 billion. **Five-Year Revenue Growth:** 176%.

Description: A U.S. Congress-chartered corporation that acts as an intermediary for educational financing.

Common positions include: Accountant; Computer Programmer; Financial Analyst; Marketing Specialist; Systems Analyst.

Principal educational backgrounds sought: Accounting; Business Administration; Computer Science; Finance; Marketing.

Company benefits include: Medical insurance; dental insurance; pension plan; life insurance; tuition assistance; disability coverage; daycare assistance; profit sharing; savings plan; employee stock purchase plan.

How they're growing/Recent developments: Sallie Mae's importance is expected to grow to meet rising tuition costs and the greater need for assistance. The corporation has committed to improving servicing efficiency, loan Administration and communications

SULLIVAN DENTAL PRODUCTS
10920 West Lincoln Avenue
West Allis, Wisconsin 53227
(414) 321-8881

Founded: 1980. **No. of Employees:** 182. **Revenues (1990):** $47.4 million. **Revenues (1986):** $11.5 million. **Five-Year Revenue Growth:** 312%.

Description: Sullivan Dental Products is a key domestic distributor of consumable dental supplies and equipment. Founded in 1980, Sullivan's marketing strategy combines personal visits by sales representatives with a catalog of more than 7,800 items, including virtually all of the product categories used in general dentistry. The company also operates equipment sales, installation and service centers in various parts of the country. In 1990, Sullivan's sales staff totaled 121 representatives in 30 states.

How they're growing/Recent developments: During 1990, Sullivan entered the eastern market when it reached a marketing agreement with American Dental Supply Corporation of Falls Church, Virginia. Under the agreement, American's 12-person sales staff became an additional dental supplies representative for Sullivan in Virginia, Maryland and Connecticut. Future growth plans call for acquisitions, further new marketing arrangements and increased sales from existing staff. The company's staff as of December 31, 1990, includes 60 sales representatives, 27 service technicians and 95 persons in the customer service, clerical, warehouse and corporate staff.

SUMMAGRAPHICS
60 Silvermine Road
Seymour, Connecticut 06483
(203) 881-2000

Founded: 1972. **No. of Employees:** 460. **Revenues (1990):** $46 million. **Revenues (1987):** $28 million. **Four-Year Revenue Growth:** 64%.

Description: An international manufacturer of tools for computer graphics systems.

How they're growing/Recent Developments: In May, 1990, Summagraphics acquired Ametek, Inc.'s Houston Instrument Division. Summagraphics is extremely active in foreign markets, with 50% of net sales coming from overseas. Employment has grown from an estimated 182 in 1987 to 460 in 1991.

SUN MICROSYSTEMS, INC.
2550 Garcia Avenue, Mail Stop PAL1-408
Mountian View, California 94043
(415) 960-1300

Contact: Julia Erdman, Human Resources. **Founded:** 1982. **No. of Employees:** 12,508. **Revenues (1990):** $2.46 billion. **Revenues (1986):** $210 million. **Five-Year Revenue Growth:** 1,071%.

Description: One of the nation's leading manufacturers of high performance workstations. During 1991, the company reorganized its structure and now operates through five units: Sun Microsystems Computer Corporation, Sun Express, Sun Microsystem Laboratories, SunSoft and Sun Technology Enterprises.

How they're growing/Recent developments: Sun's revenues have soared over the last few years. Even as competitors like Apple and Compaq struggled in 1991, Sun forged ahead, largely because of its niche in the workstation market. Increasing competition is on the way from Hewlett-Packard, IBM, DEC, and Silicon Graphics, however, and Sun has begun to feel the effects of a weak economy. Even so, revenues for fiscal 1991 rose again to $3.2 billion. The company has an excellent record of hiring women, including many in top management positions.

SUNRISE MEDICAL, INC.
2355 Crenshaw Boulevard, Suite 150
Torrance, California 90501
(213) 328-8018

Contact: Deborah Beasley, Manager of Corporate Human Relations. **Founded:** 1983. **No. of Employees:** 1,855. **Revenues (1990):** $172 million. **Revenues (1986):** $85.6 million. **Five-Year Revenue Growth:** 101%.

Description: Manufactures medical products such as wheelchairs and special mattresses, used in rehabilitation, home care and hospital settings with an emphasis on the disabled, the geriatric and bed confined patient.

Common positions include: Accountant; Marketing Specialist; Public Relations Specialist.

Principal educational backgrounds sought: Accounting; Business Administration; Liberal Arts; Marketing.

Company benefits include: Medical insurance; dental insurance; life insurance; disability coverage; profit sharing; savings plan.

Operations at this facility include: Corporate headquarters; administration.

How they're growing/Recent developments: One of Sunrise's most recent products is Sprint, a new portable, folding power wheelchair. The company also formed alliance with Hoyer Products, the leading brand of patient lifters in hospital and home care settings. Sunrise announced on January 16, 1992, that it had acquired Sopur GmbH and Affiliates, a privately held German wheelchair manufacturer. Sopur is the German market leader in custom manual wheelchairs and distributes them to dealers throughout Germany and 15 foreign countries, including Eastern Europe. The acquisition represents the cornerstone of the company's European expansion strategy. On January 3, 1992, the company announced that it had signed a contract to acquire Dufco Electronics, Inc. a Cambria, California based manufacturer of specialty electronics for power wheelchairs. Revenues rose to $204 million in fiscal 1991.

SUPER RITE FOODS, INC.
P.O. Box 2261
Harrisburg, Pennsylvania 17105
(717)232-6821

Founded: 1927; **No. of Employees:** 2,602; **Revenues (1990):** $876.8 million; **Revenues (1987):** $602.6 million; **Four-Year Revenue Growth:** 46%.

Description: Super Rite Corporation is a full-service grocery wholesaler and retailer, serving customers in Pennsylvania, New Jersey, Maryland, Delaware, Virginia, and West Virginia. As one of the largest grocery wholesalers in the Middle Atlantic region, the company supplies more than 13,000 regional brand and 1,000 private label grocery items to more than 200 supermarkets. The company's retail grocery division currently operates supermarkets under the name "Basics" in the metropolitan Baltimore and Washington, D.C. markets.

How they're growing/Recent developments: In June, 1991, the company entered into an agreement with Shoppers, a chain of 25 high volume supermarkets in metro Washington to supply the chain with virtually all of its dry grocery, frozen food and dairy products for a 51 month period. Super Rite announced in January, 1992 that sales for the third quarter of 1991, ending September 30 rose 22.8% for the thirteen week period. Management attributed the gains to continued strength on the wholesale segment, which increased sales by 47% in 1991.

SUPER VALU STORES, INC.
11840 Valley View Road
Eden Prairie, Minnesota 55344
(612) 828-4000

Founded: 1925. **No. of Employees:** 42,900. **Revenues (1990):** $11 billion. **Revenues (1986):** $7.9 billion. **Five-Year Revenue Growth:** 39%.

Description: One of the country's largest wholesale food distributors, selling to independently owned and operated food stores as well as to stores owned by the company. Shopka division sells general merchandise.

How they're growing/Recent developments: In October, 1991, the company agreed to acquire Scott's Food Stores, Inc., a supermarket chain. Twenty Cub Food Stores are planned to open over the next 18 months.

SUPERIOR TELETEC INC.

150 Interstate North Parkway
Suite 300
Atlanta, Georgia 30339
(404) 953-8338

Founded: 1985. **No. of Employees:** 690. **Revenues (1990):** $138 million. **Revenues (1986):** $47 million. **Five-Year Revenue Growth:** 194%.

Description: Manufacturers of telephone cable and wires.

How they're growing/Recent developments: In June, 1990, the company acquired the telecommunications division of Lear-Siegler. The division makes communications transmission equipment. Superior Teletic has taken an aggressive acquisitions stance and has seen an increased demand for services.

SUPERMAIL INTERNATIONAL INC.

2201 Park Towne Circle, Suite 200
Sacramento, California 95825
(916) 483-1131

Founded: 1985. **No. of Employees:** 100. **Revenues (1990):** $3.5 million. **Revenues (1986):** $1.9 million. **Five-Year Revenue Growth:** 84%.

Description: Supermail International is the largest independent Western Union agent on the West Coast and provides the general public, government agencies and the business community with a wide variety of communications, financial, and other services, including telegrams, mailgrams, facsimile transmission, postal services, overnight courier services, messenger services, check cashing, money transfer services, peso exchange, food stamps, utility payments, money orders, California lottery ticket sales. transit passes and packaging and wrapping. These services are provided through centers in Reno, Nevada and throughout California.

How they're growing/Recent developments: In 1987, the company expanded its services to include financial services such as check cashing, money orders, California Lotto and lottery, BASS Ticketmaster sales, food stamps, peso exchange, utility payments and transit passes. The company expects to continue its expansion of services through the acquisition of existing profitable check cashing operations. Plans have been completed for the construction of high visibility convenience centers. These "super stores" will provide all of the services currently available along with automated teller machines.

SURGICAL CARE AFFILIATES
102 Woodmont Boulevard, Suite 610
Nashville, Tennessee 37205
(615) 385-3541

Contact: Tammy Howell, Director of Human Resources. **Founded:** 1982. **No. of Employees:** 400. **Revenues (1990):** $124 million. **Revenues (1986):** $23 million. **Five-Year Revenue Growth:** 439%.

Description: Operates outpatient surgical centers.

How they're growing/Recent developments: Management has spurred growth through an aggressive expansion and acquisitions program. Revenues grew another 39% year to year during the first half of 1991. The company has recently acquired control of the Surgery Center in Fort Myers, Florida. In 1992, the company plans to open 8 to 10 new centers. Employment has grown from an estimated 150 in 1987 to 400 in 1991.

SURGICAL LASER TECHNOLOGIES
200 Cresson Boulevard
Oak, Pennsylvania 19456
(215) 666-5400

Founded: 1984. **No. of Employees:** 160. **Revenues (1990):** $38.4 million. **Revenues (1986):** $299 thousand. **Five-Year Revenue Growth:** 12,742%.

Description: Manufacturers of contact surgical lasers.

How they're growing/Recent developments: The company has agreed to acquire exclusive worldwide rights to all technologies of Advanced Systems Technology, Inc. for use in the medical and dental fields.

SWIFT ENERGY COMPANY
16825 Northchase Drive
Suite 400
Houston, Texas 77060
(713) 874-2700

Founded: 1979. **No. of Employees:** 164. **Revenues (1990):** $19 million. **Revenues (1986):** $4 million. **Five-Year Revenue Growth:** 375%.

Description: Crude petroleum and natural gas exploration.

How they're growing/Recent developments: In 1990, Swift acquired oil and gas reserves aggressively. It plans to possess corporate reserves valued between $200 million and $250 million by 1995. Activities are conducted through joint ventures and limited partnership programs. Employment has grown from an estimated 94 in 1987 to 164 in 1991.

SYBASE, INC.
6475 Christie Avenue
Emeryville, California 95014
(415) 596-3500

Founded: 1984. **No. of Employees:** 750. **Revenues (1990):** $103 million. **Revenues (1986):** $1 million. **Five-Year Revenue Growth:** 10,200%.

Description: A producer of software for making databases easier to use. Customers include range from Wall Street traders to manufacturers like Sun Microsystems.

How they're growing/Recent developments: Sybase has grown through a high emphasis on research and development. In addition, during 1991, Sybase purchased Deft Software. Revenues for the six months ending June 30, 1991, jumped 73% year to year, spurred by major increases in licensing fees and services. Demand is increasing quickly for the company's products, and new enhancements and products have helped increase licensing fees. Additional services revenues stemmed from the acquisition of SQL Solutions in 1990.

SYMANTEC
10201 Torre Avenue
Cupertino, California 95014
(408) 253-9600

Founded: 1982. **No. of Employees:** 240. **Revenues (1990):** $50 million. **Revenues (1989):** $39.9 million. **Two-Year Revenue Growth:** 25%.

Description: An international software company that provides application and systems software for IBM PC and Apple Macintosh users.

How they're growing/Recent developments: Symantec recently acquired Zortech, Inc. and Peter Norton Computing, a leading developer of systems management software. Revenues jumped in 1991 to over 116%, largely due to the release of an upgraded version of the Norton Utilities systems software.

SYMBOL TECHNOLOGIES, INC.
116 Wilbur Place
Bohemia, New York 11716
(516) 563-2400

Founded: 1973. **No. of Employees:** 2,100. **Revenues (1990):** $240 million. **Revenues (1986):** $23 million. **Five-Year Revenue Growth:** 943%.

Description: Symbol Technologies manufactures computer peripheral equipment, radio broadcasting equipment and communications equipment and bar code scanning equipment.

How they're growing/Recent developments: Sales of bar code scanner and portable terminals are increasing. In August, 1991, the company announced it was supplying laser radio terminals to K mart. In, March 1991, Symbol Technologies formed a joint venture with Japanese Olympus Symbol Inc. In November, 1990, the company signed a contract with UPS to deliver 45,000 bar code laser scanners over the next year. Employment has grown from an estimated 500 in 1987 to 1,700 in 1991.

SYNERGICS
191 Main Street
Annapolis, Maryland 21401
(301) 268-8820

Founded: 1980. **No. of Employees:** 120. **Revenues (1990):** $18 million. **Revenues (1986):** $6 million. **Five-Year Revenue Growth:** 200%.

Description: Synergics is a developer, builder, owner, and operator of independent power generating plants with emphasis on hydroelectric power.

Common positions include: Accountant; Administrator; Attorney; Draftsperson; Civil Engineer; Electrical Engineer; Mechanical Engineer; Financial Analyst; Operations/Production Manager.

Principal educational backgrounds include: Accounting; Business Administration; Engineering; Finance.

Company benefits include: Medical insurance; dental insurance; life insurance; tuition assistance; disability coverage.

Operations at this facility include: National headquarters.

SYNETICS
540 Edgewater Drive
Wakefield, Massachusetts 01880
(617) 245-9090

Founded: 1984. **No. of Employees:** 285. **Revenues (1990):** $25.5 million. **Revenues (1986):** $2 million. **Five-Year Revenue Growth:** 1,175%.

Description: Synetics provides engineering consulting services.

How they're growing/Recent developments: Employment has grown from 43 in 1986 to 285 in 1991.

SYNOPTICS COMMUNICATIONS
501 E. Middlefield Road
Mountain View, California 94043
(408) 988-2400

Founded: 1985. **No. of Employees:** 405. **Revenues (1990):** $176 million. **Revenues (1987):** $7 million. **Four-Year Revenue Growth:** 2,414%.

Description: A manufacturer of computer integrated network systems, especially LAN systems geared toward reducing cost and complexity.

How they're growing/Recent developments: SynOptics pioneered LAN systems that use ordinary telephone lines. The company recently introduced new products that allow systems to interact with IBM's global network management system. In October, 1991, the company signed a joint venture contract with Cisco Systems to provides a computer network called the RubSystem.

SYNTEX CORPORATION
3401 Hillview Avenue
Palo Alto, California 94304
(415) 855-5050

Founded: 1944. **No. of Employees:** 10,300. **Revenues (1990):** $1.521 billion. **Revenues (1986):** $980 million. **Five-Year Revenue Growth:** 55%.

Description: Syntex is a leading manufacturer of pharmaceuticals and the pioneer of the birth control pill.

How they're growing/Recent developments: The company has a steady stream of new drugs entering the market, bolstered by the strong support of the research and development sector (18% of sales is spent on R&D). Despite its success with "the pill," Syntex continues to diversify. 1991 was a banner year as sales increased 19.5%.

SYSCO CORPORATION
1390 Enclave Parkway
Houston, Texas 77077-2027
(713) 584-1390

Founded: 1962. **No. of Employees:** 20,000. **Revenues (1990):** $7.6 billion. **Revenues (1986):** $3 billion. **Five-Year Revenue Growth:** 153%.

Description: Distributor of food and related products to restaurants, hospitals, nursing homes and motels.

How they're growing/Recent developments: Growth has benefitted from acquisitions. Revenues are expected to grow due to increased market penetration. The company's ongoing construction and modernization programs on schedule. Employment has grown from an estimated 12,000 in 1987 to 20,000 in 1991.

SYSTEM SOFTWARE ASSOCIATES
500 West Madison Street, Suite 3200
Chicago, Illinois 60661
(312) 641-2900

Founded: 1981. **No. of Employees:** 400. **Revenues (1990):** $124 million. **Revenues (1987):** $16 million. **Four-Year Revenue Growth:** 675%.

Description: Develops and markets business planning, control system and software engineering products for IBM mid-range computers.

How they're growing/Recent developments: System Software's product line is licensed worldwide. For the nine months ending July, 31, 1991, revenues rose 20%, aided by an increase in software revenues and growth in client services. Employment has grown from an estimated 280 in 1987 to 400 in 1991.

T^2 MEDICAL
1121 Alderman Drive
Alpharetta, Georgia 30202
(404) 442-2160

Founded: 1984. **No. of Employees:** 602. **Revenues (1990):** $70.6 million.
Revenues (1986): $1.4 million. **Five-Year Revenue Growth:** 4,942%.

Description: A home health care provider specializing in intravenously feeding patients antibiotics and nutrients.

How they're growing/Recent developments: Analysts believe that new therapies for cancer should boost T^2's earnings even more. The company has grown largely through acquisitions, including the November, 1990 purchase of Extendacare Health Services of Dallas. In June, 1991, T^2's signed a joint venture agreement with Tokos Medical Corporation to specialize in the management of physician-owned companies that participate in home uterine activity monitoring.

TAMBRANDS, INC.
777 Westchester Avenue
White Plains, New York 10604
(914) 696-6060

Founded: 1936. **No. of Employees:** 4,700. **Revenues (1990):** $632 million.
Revenues (1986): $487 million. **Five-Year Revenue Growth:** 30%.

Description: The nation's leading manufacturer of tampons; makes Tampax and Maxithins.

How they're growing/Recent developments: Tambrands controlled 59% of the market in 1990. The company's international sales are also increasing, and will be boosted further by the company's 1990 acquisition of a German tampon company.

TANDEM COMPUTERS, INC.
19333 Vallco Parkway, Mail Stop 229-17
Cupertino, California 95014
(408) 725-6000

Founded: 1974. **No. of Employees:** 10,936. **Revenues (1990):** $1.9 billion.
Revenues (1986): $768 million. **Five-Year Revenue Growth:** 147%.

Description: Company provides computers, peripherals and pre-packaged software.

How they're growing/Recent developments: Growth is expected to climb with the start of a strong product cycle, with the introduction of new products, including one that increases the performance of company's mid-range systems by 50%. As the company's largest market is the banking industry, which has continued to cut back capital spending, Tandem will compensate by diversifying to other industries and emphasizing cost control. Employment has grown from an estimated 5,223 in 1987 to 10,936 in 1991.

TANDY CORPORATION
1800 One Tandy Center
Fort Worth, Texas 76102
(817) 390-3700

Contact: George Berger, Vice President of Human Resources. **Founded:** 1899. **No. of Employees:** . **Revenues (1990):** $4.5 billion. **Revenues (1986):** $3.04 billion. **Five-Year Revenue Growth:** 48%.

Description: A leading consumer electronics retailer and manufacturer.

How they're growing/Recent developments: Although Tandy has been hurt by a slumping consumer electronics market, the company announced that it planned to open eight Computer City Supercenters before the end of 1991, after originally planning only six. The company is looking to the future and the emergence of new technologies such as Digital Audio Recording and multimedia computing. In preparation, they have upgraded manufacturing and research and development operations.

TCBY ENTERPRISES
1100 TCBY Tower
425 West Capitol Avenue
Little Rock, Arkansas 72201
(501) 688-8229

Founded: 1984. **No. of Employees:** 2,087. **Revenues (1990):** $151 million. **Revenues (1986):** $40 million. **Five-Year Revenue Growth:** 277%.

Description: Franchise of soft serve frozen yogurt stores.

How they're growing/Recent developments: Due to increased competition and weaker economy, TCBY has introduced new marketing strategies, food items, and cost controls to restore previous levels of profitability. Introduced new products made with TCBY nonfat yogurt and Ultra Slimfast. Employment has grown from an estimated 255 in 1987 to 2,087 in 1991.

TCI INTERNATIONAL, INC.
34175 Ardenwood Boulevard
Fremont, California 94555-3605
(415)795-7800

Founded: 1968. **No. of Employees:** 367. **Revenues (1990):** $59 million. **Revenues (1986):** $41 million. **Five-Year Revenue Growth:** 44%.

Description: Produces and markets signal-collection systems, special purpose communication systems, and high-frequency antenna systems.

How they're growing/Recent developments: Company received a $9.9 million contract from U.S. Information Agency to provide radio station for Voice of America in Botswana. Most of the company's business is with government, military, and diplomatic operations.

TECH DATA CORPORATION
5350 Tech Data Drive
Clearwater, Florida 34620
(813) 539-7429

Contact: Tom Ginetti, Employment Manager. **Founded:** 1974. **No. of Employees:** 710. **Revenues (1990):** $348 million. **Revenues (1986):** $38 million. **Five-Year Revenue Growth:** 815%.

Description: Distributes microcomputers and related hardware and software products.

Common positions include: Accountant; Administrator; Advertising Worker; Blue Collar Worker Supervisor; Buyer; Computer Programmer; Credit Manager; Customer Service Representative; Financial Analyst; Branch Manager; Department Manager; Management Trainee; Operations/Production Manager; Marketing Specialist; Purchasing Agent; Sales Representative; Systems Analyst; Technical Writer/Editor; Technical Support Specialist.

Principal educational backgrounds sought: Accounting; Business Administration; Communications; Computer Science; Finance; Liberal Arts; Marketing.

Company benefits include: Medical insurance; dental insurance; tuition assistance; disability coverage; daycare assistance; profit sharing; employee discounts; savings plan; fitness center.

Operations at this facility include: Administration; service; sales.

How they're growing/Recent developments: Tech Data has grown through its network of distribution centers in key U.S. and Canadian markets. The company has signed agreements with Toshiba, Compaq and other manufacturers to distribute a complete line of laptop and portable computers, hardware and software. Employment has grown from an estimated 360 in 1987 to 710 in 1991.

TECHNE CORPORATION
614 McKinley Place NE
Minneapolis, Minnesota 55413
(612) 379-8854

Founded: 1981. **No. of Employees:** 131 full-time, 26 part-time. **Revenues (1990):** $15.7 million. **Revenues (1986):** $9.1 million. **Five-Year Revenue Growth:** 73%.

Description: TECHNE Corporation is a Minnesota-based holding company with one U.S. operating subsidiary, Research and Diagnostic Systems, Inc. (R&D Systems). R&D Systems' biotechnology products fall into three categories: genes, cytokines and polyclonal and monoclonal antibodies; diagnostic kits for use in clinical research; and diagnostic kits for the clinical diagnostic marketplace, including in particular, the Clinigen Erythropoietin kit recently acquired from Amgen, Inc. (Cytokines are biological proteins found in very small quantities in blood. They are literally the messengers of the cell, sending signals to the cell's genetic machinery that cause it to grow, stop growing or differentiate.) Hematology products include more than a dozen controls and calibrators, in approximately 90 configurations. These products are used throughout the world in hospital and clinical laboratories, on a broad range of automatic and semiautomatic blood cell counting instruments, to verify hematology instrument calibration and to assure the continued quality of hematology test results.

How they're growing/Recent developments: TECHNE's goal is to become the premier supplier of cytokines for research and the dominant supplier of clinical diagnostic kits for the measurement of cytokines. Both the hematology and biotechnology divisions of R&D Systems showed strong sales during 1991. The company recently announced its purchase of Amgen Inc.'s research reagent and diagnostic kit business, thus establishing the company as a leader in cytokine diagnostic assays. The company has also recently signed an agreement with Synergen, Inc. to develop, market and distribute their cytokine proteins as reagents and diagnostic kits. Both Amgen and Synergen are focusing efforts on the development of cytokines for human therapeutic use and are working with R&D Systems to develop the required clinical diagnostic kits for a number of these cytokines. Revenues for 1991 rose to $19.3 million

TECHNICAL AND MANAGEMENT SERVICES (TAMSCO)
4041 Powder Mill Road, Suite 500
Calverton, Maryland 20705
(301) 595-0710

Founded: 1982. **No. of Employees:** 500. **Revenues (1990):** $31.6 million. **Revenues (1986):** $6.3 million. **Five-Year Revenue Growth:** 402%.

Description: TAMSCO'S products and services cover the entire spectrum of disciplines oriented to ADP and telecommunications system development, manufacturing and integration. These include requirements definition, system engineering, systems design, telecommunications network design, software development, electronics and telecommunications equipment hardware development and manufacturing, systems integration, and implementation.

How they're growing/Recent developments: TAMSCO was recently cited by both *Business Week* and *Inc.* magazines as one of the nation's fastest growing high-tech companies. The Federal Aviation Administration selected the company to improve air traffic management through implementation of the company's Dynamic Ocean Track System (DOTS). TAMSCO's staff has risen from 120 employees in 1986 to an estimated 480 in 1991. Sixty-five percent of the company's staff holds undergraduate degrees, and twenty-three percent hold post graduate degrees. The average level of experience is 15 years.

TECHNITROL INC.
1210 Northbrook Drive, Suite 385
Trevose, Pennsylvania 19053
(215) 355-2900

Founded: 1947. **No. of Employees:** 871. **Revenues (1990):** $84 million. **Revenues (1986):** $37 million. **Five-Year Revenue Growth:** 127%.

Description: Produces electrical components and mechanical assemblies.

How they're growing/Recent developments: Technitrol more than doubled its sales base through the 1988 acquisition of GTE's Technical Products unit, a manufacturer of electrical contacts and thermal metal products. In September, 1991, the company acquired Engelhard Corporation's electrical contract business. Also purchased Lloyd Instruments, Ltd., a U.K company with sales of approximately $10 million. Employment has grown from an estimated 667 in 1987 to 871 in 1991.

TEKELEC
26580 West Agoura Road
Calabasas, California 91302
(818) 880-5656

Founded: 1971. **No. of Employees:** 301. **Revenues (1990):** $42.1 million. **Revenues (1986):** $14 million. **Five-Year Revenue Growth:** 201%

Description: Tekelec designs, manufactures and markets diagnostic systems worldwide for the intelligent communications network. Tekelec's products provide monitoring for the major components of the Intelligent Digital Network: protocols, transmission, signaling and cellular. Tekelec's customers include telephone operating companies, equipment manufacturers and corporations that use its systems to design, install, maintain and repair telecommunications and computer equipment. Tekelec products improve the quality and performance of communications networks for the present and the future.

Common positions include: Of the company's 301 employees, 91 are in marketing, sales, and support, 63 in manufacturing, 118 in research, development and engineering and 29 in management, administration, and finance.

How they're growing/Recent developments: During 1990, Tekelec continued its global expansion with 53% of revenues coming from the international marketplace. The company secured several new customers, including Motorola and Bell South. In addition, the company acquired Hard Engineering, a developer and manufacturer of field service protocol analysis systems, and introduced several new products, including the ChameLAN 100 FDDI network analysis system, which is Tekelec's first product in the LAN market.

TELE-COMMUNICATIONS
P.O. Box 5630
Denver, Colorado 80217-9523
(303) 721-5500

Founded: 1968. **No. of Employees:** 34,000. **Revenues (1990):** $3.6 billion. **Revenues (1986):** $646 million. **Five-Year Revenue Growth:** 457%.

Description: Company provides cable and other pay TV services; the largest operator of cable TV systems in the United States.

How they're growing/Recent developments: Company acquired United Artists Entertainment in June, 1991. Also sees growth in subscription levels and higher monthly rates for customers. Also created a spin-off company, Liberty Media Corporation. Employment has grown from an estimated 3,500 in 1987 to 34,000 in 1991.

TELERATE
Harborside Financial Center, 600 Plaza 2
Jersey City, New Jersey 07311
(212) 938-5200

Founded: 1969. **No. of Employees:** 1,900. **Revenues (1990):** $440 million. **Revenues (1987):** $335.7 million. **Four-Year Revenue Growth:** 31%.

Description: Provides data processing and preparation services.

How they're growing/Recent developments: Employment has grown from an estimated 1,200 in 1987 to 1,900 in 1991.

TELXON
P.O. Box 5582
Akron, Ohio 44334-0582
(216) 867-3700

Founded: 1969. **No. of Employees:** 1,270. **Revenues (1990):** $185 million. **Revenues (1986):** $101 million. **Five-Year Revenue Growth:** 83%.

Description: Telxon Corporation designs, develops, manufactures, markets, sells, and services portable, hand-held computer systems.

How they're growing/Recent developments: The company was recently awarded a $3.2 million contract to supply Canada's Purolator Courier with portable computers. Telxon recently introduced its POSXPRESS portable point-of-sale terminal. In addition, the PTC-860 and 960 products introduced in October of 1990, began shipping in June, 1991 and have been very well received. Employment has grown from an estimated 800 in 1987 to 1,270 in 1991.

TERADATA CORPORATION
100 North Sepulveda Boulevard
El Segundo, California 90245
(213) 524-5000

Founded: 1979. **No. of Employees:** 1,644. **Revenues (1990):** $224 million. **Revenue (1987):** $17 million. **Four-Year Revenue Growth:** 1,217%.

Description: Manufacturer and marketer of a high-performance computer systems used in relational database management.

Common positions include: Computer Programmer; Sales Representative; Software Developer.

Educational backgrounds sought include: Computer Science; Engineering.

Company benefits include: Medical insurance; life insurance; dental insurance; tuition assistance; disability coverage; employee discounts; 401k plan.

How they're growing/Recent developments: Teradata has recently introduced a new high-end processor which increases the capability of the company's relational database computer systems. Revenues for the fiscal year ending June 30, 1991, rose 15%, year to year, largely due to the June, 1990 acquisition of Sharebase Corporation, a database manufacturing systems supplier, with revenues in 1989 of $29 million. Earlier in the year, Teradata formed a joint venture with NCR Corporation to develop parallel processing business computer systems. Revenues of fiscal 1991 rose to $258 million. Employment has grown from an estimated 410 in 1987 to 1,644 in 1991.

TEREX CORPORATION
201 West Walnut Street
Green Bay, Wisconsin 54303
(414) 435-5322

Founded: 1925. **No. of Employees:** 8,000. **Revenues (1990):** $1.1 billion. **Revenues (1986):** $33 million. **Five-Year Revenue Growth:** 3,233%.

Description: Provides a wide range of construction, industrial and mining machinery for the mining, logging, and construction industries.

How they're growing/Recent developments: Revenues are boosted by Fruehauf Trailer Corporation, the largest maker of truck trailers in the United States Fruehauf Trailer is 59%-owned by Terex.

TETRA TECHNOLOGIES
25231 Grogans Mill Road, Suite 100
The Woodlands, Texas 77380
(713) 367-1983

Founded: 1981. **No. of Employees:** 371. **Revenues (1990):** $58.1 million. **Revenues (1986):** $22.5 million. **Five-Year Revenue Growth:** 158%.

Description: Waste recycling and treatment service.

How they're growing/Recent developments: In 1991, TETRA acquired TSI, which served the oil industry. The goal is to increase sales to that market. The company has seen major gains in its waste treatment and specialty chemical recycling operations.

THERMO ELECTRON CORPORATION
81 Wyman Street
Waltham, Massachusetts 02254
(617) 622-1000

Founded: 1956. **No. of Employees:** 6,061. **Revenues (1990):** $708 million. **Revenues (1986):** $332 million. **Five-Year Revenue Growth:** 113%.

Description: Develops and sells analytical instruments used to detect and monitor air pollution, radioactivity, toxic metals and other elements. The company also provides environmental and engineering services and lab-based testing.

How they're growing/Recent developments: The company received a service contract worth an estimated $30 million during 1991. In addition, the company recently introduced a new mass spectrometer that should bring in annual revenues of $20 million by 1993. Employment has grown from an estimated 3,899 in 1987 to 6,061 in 1991.

THERMO INSTRUMENT SYSTEMS
P.O. Box 9046
Waltham, Massachusetts 02254-9046
(617) 622-1000

Contact: Fred Florio, Vice President, Human Resources. **Founded:** 1986. **No. of Employees:** 2,640. **Revenues (1990):** $285 million. **Revenues (1986):** $79 million. **Five-Year Revenue Growth:** 261%.

Description: The company develops and sells analytical instruments used to detect and monitor air-pollution, radioactivity, toxic metals, and other elements. The company also provides environmental and engineering services and lab-based testing. Thermo Electron Corporation, also of Waltham, has a controlling interest in the company.

Common positions include: Sales Representative; Marketing Specialist; Scientists; Technical Personnel.

How they're growing/Recent developments: During 1991, the company received a $30 million service contract. In addition, the company's new mass spectrometer is expected to bring in as much as $25 million a year by 1993. Thermo Instrument has its own sales and marketing staff throughout North America, Asia, and Europe. Employment has grown from an estimated 675 in 1987 to 2,640 in 1991.

3COM CORPORATION
5400 Bayfront Plaza
Santa Clara, California 95052
(408) 764-5000

Founded: 1979. **No. of Employees:** 380. **Revenues (1990):** $419 million. **Revenues (1986):** $64 million. **Five-Year Revenue Growth:** 554%.

Description: Manufacture and sale of computer communications systems.

How they're growing/Recent developments: Growth in recent years has been spurred by new product development and by a 1987 merger with Bridge Communications. Revenues however, fell in the 1990-91 fiscal year, and may continue to do so in the short run as the company de-emphasizes the sale of client server products in order to focus on connectivity and inter-networking products.

TIME-WARNER INC.
75 Rockefeller Plaza
New York, New York 10019
(212) 275-8000

Founded: 1922. **No. of Employees:** 35,000. **Revenues (1990):** $11.5 billion. **Revenues (1986):** $3.8 billion. **Five-Year Revenue Growth:** 203%.

Description: A worldwide media and entertainment company with operations in publishing, film, cable television, and music recording. The company publishes 25 magazines including *Time, Sports Illustrated, Life, People,* and

Fortune. Book publishing operations include Little Brown & Co., Warner Books, Book-of-the Month Club and TimeLife, Inc. The film segment includes Warner Bros. and Lorimar Television. Cable includes American Television and Communications and Warner Cable Communications, Home Box Office and Cinema. Music recording includes Warner Bros., Elektra, and Atlantic labels.

How they're growing/Recent developments: When Time Inc. bought Warner Communications, it was one of the biggest mergers of all-time. Revenues have continued to rise since. The merger left the company with a great deal of debt, which in the short term may hamper employment opportunities. But in the long term, new technologies in entertainment and publishing will brighten prospects. In October, 1991, Time-Warner agreed to form a limited partnership with C. Itoh & Co. and Toshiba Corporation, to be called Time-Warner Entertainment. This will include the company's filmed entertainment, cable programming, and cable systems operations.

TJ INTERNATIONAL, INC.
380 East Park Center Boulevard, Suite 300
Boise, Idaho 83706
(208)345-8500

Founded: 1960. **No. of Employees:** 2,700. **Revenues (1990):** $327 million. **Revenues (1986):** $180 million. **Five-Year Revenue Growth:** 82%.

Description: Manufacturer of high-quality wood windows and doors. The company also makes structural items for the light construction industry.

How they're growing/Recent developments: After entering into a joint venture with MacMillan Bloedel, Ltd., a British Columbia-based forest products company, the partnership then acquired Nordel, Inc., a Canadian lumber manufacturer with annual sales of approximately $5 million.

TOKOS MEDICAL
1821 East Dyer Road
Santa Ana, California 92705
(714) 474-1616

Founded: 1983. **No. of Employees:** 1,200. **Revenues (1990):** $75.4 million. **Revenues (1986):** $16.6 million. **Five-Year Revenue Growth:** 354%.

Description: Tokos Medical is home health care services firm dedicated to enhancing medical outcomes for women with complicated obstetrical and gynecological problems.

How they're growing/Recent developments: In August, 1990, Tokos acquired Physiological Diagnostic Service, Inc., a provider of home uterine activity monitoring and perinatal nursing services for high-risk pregnant women. Tokos is currently investing in the development of new technologies that will allow it to expand its obstetrical and gynecological home care services, and to fund research and development of new applications for its products and services. For the six months ending June 30th, 1991, net patient service revenues climbed 43%, year to year.

TOOTSIE ROLL INDUSTRIES
7401 South Cicero Avenue
Chicago, Illinois 60629
(312) 838-3400

Founded: 1919. **No. of Employees:** 1,450. **Revenues (1990):** $194 million. **Revenues (1986):** $111 million. **Five-Year Revenue Growth:** 75%.

Description: A manufacturer and distributor of candy, for the most part under the Tootsie Roll and Charms names.

How they're growing/Recent developments: Acquired Charms Co. in 1988, largest distributor of lollipops in the United States. Tootsie Roll gained record sales in 1990 and during the first quarter of 1991 due to promotions. The company has also been setting sales records in international markets. Employment has grown from an estimated 1,100 in 1987 to 1,450 in 1991.

TOTAL SYSTEM SERVICES, INC.
P.O. Box 120
Columbus, Georgia 31902
(404) 649-4836

Contact: Joyce L. Fowler, Recruiting Director. **Founded:** 1982. **No. of Employees:** 1,264. **Revenues (1990):** $83.9 million. **Revenues (1986):** $36.4 million. **Five-Year Revenue Growth:** 130%

Description: A bank and private label credit card data processing services company.

Common positions include: Computer Programmer; Quality Control Supervisor; Systems Analyst; Technical Writer/Editor.

Educational backgrounds sought include: Computer Science.

Company benefits include: Medical insurance; dental insurance; life insurance; tuition assistance.

Operations at this facility include: Service.

How they're growing/Recent developments: Increases in the number of credit card holders and the addition of new credit card services have pushed revenues to record levels for seven consecutive years. A new facility and new equipment further aid strong sales expectations. Employment has grown from an estimated 300 in 1987 to 1,264 in 1991.

TOYS 'R' US
461 From Road
Paramus, New Jersey 07652
(201) 262-7800

Founded: 1928. **No. of Employees:** 41,000. **Revenues (1990):** $5.5 billion. **Revenues (1986):** $2 billion. **Five-Year Revenue Growth:** 175%.

Description: The largest toy retailer in the nation.

How they're growing/Recent developments: Toys 'R' Us plans aggressive expansion of domestic and international toy operations, as well as their clothing division. The company plans to open 80 stores fiscal 1991-92, including in international markets like Japan and Spain. The company plans an expanded use of high-technology distribution centers to increase productivity.

TRADITIONAL INDUSTRIES, INC.
5155 North Clareton Drive
Agoura Hills, California 91301
(818) 587-6700

Founded: 1976. **No. of Employees:** 160. **Revenues (1990):** $62 million. **Revenues (1986):** $35.85 million. **Five-Year Revenue Growth:** 73%.

Description: Distributor of photography equipment and supplies.

TRANZONIC COMPANIES
30195 Chagrin Boulevard
Pepper Pike, Ohio 44124
(216) 831-5757

Founded: 1946. **No. of Employees:** 842. **Revenues (1990):** $97 million. **Revenues (1986):** $54 million. **Five-Year Revenue Growth:** 80%.

Description: Personal care and home products.

How they're growing/Recent developments: In June, 1988, Tranzonic acquired American Hardware, Inc. and formed its own Housewares Division. In 1989, the company acquired J.C. Baxter Co., a maker of spiral paper tubes. The company's personal care division provides the bulk of the company's profits, through sales of disposable diapers, tampons, condoms and condom dispensing machines. Employment has grown from an estimated 750 in 1987 to 842 in 1991.

TRIAX COMMUNICATIONS
100 Fillmore
Suite 600
Denver, Colorado 80206
(303) 333-2424

Founded: 1982. **No. of Employees:** 461. **Revenues (1990):** $88 million. **Revenues (1986):** $4 million. **Five-Year Revenue Growth:** 2,100%.

Description: Operates cable television systems.

How they're growing/Recent developments: Employment has grown from 141 in 1986 to 461 in 1991.

TRICARE
17101 Armstrong Avenue, Suite 200
Irvine, California 92714
(714) 250-4092

Founded: 1976. **No. of Employees:** 180. **Revenues (1990):** $24.46 million. **Revenues (1988):** $12.98 million. **Three-Year Revenue Growth:** 88%.

Description: Provides occupational health care evaluation services, whose stated purpose is to improve the effectiveness of the delivery of medical services through the California worker's compensation system.

How they're growing/Recent developments: In May, 1990, Tricare acquired Occu-Care, Inc. Between 1988 and 1990, net income rose from $633,000 to $1.6 million.

TRI-COUNTY SECURITY
22930 Woodward
Ferndale, Michigan 48220
(313) 545-7100

Founded: 1984. **No. of Employees:** 419. **Revenues (1990):** $4 million. **Revenues (1986):** $329 thousand. **Five-Year Revenue Growth:** 1,116%.

Description: Provides security and investigative services.

How they're growing/Recent developments: Employment has grown from 97 in 1986 to 419 in 1991.

TRIGEN ENERGY CORPORATION
1 Water Street
White Plains, New York 10601
(914) 948-9150

Founded: 1986. **No. of Employees:** 176. **Revenues (1990):** $31 million. **Revenues (1986):** $957 thousand. **Five-Year Revenue Growth:** 3,139%.

Description: Trigen is an international developer and operator of cogenerated district heating and cooling (DHC) facilities that provide economical heating and cooling to municipalities, commercial builders, industries and institutions.

How they're growing/Recent developments: DHC is energy efficient because fuel is burned at one central source in efficient, manned boilers, and environmentally acceptable because central plants save fuel and have better emissions control than do boilers in individual buildings. Employment has grown from 25 in 1986 to 176 in 1991.

TRIMAS CORPORATION
315 East Eisenhower Parkway, Suite 300
Ann Arbor, Michigan 48108
(313) 747-7025

No. of Employees: 1,600. **Revenues (1990):** $328 million. **Revenues (1987):** $52 million. **Four-Year Revenue Growth:** 531%.

Description: A manufacturer of specialty container products and towing systems.

How they're growing/Recent developments: Management's aggressive acquisitions strategy has been the main force behind the company's growth. In June, 1990, the company acquired Draw-Tite. Sales for the first half of 1991 rose 7.4%, largely due to the Draw-Tite acquisition, which buffered the company from less profitable businesses.

TRIMBLE NAVIGATION, LTD.
585 North Mary Avenue
Sunnyvale, California 94086
(408) 730-2900

Contact: Vickie Fontela, Employment Representative. **Founded:** 1978. **No. of Employees:** 356. **Revenues (1990):** $63.3 million. **Revenues (1986):** $7.4 million. **Five-Year Revenue Growth:** 755%.

Description: Trimble Navigation Limited is a leader in the emerging commercial markets for navigation and positioning data products using the satellite-based Global Positioning System (GPS) technology.

Common positions include: Accountant; Administrator; Computer Programmer; Electrical Engineer; Mechanical Engineer; Operations/Production Manager; Marketing Specialist; Quality Control Supervisor; Sales Representative; Systems Analyst; Technical Writer/Editor.

Principal educational backgrounds sought: Computer Science; Engineering.

Company benefits include: Medical insurance; dental insurance; life insurance; tuition assistance.

Operations at this facility include: Manufacturing; research and development; administration; service; sales.

How they're growing/Recent developments: Trimble is a world leader in satellite-based navigational systems. The company has recently agreed to acquire Avion Systems, a developer of air collision avoidance systems. For the nine months ending September 30, 1991, revenues more than tripled year to year, with growth in all product markets, especially in the area of military systems.

TRINITY INDUSTRIES
2525 Stemmons Freeway
Dallas, Texas 75207
(214) 631-4420

Contact: Jack Cunningham, Vice President of Human Resources. **Founded:** 1933. **No. of Employees:** 9,800. **Revenues (1990):** $1.263 billion. **Revenues (1986):** $436 million. **Five-Year Revenue Growth:** 190%.

Description: Trinity is engaged in the construction and leasing of rail cars and containers, and the manufacture of commercial boats and barges.

How they're growing/Recent developments: The company has been investing heavily to position itself for fast growth in the next few years. Although it has been slowed by the recession and rail car profits will remain flat in 1992, the company's marine division will bounce back strongly. In September, 1991, the company was awarded a major contract from Marine Spill Response Corporation to build 16 vessels. In addition, the company also received a $90 million contract from the U.S. Navy to build two oceanographic survey ships.

TSI, INC.
500 Cardigan Road
Shoreview, Minnesota 55112
(612) 483-0900

Founded: 1961. **No. of Employees:** 370. **Revenues (1990):** $39.7 million. **Revenues (1986):** $20 million. **Five-Year Revenue Growth:** 98%.

Description: The company makes and markets sophisticated instruments and systems for the measurements of flow and flow characteristics of gases, liquids and small airborne particles.

How they're growing/Recent developments: During 1991, TSI signed an agreement with two Japanese firms under which TSI was granted an exclusive license under a U.S. patent to manufacture and sell instruments for the measurement of contamination in ultra-pure water. TSI's license covers the entire world with the exception of East Asia. Employment has grown from an estimated 350 in 1987 to 370 in 1991.

20TH CENTURY INDUSTRIES
Suite 700
6301 Owensmouth Avenue
Woodland Hills, California 91367
(818) 704-3700

Contact: Richard Andre, Vice President of Human Resources. **Founded:** 1967. **No. of Employees:** 1,865. **Revenues (1990):** $715 million. **Revenues (1986):** $366 million. **Five-Year Revenue Growth:** 95%.

Description: 20th Century sells auto and home owners insurance in California, directly to the consumer.

How they're growing/Recent developments: Revenues for the six months ending June 30, 1991, advanced 14% year to year on an increase in policies in force. In August, 1991, the company announced that it had experienced an underwriting profit of $13.2 million in the first half of 1991, up from a loss of $447,000 a year earlier. Employment has grown from an estimated 1,500 in 1987 to 1,865 in 1991.

TYCO LABORATORIES INC.
3 Tyco Park
Exeter, New Hampshire 03833
(603) 778-9700

Founded: 1962. **No. of Employees:** 14,400. **Revenues (1990):** $2.1 billion. **Revenues (1986):** $796 million. **Five-Year Revenue Growth:** 164%.

Description: Manufacturer of fire protection/flow control systems.

How they're growing/Recent developments: Tyco expanded international operations with the August, 1990 acquisition of a large Australian fire protection and detection company. Operations outside of the United States accounted for 30% of sales in fiscal 1991. Revenues jumped to $3.1 billion in 1991. Employment has grown from an estimated 11,000 in 1987 to 14,400 in 1991.

TYSON FOODS
P.O. Box 2020
Springdale, Arkansas 72765
(501) 756-4000

Founded: 1934. **No. of Employees:** 25,000. **Revenues (1990):** $3.8 billion. **Revenues (1987):** $1.5 billion. **Four-Year Revenue Growth:** 153%.

Description: Producers of poultry products, including broiler, fryer, and roaster chickens.

How they're growing/Recent developments: Tyson acquired Holly Farms Corporation in 1989, and thus strengthened its leading position in poultry while also expanding into the beef and pork markets. Sales are expected to continue increasing due to higher poultry sales. Increased operating margins will boost profits.

ULTIMATE CORPORATION
717 Ridgedale Avenue
East Hanover, New Jersey 07936
(201) 887-9222

Founded: 1978. **No. of Employees:** 494. **Revenues (1990):** $186 million. **Revenues (1986):** $138 million. **Five-Year Revenue Growth:** 35%.

Description: Company interprets and designs mini-computer systems for use in business applications.

How they're growing/Recent developments: Although the company suffered a fiscal 1990-91 loss due to soft markets, it has returned to profitability, aided by cost controls. Early results of a new product, Ultimate PLUS Business Operating Environment have been outstanding. Employment has grown from an estimated 450 in 1987 to 494 in 1991.

UNIFORCE TEMPORARY PERSONNEL, INC.
1335 Jericho Turnpike
New Hyde Park, New York 11040
(516) 437-3300

Founded: 1961. **No. of Employees:** 80. **Revenues (1990):** $113.4 million. **Revenues (1986):** $60.2 million. **Five-Year Revenue Growth:** 88%.

Description: Provides temporary personnel services through a network comprised of 97 (predominantly licensed) independently owned and operated temporary personnel offices, supplemented by a small core of company owned units.

How they're growing/Recent developments: Management feels that its structure is centered around the company's "partnership" with its licensees. Licensees retain total equity and autonomy in their local businesses, while the headquarters offers centralized services where necessary. Uniforce's growth strategy incorporates its "Santa Claus Program" in which Uniforce licensees can acquire independent temp services in their territories and pay only half of the cost. The corporate office pays the rest of the acquisition cost.

UNITED GAMING, INC.
4380 Boulder Highway
Las Vegas, Nevada 89121
(702) 435-4200

Founded: 1968. **No. of Employees:** 962. **Revenues (1990):** $89 million. **Revenues (1986):** $34 million. **Five-Year Revenue Growth:** 162%.

Description: United Gaming is the largest gaming machine route vendor in Nevada. The company also makes and markets video games and operates a casino.

How they're growing/Recent developments: The company makes 90% of machines used in route sales. In 1990, the company bought the Plantation Casino in Sparks, Nevada.

UNITED PARCEL SERVICE OF AMERICA, INC.
Greenwich Office Park 5
Greenwich, Connecticut 06831
(203) 862-6000

Founded: 1907. **No. of Employees:** 246,800. **Revenues (1990):** $13.606 billion. **Revenues (1986):** $8.620 billion. **Five-Year Revenue Growth:** 58%.

Description: The world's largest package delivery service.

How they're growing/Recent developments: UPS is growing through acquisition and expansion. Employment has grown by 78,600 between 1986 and 1990. The company obtained 9.5% of Mail Boxes, Etc., the nation's leading neighborhood mailing and business service center franchise. UPS has expanded into Poland, Czechoslovakia, Hungary, Yugoslavia, Romania, and the former Soviet Union, and has obtained a piece of the Japanese market through a joint venture formed with Yamato Transport in 1990. Employment has grown from an estimated 191,000 in 1987 to 246,800 in 1991.

UNIVAR CORPORATION
P.O. Box 34325
Seattle, Washington 98124-1325
(206) 889-3400

Founded: 1966. **No. of Employees:** 2,833. **Revenues (1990):** $1.38 billion. **Revenues (1986):** $693 million. **Five-Year Revenue Growth:** 99%.

Description: Distribution of industrial, textile, and agricultural chemicals.

How they're growing/Recent developments: The acquisition of McKesson Chemical in 1986 made Univar the largest industrial chemical distributor in the United States. Employment has grown from an estimated 2,460 in 1987 to 2,833 in 1991.

UNIVERSAL CORPORATION
P.O. Box 25099
Richmond, Virginia 23260
(804) 359-9311

Founded: 1918. **No. of Employees:** 20,000. **Revenues (1990):** $2.8 billion. **Revenues (1986):** $1.1 billion. **Five-Year Revenue Growth:** 155%.

Description: The holding company for world's largest independent tobacco dealer, Universal Leaf Tobacco Co. Also distributes lumber in Europe and sells title insurance on real estate.

How they're growing/Recent developments: Philip Morris accounted for 29% of the company's tobacco revenue. Revenues for the nine months ending March, 1991 advanced 17% year to year due to acquisitions. The company acquired a German international tobacco trading group with $200 million annual gross sales.

UNIVERSAL MEDICAL BUILDINGS L.P.
731 North Jackson Street
Milwaukee, Wisconsin 53202
(414) 278-0100

Founded: 1981. **No. of Employees:** 130. **Revenues (1990):** $96 million. **Revenues (1986):** $22 million. **Five-Year Revenue Growth:** 336%.

Description: Designs, develops, and builds a range of health care facilities from office buildings, HMOs, and urgent care centers to clinics.

How they're growing/Recent developments: As of June, 1991, the company had a development contract backlog worth over $300 million. Employment has grown from an estimated 120 in 1987 to 130 in 1991.

THE UPJOHN COMPANY
7000 Portage Road
Kalamazoo, Michigan 49001
(616) 323-4000

Founded: 1886. **No. of Employees:** 18,500. **Revenues (1990):** $3.033 billion. **Revenues (1986):** $2.291 billion. **Five-Year Revenue Growth:** 32%.

Description: A leading producer of pharmaceutical, as well as chemicals, seeds, and animal health products. The company's well known products are the pain-reliever Motrin and the baldness treatment Rogaine.

How they're growing/Recent developments: Upjohn is dedicated to new product development, spending 14% of sales on research and development. Current hopes lie in drug treatments for irregular heartbeat, cancer, diabetes, and AIDS.

US HEALTHCARE, INC.
1425 Union Meeting Road
Blue Bell, Pennslyvania 19422
(215) 628-4800

Founded: 1982. **No. of Employees:** 2,203. **Revenues (1990):** $1.3 billion. **Revenues (1986):** $502 million. **Five-Year Revenue Growth:** 159%.

Description: Owns and operates HMOs throughout the country, in the Mid-Atlantic, Greater New York and New England.

How they're growing/Recent developments: The company holds a 21% interest in U.S. Bioscience, a pharmaceuticals company formed in 1987 to develop and market new cancer drugs. Total revenues for the first half of 1991 rose 26% year to year, aided by an increase in membership. Employment has grown from an estimated 1,075 in 1987 to 2,203 in 1991.

USMX INC.
141 Union Boulevard, Suite 100
Lakewood, Colorado 80228
(303) 985-4665

Founded: 1979. **No. of Employees:** 76. **Revenues (1990):** $15 million. **Revenues (1986):** $10 thousand. **Five-Year Revenue Growth:** 14,900%.

Description: USMX is engaged in the production and development of gold properties in the Western United States.

How they're growing/Recent developments: In May, 1991, USMX announced its third discovery of the year of potentially significant gold mineralization at Alligator Ridge in White Pine Country, Nevada.

US SURGICAL CORPORATION
150 Glover Avenue
Norwalk, Connecticut 06856
(203) 845-1000

Founded: 1960. **No. of Employees:** 4,600. **Revenues (1990):** $514 million. **Revenues (1986):** $206 million. **Five-Year Revenue Growth:** 150%.

Description: Develops, manufactures, and markets Autosuture, a patented surgical stapling device.

How they're growing/Recent developments: In July of 1991, the company announced an agreement with Biomet, Inc. to jointly develop a new line of absorbable orthopedic products. The company's laparoscopy products are currently showing strong sales. Research and development is focused on a synthetic bone and hard tissue substitute.

UTAH MEDICAL PRODUCTS, INC.
7043 South 300 West
Midvale, Utah 84047
(801) 566-1200

Founded: 1978. **No. of Employees:** 319. **Revenues (1990):** $23.9 million. **Revenues (1986):** $5.7 million. **Five-Year Revenue Growth:** 319%.

Description: A provider of critical care medical equipment to hospitals.

How they're growing/Recent developments: In December, 1987, the company was awarded a six-year, $40 million contract by Baxter Healthcare Corporation. Dedication to research and development has resulted in new products like the Intran line, which is used to measure intrauterine pressure in high-risk childbirth. Employment has grown from an estimated 105 in 1987 to 319 in 1991.

UTILX
22404 66th Avenue South
Kent, Washington 98032
(206) 395-0200

Founded: 1984. **No. of Employees:** 438. **Revenues (1990):** $41 million. **Revenues (1987):** $12.8 million. **Four-Year Revenue Growth:** 220%.

Description: Cable and pipe installer.

How they're growing/Recent developments: In October, 1991, Utilx signed an agreement with Dow Corning in which Utilx became the exclusive licensee of Dow Corning's CableCure Technology. In 1990, the company acquired Revalt, a company that specializes in sealing underground manholes from gases and water.

VALLEN CORPORATION
P.O. Box 218
Carlisle, Pennsylvania 17013
(717) 766-0711

Founded: 1947. **No. of Employees:** 590. **Revenues (1990):** $99 million. **Revenues (1987):** $67.64 million. **Four-Year Revenue Growth:** 46%.

Description: Manufacturer and distributor of a wide variety of industrial safety and health products. Also makes industrial safety equipment.

How they're growing/Recent developments: The company opened a new branch in Richmond, Virginia, in 1991, and completed a building manufacturing plant in Houston. Employment has grown from an estimated 350 in 1987 to 590 in 1991.

VALMONT INDUSTRIES, INC.
P.O. Box 358
Valley, Nevada 68064-0358
(402)359-2201

Founded: 1974. **No. of Employees:** 5,030. **Revenues (1990):** $874 million. **Revenues (1986):** $313 million. **Five-Year Revenue Growth:** 179%.

Description: Manufactures steel reinforcing bars and mechanized irrigation equipment.

How they're growing/Recent developments: Valmont recently acquired a 50% interest in Rudolf Bauer, A.G., an Austrian irrigation company. Management has set its goal to be the world's top irrigation company. Employment has grown from an estimated 3,700 in 1987 to 5,030 in 1991.

VALSPAR CORP.
1101 South Third Street
Minneapolis, Minnesota 55415
(612) 332-7371

Founded: 1934. **No. of Employees:** 2,700. **Revenues (1990):** $571 million. **Revenues (1986):** $345 million. **Five-Year Revenue Growth:** 66%.

Description: A major maker of industrial coatings and consumer paints.

How they're growing/Recent developments: Valspar has acquired the powder coatings assets and operations of Reliable Coatings, Inc., and the container coatings assets from Hi-Tek Polymers, Inc.

VALUE MERCHANTS
710 North Plankinton Avenue
Milwaukee, Wisconsin 53203
(414) 274-2575

Founded: 1969. **No. of Employees:** 1900. **Revenues (1990):** $140 million. **Revenues (1986):** $22 million. **Five-Year Revenue Growth:** 536%.

Description: Operates a nationwide system of wholesale closeout toy stores.

How they're growing/Recent developments: The company completed acquisition of the Everythings-A-Dollar chain of 121 retail close-out stores. Net sales for the 16 weeks ending May 25, 1991, advanced 74% year to year, reflecting the increase in operating stores.

VANGUARD CELLULAR SYSTEMS
2002 Pisgah Church Road, Suite 300
Greensboro, North Carolina 27408
(919) 282-3690

Founded: 1983. **No. of Employees:** 580. **Revenues (1990):** $64.2 million. **Revenues (1986):** $ 2.4 million. **Five-Year Revenue Growth:** 2,575%.

Description: The fifth-largest cellular phone systems company in the United States.

How they're growing/Recent developments: A solid sales and marketing strategy has raised the company's total base of subscribers to over $5.7 million. In June, 1991, the company agreed to acquire a rural service area in Pennsylvania, covering a population of over 69,000. Employment has grown from an estimated 155 in 1987 to 580 in 1991.

VENCOR, INC.
700 Brown & Williamson Tower
Louisville, Kentucky 40202
(502) 569-7300

Founded: 1985. **No. of Employees:** 2,500. **Revenues (1990):** $78.3 million. **Revenues (1986):** $8.4 million. **Five-Year Revenue Growth:** 832%.

Description: Providers of care to chronically ill patients; the company operates 19 hospitals.

How they're growing/Recent developments: The company has an aggressive acquisitions program, having acquired six hospitals in 1991 alone. For the nine months ending September 30, 1991, net revenues advanced 73%.

VERDIX CORPORATION
14130-A Sullyfield Circle
Chantilly, Virginia 22021
(703) 378-7600

Founded: 1982. **No. of Employees:** 70. **Revenues (1990):** $11.4 million.
Revenues (1986): $3.8 million. **Five-Year Revenue Growth:** 200%.

Description: Manufacturers of computer systems and software tools, specializing in computer security and Ada computer language develop systems for government and industrial clients.

How they're growing/Recent developments: Verdix is finishing the development of a new product that will combine Verdix Ada Development System (VADS) technology with computer aided software engineering products from other suppliers. In November, 1991, the company agreed to acquire Meridian Software Systems, an Irvine, California, marketer of desktop software engineering tools. Revenue for fiscal 1991 increased another 16% over 1990 to $13.3 million. Employment has grown from an estimated 57 in 1987 to 70 in 1991.

VERIFONE, INC.
Three Lagoon Drive
Suite 400
Redwood City, California 94065
(415) 591-6500

Founded: 1981. **No. of Employees:** 900. **Revenues (1990):** $155 million.
Revenues (1986): $31 million. **Five-Year Revenue Growth:** 400%.

Description: The company produces transaction automation systems. The company manufactures its products primarily through facilities in Taiwan.

How they're growing/Recent developments: New products include transaction systems for the retail payment processing market. Management's growth strategy has been to attempt to increase the company's penetration of the U.S. payment processing market, boost the average systems sales price per transaction site, speed up the replacement of existing systems by offering new products with enhanced features and applications software programs, expand into new segments of the payment processing market by developing multi-lane retailers, fast-food restaurants, movie theaters and taxis, develop the international payment processing market, and develop new markets for transaction automation.

VESTRO FOODS, INC.
12 Corporate Plaza, Suite 100
Newport Beach, California 92660
(714) 760-0354

Founded: 1984. **No. of Employees:** 170. **Revenues (1990):** $33 million. **Revenues (1986):** $742 thousand. **Five-Year Revenue Growth:** 4,368%.

Description: Vestro Foods is engaged in the acquisition, ownership, and operation of specialty food businesses. Subsidiaries include Little Bear and Westbrae Natural, which make up the Natural Foods Group; and Heidi's Pastry, which makes up the Fine Baked Goods Group.

How they're growing/Recent developments: During 1990, sales of all subsidiaries increased, and focus on major customers and broader geographic penetration was intensified to improve coverage and service capabilities. In addition, the company acquired Jan Holzmeister Cheesecake, Ltd. in May, 1990. Employment has grown from 12 in 1987 to 170 in 1991.

VIACOM INC.
1515 Broadway
New York, New York 10036
(212) 258-6000

Founded: 1986. **No. of Employees:** 5,000. **Revenues (1990):** $1.6 billion. **Revenues (1986):** $941 million. **Five-Year Revenue Growth:** 66%.

Description: Produces motion pictures and videos, and also runs radio broadcasting stations.

How they're growing/Recent developments: Earnings are expected to grow due to as the economy strengthens and demand for television advertising improves. Proceeds from the mid-1991 sale of common shares have redeemed a large amount of debt. In August, 1991, the company acquired the 50.01% interest in MTV Europe that it did not already own. Distributes "The Cosby Show".

VIATECH, INC.
One Aerial Way
Syosset, New York 11791
(516) 822-4940

Founded: 1934. **No. of Employees:** 1,733. **Revenues (1990):** $292 million. **Revenues (1986):** $50 million. **Five-Year Revenue Growth:** 484%.

Description: Viatech is a diversified services company offering packaging, engineering, survey and mapping services.

How they're growing/Recent developments: Viatech owns a majority interest in Ferembal, the second-largest French manufacturer of food cans. Other overseas subsidiaries include packaging manufacturers in Spain and the United Kingdom. Employment has grown from an estimated 175 in 1987 to 1,733 in 1991.

VIDEO DISPLAY CORPORATION
1868 Tucker Industrial Drive
Tucker, Georgia 30084
(404) 938-2080

Founded: 1975. **No. of Employees:** 478. **Revenues (1990):** $54.5 million. **Revenues (1986):** $13 million. **Five-Year Revenue Growth:** 319%.

Description: Video Display makes and distributes rebuilt and new cathode ray tubes (CRTs) mainly for television sets.

How they're growing/Recent developments: During 1989 and 1990, the company entered into an agreement to deliver $10.3 million in goods and services for the expansion of an existing semiconductor facility in Algeria. The contract is currently nearing completion. Employment has grown from an estimated 340 in 1987 to 478 in 1991.

VIKING OFFICE PRODUCTS
13809 South Figueroa Street
Los Angeles, California 90061
(213) 321-4493

Founded: 1960. **No. of Employees:** 808. **Revenues (1990):** $158 million. **Revenues (1986):** $81 million. **Five-Year Revenue Growth:** 95%.

Description: Viking markets office products to small and mid-sized companies through direct-mail catalogs.

How they're growing/Recent developments: Viking uses innovative and aggressive direct marketing catalogs, through which most of the company's sales are made at 30% to 50% below list prices. In 1990, the company expanded overseas by setting up a major distribution center in Leicester, England.

VISHAY INTERTECHNOLOGY
63 Lincoln Highway
Malvern, Pennsylvania 19355
(215) 644-1300

Founded: 1962. **No. of Employees:** 8,500. 3,900 in the United States. **Revenues (1990):** $446 million. **Revenues (1986):** $59 million. **Five-Year Revenue Growth:** 656%.

Description: Manufacturers of resistor-based stress measurement sensors.

How they're growing/Recent developments: Acquisitions have significantly raised Vishay's sales base, and the company plans to further penetrate markets and cut costs. In April, 1991, Vishay acquired Aztronic (France) which makes insulators and transformers. Vishay's main U.S. employment centers are Malvern and Bradford, PA; Columbus and Norfolk, NE; Raleigh, NC. and El Paso, TX. Other facilities are in Colorado, Maryland, Michigan, and South Dakota. Employment has grown from an estimated 7,500 in 1987 to 12,400 in 1991.

VITAL SIGNS
20 Campus Road
Totowa, New Jersey 07512
(201) 790-1330

Founded: 1972. **No. of Employees:** 315 full-time, 110 part-time. **Revenues (1990):** $38.5 million. **Revenues (1986):** $15.5 million. **Five-Year Revenue Growth:** 148%.

Description: Designs manufactures and markets single-patient use medical products for anesthesia, respiratory and critical care applications.

How they're growing/Recent developments: Vital Signs is a pioneer in the disposable medical products market. The company was the first to introduce such products as air-filled cushion face masks and clear nonconductive anesthesia kits. These products have captured an increasing share of the medical products market, primarily because of their cost advantages and improved patient care features. The Company believes that its ability to understand the needs of hospitals, providers and patients, and develop products geared towards meeting those needs, is enhanced by its concentration on this specialized market. Revenues increased in fiscal 1991 to $49 million.

VIVIGEN INC.
2000 Vivigen Way
Santa Fe, New Mexico 87505
(505) 473-4728

Founded: 1981. **No. of Employees:** 126. **Revenues (1990):** $11 million. **Revenues (1986):** $2 million. **Five-Year Revenue Growth:** 450%.

Description: Vivigen performs clinical biochemical and molecular chromosome analysis to detect genetic diseases and some types of cancer.

How they're growing/Recent developments: In June, 1991, Vivigen signed an agreement with Baxter International-Caremark Women's Health Network to market Vivigen's products and services to group customers and doctors. Employment has grown from an estimated 76 in 1987 to 126 in 1991.

VONS COMPANIES
618 Michillinda Avenue
Arcadia, California 91007
(818) 821-7000

Founded: 1987. **No. of Employees:** 35,000. **Revenues (1990):** $5.2 billion. **Revenues (1986):** $3.0 billion. **Five-Year Revenue Growth:** 73%.

Description: Owns and operates chains of supermarkets and food and drug stores in Southern California and Las Vegas.

How they're growing/Recent developments: The company acquired Safeway's Southern California stores in 1988. Employment has grown from an estimated 22,000 in 1987 to 35,000 in 1991.

WABASH NATIONAL CORPORATION
P.O. Box 6129
Lafayette, Indiana 47903
(317) 448-1591

Founded: 1985. **No. of Employees:** 1,100. **Revenues (1990):** $170.1 million. **Revenues (1986):** $69.2 million. **Five-Year Revenue Growth:** 170.7%.

Description: Wabash National designs, manufactures and markets standard and customized truck trailers, including dry freight vans, refrigerated trailers and bimodal vehicles, as well as parts and related equipment. The company believes that it is among the three largest U.S. manufacturers of truck trailers and the leading manufacturer of both fiberglass reinforced plastic van trailers and aluminum plate trailers. In addition, the company is the exclusive manufacturer of "RoadRailer," a bimodal technology consisting of trailers and detachable rail bogies that permit a vehicle to run both over the highway and directly on railroad lines. Wabash markets its products through dealers to truckload and less-than-truckload common carriers, private fleet operators, household moving and storage companies, package carriers and intermodal carriers including railroads. Major customers include: Schnieder National, Roadway Express, K mart Corporation, Allied Van Lines, and many others.

How they're growing/Recent developments: Wabash National is now one of the largest U.S. manufacturers of truck trailers. Despite difficult times for the industry as a whole, Wabash saw its earnings advance strongly due to increased sales of higher priced new products. As of September 30, 1991, the company's order backlog stood at over $100 million, an increase of 100% over a year earlier.

WALGREEN CO.
200 Wilmot Road
Deerfield, Illinois 60015
(708) 940-2500

Founded: 1901. **No. of Employees:** 50,000. **Revenues (1990):** $6 billion. **Revenues (1986):** $3.7 billion. **Five-Year Revenue Growth:** 62%.

Description· Largest U.S. retail drug store chain.

How they're growing/Recent developments: Almost 80% of all Walgreen stores have been remodelled or opened within the last five years. One hundred million prescriptions were filled in 1990. Advances in satellite technology have allowed the company to link all stores through an intercom and online pharmacy system.

WALLACE COMPUTER SERVICES, INC.
4600 West Roosevelt Road
Hillside, Illinois 60162
(708) 449-8600

Founded: 1908. **No. of Employees:** 3,000. **Revenues (1990):** $449 million. **Revenues (1986):** $305 million. **Five-Year Revenue Growth:** 47%.

Description: A manufacturer of business forms, mainly for computer applications. Wallace also does printing and direct marketing for small businesses.

Common positions include: Accountant; Computer Programmer; Management Trainee; Sales Representative.

Principal educational backgrounds sought: Accounting; Business Administration; Computer Science; Marketing.

Company benefits include: Medical insurance; dental insurance; life insurance; disability coverage; profit sharing; savings plan.

Operations at this facility include: Manufacturing; research/development; administration.

How they're growing/Recent developments: During 1991, Wallace agreed to acquire MG Industries, Inc., a company with 1990 sales of $45 million. Wallace has spent $163 million on new facilities and equipment within last five years. Employment has grown from an estimated 2,600 in 1987 to 3,000 in 1991.

WAL-MART STORES, INC.
702 South West Eighth Street
Bentonville, Arkansas 72716
(501) 273-4000

Founded: 1969. **No. of Employees:** 328,000. **Revenues (1990):** $32 billion. **Revenues (1986):** $12 billion. **Five-Year Revenue Growth:** 167%.

Description: Wal-Mart operates a chain of retail department stores.

How they're growing/Recent developments: Strong base expansion and an aggressive pricing posture should facilitate market share gains in Wal-Mart division, while the improving profitability of the wholesale clubs should enhance longer term prospects. The company has pared operating costs and has improved inventory management. 35 more store openings planned for 91-

92, as well as the expansion of 150-160 stores and two supercenter stores. A February, 1991 merger with 28 units of The Wholesale Club was expected, along with the acquisition of McLane Co. in 1990.

WARNER-LAMBERT COMPANY
201 Tabor Road
Morris Plains, New Jersey 07950
(201) 540-2000

Founded: 1856. **No of Employees:** 34,000; **Revenues (1990):** $4.687 billion; **Revenues (1986):** $3.103 billion; **Five-Year Revenue Growth:** 51%.

Description: A major producer of pharmaceuticals and over-the-counter health care products.

How they're growing/Recent developments: Warner-Lambert sells the most breath mint and gum brands in the world. In 1990, the company invested $379 million (8% of sales) in research and development, and plans to spend $2 billion in that area over the next five years. Warner is waiting for FDA approval on Cognex, the first drug to treat Alzheimer's disease. Through subsidiaries, the company holds the number one position in the aquarium products industry, and is the leader in gelatin capsules for the pharmaceutical industry.

WASTE MANAGEMENT INC.
3003 Butterfield Road
Oak Brook, Illinois 60521
(708) 572-8800

Founded: 1968. **No. of Employees:** 62,050. **Revenues (1990):** $6 billion. **Revenues (1986):** $2 billion. **Five-Year Revenue Growth:** 200%.

Description: The nation's largest provider of waste management services; engages in the collection and disposal of solid, liquid, chemical, nuclear, and hazardous waste. Also provides environmental services to Europe, Australia, Saudi Arabia, and Venezuela.

How they're growing/Recent developments: The company expects more municipal contracts, and continued international expansion. Employment has grown from an estimated 30,000 in 1987 to 62,050 in 1991.

WATSCO, INC.
2665 South Bayshore Drive
Coconut Grove, Florida 33133
(305) 858-0828

Contact: Ray Koniecke, Director of Recruitment. **Founded:** 1956. **No. of Employees:** 680. **Revenues (1990):** $118 million. **Revenues (1986):** $15 million. **Five-Year Revenue Growth:** 687%.

Description: A holding company whose subsidiaries distribute residential central air conditioners, manufacture climate control equipment and run temporary and permanent placement offices.

Common positions include: Accountant; Draftsperson; Industrial Engineer; Purchasing Agent.

Principal educational backgrounds include: Accounting; Business Administration; Engineering.

Company benefits include: Medical insurance; dental insurance; pension plan; life insurance; tuition assistance; disability coverage.

Operations at this facility include: Manufacturing; sales.

How they're growing/Recent developments: Through 1990 acquisition of Heating and Cooling Supply, Inc., became largest independent distributor of central AC equipment. Acquired Dunhill Personnel in 1988. The company expects revenue increases due to come with an improved economy. In June, 1991, the company opened its first Nevada distribution facility in Las Vegas. Employment has grown from an estimated 300 in 1987 to 680 in 1991.

WATTS INDUSTRIES
P.O. Box 628
Lawrence, Massachusetts 01842
(508) 688-1811

Founded: 1874. **No. of Employees:** 2,650. **Revenues (1990):** $292 million. **Revenues (1986):** $137 million. **Five-Year Revenue Growth:** 113%.

Description: Makers of a line of valves for the water safety and flow control, water quality and industrial markets.

How they're growing/Recent developments: Business has continued to improve, largely on the strength of acquisitions. In September, 1991, for example, Watts acquired Henry Pratt Co., a water distribution valve maker. Employment has grown from an estimated 1,500 in 1987 to 2,650 in 1991.

WAXMAN INDUSTRIES, INC.
24460 Aurora Road
Bedford Heights, Ohio 44176
(216) 439-1830

Founded: 1962. **No. of Employees:** 1,796. **Revenues (1990):** $449 million. **Revenues (1986):** $98 million. **Five-Year Revenue Growth:** 358%.

Description: Provides plumbing and hydronic heating supplies in United States and Canada.

How they're growing/Recent developments: K mart Corporation recently selected Waxman as its vendor for K mart's national program for "carded" plumbing products. The first shipments to K mart were expected early in 1992. Employment has grown from an estimated 800 in 1987 to 1,796 in 1991.

WERNER ENTERPRISES
P.O. Box 37308
Omaha, Nebraska 68137
(402) 895-6640

Founded: 1956. **No. of Employees:** 1,965. **Revenues (1990):** $251.6 million. **Revenues (1987):** $94.4 million. **Four-Year Revenue Growth:** 167%.

Description: Werner Enterprises is a leading truckload carrier transporting a wide range of commodities throughout the continental United States and portions of Canada.

How they're growing/Recent developments: Despite an industry-wide slowdown and a surge in fuel prices, Werner had another record year in 1991. Revenues grew 21%, reaching $305.3 million. The increase in revenues was largely due to increased rates and a fuel surcharge. Werner won the Chilton's Quality Carrier award for the second year in a row; the award reflects the opinions of about 2,300 shippers throughout the United States who rank carriers based on service, convenience, price, and sales criteria. In addition, the company has improved the quality of its driver workforce by adjusting its pay scale to attract more experienced drivers. The company also added about 100 new tractors to its fleet.

WET SEAL, INC.
64 Fairbanks
Irvine, California 92718
(714) 583-9029

Founded: 1962. **No. of Employees:** 350. **Revenues (1990):** $107 million. **Revenues (1986):** $11 million. **Five-Year Revenue Growth:** 873%

Description: Retailers of women's clothing and accessories.

How they're growing/Recent developments: Since its acquisition by a Canadian retailer in 1989, Wet Seal has expanded rapidly. The company expected to open 15 stores during the remainder of 1991-92.

WILLIAMS-SONOMA, INC.
100 North Point Street
San Francisco, California 94133
(415) 421-7900

Founded: 1956. **No. of Employees:** 2,500. **Revenues (1990):** $287 million. **Revenues (1986):** $104.6 million. **Five-Year Revenue Growth:** 174%.

Description: Williams-Sonoma, Inc. operates three retail concepts (Williams-Sonoma, Pottery Barn, and Hold Everything), one direct sales organization (California Closet Company) and five mail-order businesses (Williams-Sonoma, Hold Everything, Gardener's Eden, Pottery Barn and Chambers).

How they're growing/Recent developments: In May, 1988, the company entered into a joint venture agreement with Tokyu Department Store Company to establish Williams-Sonoma Japan. Employment has grown from an estimated 800 in 1987 to 2,500 in 1991.

WINDMERE CORPORATION
5980 Miami Lakes Drive
Miami Lakes, Florida 33014
(305) 362-2611

Founded: 1963. **No. of Employees:** 350. **Revenues (1990):** $155 million. **Revenues (1986):** $95 million. **Five-Year Revenue Growth:** 63%.

Description: Produces and sells health care products, electric appliances, and personal care items.

WORDPERFECT CORPORATION
1555 North Technology Way
Orem, Utah 84057
(801) 222-4000

Founded: 1979. **No. of Employees:** 1,600. **Revenues (1990):** $452 million.
Revenues (1986): $52 million **Five-Year Revenue Growth:** 769%

Description: Providers of business-oriented word processing computer software.

How they're growing/Recent developments: Improving upon its immensely popular word processing program with office for Macs version 3.0, which enables users to exchange messages with PC users. Version 3.02 adds remote messaging and message organizing capabilities. The company provide a toll free service, whose 680 operators handle 14,000 calls a day. In July, 1991, WordPerfect Office for Macs version 3.0 garnered praise among its early users. Revenues for 1991 reached $532 million

WM. WRIGLEY JR. COMPANY
410 North Michigan Avenue
Chicago, Illinois 60611
(312) 644-2121

Founded: 1898. **No. of Employees:** 5,463. **Revenues (1990):** $1.11 billion.
Revenues (1986): $699 million. **Five-Year Revenue Growth:** 59%.

Description: Having celebrated its 100 year anniversary in 1991, Wrigley remains the world's foremost producer of chewing gum.

How they're growing/Recent developments: Wrigley is famous for its fiscally conservative management. The company responds cautiously to the marketplace before making any moves, and is free of long-term debt. In 1991, Amurol Products, the Wrigley subsidiary that produces the well known Hubba Bubba gum, introduced Michael Jordan Hang Time shredded gum. Both foreign and domestic sales are increasing.

XILINX, INC.
2100 Logic Drive
San Jose, California 95124
(408) 559-7778

Founded: 1984. **No. of Employees:** 332. **Revenues (1990):** $49.9 million. **Revenues (1987):** $4.4 million. **Four-Year Revenue Growth:** 1,034%.

Description: Xilinx is a designer and manufacturer of proprietary field programmable gate arrays (FPGAs), and related development system software. These products provide significant time and cost savings and increased flexibility over traditional logic solutions.

How they're growing/Recent developments: Xilinx is one of the fastest growing companies in the semiconductor industry. Xilinx's revenues rocketed to $97.6 million in 1991, a 95% increase over 1990. 1990 revenues had increased 65% over those for 1989. The company shipped a record number of FPGAs in 1991. Xilinx now has more than 10,000 development systems installed at more than 3,500 customers worldwide. European sales contributed $16 million to 1991 revenues, and Japanese and Far East sales were $15 million. With more than 50% of Xilinx's development system software installed outside North America, the company expects the international marketplace to continue to be a major contributor to corporate growth. Between March, 1990 and March, 1991, the company's employee population grew by 39%, from 239 to 332 employees. In 1989, the company employed 152.

XL DATACOMP, INC.
908 North Elm Street
Hinsdale, Illinois 60521
(708) 323-1200

Founded: 1979. **No. of Employees:** 1,200. **Revenues (1990):** $449.6 million. **Revenues (1987):** $93.8 million. **Four-Year Revenue Growth:** 379%.

Description: XL/Datacomp is one of the nation's largest full-service distributors of IBM midrange computer systems, applications software, and support services.

Common positions include: Accountant; Administrator; Advertising Worker; Architect; Attorney; Computer Programmer; Credit Manager; Customer Service Representative; Financial Analyst; Branch Manager; Marketing Specialist; Public Relations Specialist; Sales Representative; Systems Analyst; Technical Writer/Editor.

Educational backgrounds sought: Accounting; Art/Design; Biology; Business Administration; Chemistry; Communications; Computer Science; Economics; Engineering; Finance; Geology; Liberal Arts; Marketing; Mathematics; Physics.

Operations at this facility include: Regional headquarters; administration; service; sales.

How they're growing/Recent developments: In August, 1991, the company announced that it would be merging with Storage Technology Corporation of Colorado. According to XL/Datacomp chairman Thomas Owens, "The products StorageTek has under development for the AS/400 market will fit well into our sales and service activities. The benefits for our customers are significant. The continuity of doing business with the XL/Datacomp people they know and trust is important, and we'll be able to provide them with StorageTek's leading edge technology." Employment has grown from an estimated 750 in 1987 to 1,200 in 1991.

X-RITE
3100 44th Street SW
Grandville, Michigan 49418
(616) 534-7663

Founded: 1958. **No. of Employees:** 248. **Revenues (1990):** $23.6 million. **Revenues (1986):** $14.3 million. **Five-Year Revenue Growth:** 65%.

Description: Produces quality control instruments for the graphic arts, photographic, medical, packaging and microfilm industries, including desitometers, sensitometers, shrink packaging equipment, silver recovery equipment and X-ray marking systems.

Common positions include: Accountant; Electrical Engineer; Mechanical Engineer.

Educational backgrounds sought: Computer Science; Engineering.

Company benefits include: Medical insurance, dental insurance; life insurance; tuition assistance; disability coverage; profit sharing; savings plan.

How they're growing/Recent developments: X-Rite's revenues have increased largely on the strength of new product releases. The trend continued well into 1991 as sales for the year ending September 30, 1991, rose 24%. The company's profitability also has been improving due to improved design and assembly efficiency. Exports accounted for 28% of sales in 1990. In October, 1991, the company announced a $2.5 million contract with a Japanese photography equipment manufacturer to supply quality control instruments. Employment has grown from an estimated 138 in 1987 to 248 in 1991.

ZENITH NATIONAL INSURANCE CORPORATION
21255 Califa Street
Woodland Hills, California 91367
(818) 713-1000

Founded: 1971. **No. of Employees:** 1,270. **Revenues (1990):** $468 million. **Revenues (1986):** $411 million. **Five-Year Revenue Growth:** 14%.

Description: Through Zenith Insurance, Calfarm and Calfarm Life Insurance, this company writes worker's compensation, reinsurance and other property, casualty, and life and health insurance.

How they're growing/Recent developments: Earnings for the first nine months of 1991 rose dramatically, reflecting improved property/casualty underwriting. The reinsurance business is expected to be hurt in the short run, however, in light of recent fires in Oakland and Berkeley, California . Employment has grown from an estimated 360 in 1987 to 1,270 in 1991.

ZEOS INTERNATIONAL
530 Fifth Avenue NW
St. Paul, Minnesota 55112
(612) 633-4591

Founded: 1983. **No. of Employees:** 219. **Revenues (1990):** $127.9 million. **Revenues (1987):** $1.7 million. **Four-Year Revenue Growth:** 7,629%.

Description: Designs, manufactures, markets and supports a broad line of high performance microcomputers and related hardware products compatible with industry standards. The company ships through the mail, following Dell Computer's lead. Customers include Pfizer.

How they're growing/Recent developments: During 1990, Zeos entered the transportable computer market with the introduction of a 6.5-pound notebook product.

PART II

Ten Industries for the 1990's:
An Economic Survey

BIOTECHNOLOGY

The new tools of biotechnology are revolutionizing our understanding of the origin, structure, and biochemical pathways of diseases. This knowledge has resulted in breakthroughs in designing diagnostic methods and treatments that prevent or intervene in disease progression. Biotechnology is finding applications in other fields as well, to develop new substances of commercial value, produce large quantities of rare substances, improve manufacturing processes, develop better tasting and more nutritious foods, reduce reliance on pesticides, and clean up on environmental wastes.

Biotechnology is an umbrella term that refers to biological processes and techniques that use organisms or their cellular, subcellular, or molecular components to make products or modify plants and animals to carry desired traits. Micro-organisms have been used for thousands of years to make bread, fermented beverages and foods, and, in modern times, to produce antibiotics, enzymes, vitamins, and amino acids. The development of "new" biotechnologies in the past 20 years draws on many scientific and engineering disciplines. These techniques, including recombinant DNA (genetic engineering) and monoclonal antibody technologies, provide the ability to modify with far greater precision and speed the genetic materials of organisms, and to produce desired products in large quantities. The focus of this discussion is on the impact of modern biotechnology.

Recombinant DNA technology makes it possible to transfer specific genetic messages from one organism to another and stimulate the second organism to produce large quantities of rare proteins such as interferon and growth hormone. Chemically identical or monoclonal antibodies (MAbs), designed to recognize and bind to specific molecules, are most commonly used in *in vitro* diagnostic tests to identify with greater sensitivity the presence of antigens associated with diseases or conditions. MAbs are also used in treating organ transplant rejection, and are widely applied in industry and molecular biology research to extract and purify target substances from mixtures and vaccines.

DNA probe diagnostics make confirmations through genetic information in cells, rather than detecting the presence of antibodies, and thus offer even greater accuracy than other diagnostic technologies. DNA probes are finding use in forensic testing to solve crimes and paternity cases, and in testing for diseases and food contaminants.

Gene therapy may enable doctors to treat hereditary diseases and cancers by replacing defective genetic material with normal DNA or by delivering therapeutic substances within the body. The first human gene therapy trials to treat patients with severe immune comprised disease (a hereditary disease that destroys the immune system) and advanced melanoma (a lethal type of skin cancer) have been encouraging.

Industrial Structure

The total number of firms working in biotechnology has been fairly constant. The formation of new companies has offset the number of firms being acquired or merged with other companies. Acquisitions, mergers, equity purchases, and alliances between the small companies and larger manufacturing firms are contributing to an industry consolidation of sorts. The high cost of research and development, especially in human therapeutics, and the need of small companies to gain access to distribution networks and obtain funding, provide the impetus for forming business alliances. Larger companies often enter into partnerships with small biotechnology firms to find new products or to keep up with technical developments. Although alliances among domestic firms predominate, collaborations between U.S. biotechnology firms and foreign firms are increasing. The General Accounting Office reports that the share of business alliances in biotechnology between U.S. and foreign firms rose from 30 percent in 1981 to 45 percent in 1988.

Industrial Production

Sales data on products developed through biotechnology are neither sufficiently broken down in company reports nor collected by the Government in sufficient detail to assess the size of industrial production. Unofficial estimates indicated that U.S. firms' shipments of products developed specifically through recombinant DNA and monoclonal antibody technologies could have reached $3 billion by the end of 1991. Sales of pharmaceuticals and diagnostics for human health care will account for most of the total. Estimates for previous years are 1990--$2.2 billion, 1989--$1.5 billion, 1988--$1 billion, 1987--$600 million, and 1986--$350 million.

Sales have grown dramatically over the past few years because the new products are not only useful, but they often offer the only available source of treatment. Development times for human therapeutics have been lengthy because testing and regulatory review procedures are complex. In contrast, diagnostic tests are approved faster. Since 1981, the Food and Drug Administration has approved more than 520 diagnostic tests are approved faster. Since 1981, the Food and Drug Administration has approved more than 520 diagnostic kits using MAbs and DNA probes.

Biotechnology has been responsible for some major life-saving products: a MAb that purifies a blood clotting factor of the AIDS virus; colony stimulating factors to reduce the threat of infections that frequently afflict patients undergoing chemotherapy and bone marrow transplants; alpha interferon to treat several viral infections; and a safe version of human growth hormone to replace the natural hormone withdrawn from the market because of possible contamination with a deadly virus. Biotechnology has also been indispensable in AIDS research since the discovery of the virus, deciphering the virus' structure, and as a tool in designing drugs and vaccines. Development of screening tests for the AIDS virus in 1985 and hepatitis C virus in 1990 have helped ensure the safety of the nation's blood supply.

Transgenic animal models are beginning to used in medical research to study specific human diseases, such as Alzheimer's disease and breast cancer, and to test experimental drugs and carcinogens. DNA probes have allowed diagnoses of pathogenic diseases and proven invaluable in forensics, resolving criminal cases and identifying relatives.

Veterinary products derived from biotechnology include vaccines against pseudorabies, scours, and feline leukemia, and diagnostics. Faster, more accurate tests for such food contaminants as salmonella, aflatoxin, and listeria are contributing to safer foods. In 1990, chymosin (or rennin), became the first genetically engineered food processing product approved in the U.S. This version offers cheese producers a less costly alternative to the less pure natural product derived from the stomach lining of calves. Another enzyme, alpha amylase used in the textile and corn syrup industries, is being produced by a micro-organism that has been modified to make larger quantities of the enzyme. A genetically engineered baker's yeast that decreases breadmaking time was approved for use in the UK in 1990. In agriculture, the first genetically engineered pesticide, using killed bacteria containing a natural toxin, was approved for marketing in the U.S. in 1991. Enzymes genetically engineered to break down fats are being used to manufacture laundry detergents in Japan and Denmark.

International Competitiveness

The United States leads the world in most commercial applications in biotechnology, due to its massive investment in biomedical research. Although the United States predonimates, commercial application of the new biotechnologies worldwide is in its infancy. Western Europe and Japan have strengths in many scientific and engineering disciplines underlying biotechnology and in industries that are applying biotechnology. To cite a few examples, Germany and Switzerland are noted for their strength in developing pharmaceuticals, the Netherlands and Denmark in enzymes, Sweden in separation and purification technology, and Japan in amino acids, biosensors, fermentation processes, and marine biotechnology.

While there are no official trade statistics for biotechnology, surveys of export earnings reported by U.S. firms from biotechnology-related products and services, and royalties from licenses show a growing trend in foreign sales. Sales by 48 biotechnology companies were worth $180 million in 1989, accounting for a quarter of their total sales. Furthermore, a study by Ernst and Young indicates that foreign sales account for one-fifth of all sales by U.S. biotechnology companies, and this figure is expected to increase to one-third in five years.

Industrial Research & Development

Industry is increasing research and development in biotechnology. According to unpublished data provided to the NSF, industry spent about $2.3 billion on R&D in 1990, compared to $1.4 billion spent in 1987. Seventy-seven percent of industrial research funds is now spent on human health care, the fastest growing field (therapeutics, 63 percent; diagnostics, 14 percent). The remainder goes to plant agriculture (10 percent), animal agriculture (5 percent), chemicals and food additives (4 percent), biosensors and bioin-struments (3 percent), and other (1 percent).

The Government also allocates most of its $4 billion biotechnology-related budget to health care research. Government support for biomedical research over the past several decades and the high value-added nature of medical products are why most commercial applications of biotechnology are occurring in health care. More than some 132 biotechnology-derived medicines are in clinical trials or awaiting final approval, according to the Pharmaceutical Manufacturers Association. The major categories are treatments for cancer, AIDS, cardiovascular diseases, and arthritis; artificial blood; safer, more effective versions of vaccines such as the cholera vaccine; and new vaccines against such diseases as malaria and AIDS. One example of the focus on health care is the development of anti-sense drugs that are designed to bind to their defective mirror-image opposites and block the production of disease-causing proteins by abnormal genes.

Diagnostic testing is one of the fastest growing applications of biotechnology. Techniques that amplify minute amounts of genetic material into larger quantities of analyzable material are revolutionizing the speed and accuracy of testing and many areas of scientific research. New techniques for producing MAbs will make more varieties available at lower costs and provide MAbs more compatible with the human immune system. Most MAbs are used in *in vitro* (test tube) diagnostic tests but industry is developing MAbs for *in vivo* (inside the body) imaging to detect cancers, and therapeutic MAbs linked to toxins as drug delivery agents. MAbs have promising applications in detecting the remission, relapse, or outcome of drug therapies in cancer patients.

Molecular biology and gene amplification techniques have accelerated the discovery of disease-causing genes since the early 1980's. The genes identified to date include: Alport's syndrome, Alpha 1-antitrypsin deficiency, Lesch-Nyhan syndrome, sickle cell anemia, hemophilia, retinoblastoma, Duchenne muscular dystrophy, cystic fibrosis, retititis pigmentosa, chronic myelogenous leukemia, neurofibromatosis (or elephant man's disease), osteoarthritis, p53 tumor suppressor gene, a hereditary form of Alzheimer's disease, non-insulin-dependent diabetes, two forms of epilepsy, fragile X syndrome, Mafran's syndrome, and familial adenomatous polypsosis (colorectal cancer). By understanding the biochemical progression of these diseases, therapies might be developed for early intervention or treatment. For example, researchers are investigating nasal sprays to deliver new genes to patients suffering from cystic fibrosis and other lung disorders.

Animals

Animal health care is benefiting from advances made in human health care. Veterinary products now being developed include diagnostic tests, vaccines (rabies, mastitis, and rinderpest), drugs (alpha interferon for treating shipping fever in cattle), and drug delivery systems. A recombinant oral rabies vaccine to protect wild raccoons is being tested in parts of the United States.

Biotechnology is being used to identify genes in livestock animals for such desired trait as improved disease resistance, faster growth, and better quality meat (lower fat, lower cholesterol) for selective breeding. Transplanting such genes into livestock will develop improved livestock faster than can be accomplished through traditional breeding. Embryo multiplication and transfer can then be used to speed up production of high-quality animals. One of the most promising developments is transgenic chickens that have inherited a resistance to avian leukosis virus, a disease that costs U.S. egg producers $50-to-$100 million a year.

To improve animal husbandry, growth hormones have been developed that increase milk production in dairy cows, and promote fast growth and leanness in pigs. Epidermal growth factor is being investigated in Australia that causes sheep to shed its wool, reducing the cost of shearing. In the Netherlands, researchers are developing processes to use modified micro-organisms to recycle manure into animal feed, and simultaneously reduce environmental pollution caused by farm animals. The micro-organisms convert the ammonia component of manure into lysine, an important amino acid used in feed additives. Transgenic animals have been developed that can produce human proteins in milk, such as TPA, blood clotting factors, and hemoglobin. The eventual goal of extracting targeted proteins in sufficient quantities and ensuring necessary purity and efficacy for use in drugs, however, is at least several years off.

In marine biotechnology, work is focused on improving fish and shellfish for the aquaculture industry. Commercial goals are to increase size and growth rate, improve resistance to diseases and frigid temperatures, and increase the proportion of female fish. Fish genetically engineered to grow 20-to-40 percent faster could be on the market in the near future if they prove economical.

Plants

In plant agriculture, biotechnology is providing tools to develop new crops with improved resistance to pests, diseases, herbicides, pesticides, and environmental stresses (drought, freeze/thaw climatic changes, saline soils), and to improve their nutritional content. New varieties of fruits and vegetables are being developed for enhanced flavors and such improved commercial characteristics as higher solids content, controlled ripening, and seedless varieties. The long-sought goal of transforming valuable cereal crops (rice, corn) with new genes has recently become possible through new methods of direct DNA delivery. Other commercial targets are diagnostics for plant diseases, new varieties of ornamental flowers, and nutritious oilseeds. Micro-organisms are being developed for use in agriculture that increases nitrogen intake by plants, reduce frost damage in crops, and kill pests.

Tobacco plants have been engineered to mass-produce commercially valuable substances such as drugs, enzymes, flavors and fragrances. Field tests are underway to grow tobacco plants and extract proteins of interest from them.

Food Processing

In food processing, the application of genetic and protein engineering will yield many improved enzymes, amino acids, starter cultures for fermented foods, vitamins, flavoring and food coloring agents, thickeners, emulsifiers, and vegetable oils. Baker's yeast transformed with an anti-freeze gene isolated from fish could improve the quality of frozen dough currently on the market. Products nearing the market include vitamin C, glucose isomerase (an enzyme used to produce high fructose corn syrup), low-calorie beer, and various food flavors. Faster, more accurate diagnostic tests to detect bacterial contamination and pesticide residues in food products are another important area of research.

New Materials

In material science, a super-adhesive derived from mussels is being tested for surgical use. Research areas include high-tensile strength fibers, anticorrosive coatings for marine vessels, and cellulose fibers for a variety of industrial processes. Biodegradable plastics produced by bacteria are available but too expensive to compete with petroleum-derived plastics; the cost differential might be overcome by transforming corn or potatoes to produce biodegradable plastics, but this is some years off.

Biosensors

Biosensors--devices that combine biological and electrical components--can provide highly specific detection of targeted substances, feedback, and control. Biosensors are promising for use in medical diagnostics testing, *in situ* drug delivery, monitoring industrial processes such as contamination in bioreactors, narcotics detection, and monitoring air, water, and soil for the presence of toxins and pollutants.

Bioremediation and Natural Resources

Bioremediation, using micro-organisms to clean up wastes, has been practiced for many years to treat sewage and more recently in eliminating or reducing contaminated soil, water, or waste streams of petroleum products, chemicals used to preserve woods, pesticides, solvents, certain PCB's, and other hazardous wastes. In the past few years, research and application of bioremediation have grown in response to regulatory pressures to cleanup toxic waste sites, the high cost of operating landfills, increasing space shortages, concerns about incinerating toxic chemicals, and the need to degrade contaminants permanently.

The most common method of bioremediation is to apply nutrients, oxygen, and water at waste sites to stimulate indigenous micro organisms to consume the contaminants. Another method is to add to the waste site naturally occurring micro-organisms that have been selectively bred for specific advantages. Although natural organisms have provided plentiful research targets, recombinant organisms are being developed to tackle contaminants which persist in the environment because few micro-organisms have evolved to degrade them. Other research targets are to overcome the limitations of natural organisms, which tend to work slowly, require minimum temperatures, die cast, and degrade only one type of contaminant. However, the additional cost of more complex regulatory approval procedures for recombinant, as opposed to natural, organisms, and possible adverse public reactions could inhibit its development. Thus recombinant organisms initially will be used in closed bioreactor systems.

In energy, a microbe has been developed that removes sulphur from petroleum and it may be useful in processing cleaner-burning fuels. Converting biomass--organic material such as wood, grass, and grain--into fuel has not been sufficiently cost-effective to compete with petroleum-derived fuels, but a new recombinant micro-organism promises to convert most organic materials into ethanol at a significantly lower costs. Regulatory pressures stemming from the 1990 amendments to the Clean Air Act are expected to help spur demand for ethanol in cities that do not meet EPA air quality standards.

Natural micro-organisms are being used by mining companies to leach metals and minerals. Bioleaching accounts for about 25 percent of the copper produced in the U.S. and is beginning to be used in mining gold, uranium, and other precious metals. The use of micro-organisms will increase as a method to obtain metals and minerals from mines that have been exhausted using conventional methods. The economic feasibility of bioleaching varies with the site and depends on metal prices. Genetically engineered micro-organisms are being investigated to speed the process of leaching.

Commercialization

Future commercial application of biotechnology will depend on a number of factors. Much research is needed in basic and applied areas to understand the genetic makeup, structure, and metabolism of micro-organisms, plants, and animals, including those from marine environments. Advances in bioprocess engineering--for example, large-scale production, monitoring, separation, and purification technology; bioreactor design; biosensor design; and enzymology--will determine product cost, quality, and competitiveness. Despite some companies' success in raising a record amount of financing through public stock offerings in 1991, access to affordable capital to fund the often lengthy research and development and regulatory approval process remains the most significant problem for most biotechnology companies. Industry is also concerned about a growing backlog of patent applications in the Patent and Trademark Office, inconsistencies in patent approvals, and uncertain regulatory processes for recombinant DNA-derived products used in the environment or as foods.

The ability to obtain prompt patent protection to enforce intellectual property rights is especially important to small companies that rely on revenues from technology licensing and to attract investment. The United States offers the most comprehensive patent protection in the world for biotechnology inventions; micro-organisms, plants, and animals are patentable, practical application. The Government is attempting to gain greater international protection for biotechnology inventions, particularly in developing countries, harmonize patenting procedures with Europe and Japan, and reduce the backlog of patent applications.

Lack of affordable product liability insurance could raise production costs as biotech firms develop such products as drugs, vaccines, and chemicals that traditionally have been subject to greater product liability risks. Insurers are uncertain as well about the risks and the liability of insuring genetically engineered organisms used in the environment.

Other factors influencing the adoption of biotechnology are the political and socio-economic effects of a new product on employment and price levels (the impact of bovine growth hormone on the dairy industry, for example). Public concerns about the safeness of genetically engineered foods and products released in the environment will continue to influence government regulatory attitudes and sales. Improved communications with the public about the safety aspects of genetically engineered products and improved education in the schools could alleviate this situation over the longer term.

Long-Term Prospects

Long-term predictions are difficult to make because, potentially, biotechnology processes can be applied by many industries. Even those products in the advanced stages of development face uncertain prospects because of questions concerning the timing of regulatory approval, cost-effectiveness, competitiveness with existing products, and Medicare cost reimbursement limits. Based on the large number of promising products in the research and development pipeline, however, market values of products derived through the application of biotechnology could reach $6 billion by 1995 and several tens of billions by the early 21st century. Human health care products will continue to dominate the market, followed by products derived from animal and plant agriculture.

Market values of products for non-medical uses will be much smaller, at least for the next 5 years. The economic constraints are more severe, and, although significant research is needed, industry is investing far less than in biomedical R&D. Several conditions influence development of biotechnology in plant agriculture. One, several growing seasons are needed for evaluating the performance of targeted genes and producing commercial-scale quantities of seeds. Two, sales of biotech-derived plants intended as food for people or livestock hinge on whether buyers will accept products made through novel processes. Three, Government agricultural subsidies weaken the financial incentives that can make production of innovative crops attractive to farmers.

The next few years should see the first genetically engineered crops trickling onto the market, followed by many more products that eventually could challenge the strong current market focus on biotechnology for human health care.

COMPUTER EQUIPMENT AND SOFTWARE

Computer equipment and software includes seven specific industries: electronic computers; computer storage devices; computer terminals; computer peripheral equipment; and software/computer programming services, prepackaged software, and computer integrated systems design.

Electronic computers include digital computers of all sizes, as well as computer kits assembled by the purchaser. Computer storage devices are such equipment as magnetic and optical disk drives and tape storage units. The category for computer terminals also covers teleprinters. Computer peripherals are printers, plotters, graphic displays, and other input/output equipment.

The U.S. computer equipment industry continued to face slack demand and intense price competition in several product sectors during 1990. Shipments rose only 4 percent to $71 billion, below the 1989 growth rate. First half revenue results for many leading U.S. firms were mixed. Sales remained sluggish for mainframes, minicomputers, and personal computers, but recovered for disk storage devices and continued to be strong for workstations, laptop computers, and local area network (LAN) equipment. Efforts to cut the Federal budget deficit, particularly defense spending, had a dampening effect on the industry's revenues. New orders rose 6% through June, 1990, compared with a relatively flat first 6 months of 1989, indicating that a turn around in shipments growth might occur by the end of the year.

Ongoing efforts of computer equipment firms to cut costs and increase profits in a weak domestic market continued to adversely affect employment. Total employment declined by 4%, to an estimated 277,000 workers; the 12,000 lost jobs were mainly administrative and non-technical personnel. Of this total, only 2,000 were production workers laid off during plant closings. A number of companies managed to reduce their work forces through attrition and early retirement rather than layoffs. The Northeast region of the country was particularly hard hit by employment cutbacks because of stagnant minicomputer sales.

The computer equipment industry spends enormous sums on R&D to maintain its technological leadership. According to Business Week's R&D Scoreboard, the R&D expenses of a combined sample of 94 computer systems, peripheral, and communications firms reached $13.4 billion in 1989, the latest year for which information is available. This amount substantially exceeded spending in such other major industries as automotive, health care, and chemicals. The computer equipment industry's average R&D investment as a percentage of total revenues was 8.4 percent, more than twice the composite figure of 3.4 percent for all industries.

U.S. corporate and university research laboratories have been working on several projects that may affect the development of computer systems throughout this decade and into the next century. In terms of breakthroughs that may lead to advanced circuitry, university researchers have experimented with quantum-effect electronic devices that have features 3,000 times smaller than the diameter of a human hair (molecular electronics). A private sector laboratory has also used a scanning tunneling microscope to maneuver and position individual atoms on a surface, holding out the promise of manufacturing microscopic electric circuits and extremely dense data storage devices. At the systems level, other private sector researchers have successfully demonstrated a prototype optical computer using lasers, lenses, and mirrors, rather than electronic circuitry to move, retrieve, and process data. These developments may pave the way for computers that are substantially smaller and orders of magnitude faster than machines currently on the market.

Capital expenditures in the industry slowed in 1989. The annual survey by *Electronics Business* magazine showed that worldwide capital expenditures of a combined sample of 34 leading U.S. computer hardware firms for plant and equipment rose only 9 percent, to just below $12 billion. This growth was less than half that of 1988. Within the sample, desktop computer suppliers boosted spending an average of 38%, while a significant number of minicomputer and peripheral equipment manufacturers cut back their expenditures sharply. IBM played a particularly important role by investing $6.4 billion, more that half of the entire sample's total spending, to improve its production facilities around the world. Several industry observers expected growth in capital spending to continue in 1990.

International Competitiveness

Total U.S. computing equipment exports grew by 15% to $24.7 billion in 1990, signifying an increase in overseas demand. Canada and Japan each accounted for 13% of total U.S. electronic computing equipment exports in 1990. As expected, exports to Eastern Europe surged, although they remained a small portion of total U.S. trade. The Western European market bought 47% of U.S. exports, up 6% over 1989, and should continue to increase its computing equipment purchases, albeit at a slower rate than expected as a result of the integration of the European Community (EC) in 1992. EC92 is the merger of the 12 Western European countries, which constitute a single market of 325 million people with a Gross Domestic Product of $4.5 trillion and a 1988 per capita income of $13,770.

Imports increased by 8% over 1989 to roughly $25.2 billion in 1990, most of that due to significant growth in imports of peripherals and parts. Imports of peripherals and parts from Canada jumped 59%, peripherals from

Japan rose by 20%, peripherals and parts from Singapore increased by 26%, and parts from Taiwan expanded by 75%. Offshore investment in manufacturing facilities by U.S. firms contributed to the rapid growth of imports from Singapore.

This trade activity led to the first overall U.S. trade deficit in electronic computing equipment. While the movement into deficit was led by the strong growth in peripheral and parts imports, imports of computers actually declined. This situation reflected the comparative strength of U.S. systems suppliers, who often manufacture complete systems in the United States from imported parts and subsystems. U.S. computing equipment trade data reflect the overseas sourcing patterns and subsidiary operations of this globally-based industry. For example, in 1990, computers represented 32% of U.S. exports but only 10% of the imports. The overseas sourcing of peripherals was evidenced by the fact that these products represented 55% of the total equipment imports.

Foreign manufacturing facilities in the United States, with their related exports and imports, complicate the use of trade data as a measure of the U.S. based industry's competitive status. For example, although the trade deficit suggests that the production base in the U.S. is eroding, the true competitive picture of the U.S. computer industry can only be found by excluding foreign manufacturing facilities located on U.S. soil and including U.S. owned foreign production.

Rising imports and slow growth in the U.S. market combined to increase the share of imports as a percentage of apparent domestic consumption from 35.7% in 1989 to 40% in 1990. Apparent domestic consumption grew by only 4% in 1990, compared to previous rates of 17% and 10% in 1988 and 1989 respectively.

Foreign firms have continued to invest in the U.S. computer industry at a rapid pace. Cumulative foreign direct investment within the office and computing machines sector, which consists largely of computer manufacturers, rose nearly 50% to $4.1 billion in 1989 alone. In particular, outlays by foreign companies to acquire U.S. firms and to establish businesses and plants in the United States increased by roughly $500 million. Among the factors contributing to this surge in investment were a weak dollar relative to other major currencies, which lowered the cost of U.S. assets; the need of cash poor firms in the U.S. to obtain abundant, cheap capital to finance their R&D and operational expenses; and foreign interest in gaining access to the latest technological advances.

The Japanese have emerged as major foreign investors. They have acquired equity positions in 53 U.S. computer equipment and 11 software firms since 1980, with most of that activity taking place during the last 5 years. They have also substantially expanded their manufacturing and research in the United States. According to a recent Commerce Department study, Japanese suppliers wholly own 13 plants producing such computer peripherals as printers, keyboards, and disk drives. Seven plants produce computer-related components; another 3 manufacture personal computers and laptops. Their more than 20 R&D centers are located mainly in California and the Northeastern states, where they can monitor important technological developments within leading U.S. companies and university research laboratories. The research efforts of these Japanese-owned facilities have been largely focused on software, data storage, and workstation development.

Many industry groups in 1990 become increasingly concerned about such competitiveness issues as the high cost and lack of availability of capital in the United States, antitrust constraints against joint production, the decline in the quality of the U.S. educational system, unfair trade practices, and the industry's growing dependence on foreign suppliers for critical components and subassemblies. They generally expressed strong support for proposed federal legislation that would stimulate corporate R&D and ensure a healthy business climate. These proposals include a permanent but modified R&D tax credit, a reduction in the capital gains tax, and clarification of antitrust laws to allow joint production consortia. The groups also reached a consensus on the need for better science and mathematics education, and the importance of maintaining an open and fair world trading system.

The world computer systems market increased in value almost 10% in 1990, to an estimated $150.9 billion, according to International Data Corporation. The United States was the single largest country market, representing more than a third of this total. Japan followed with $29 billion in computer systems sales, and the combined Western European market was nearly as big as the United States, at $50 billion. Markets in both Japan and Europe grew more than twice as fast as the United States, at 13.5% and 10%, respectively. Personal computers and workstations accounted for approximately half of computer systems sales in all world markets, and their 15 percent increase over 1989 in value of shipments substantially outpaced the growth rates of other types of computers. Japan remained oriented toward larger systems such as mainframes and minicomputers.

A report in mid-1990 by the Computer Systems Policy Project, a coalition of chief executive officers from 11 major U.S. computer firms, noted that foreign competition has seriously eroded the industry's strong position in the world market and its technological leadership over the past decade. The U.S. share of world computer systems sales declined from 81% in 1983 to 61% in 1989. By contrast, Japan's share grew from 8% to 22% and Europe's from 10% to 15% during the same period. U.S. capabilities have already either fallen behind or are being overtaken by the advances made by foreign firms in capital intensive technologies. These include displays, storage devices, microelectronics, and electronic packaging and manufacturing technology. The United States is still clearly ahead of its foreign competitors in technologies that stress creativity and are not capital intensive, such as software engineering, systems and applications software, data base systems, and processor architecture. However, this lead is expected to rapidly diminish if current trends continue.

Long-Term Prospects

The U.S. computer equipment industry should experience further consolidation over the next five years through ongoing mergers and acquisitions, and the departure of technologically weak and cash poor firms. It should also become even more international in character. Strategic alliances with foreign companies will probably increase as U.S. firms seekout European and Asian partners to share mounting R&D costs through joint research and product development, and to gain access to low-cost, high-volume manufacturing capacity. Foreign participation in U.S. manufacturing may grow in turn. Subsidiaries of foreign companies may expand their U.S. operations by electing to locally produce some of the components and subassemblies used in their computer systems, as well as a wider range of peripherals. At the same time, U.S. offshore production may continue to expand to meet the particular needs of customers in key overseas markets and within major regions, such as the European Community after 1992.

If current trends continue, the U.S. computer skills and production base will favor design, systems integration, parts assembly, and software development. With semiconductors incorporating increasing amounts of a system on a single die, systems suppliers will work ever more closely with semiconductor firms to create new products. For example, by the mid-1990s, microprocessors will contain nearly 10 million transistors on a chip, or 10 times today's densities. This level of integration will allow manufacturers to place on a chip all of the elements of a 200 million instructions per second (MIPS) workstation.

Demand within the world information technology market will shift more toward software and computer services during the early 1990s, according to International Data Corporation's projections. Computer system (hardware) sales should only grow 9 percent annually, to around $212 billion by 1994, and represent less than 45 percent of this world market. The U.S. computer systems market will also decline in importance relative to other major overseas markets. It will still equal Western Europe in the total value of computers sold, but will be outstripped in growth by Japan and key markets in Asia, Latin America, and possibly Eastern Europe. Personal computers and workstation sales will continue to play a dominant role in the world computer systems market, accounting for 52 percent of its value.

Supercomputers

Supercomputers are traditionally defined as computers with the highest processing speed and selling for the highest prices in any given period of time. The super computer industry experienced mild growth in 1990, bolstered mainly through increased sales of both mini-supercomputers (systems with operational speeds between 100 and 350 floating point operations per second, or megaflops), and massively paralled systems (computers with more than one 1,000 processors). Supercomputer shipments worldwide reached a total value of $1.5 billion, up 13 percent from 1989. Shipments of high-end super-computer systems with operational speeds of over 350 megaflops posted an-other approached sixty. Industry sources estimated that 600 mini-supercom-puter and massively paralled systems have been shipped -- 10 times the num-ber of high-end systems -- although Dataquest Incorporated puts the figure at about 800. There was one new entrant in the field, but no major new super-computers were introduced by existing vendors.

Long-Term Prospects

The Defense Advanced Projects Research Agency (DARPA) has awarded two U.S. high performance computer firms multimillion dollar con-tracts to jointly build a computer system with a theoretical peak performance of 1 trillion operations per second (teraops), about 250 times faster than cur-rently available supercomputers, by the mid-1990s. The actual performance of this system will be considerably slower, but the architectural models which will result from the development program should lead the way to the next generation of super computing. In conjunction with the National Research and Education Network (NREN), DARPA has also teamed up with the NSF to provide $15.8 million over the next three years to the newly formed Corpo-ration for National Research Initiatives, which will coordinate research groups developing the hardware and software for a computer network capable of transmitting data at the rate of 1 billion bits (gigabits) per second.

Supercomputers with large numbers of processors will continue to make their way into the mainstream of the industry, dependent upon the ability of companies to develop software applications. Those systems defined as moderately parallel, having around 25 processors or less, will maintain their superior performance capability as multi-usage systems and be especially successful as workhorses at the high-end of the market.

Mainframes

Mainframes are high performance computers used principally for such large-volume, general-purpose applications as on-line transactions, batch, decision support, and interactive processing. Low-end, uniprocessor models range in price from approximately $600,000 to a few million dollars. High-end mainframes with up to six central processing units can exceed $15 million. The market consists largely of users who upgrade to these higher performance systems or purchase mainframes to augment their existing sys-tems.

The performance of these computers is often measured in millions of instructions per second (MIPS). The fastest U.S. systems on the market through mid-1990 had processing speeds of around 120 MIPS. However, leading U.S. companies began introducing new families of computers in the third quarter that offered approximately twice this performance in six to eight processor configurations. Two Japanese suppliers announced new mainframe lines with high-end multiprocessor models that will reportedly operate at 500 MIPS; these will be shipped in 1991.

Mainframes achieve their high speeds through advanced computer design; high-density packaging; and very large scale integration (VLSI) emitter coupled logic (ECL) chips. The cycle time of several systems is now down to 10 nanoseconds. Their main memory capacity is considerably larger than other types of commercial computers; it can reach up to two billion bytes (gigabytes) through the use of the latest dynamic and static random access memory (DRAM and SRAM) devices. Mainframes can be either air or water cooled. The cost of research and developed for a new generation system averages about $500 million, but can reach as high as $1 billion.

Long-Term Prospects

Mainframe vendors may experience a resurgence in demand for their systems beginning in 1992, benefitting from the trend toward "enterprise-wide" computing within major corporations. Large scale mainframes will not only continue to play a significant role in on-line transaction processing, but will also handle massive data bases and manage complex networks of workstations and personal computers. If vendor efforts in software and networking technology bear fruit, processors and storage devices will reside in different geographical locations within an enterprise and be linked together by very high-speed fiber optic channels. Corporate mainframe users will have access to all of these computing and storage resources which will appear to the user to be a single computing system.

Midrange Computers

The midrange segment of the computer industry consists of multiuser systems, ranging in price for $25,000 to $500,000, with 16- to 64-bit processors. Some of these machines are designated general-purpose computers; others are designed for specific applications. Midrange computers serve a broad spectrum of applications, but are used predominantly in services and durable goods manufacturing, and to a lesser degree, in the education and government markets.

The midrange market remained at approximately $20 billion in 1990. The midrange environment continues to undergo changes in its fundamental structure. Traditional midrange vendors are reducing their workforce through layoffs, early retirements, and attrition. Previous years of austerity have paid off for a number of the suppliers, who have reported significant strengthening of their financial positions. However, some midrange players continue to struggle, and an industry shake-out is likely.

Most midrange vendors have broadened their offerings to include networking equipment, software, technical workstations, portables, and system integration services. Many midrange suppliers have focused on specific market niches. Many offer their midrange computers as network servers, but competition for this application comes from the powerful new dedicated network servers described in the Local Area Networking section of this chapter. Most analysts feel that both midrange systems and dedicated network servers have their roles, due to differences in capacity and software availability.

Users of midrange systems are carefully watching the development of open systems -- those employing nonproprietary or standardized hardware components and operating systems. Most suppliers, while seeking to preserve their installed base of proprietary systems, have also introduced some form of open system. Open systems have garnered a share of the midrange market, and as such limitations as the lack of specific applications software are overcome, these systems will account for an even larger share.

Open systems, which are not as profitable as proprietary systems, have made pricing in the midrange segment more competitive. Open systems also contribute to the increasing importance of value-added resellers (VARs), who bundle each system with applications software for specific user needs. In 1990, approximately 17 percent of all midrange systems were sold through VARs, compared to 11 percent in 1987. Many midrange suppliers are broadening their range of products through strategic relationships with other suppliers.

Midrange users are turning to laser-printing rather than traditional high-speed impact printers. Small- and medium-size computer users are finding the high-end of laser printers (36-79 pages per minute) well-suited to their needs for print quality, flexibility, and consistency.

Long-Term Prospects

In the long term, software will drive increases in the demand for midrange systems, particularly software that facilitates the connectivity of incompatible systems. Until this happens, open systems will continue to slowly increase their installed base, while seriously competing with proprietary systems. Midrange systems will provide functionality to large networks until dedicated network server hardware and software is developed that can handle large networks.

Workstations

Workstations are single-user computer systems with advanced graphics capabilities that, in price and performance, compete with the fastest personal computers at the low end and mini-supercomputers and superminicomputers at the high end. They have been purchased mainly for occupationally intensive scientific and engineering applications since their introduction in the early 1980s, but in recent years have moved into such commercial markets as electronic publishing, business graphics, financial services, mapping, and office automation. Their most significant features are the use of high-performance, 32-bit microprocessors; large, high-resolution monochrome or color monitors; and sophisticated software capable of handling multi-tasking (more than one task at a time) and networking (communications with other computers). Graphics supercomputers are a class of 64-bit workstations introduced at the high end in 1988, priced around $100,000. These systems have scalar and vector processing performance levels well above traditional technical workstations and superworkstations, and graphics capabilities that enable scientists and engineers to view 3-D simulations of complex mathematical models in real time.

In contrast to the sluggishness of some segments of the computer industry, U.S. workstation vendors enjoyed another year of strong demand for their systems from both domestic and foreign customers in 1990. Their worldwide shipments reached 5,000,000 units valued at an estimated $8.5 billion, a 37 percent increase over 1989. U.S. suppliers stimulated demand by continuing to announce new products with substantial improvements in their price performance ratios, and by slashing prices as much as 25 to 40 percent on selected existing entry-level and high-end systems. The battle for market share among leading manufacturers, their efforts to displace personal computers in certain commercial accounts and to stave off encroachment by X-windows terminal firms, drove the price per MIPS (millions of instructions per second) for a low-end workstation to under $400 retail and to below $240 after volume discounts. Competition across the product spectrum intensified with the entry of semiconductor houses and the introduction of a new workstation family by IBM, signaling its intent to play a major role in this market. The rapid pace of new product introductions has reduced the product life cycle of traditional 32-bit workstations to only a year. Models introduced on the market in 1990 had at least 12 MIPS performance, a minimum of 8 megabytes (MD) of main memory, and an average of 120 MB of auxiliary storage. The majority of these new systems used reduced instruction set chip (RISC) microprocessors as their central processing units and UNIX as their operating system environment. Some workstations featured superscalar architectures in which several instructions could be executed simultaneously per clock cycle, resulting in a significant boost in system performance over competitive products. A number of suppliers marketed models with 3- dimensional graphics capabilities for under $10,000. At the high end, a graphics supercomputer system with up to 8 central processing units operating at more than 230 MIPS and with 128 MB of main memory was introduced for approximately $200,000.

Workstation vendors have begun to broaden their distribution channels in the United States to compete with high-end personal computer manufacturers. Although original equipment manufacturers (OEMs) and value-added resellers have been their principal sources for sales, U.S. firms have increasingly turned to retail dealers to lure commercial customers away from personal computers and to counteract the forays of PC suppliers into traditional workstation markets. Almost 250 dealers now distribute workstation products, according to a recent report from Summit Strategies, a Boston-based consulting group.

Long-Term Prospects

The U.S. workstation industry can expect significant challenges to both its market and technological leadership over the next five years. At the low end of the market, it will face growing competition from personal computer suppliers and Asian clone manufactures offering systems with comparable processing power, memory, and graphics capabilities. In the more advanced workstation market, U.S. manufacturers will have to contend mainly with large, vertically integrated Japanese companies which will try to win control of these markets through a 2-pronged strategy of targeting certain RISC microprocessors and versions of UNIX, and by using their manufacturing prowess in semiconductor and display technologies. The ability of U.S. firms to protect intellectual property rights, provide customers with better service and support, and keep the lead in software development, will determine whether they remain dominant in workstations. Particularly important will be their efforts to develop software that will make their machines easier to use and network together in an integrated computing environment that employs proprietary and open systems from different vendors. The world market for workstations could exceed $30 billion by 1995, if average growth rates of 30 percent per year are maintained.

Personal Computers

Personal computers (PCs) are single-user, general application computers based on a single microprocessor chip with a resident operating system and local programming capability. Typical units with monitor sell for $2,000 to $4,000, although prices range from $500 for some home computers to $30,000 for the most sophisticated, fully-configured systems. Although high-end PCs are approaching the performance levels of low-end workstations, they typically are single task oriented and have slower processors, less graphics capability, and lower resolution displays. Personal computers include two categories: desktops and portables. Stationary desktop systems include floor-standing or "tower" configurations; portable computers include transportable, laptop, notebook and hand-held models.

The trends in the U.S. industry toward less concentration and more internationalization continued in 1990. New firms entered the U.S. PC market, while some firms lost market share. From 1985 to 1990, according to Dataquest, the share of unit shipments of the top ten vendors decreased from 80 to 56 percent. Buyer demand for standardized technology and the continued availability of off-the-shelf components and circuit boards, especially from the Far East, makes market entry easier for small firms. However, new entrants must stay competitive in service, support, and price in this increasingly commoditized industry. Foreign vendors' penetration of the U.S. market also increased. Overseas suppliers marketed their products more aggressively and purchased U.S. computer firms to obtain new technology and distribution channels. From 1985 to 1990, these companies increased their share of the U.S. market form 10 to 26 percent; this increase was driven by strong sales of laptop computers. This trend should continue over the next several years. Forty percent of the fifty largest PC vendors selling in the United States are currently foreign owned. As worldwide market competition increases, domestic and foreign suppliers will increasingly look beyond their home borders for new markets.

Shipments of desktop and portable computers to the U.S. market in 1990 exceeded 10.7 million units, up about 7 percent from 1989. These included computers manufactured and assembled in the United States by domestic firms and U.S. subsidiaries of foreign companies; and imported systems produced offshore by either U.S. or foreign-owned companies. The value of the U.S. market increased 13.6 percent to around $31.8 billion. The growth in sales was unchanged form 1989.

In 1990, there were no spectacular product or technology introductions that dramatically spurred sales, nor major changes in consumption patterns. It was another year of transition for buyers and aggressive competition and price-cutting for suppliers. The user base continued to move gradually but resolutely toward the world of 32-bit high speed processors, multimegabyte memories and multiasking operating systems. Purchasers continued to respond as much to technical issues as to economic cycles. For example, buyer confusion over the myriad of technical and purchase options -- processor type and speed, packaging style (portable versus desktop), memory and storage capacity, type of peripherals and controller boards, operating system and application software, user interface, price distribution channel and vendor -- continued unabated. This confusion, compounded by a general economic slowdown in both capital and consumer spending, contributed to sales that were below historical trends.

A breakdown of PC sales by application shows that business/professional usage represented about two-thirds of the market in 1990, in terms of units sold and value, according to the International Data Corporation (IDC). The 9 percent increase in units sold in 1990, to 6.9 million, was slightly less than 1989 growth. Unit shipments for scientific/technical and educational consumption grew 21 percent and 7 percent respectively. By contrast, sales of PCs for very limited entertainment, hobby, and home management uses (i.e. balancing checkbooks) declined 26 percent in 1990, to around 900,000 units.

As computer suppliers searched for new markets in 1990 because of the slowing of the business sector, they focused on the estimated 94 million U.S. households, which are a growing market for home business computing. Several major PC manufacturers introduced new models in the sub-$1,000 price range specifically targeting this large and unsaturated market segment. Others promoted their lowest-cost machines through mass merchandising channels. Promotional campaigns offered reduced prices, longer warranties, bundled software, and expanded training and support packages. According to Link Resources, only 24 percent of U.S. families now own personal computers.

Sales of PCs like the Mactinosh, based on Motorola's 68xxx microprocessors, held about one-tenth of the 1990 market, a 15 percent rise over the previous year. Shipments of PCs using Intel 80386 and 486 processor chips, which include all IBM PC-compatible computers, grew around 12 percent, and represented about 80 percent of the market. Shipments of 8088/86-based PCs-- former mainstays of the market --continued the decline that began in 1986 when computers with these chips were replaced by a newer generation. However, the use of these chips in hand held portables may cause a rise in shipments after 1992.

PC-AT computers, based on the 80286 processor, accounted for a third of U.S. sales, and have dominated sales since surpassing the PC-XT in 1988. These sales may now have peaked as buyers are demanding even higher performance computers to run more complex software. But demand for 80286 processors will continue through their use in laptops and notebooks, and in other less demanding processing applications.

The new 80386sx computers, powered by a less expensive version of the 80386 microprocessor and capable of running new 32-bit software, are replacing the ATs as the predominant system in the market. Billed as the new entry-level computer for the commercial sector, shipments of these units exceeded 2 million in 1990 and surpassed sales of regular 80386dx-based computers. Competition in 1990 continued between competing 32-bit bus technologies used to transfer information and commands among elements of a computer system. More PC models and plug-in boards were introduced that were based on the Extended Industry Standard Architecture (EISA) and the Micro Channel Architecture (MCA) buses. EISA is an extension of the current AT standard, while MCA is the new IBM standard. These new products provide more robust performance levels for data-intensive and complex communication functions, but represent only about 10 percent of the market, most of which are MCA based-computers made by IBM. Initial EISA boards have been designed for file server-type systems based on Intel's 80486 chip, and sell for over $10,000; however, the technology is expected to migrate down into the 80386 arena, with resulting price decreases. While some system and board manufacturers prefer one technology over the other, many are supporting both architectures.

As personal computers become more widely dispersed among all segments of society, the design of human interfaces becomes increasingly critical to their utility and popularity. Interface issues range form the design of such physical input devices as keyboards, point-and click mouse devices, and light pens, to a user's mental interaction with the computer. Since the introduction of the Macintosh in 1984, its graphical user interface (GUI) has become very popular. The GUI system uses icons (symbols) to represent available functions; these icons are generally manipulated by a mouse in conjunction with a keyboard. This approach is in contrast to the more traditional method of using typed commands and character-based software, which has been characteristic of DOS and other operating systems. Such GUI software as Windows 3.0, introduced in May, 1990, for the DOS environment, is increasing in popularity, and should be a key factor in making computers easier to use. More GUI-compatible applications software is being developed.

Long-Term Prospects

The U.S. PC market may exhibit somewhat higher growth rates in 1992, as pressure to upgrade to more powerful machines intensifies. Demand should be led by the need for and availability of more powerful applications software. Migration from DOS to the OS/2 operating system by local area networks (LAN) and more sophisticated users will also increase demand for higher performance computers. However, a return to the double-digit growth rates of the past will depend upon the increased use of computers in schools and homes. Widespread use of instructional computers in schools, especially below the college level, awaits additional funding, the creation of more educational software, and the development of multi-media technologies.

Major producers expect the home market to continue to grow because of increased computer literacy and awareness, the introduction of new easier-to-use software, and the widening use of home computers for business and education. Dataquest projects that sales of home computers could reach 47.4 million by 1994. In the long term, the viability of this market will depend upon the development of relevant software programs; multimedia applications integrating audio, video, text and graphics; on-line systems providing information and personal services; and integrated home management networks that control communications, security, and energy consumption.

Another potential growth area is overseas, where future PC and workstation sales are expected to grow faster than in the United States. The compound annual growth over the next five years is projected to be 11 percent in Europe and 18 percent in Japan. PC shipments outside the United States should exceed $70 billion by 1994. As a result, U.S. firms will place more emphasis on investing abroad, and on developing and adapting products for foreign markets.

As 1992 approaches, more computer and software producers are expected to locate within the European community (EC) to take advantage of the opportunities that this large, integrated European market will offer by establishing plants and distribution channels in Europe, companies can better benefit from EC efforts to harmonize national standards and regulations. The European Community has an estimated installed base of 24 million PCs, about half of the U.S. total. With a population that exceeds that of the United States by more than 80 million people, the EC market had great potential.

As a result of continual advances in systems and component technology and software development, significantly more powerful, functional, and easy-to-use personal computers will be introduced over the next five years. By 1995, the performance of an average system should reach at least 50 megahertz (MHz), or 5 times what currently exists. Typical memory capacity will equal 16 megabytes (MB), and access times may fall below 60 nanoseconds with the advent of faster, 16 megabit dynamic random access memory (DRAM) chips.

Developments in systems software should result in PCs that offer multiasking and advanced networking and graphics capabilities.

Portables

A portable is a personal computer which has all the functions of a desktop computer; is rugged enough for travel; and has a full-sized keyboard in the same physical unit as the display, the motherboard, and some type of mass storage device.

The U.S. portable computer market was worth $5.4 billion in 1990, a 30 percent increase over 1989. The United States is the largest single market for portables, with about 50 percent of total worldwide sales. The Japanese market accounts for 18.3 percent, and the Western Europe, 19.5 percent. In Japan, shipments of portables exceeded shipments of desktop personal computers in 1990. In the United States, with its large installed base of desktop systems, portables made up only about 11 percent of all personal computers sold. In Western Europe, the figure was 7 percent. The Western European market is quite similar to the U.S. market, and except for some software changes, demands similarly configured machines.

Almost all portables for the United States market that are more powerful than those based on Intel's 8088 microprocessor are manufactured in the U.S., to avoid the 100 percent duty on Japanese portable imports resulting from the semiconductor trade sanctions imposed by the U.S. government in 1986. Most portables sold in the United States are assembled in the United States using foreign, primarily Japanese, components. Both Japanese and U.S. companies have recently built or acquired facilities in Europe to take advantage of the rapidly growing EC92 market.

As in previous years, portables continue to find their strongest market among professional users. Although portable computers can have all functionality of a desktop computer, most are used only as a second computer which is periodically downloaded onto a desktop or larger system for integration into master files. But even limited to these functions, portables have become indispensable to many firms, which have expanded their technical staff to support the fleet of portables, update their communication capabilities, and provide maintenance and security.

The "docking station" concept, introduced by a number of portable vendors, combines a high-performance laptop with a docking station unit containing peripheral ports, additional drive slots, and expansion board slots. These systems occupy the high end of the portable spectrum, but are probably the architecture of the future, since they combine portability with maximum storage.

Portables have made an impact on the same markets as the desktop computer. Although the office/professional segment was the first to use portable technology extensively, the home and student markets grew by 20 percent form 1989 to 1990, the largest increase in any of the end-use groups. The number of users in this segment has increased sharply with the introduction of "notebook" style portables which can fit in a briefcase; use will accelerate as these systems decrease in price.

The portable workstation, or "lapstation," brings a new user group to the portable market. Introduced in 1990, these systems have the processing and storage capacity for many design and engineering functions. Although restricted due to limitations on display resolution and a dependence upon AC power, the systems enable engineers to run simulations away from the office.

Portable vendors all use similar technology and basic componentry, differentiating their systems by industrial design, power supply, and display functionality. Theoretically, all components are available to any portable designer. However, the most advanced displays are available in very limited quantities due to low yields in the manufacturing process. Some specific technologies that are imperative to the success of the portable computer in the marketplace are those that decrease weight to the 4-8 pound range, extend operating time up to 8 hours on battery power, and give optimum display resolution.

Advanced displays meet many of the visual and interactive needs of the users. Even the newest flat-panel displays for portables, however, are not equal in quality or price with the cathode ray tube (CRT). The active matrix liquid crystal display (LCD) technology, which is the closest in resolution, color, and brightness to the CRT, was introduced to the U.S. market in the Apple Macintosh portable in 1990. The display is somewhat cost-prohibitive at this time due to low yields in the manufacturing process.

Such slightly older, passive LCD technologies as twisted, double-twisted and superdouble-twisted nematic, are available in large quantities, since they have advanced along the manufacturing learning curve. The addition of a backlight has dramatically improved the quality of these screens, although many portable vendors have chosen not to incorporate a backlight in order to preserve battery life. Color and gray-scale displays will be available on portables in early 1991, at a premium price.

Promising advances in plasma and electroluminescent flat-panel displays give vendors an alternative to LCD technology. Both these technologies now have sufficient brightness and resolution, and are advancing in the areas of power usage and color capabilities.

Power management techniques continue to be developed for maximizing battery life and extending true portability. One promising new development in batteries is nickel hydride, slated to replace the dominant nickel cadmium. Some of the advantages of the nickel hydridecell are quick charge, a favorable discharge curve, and weight 30 to 40 percent less than nickel cadmium battery.

Until an alternative technology is developed, the keyboard remains a hurdle to further miniaturization. One step toward miniaturization is an alternative input device called the "electronic tablet," which can recognize characters written on the screen. This has already been accepted in the Japanese market, where the characters are more formalized and easier for a computer to recognize than Western script. A number of portables incorporate pointing mechanisms for data manipulation--either a roll ball or a pointing bar somewhere on the keypad. With the wider usage of the Windows 3.0 program in MS-DOS-based computers, demand for these pointing methods or touch screens will grow. Voice recognition, which currently hosts with a 30,000 word capacity, is another alternative to the keyboard. Modem and FAX boards, common in desktop computers, are now available in portables. A number of companies have included cellular capability in their latest offerings.

Long-Term Prospects

Within the next five years, voice recognition will be introduced in portables, redefining their size and shape. Powerful communication capacities will be added in the search for true portability. Battery size, weight, and strength will be other hurdles crossed in expanding portable functionality by 1996. By 1994, an equal number of portable and desktop computers will be sold in the United States. Annual growth is expected to remain around 25 percent for the next five years.

Magnetic and Optical Disk Optical Storage

Major U.S. disk storage manufacturers made significant mergers, acquisitions, and consolidations in 1990. Optimem, a disk drive and media manufacturer, was acquired by Archive Coproration; the acquisition enabled Optimem to revive its discontinued optical products. Other consolidations included Western Digital Corporation's purchase of Tandon's disk storage operation, and Maxtro's acquisition of Miniscribe, a manufacturer of rigid diskdrives. Several other financially troubled U.S. disk storage manufacturers were unable to find "white knights" to rescue them. For example, Priam, known for its high-capacity, high-performance 5.25-inch drives, went into Chapter 11 bankruptcy, and its operations were sold separately to several companies.

Total employment in the U.S.-based disk storage industry declined an estimated 10 percent from 1989 to 1990, to 31,000 units. The decline was due to several corporate failures and to the continued expansion of offshore production.

End users continued to demand increased capacity and lower prices. Dataquest estimates that the average capacity for 3.5-inch magnetic disk drives nearly doubled from 1989 to 1990, to 80 megabytes. The 5.25-inch drives increased to over 200 megabytes compared to 126 megabytes in 1989. The highest capacities for both 3.5-inch and 5.25-inch were offered by Seagate Technology, 426 megabytes and 1.2 gigabytes, respectively. As the storage capacity increased, the factory cost per megabyte dropped between

1989 and 1990 from $3.96 to $3.11 for 5.25-inch disks, and from $5.86 to $4.65 for 3.5-inch disk form factors.

The trend toward miniaturization and higher capacity in disk storage continued in 1990. According to the Disk/Trend Report, worldwide sales of 3.5-inch drives with capacities of 300-500 megabytes increased nearly tenfold, from 40,000 units in 1989 to 373,000 units in 1990. Sales of 5.25-inch drives with capacities of 500 megabytes-1 gigabyte increased 203 percent, from 158,000 to 480,000 units.

The 3.5-inch form factor drives accounted for 71 percent of all rigid disk drive shipments, followed by 5.25-inch at 23 percent, and less-than-3-inch disk drives at 2 percent. Larger form factors, 8- to l0-inch drives and 14-inch drives, each accounted for only 1 percent of total shipments.

While shipments of 3.5-inch drives showed a healthy increase due to increased market demand for 3.5-inch drives by desktop and laptop owners, the 5.25-inch segment of the storage industry dropped significantly. In 1990, 19 million units of 3.5-inch units were shipped, an increase of 44 percent over 1989. By comparison, shipments of 5.25-inch drives were 4.8 million units, a sharp decline of 31 percent from the previous year. The increased sales of 3.5-inch drives boosted revenues for U.S. manufacturers, as over 90 percent of revenues generated from the sales for these devices went to U.S. firms. About 500,000 2.5-inch drives, which first entered the commercial markets in 1989, were sold in the United States in 1990. The average capacity of these drives was 30 megabytes. Two U.S. companies, Conner Peripherals and PrairieTec, and one Japanese firm, JVC, dominated the 2.5-inch drive market. Substantial growth in the demand for notebook-size personal computers (weighing less than seven pounds) also motivated several other companies, including Areal Technology and Quantum, to begin manufacturing the 2.5-inch disk drive in 1990.

The optical drive industry also introduced an advanced phase change recording technology for erasable drives in 1990. This type of technology allows the media to interchange between write-once and erasable on a single drive. Other advances were higher capacities and faster access times, equivalent to today's small form factor magnetic drives; these pose the best possibility of displacing magnetic drives in the marketplace. The current price/performance ratio of erasable optical drives, however, makes them uncompetitive with magnetic drives for the present.

Long-Term Prospects

Capacities for all form factors will continue to increase by the mid-1990s, the average capacity for 5.25-inch drives should climb to over 900 megabytes, and for 3.5-inch drives to about 140 megabytes. Consolidation of U.S. disk drive vendors may continue. The market for 5.25-inch disk drives should continue to decline. Competing technologies like 2.5-inch disk drives and erasable optical disk drives are expected to enter the mainstream market for portables and desktop computers. Several critical technologies including dye-based media -- which uses less expensive materials such as a dissolvable coating on media -- should migrate from R&D status to practical applications in the erasable optical disk drive industry. This should improve the cost/performance of erasable drives, making them serious contenders for displacing high capacity magnetic drives by mid-1990.

Printer Industry

The U.S. printer market was valued at $11 billion if-sold-value (list price times number of units sold) in 1990, an increase of nearly 7 percent over 1989, according to BIS CAP International, a market research and consulting company. Virtually all 1990 growth in the printer industry stems from the nonimpact printer segment, which grew almost 20 percent above 1989, to $6 billion. The shift to ink jet and laser technology, which began in the mid-1980s, continued due to falling prices and to increased demand for desktop publishing and high quality copies. Desktop laser printers accounted for more than 60 percent of the total value in the non-impact category.

BIS CAP International estimates that the color segment of the non-impact printer market, which appeals to selective industries such as publishing, totaled only $5 million in 1990, representing 45 percent growth over 1989. Although ink jet color printers accounted for more than 71 percent of unit shipments in this category in 1990, thermal transfer color printers supplied nearly half the value. The average price of an ink jet color printer was about $2,750, compared to $7,500 for a thermal transfer color printer, which produces copies with better resolution and deeper, richer colors. Progress in color laser technology is slow. Aside from the enormous costs, the single greatest obstacle is the difficulty in achieving precise color placement. Recent breakthroughs allow some intelligent color copiers, with the proper software and add-on components, to be transformed into color laser printers. The main add-on component, know as the intelligent processing unit (IPU), functions as the connection between the computer and the copier. Converting an intelligent color copier into a color laser printer can cost anywhere from $30,000 to $100,000, depending on the configuration and the specific needs of the user. Dataquest, a market research firm, reported that shipments of impact printers totaled about 5.3 million units in 1990, representing a decline of almost 5 percent over the 1989 level. Dot matrix printers accounted for almost 98 percent of all impact printers sold. Although non-impact printers are the fastest growing segment of the printer industry, impact printers still account for 29 million units or almost 80 percent of the U.S. installed-base.

Long-Term Prospects

New product developments will continue to shape the printer industry. Through 1996, laser technology will be preferred in the monochrome segment, and laser revenues will rise 12 to 17 percent annually. In the color segment, ink jet technology will dominate the market. Shipments of impact printers are expected to drop below 3 million units, but will still represent 50 to 60 percent of the U.S. installed base over the next five years.

Local Area Networking

The local area network (LAN) market has continued to expand since the early 1980s as user needs have become more sophisticated. LANs allow users to share such expensive resources as storage devices and peripherals, while providing efficiency, database integrity, and security. LANs, once predominantly found on the departmental level, are now working their way into the management information systems (MIS) level and becoming part of enterprise-wide networks. They are becoming the preferred platform for such corporate mission critical applications as on-line transaction processing and computer integrated manufacturing.

The worldwide LAN market grew by 25.5 percent in 1990, reaching $6.4 billion, according to Dataquest. (These numbers are for hardware excluding both gateways and LAN software applications). The U.S. market share was $2.6 billion. Among the major worldwide market segments are PC LANs and enterprise LANs. The PC LAN segment, including network operating systems (NOS), dedicated servers (hardware designed to run network-oriented operating systems and server-based applications), and network interface cards (NIC), grew by 32.5 percent to $4.4 billion. Revenues in the enterprise LAN segment, which includes LAN interconnects (bridges and routers), terminal servers, host-based boards, and wiring centers, grew by 12 percent to $2 billion. Areas experiencing major growth in 1990 include NOS, dedicated servers, LAN interconnects, and unshielded-twisted pair connections.

The worldwide LAN network operating systems market is estimated at $1.2 billion for 1990, according to a report by Salomon Brothers. Major NOS vendors include Novell, with approximately 55 percent of the market, 3Com with 13 percent, IBM with 12 percent, Banyan with 6 percent, and Apple with 3 percent. NOS vendors, responding to the need for connectivity between different protocols, are supporting such open standards as Open Systems Interconnection (OSI), and delivering software for each other's proprietary protocols.

The market for dedicated LAN servers grew by 70.7 percent in 1990, to $542.8 million, according to Dataquest. Server vendors are introducing a new generation of network servers capable of handling more users and more traffic, and performing other tasks beyond the simple activities of file transfer and peripheral sharing. The market is being driven by the sheer number of PCs and workstations on networks, and by the trend toward client-server computing (where processing of an application is split between the front-end PC or workstation and the back-end server.) The new Intel 386 and 486 microprocessor based servers can provide peak internal transfers at speeds comparable to many mainframes.

The market for network interface cards (NIC) grew by 22.3 percent in 1990, reaching $2.5 billion. Close to 4.0 million NICs were shipped to the U.S. market. More than 45 percent of NIC shipments in the United States are based on Ethernet; in 1990, these shipments of NICs running on Ethernet totaled about 1.8 million units. Ethernet should remain in fairly strong demand with the advent of the lOBase-T standard, which allows Ethernet LANs to transmit at 10 megabits per second (mbps) across standard unshielded twisted-pair wiring. The lOBase-T hardware market reached $460 million in 1990 and will experience a compound annual growth rate of 21.9 percent between 1989 and 1996, according to Market Intelligence Research Corporation (MIRC). Token ring connections are on the rise, comprising about 30 percent of units shipped to the market in 1990.

Unshielded-twisted pari (UTP), a common telephone-type wire, is becoming the media of choice for Ethernet connections. UTP connections for Ethernet triplet between 1989 and 1990, and now make up close to 35 percent of the total quantity of Ethernet NIC shipments. The ability to use already installed telephone wire for connecting LANs is one reason for this rapid growth in UTP connections. Shipments of NICs over fiber optic connections for Ethernet doubled in 1990, yet make up only 2 percent of the total quantity of Ethernet NIC shipments. Coaxial cable connections make up the remaining 63 percent of Ethernet NIC shipments.

Corporate executives see LANs as valuable assets, and are demanding total enterprise connectivity and control. As the market for enterprise networks increases, so does the demand for such internetwork devices as gateways, routers, and bridges. In 1990, the worldwide LAN interconnect market grew to $562 million, about 10 percent of total LAN revenues, according to Dataquest. (This number excludes gateways.) The sale of remote bridges, which link geographically separate LANs over telecommunication lines, grew 37.7 percent over the 1989 level, reaching $207 million. The sale of routers, which selectively forward data from different protocols, grew to $226 million, a 47 percent increase over 1989. End users are interested in moving toward enterprise-wide networking and maintaining their already existing installed base of computers. With the trend toward connectivity, the market for gateways has increased. Gateways connect users of different computer architectures, allowing access to other LANs, minicomputers, mainframes, LAN facsimiles, and electronicmail (E-mail) systems.

The trend toward enterprise-wide networking has fueled the rapid growth of wiring hubs, which combine different topologies (configurations) and media into one concentrator. Until recently, most wiring hubs were media-distribution systems providing connectivity between fiber, twisted pair, and coaxial cables for Ethernet. "Smart hubs" have now evolved, which are sophisticated architectures handling such multiple access methods as Ethernet, token ring, and fiber distributed data interface (FDDI), under a common system of management and control. The worldwide market for wiring centers in 1990 reached $495 million.

In 1990, more software applications were introduced to enable users to reap the benefits of network computing. In the early days of LANs, existing single-user software was simply modified to run on a LAN. Now software is being designed to take advantage of the distributed processing capabilities of local area network, allowing several workstations to access and use the same data files at the same time. Some popular LAN software applications are database management, accounting, E-mail and text processing. The total LAN application software market was about $681 million in 1990, according to International Data Corporation (IDC). The PC LAN E-mail market is growing, but only 14 percent of all PC LAN users in 1989 had access to an E-mail package.

An important area of interest in 1990 was network management software, which, unlike other networking software packages, is designed exclusively to assist the network manager in controlling the activities of the network. There are currently a number of competing architectures for network management; there is also an industry-wide effort to standardize network management protocols. The network protocol used by most managers is called simple network management protocol (SNMP), which runs on transmission control protocol/internet protocol (TCP/IP) networks. Many other managers use common management information protocol (CMIP), which runs on open systems interconnect (OSI) networks. U.S. vendor sales of integrated network management systems more than doubled over their 1989 level, to $75 million in 1990.

Distribution channel revenues for LANs have shifted toward non-direct channels. According to LAN Magazine, the LAN value-added reseller market is growing at 40 percent a year, with combined sales of the top LAN suppliers surpassing $1 billion in 1990. The LANVAR industry is experiencing consolidation as smaller VARs are acquired by larger ones. This is in direct response to changes in the end user environment, where MIS (management information systems) managers are becoming more involved in the LAN buying decisions of large corporations, and are buying from dealers who have greater resources.

In 1990, major vendors announced their commitment to OSI as a key component of enterprise networking. Governments and corporations in the U.S. and abroad are now taking steps to incorporate this network protocol into their existing systems. For example, the U.S. Government has implemented the U.S. Government OSI Profile (GOSIP). The GOSIP mandate, which came into effect August 15, 1990, requires federal agencies to purchase only network products complying with OSI standard specifications. Although OSI is part of the strategic planning of many network users since it allows for more open connectivity, the lack of OSI applications and the established success of TCP/IP applications hinder OSI growth. Consequently, TCP/IP continues to grow.

FDDI technology is gaining acceptance for corporate backbone networks because of its 100 mbps data transfer rate, low noise level, and advanced network management capabilities. More than 80 leading computer and telecommunications companies support FDDI products. A second generation of FDDI chips was introduced in 1990. These new chips offer improved integration and network management support.

Long-Term Prospects

The 1990's will see the evolution of "networking computing," a phrase describing the trend in which workgroup LANs become integrated into enterprise-wide, multivendor networks. This trend will lead to real distributed processing and client-server computing used for mission critical applications.

The demand for dedicated servers, which are key in client-server computing, will rise as users move away from non-dedicated, minicomputer and mainframe servers. Client-server applications such as database management systems will also proliferate. Once the number of application servers increases, vendors will produce tools to help managers deal with client-server applications.

The market will continue to determine which standards are eventually accepted. FDDI products will increase. Infonetics Research Institute predicts that the FDDI market will reach over $1.3 billion in 1993. OSI products will continue to appear on the market, competing alongside TCP/IP products. Network management platforms will make a transition into SNMP and CMIP. As the market accepts standards, one of the main challenges will be the integration, sale and servicing of these multivendor solutions.

SOFTWARE

The U.S. software industry remained the world leader and experienced relatively healthy growth, attaining sales of almost $29 billion, or 20 percent above its 1989 level. Software markets continued to be healthy overall, with new product announcements across the range of computer system sizes, from micro to mainframe. According to International DataCorporation, the total world market for packaged software reached $43.0 billion in 1990. Of this total, the United States market represented $18.0 billion, or 42 percent. The European market stood at 17.3 billion, or 40 percent. In Japan, where custom software still represents a major percentage of that market, the packaged software market reached only $3.9 billion, or 9 percent of the world total.

In the personal computer segment of the market, Microsoft announced Windows 3.0, a graphical user interface, which works with the popular DOS operating system from the same company. The use of Microsoft's multiasking operating system, OS/2, continued to spread, although more slowly than most forecasters had predicted. Microsoft and IBM announced an agreement by which certain aspects of the future development of OS/2 will be divided between the two companies. The agreement was designed to speed the use of the operating system throughout the various segments of the personal computer market.

Operating systems for personal computers are often categorized hierarchically by their ability to handle users and tasks concurrently. The DOS operating system is single-user; OS/2, single-user, multiasking. UNIX continued to be the operating system of choice in scientific and engineering applications, with its move into the business and communications markets continuing. Estimates placed UNIX at 10 to 12 percent of the market and DOS/OS/2 at about 25 to 30 percent. Proprietary operating systems such as Apple Computer Corporation's operating system for its MacIntosh line of personal computers represented 5 to 10 percent of the market.

In the larger computer systems sectors, new hardware announcements were accompanied by significant new software announcements. Both enhanced proprietary operating systems and so-called open systems, based on UNIX, formed the core of the new software products.

INTERNATIONAL COMPETITIVENESS

Intellectual property rights protection continued to be of concern to software suppliers worldwide. The European Community's Software Directive, arising from the move toward economic integration under EC92, raised the issues of copyright protection of software interfaces and the unauthorized decompilation of these interfaces in the course of "reverse engineering" efforts by competitors. By late 1990, the issues remained unresolved, although the U.S. Government had expressed its desire to the EC Commission that the two issues be resolved in such a manner as to ensure continued growth in the world's software industry.

Long-Term Prospects

By 1995, the world packaged software market could approach $100 billion, with the U.S. and European markets in the forefront. The Japanese market should also show significant growth, due to the increasing competitiveness of Japanese suppliers and the continued shift of users toward packaged solutions and away from custom software.

COMPUTER SERVICES AND CONSULTING

Computer professional service providers advise on such problems as the design and selection of computer and peripheral systems, computer and telecommunications linkages, and systems and network management. They also train people in how to use computer systems, software, and combined computer and telecommunications networks. Computer professional services companies provide specific solutions to clients' business needs. Revenue figures cited in this section include all earnings derived from computer professional services, regardless of the provider.

Computer and telecommunications services represent the infrastructure of the information age. The growing importance of service industries in the U.S. and world economies will increase dependence on this infrastructure for at least the next decade. Providers of computer professional services have a comparatively bright future, even though revenues will not meet earlier high expectations.

During 1991, most individual firms and segments of the computer professional services sector did not achieve their predicted current dollar growth projections. In a surprising number of firms, senior managers had never held management positions during a national economic downturn and reacted inappropriately to changes in the market. Many were slow to reduce overhead, both employees and inventory, which significantly reduced profit margins for the year. Their rapid resort to price cutting not only reduced revenues in 1991, but sufficiently changed customer expectations so that aggregate revenues may be adversely affected during the next three to four years, most notably in 1992.

Revenues in 1992 will also be constrained by industrial restructuring trends that will reduce the number of managers, who usually are heavy consumers of these services; unfavorable exchange rate differentials in foreign markets (most notably Germany and Japan); and slower economic growth rates than in the past in selected economic sectors, such as automobiles and financial services, which are normally leading growth markets for information services.

With the rapid advances in computer technologies, the professional services associated with them have also changed. Compared with five years ago, a markedly advanced level and mix of skills are needed to provide these professional services. For example, the increasing use of custom programming requires broader and more extensive computer knowledge and training.

Industry Structure

In the United States, most firms in this sector remain independent, providing combinations of professional services and frequently offering other types of services and goods. In Western Europe and Japan, a larger percentage of computer professional services firms are subsidiaries of corporate conglomerates and account for an even greater percentage of sector revenues.

In 1991, about 3,700 U.S. firms (other than sole proprietorships) primarily provided computer professional services. The principal offerings of more than 1,700 of these firms were systems integration services; the remaining 2,000 mostly offered other kinds of computer professional services. Most of the net increase over 1990 came from the incorporation of sole proprietorships, in large part because of changes in tax laws and regulations regarding the status of consultants.

Although start-up costs have been reasonably low for these firms, annual increases in the total number of companies have been modest in recent years. New entrants have tended to be matched by losses in the number of firms through mergers and acquisitions.

The recent decrease in the availability of venture capital hastened to reduce the size, rather than the number, of start-up firms offering computer professional services. In contrast, a lack of venture capital has seriously affected the establishment of new companies producing hardware equipment.

According to trade association data, 1988 was the record year in both numbers and dollar values for mergers and acquisitions of computer professional services firms in the United States. In 1989 through 1991, the pace slackened somewhat but remained ahead of overall economic trends. In response to diminished revenue growth rate projections, 1992 is anticipated to set new records for mergers and acquisitions of these firms.

In addition to those companies mainly providing computer professional services, there are companies and sectors that earn significant revenues from such services. Manufacturers and distributors of computer and peripheral equipment, for example, increased their sales of services in the Unitod States and in Western Europe. A growing number of telecommunications firms are providing computer services, especially systems integration services, as outgrowths of their own equipment-marketing efforts, as well as from acquisitions. A number of nonprofit institutions and accounting and auditing firms are active participants in thc market.

Automating for Competitiveness

Despite significantly lower growth rates than in the past, the domestic market for computer professional services remains one of the faster growing segments of the U.S. economy. This market is expanding because organizations in both public and private sectors face increasingly complex problems of office and factory automation. These organizations have to rely upon outside help in designing appropriate automated systems and in making them work.

The need for these systems is fueled by increased foreign competition, especially from Japanese companies; changes in patterns of national growth and consumption, such as the comparatively low capital investment in U.S. services industries; and changes in government regulations. All these factors affect patterns of commercial interaction among companies, their suppliers, and customers.

Computer professional services continue to benefit from steady growth in the numbers and features of personal computers, workstations, and network terminals. Since 1990, the use of electronic mail systems (including digitized voice mail) and services was the fastest-growing source of revenues from professional services. There are about 5 million electronic mail-boxes in the United States. A small but strategically significant number of these mail-boxes are on international networks operated by multinational corporations.

Demographic and technological changes (such as greater computer literacy of U.S. managers in comparison with their foreign counterparts) have created notable economic advantages for U.S. firms that contract out for computer professional services. This customer base helps U.S. firms develop competitive advantages in offering services internationally, although the edge is diminishing over time.

Market Changes

Custom programming--by either in-house staffs or contractors has grown at a slower rate than other subsectors. In addition to less growth in the overall economy, this slowdown is due largely to the proliferation of prepackaged software, fourth generation languages, and computer-assisted software engineering tools. At the same time, this software proliferation has increased the need for outside professional training services. The wide availability of prepackaed software has led many providers of custom software to move from software development to software enhancements and modifications as their primary sources of revenues. Also, the importance of documentation service--custom software manuals showing how to modify software--is growing. These trends are anticipated to continue for at least the next five years.

Training services revenues have been growing fastest in computer-aided design/computer-aided manufacturing (CAD/CAM) and computer-aided engineering (CAE) applications particularly for training in the use of graphics software in the automotive and aerospace sectors. At the same time, the growth of revenues in training from word-processing and data-transaction systems has slowed because the software has become more user friendly.

There is a notable increase in the share of training provided by both interactive and digital video instruction. Systems vendors remain the preferred suppliers of computer education and training services for product-related services, which remain the primary market segment.

Systems Integration

In addition to firms that specialize in providing turnkey computer systems, data processing services companies, hardware and peripherals manufacturers, and software developers have found systems integration to be a lucrative business. Many of these firms are entering the field through new or expanded operating units; others are acquiring existing providers of services or merging to create new packages of offerings.

U.S. Government procurement has been an important element in the growth of integrated systems services. However. the Federal share of the systems integration market has been declining and is expected to continue to decrease through 1995 at least. State and local government procurements are expected to do no better than to maintain their small market share.

The growth of systems integration services, both in the United States and abroad, is difficult to assess on the basis of revenue data alone. Longitudinal growth rates were traditionally understated because they included a declining share of equipment costs. The value-added services component of turnkey systems continues to increase, but the cost per Calculation or function of computer memory is continuing a dramatic long-term decline. On the other hand, an increasing share of the total revenues of a firm is derived from repair and maintenance serrvices embedded in systems integration contracts.

The increasing use of single-procurement contracts for integrated computer-related services obscures trends in the revenues for any one component of those services. This use has changed competition patterns in the subsector. Only a few very large firms can afford to prepare bids on the largest projects, medium and small firms must increasingly form strategic alliances to make such bids jointly.

The most notable growth segment in U.S. systems integration in 1987 and 1988 was desktop publishing systems. During 1989, their significance with in this subsector slowed in the United States but began to gain prominence in Western Europe. During 1988 and 1989, the fastest-growing industrial sectors served by systems integrators was telecommunications. In both 1990 and 1991, no single sector had prominently high growth rates in the United States. By contrast, in the EC, financial services institutions (especially banks and insurance firms) were growth leaders.

Customer uncertainty about making purchases becomes greater as the time lag increases between announcements of new computer hardware and prepackaged software, and product release. Computer professional services firms are concerned that this time lag, which has increased throughout the 1980's, will continue and will reduce the information services growth rates throughout the 1990's.

Outlook for 1992

Revenues from computer professional services are expected to reach $56.3 billion, an increase of 13.9 percent in current dollars. Systems integration revenues will be a projected $17.8 billion; computer consulting and training services, more than $20.5 billion; and custom programming, nearly $18 billion, an increase of 14.9 percent. Mergers and acquisitions of computer professional services firms are expected to set a new record in 1992.

In 1992, more than 38 percent of all revenues for programming services--and a larger share of total profits--are expected to come from foreign clients, primarily in Western Europe and East Asian/Pacific countries. There are more foreign subsidiaries of multinationals based in the United States. Services provided to them will continue to create opportunities for U.S. custom programming and design services to enter markets abroad.

Expanding computer-related training in secondary schools, colleges, and universities, combined with increased numbers of software-based and video cassette tutorials available in retail stores, will continue to limit the growth of computer training firms. Nevertheless, revenues of this subsector will continue their dynamic growth; the increase for U.S. firms in 1992 is estimated to be 16.3 percent. According to one research firm: "Quantifying time and labor savings is now being used as a key element in many vendor's marketing strategies." This means that computer services are not just considered to be new and different. Rather, they are being marketed as a key contribution to increasing worker productivity and making a firm more effi-cient. This is a significant, and positive, change in market focus.

In 1992, it is estimated that more than 27 percent of computer education and consulting services revenues will come from abroad, although such revenues will accrue mainly to the largest 50 U.S. providers of such services.

Long-Term Prospects

Compound annual growth rates (in current dollars) for computer professional services exceeded 15 percent in the 1980's, despite variable economic conditions in the United States. Annual growth rates approached 20 percent from 1986 through 1989. Looking to the future, if the national economy and foreign sources of revenue continue to increase, this industry sector should achieve average annual growth rates (in current dollars) that will exceed 13 percent through 1996, and total revenues exceeding $95 billion in 1996.

The Western European market looks especially promising in the 1990's. A U.S. research firm projected that the West European market for computer professional services would grow an average of 24 percent annually and would reach $23.2 billion by 1992. This is a much faster rate of growth than that projected for the U.S. market. Although changing exchange rates cloud the picture, even faster growth rates are projected for the Japanese and South Korean markets.

Computer training and consulting will continue to gain market shares within this expanding services sector, both in the United States and abroad. Growth rates abroad, especially in Japan, are expected to exceed those in the United States. The acquisition and use of computers by those who are marginally computer-literate will increase and will continue to restructure the professional services market.

The development of integrated services digital networks (ISDNs) in telecommunications, which adds more computer intelligence into the network, will further blur distinctions between computer and telecommunications technologies. Development of these networks continues to proceed more rapidly in Western Europe than in the United States. Both U.S. and foreign businesses will need to purchase increasing amounts of computer professional services to adapt to this new environment and to increase organizational productivity.

FINANCIAL SERVICES: MUTUAL FUNDS

Despite setbacks in securities markets in the second half of 1990, mutual fund assets remained above the trillion dollar mark first reached in January, 1990. By the end of 1990, mutual funds had also posted new records, both in the number of funds (3,108) and in the number of individual acccounts (62.6 million). Total mutual fund assets continued to reach new highs in the first half of 1991 reflecting the recovery of the securities market and the infusion of new investments. Modest gains in new sales of equity funds were overshadowed by substantial gains in new investments in fixed-income funds as bank certificates of deposit (CDs) offered less attractive yields. The Dow Jones industrial average, the markets most closely watched indicator, closed above 3,000 and set new highs several times during the year. The growth in equity portfolios, combined with the extremely strong inflows into bond and other income funds contributed to higher total fund assets. By mid-1991, total mutual fund assets reached $1.19 trillion up from $1.07 trillion at the end of 1990.

Industry Description

The mutual fund industry consists of investment companies that sell shares in one or more mutual funds. A mutual fund is a pool or portfolio, of financial assets. So-called open-end funds are sold publicly and their shares must be redeemed by the investment company upon request of the shareholder. The value of the shares rises and falls with the value of the pool of financial assets. Shareholders rely on the investment company to gain a favorable return on their investment instead of operating directly in the market themselves.

A fund manager determines the composition of the portfolio, which may include stocks, bonds, Government securities, shares in precious metals, and other financial assets selected to meet the stated objective of the fund.

Mutual funds are commonly categorized by their general investment objectives. Equity funds consist mainly of common stocks and are organized primarily to achieve capital appreciation, or growth, rather than periodic distribution of income. Bond funds, on the other hand, are composed predominantly of corporate, U.S. Government, or municipal bonds and emphasize regular income rather than growth. Income funds have the same objectives as bond funds but include Government National Mortgage Association securities, Government securities, and common and preferred stocks as well as bonds. Money market mutual funds consist of short-term instruments, such as U.S. Government securities, bank CDs, and commercial paper. Short-term municipal bond funds are composed predominantly of tax-exempt short-termmunicipal securities.

Investment companies sell shares directly to the public or through agents. Registered representatives of brokerage firms, insurance agencies, and financial planning firms, among others, sell mutual fund shares as part of their overall financial service. The funds usually add a sales charge, or "load" which is used to compensate agents.

Many investment companies sell shares in funds directly to the public by mail and by telephone. These shares are usually sold "no load", that is with no sales charge or a nominal (less than 3 percent) sales charge. About a third of mutual funds do not carry a load. Revenue for investment companies from these funds is usually provided by management fees based on the size of assets, performance, or both. Some funds. known as 12b-1 funds, use a portion of their assets for marketing and distribution expenses.

A mutual fund must meet specific regulatory requirements. It must register with the Securities and Exchange Commission (SEC), issue a prospectus giving a detailed report of its operations, and adhere to strict accounting and valuation rules. A number of regulations exist to prevent conflicts of interest among officials of investment companies.

Mutual funds are also governed by state regulations and securities laws. Because of the fiduciary nature of mutual funds, they are subject to closer scrutiny than the operations of other financial institutions.

Closed-end funds

Closed-end funds are similar to open-end mutual funds in that both invest in various securities on behalf of investors sharing a common objective. Both provide professional management and seek to reduce risk through diversification. But while open-end funds continuously offer new shares to new investors and buy back (redeem) shares, closed-end funds usually have a fixed number of shares, which are sold through initial public offerings and subsequently trade on the open market.

Closed-end funds became more popular in the late 1980's. New issues climbed from less than $1 billion in 1985 to $21 billion in 1988, when closed-end income funds in particular offered strong appeal following the market drop of 1987. Initial public offerings have declined to a level estimated at less than $10 billion in 1991. The decline is attributed to a variety of factors, including the saturation of the market, renewed strength of the securities markets, and the increased popularity of other types of investments, including open-end funds.

Regulatory Changes

The mutual fund industry generally supports sections of a pending Administration banking bill that would change the financial services industry by among other things, ending the 1933 Glass-Steagall Act separation of banking and securities activities. The measure also would allow qualified banks to sell mutual funds through affiliates, provided they erect "firewalls" to separate them from the affiliates. Understandably, mutual funds favor the reciprocal ability to establish banks.

The Treasury Department, the SEC, and the mutual fund industry also support a proposal that provides more flexibility for mutual funds to engage in short term trading. The measure, part of a tax simplification bill introduced in mid-1991, would repeal a 1936 rule under which funds lose their tax exempt status if they receive more than 30 percent of their annual profit from trading securities held less than three months. This "short-short" rule as it is known, has restricted the ability of funds to move in and out of stocks. Under the proposed rule funds would be able to execute orders solely on the basis of investment merit and without considering the tax consequences.

Other regulatory changes should also be forthcoming. In 1990, the SEC began an in-depth review of the 50-year-old Investment Company Act and the Investment Advisors Act to determine what changes are needed in light of developments in the financial services industry. The SEC sought and received substantial comment from the industry and investing public. Due to the high level of interest, the Commission had to extend the original comment deadline.

Among the changes likely to grow out of the study is one that will require funds to disclose more information about persons on whom they rely for investment advice. Concerns about the safety of money market funds will probably lead to a rule requiring the funds to disclose that their underlying securities are not insured and that shareholders have no guarantee against a drop in the value of their accounts. The SEC also may impose limits on the investments money market funds can make, such as by limiting how much of their assets can be in other than top rated money market instruments. The SEC will also concentrate on those sections of the Investment Company Act that affect international mutual fund sales. A North American Free Trade Area may include a provision allowing the reciprocal establishment and sale of mutual funds among Canada, Mexico, and the United States.

Global Outlook

The popularity of mutual funds is not confined to the United States. Mutual funds have enjoyed worldwide growth that closely parallels their growth in the United States. Assets of all non-U.S. mutual funds totaled $1.09 trillion in 1990, slightly higher than the $1.07 trillion in assets held by U.S. funds. Assets of European Community (EC) funds totaled $644 billion in 1990. France had the largest EC asset pool with $383 billion, followed by the

United Kingdom ($92 billion) and Germany ($83 billion). Japanese funds had an impressive $354 billion. Other countries have also begun to develop mutual funds. The rapid development and growth of foreign mutual funds represents an attractive potential market for U.S. mutual fund sales in the years ahead.

Consistent with the move toward a global securities market, the mutual fund industry and the SEC are working to liberalize international fund sales by eliminating various barriers to effective competition. Tax requirements for U S investment companies constitute the single biggest impediment for funds seeking to market their shares abroad. One possible solution is to accord a more favorable tax treatment to foreign investors by allowing them a tax-free buildup of interest income and capital gains until shares are sold. U.S. mutual fund investors are subject to tax withholding. Other areas for consideration include the dissimilarity in structure of foreign funds which do not always exist as separate corporate entities with boards elected by shareholders. Definitions of mutual funds are somewhat different, too, as are requirements for accounting and disclosure. The U.S. also requires the forward pricing of funds whereas some countries permit the purchase at the previous day's market price. Affiliated party transactions are quite commonplace abroad whereas they are prohibited in the United States.

The mutual fund industry estimates that foreign shareholders account for less than one half of one percent of U.S. mutual fund shares. With the increased awareness of foreign markets and export sales for financial services, interest in marketing U.S. funds abroad is growing. The U.S. mutual fund industry continues to explore with its foreign counterparts ways to internationalize the market along the line of the new European Undertakings for Collective Investments in Transferable Securities (UCITS) This liberalized system makes possible the free marketing of mutual fund shares within the 12-member European Community (EC). UCITS, which are open-end investment companies or unit trusts, correspond in general to open-end mutual funds in the United States.

A 1988 EC directive allows a UCITS registered in one EC country to market its units in other EC member states by coordinating national laws and ensuring more effective and uniform protection of investors. The UCITS remain under the supervisory control of home country authorities, but they are subject to the marketing rules of the other member states. The UCITS directive became effective on October 1, 1989 for 10 member states of the EC, and on April 1, 1992 for Portugal and Greece.

There is no provision in the EC directive for the sale of third-country mutual funds. Accordingly, any U.S. fund that wants to establish itself and market within the EC is required to reregister within the individual member states. EC fund managers find it virtually impossible to establish funds in the United States because of strict SEC requirements. Congress could amend the Investment Company Act by giving the SEC authority to approve foreign funds for sale in the United States if the Commission determined they were subject to comparable regulations in their home country. New legislation could be introduced after the international industry and regulatory groups agree on a plan acceptable to The SEC. Once implemented,(perhaps during the mid-1990's) the internationalization of fund sales would create a competitive global environment and give U.S. mutual funds new opportunities for sales.

Outlook for 1992

Barring a deep recession or prolonged declines in the securities markets, the prospects for mutual funds remain upbeat. As the population continues to grow older there will be more people with higher incomes to invest as they focus on retirement savings. Balanced funds, which are composed of both equity and debt issues, became increasingly popular in 1991 and they should remain attractive in 1992.

Long-Term Prospects

The phenomenal growth of the mutual fund investing of the 1980's will not be sustained. The industry anticipates a slower but steady growth. Demographics should sustain interest in funds. As the baby boomers age, new opportunities will open for financial service firms that can assist them in planning for retirement.

Although there will probably be fewer investment vehicles, many mutual funds will re-package their products to appeal to specific markets. They will also change distribution methods to make investing easier. Electronic transactions will become more widespread as will sales through automatic withdrawal from bank accounts and payroll deduction. Banks will become a significant distribution channel of mutual funds for their own customers.

The industry is designing variations in sales charges and the distinction between load and no-load funds will become more blurred. Some load funds are already reducing sales charges in response to a better informed and cost-conscious investing public.

Funds will continue to emphasize good service and cost-efficiency. In the process, they will have to trim the high cost of those services and the larger marketing and public relations efforts that tend to squeeze their profit margins. As part of the industry effort to become more efficient and reduce operating costs, some funds are moving their transfer and shareholder relations operations in-house. Other funds will be merged, either within the same family of funds or with outside funds, including foreign funds seeking to increase their U.S. presence.

The move toward 24-hour securities trading would not materially affect mutual funds. However, a special provision would have to be made for The pricing of funds since the net asset values that funds use to determine purchase and redemption prices are based on the daily closing prices of their underlying securities.

HEALTH CARE

The providers of health and medical services include public and private health care institutions such as hospitals, offices and clinics of physicians and other health care professionals, nursing homes, other specialized facilities, and managed-care establishments. The health and medical services industry is made up of thousands of independent medical practices and partnerships, several large public and not-for-profit private hospitals, and a rising number of for-profit hospitals and managed-care and other health and medical service establishments.

Health Care Expenditures

U.S. health care outlays, accounting for approximately 13 percent of the Gross National Product, totaled $738 billion in 1991, up about 11 percent from $666 billion in 1990. Private sector health care expenditures made up about 58 percent of the total, while the public sector accounted for the remainder. Medicare and Medicaid make up the principal public source of these expenditures.

Expenditures for hospital care totaled an estimated $282 billion in 1991, up more than 10 percent from $256 billion in 1990. This represented 38 percent of total health care spending. Physicians' services, the second largest item, rose 11 percent to about $140 billion, while expenditures for nursing-home care, the third largest sector, gained 12 percent to an estimated $59 billion. Home health care, one of the fastest growing areas, is projected to show a year-to-year increase of approximately 26 percent from 1990, with expenditures totaling an estimated $9 billion in 1991. Expenditures for dental care, other professional services, and other health services are projected to come to $86 billion in 1991.

Employment

Employment in the health care industry has gone up steadily, from 7 million in 1988 to more than 9 million by July, 1991, an average annual growth rate of 8 percent. These numbers are exclusive of employment in the health insurance, medical equipment and supplies, and pharmaceutical industries.

Employment has grown fastest in offices of physicians and surgeons -- by 200,000 between 1988 and 1990. Hospital employment, the largest source of jobs in the health care sector, increased by 409,000 between 1988 and 1990. Private hospitals accounted for most of this increase. Nursing and personal care facilities also are important sources of jobs for skilled nursing personnel and medical technologists, among others.

Cost Factors

Many factors have contributed to the rising cost of health care, including so-called defensive medicine; increasing reliance on sophisticated and expensive equipment; innovative treatment of such illnesses as heart disease, end-stage renal disease, AIDS, and cancer; and an aging population, which adds to Medicare and Medicaid expenditures.

Another factor behind the rising cost of health care has been the rise in malpractice suits. One major insurance company reports that claims increased from 11.3 per 100 doctors in 1981 to a peak of 17.8 in 1985. Since then, however, the rate has dropped. According to the American Medical Association (AMA), 8 malpractice claims per 100 physicians were paid in 1989, the last year for which data are available. This is a reduction of nearly one-third from the peak rates of the mid-1980s.

Malpractice premiums for self-employed physicians rose at an average annual rate of about 18 percent between 1982 to 1988, to an average of $15,900. Since then, as the rate of malpractice claims has dropped, several major insurers have reduced premiums. Nevertheless, the AMA estimates that malpractice premiums totaled almost $6 billion in 1990.

The increase in medical malpractice suits and claims has brought with it a greater reliance on defensive medicine, such as duplicate tests and diagnostic procedures; the use of consultants; more hospitalization; and extensive documentation. The AMA estimates defensive medicine alone adds $15 billion to the nation's health care costs.

The increase in the number and size of malpractice awards has led some states to cap awards, particularly for pain and suffering. In addition, the insurance industry has joined forces with the medical community in pushing for reforms of the tort system. As a result, both the number of malpractice claims and the rate of increase in malpractice premiums have been reduced.

Psychiatric Care

A National Medical Enterprises Inc. report shows that the number of private psychiatric hospitals rose from 220 in 1984 to 403 in 1989, an 83 percent increase. During the same period, the number of psychiatric units in general hospitals increased from 1,259 to 1,858, a 47 percent increase, while state and county psychiatric hospitals decreased 23 percent, from 277 to 212. Department of Veterans Affairs medical centers, residential centers for emotionally disabled children, and multi-service mental health organizations all remained stable.

The American Psychiatric Association estimates that the United States spent $50 billion on hospital-based psychiatric care in 1989. This includes $16 billion for substance-abuse services. Private insurance paid about 67 percent for inpatient psychiatric care, Medicare and Medicaid accounted for 17 percent, and the remaining 16 percent was paid by others. During the past decade, psychiatric hospitals had an average annual occupancy rate of 85 percent. Although about 10 million Americans are being treated for psychiatric and substance-abuse problems, another 40 million are in need of treatment, according to some estimates. Among the reasons that demand for psychiatric care services is increasing are that treatment is becoming more effective, insurance coverage for mental illnesses is becoming more prevalent, and society is becoming more accepting of psychiatric and substance-abuse services. In addition, many states now require insurance companies to cover psychiatric care.

Medicare Spending

Medicare is the Federal health program for patients who are at least 65 years old or disabled. More than 35 million persons are enrolled in Medicare, of whom 32 million are elderly and 3 million disabled. Medicare spending rose from $100 billion in 1989 to $108 billion in 1990, an increase of 8 percent. At the same time, the number of beneficiaries increased by only 2 percent. Hospital insurance under Medicare is funded primarily by Social Security payroll taxes. Medicare consists of two basic programs, Hospital Insurance (HI), and Supplementary Medical Insurance (SMI). HI pays for hospital care, skilled nursing, home health care, and hospices. HI outlays totaled an estimated $65 billion in 1990, an increase of more than 6 percent over 1989. SMI outlays grew from $39 billion in 1989 to $43 billion in 1990, a 10 percent increase. SMI pays for doctors, hospital outpatient and laboratory services, end-stage renal disease treatment, and durable medical equipment. Enrollees pay about 25 percent of SMI costs; the rest comes from general revenues.

Profit Margins

There is no uniform way of reporting the industry's profitability. Fragmentary information indicates that nearly 9 of 10 hospitals, the dominant group of health care providers, do not operate for a profit. Information on other health care providers, including physicians and dentists, nursing homes, and managed-care organizations is sparse. This lack of information is compounded by the current wave of mergers among private hospitals and other health care organizations.

According to one estimate, profit margins of all for-profit hospitals declined during the first four years of the Prospective Payment System (PPS). Under PPS, fees for services rendered are replaced with a scale of fixed payments based on the patient's illness. According to the Prospective Payment Assessment Commission (ProPAC), profit margins dropped from 7.3 percent in 1984, the first year of PPS, to 3.5 percent by 1988. Since then, margins have barely changed, reaching an estimated 3.8 percent by 1990. In the aggregate, however, hospital margins are considerably higher now than at any time during the 1970's.

Home Health Care

One way of containing health care costs that is catching on fast is by providing care in a patient's home. More than 5 million people in the United States require home care services. At-home care is less extensive than institutionalization and may often be less traumatic.

During 1990, there were about 11,000 home health service providers in the United States, of which 5,700 were Medicare-certified and more than 1,780 hospitals provided home health care services. Since the start of the Prospective Payments System, hospital-based home health services providers have increased significantly, from 1,167 in 1984 to 1,784 in 1989.

Expenditures for home-care services totaled an estimated $7 billion in 1990, exclusive of home health care products. Medicare expenditures for home care amounted to about $4 billion, an increase of 24 percent from 1989.

Although still a small portion of all U.S. health care expenditures, spending on home health care has been growing at an annual rate of about 20 percent for the past few years. This rapid growth reflects the increasing number of older Americans; the lower average cost of home care ($750 per month for routine skilled nursing care at home compared with $2,000 in an institution); active insurance industry support for home care; and Medicare promotion of home health care as an alternative to institutionalization.

Other programs to help reduce Medicare costs seek to shift a greater proportion of health care to outpatient services and to discourage hospitals from making unnecessary capital outlays.

Under Medicare, the length of hospital stays is decreasing. For instance, between 1964 and 1988, inpatient days decreased by almost 14 percent, while outpatient days grew by almost 35 percent. This increase is reflected in the number of elderly people making more outpatient visits and greater use of nursing homes, home-care services, and emergency health care centers.

Health Care Reform

Alternative approaches for controlling costs of health care have been proposed as part of a package of health care reforms. Among the reforms most frequently advocated are universal health insurance and restructuring Medicaid. The Bush Administration has proposed legislation that aims at, among other things, an improved health care delivery system and greater access to affordable quality health care through reduced liability costs and improved quality of care. In 1991, several proposals for expanding health insurance were being discussed in Congress, prompted by various congressional and other Government studies critical of the health care system. For instance, the U.S. Bipartisan Commission on Comprehensive Health Care for All Americans (Pepper Commission) recommended a plan for extending health care insurance coverage to the 37 million uninsured persons, including the aged, the unemployed, the employed poor, and employees of small businesses. Other recommendations included overhauling the private insurance system and restructuring Medicaid.

International Health Care Market

The international climate seems favorable for U.S. health care companies to invest abroad. The prospects in Western Europe, Mexico, Japan, Kuwait, the former Soviet Union, Poland, and Hungary are particularly promising. The governments of these nations have made health care a centerpiece of their social policy and are providing steady annual budget increases for health care. Many of these countries are also striving to modernize both the public and private health sectors and offer market opportunities for a wider range of services and medical equipment. Others are calling for decentralization of the health care industry. In both Western Europe and Japan, demographic factors, including aging populations, increased longevity, and relatively higher incomes, are creating growing demand for health care services. For example, some U.S. firms have already obtained contracts from Kuwait to provide emergency health care services there, and additional contracts may be awarded in the future.

The best opportunities are in the areas of primary care, homecare, and nursing home services. In addition, opportunities in hospital management, ancillary services, private health insurance, and drug rehabilitation programs appear promising.

In some foreign markets, U.S. firms face trade and regulatory barriers. For example, although Japan allows foreign firms to provide home care and nursing home services, foreigners are not allowed to own health care facilities or to manage hospitals. Such issues are being addressed in the Uruguay Round and the services negotiations of the prospective North American Free Trade Agreement.

Outlook for 1992

Health care expenditures in 1992 should rise to about $817 billion, a record 14 percent of GNP. Outlays for hospital care will rise by 11 percent, to $313 billion. Expenditures for physicians services will amount to an estimated $155 billion, an 11 percent increase over 1991, while spending for nursing homes and home care will approach $77 billion, a 13 percent rise.

Long-Term Prospects

Many of the proposed national health care reforms could lead to more efficient and effective services and procedures, expanded insurance coverage, wider availability of services, and more alternative health care resources.

Signs of greater diversity are already evident. Managed care such as private health maintenance organizations (HMOs) and home health care now occupy an important place in the market and will undoubtedly play major roles in the future. Other alternatives to institutional care, such as private specialized health care providers for substance abuse or psychiatric disorders, among others, also will be important.

Drugs

The United States continues to be the world's leader in discovering and developing new medicines and represents the world's largest single market for pharmaceuticals. Highly innovative and technologically advanced, the industry has consistently maintained a competitive edge in international markets and a positive balance of trade. In 1991, exports exceeded imports by about $1 billion.

Drug industry shipments increased about 9.4 percent in 1991 to about $59 billion. In constant dollars, the increase was close to 4 percent. Fueled in part by demand for new drugs, exports, valued at almost $6 billion, rose nearly 14 percent above 1990, while imports reached almost $5 billion, up almost 25 percent. For 1991, total employment in the industry reached 191,000, a slight increase over 1990.

While the pharmaceutical market again proved to be resistant to economic recession in 1990-91, the structure of the industry is changing in response to increasing research and development (R&D) costs, growing sales of generic drugs, and government regulations. Most recently, for example, the Omnibus Budget Reconciliation Act of 1990 mandated price rebates on pharmaceuticals reimbursed under Medicaid beginning in 1991. Pharmaceutical manufacturers must offer Medicaid its "best price," with rebates ranging from a minimum of 12.5 percent to a maximurn of 25 percent. By 1993, the minimum rebate will be 15 percent, and there will be no maximum.

Similarily, Food and Drug Administration regulations not only greatly affect the industry's domestic performance, but also have a direct bearing on its international competitiveness. New drug approvals are perhaps the most rigorous in the world. According to a 1990 study by the Center for the Study of Drug Development at Tufts University, it takes U.S. pharmaceutical firms an average of 12 years and $231 million to get one new medicine from the laboratory to the pharmacist's shelf. Only about one in five of the medicines that begin clinical trials make it through the approval process. In addition to the strict regulatory environment, the industry must deal with increasing legal costs growing out of product liability and medical malpractice suits.

Partly as a result of high R&D costs, mergers and acquisitions have increased as the major pharmaceutical firms seek to adjust to market conditions. In 1991, the industry's R&D expenditures increased by 13 percent to more than $9.2 billion. Drawn-out clinical trials, more complex diseases, and the growing expense of high-technology equipment all add to escalating R&D costs. Pharmaceutical R&D has grown from around 12 percent of the value of industry shipments in 1980 to more than 15 percent in 1991, one of the highest proportions of any U.S. industry.

Growing sales of lower-priced generic drugs also influence the way the pharmaceutical industry markets its products. Generic prescription drugs now account for 30 percent of total prescriptions written. While the recent recession did not slow the demand for pharmaceuticals, Americans did scale back on their visits to physicians and were more cost conscious when purchasing pharmaceuticals. Direct-to-consumer advertising for non-branded generic drugs has increased. Likewise, the brand-name firms significantly increased their marketing efforts throughout the world in response to the competition from generics.

International Competitiveness

U.S. manufacturers account for 42 percent of the major pharmaceuticals marketed worldwide. While consistently maintaining a positive trade balance, the industry faces increasing international competition. To maintain competitiveness, the industry must overcome such obstacles to U.S. sales overseas as price controls, illegal use of patents and copyrights, and foreign regulations on marketing and R&D. During the last 20 years, for example, price and profit controls in most European countries limited price increases for pharmaceuticals to less than one-half of the rate of inflation. Because of widespread piracy of product and process patents, copyrights, and trademarks, the pharmaceutical industry has initiated a number of actions against foreign countries under Section 301 of the 1974 Trade Act to obtain stronger intellectual property protection. As a result, the U.S. Government has negotiated improved patent protection in a number of countries, but there is still much work to be done on the issue of intellectual property rights.

The U.S. pharmaceutical industry does more than half of its foreign business in Western Europe. Since the European Community (EC) represents a market of 340 million consumers. The industry is closely monitoring the move toward a single EC market in 1992. A critical issue will be how the wide range of pharmaceutical pricing and reimbursment constraints in the member states consolidated into EC regulations.

Japan is the United States' largest pharmaceutical customer. With more than $30 billion in domestic pharmaceutical sales, Japan also is the world's second largest drug market, exceeded only by the United States. Japan exports less than 5 percent of the drugs produced locally and has the highest per capita consumption of drugs in the world. Japanese spend 40 percent more per capita on prescriptions than Americans. Drugs make up 17 percent of health spending in Japan, compared with 7 percent in the United States.

Although the United States has a pharmaceutical trade surplus with Japan, U.S. firms find it increasingly difficult to compete because of Japan's drug pricing system. The Japanese government not only reduces health insurance reimbursements for pharmaceutical every two years, but also makes it extremely difficult for the industry to raise prices to offset inflation. Japan is currently reviewing its mechanism for price setting and price management of pharmaceuticals, and has scheduled a full-scale price revision of its drug industry for April, 1992.

Outlook for 1992

The drug industyy is expected to continue to grow at about 9 percent during 1992. In constant dollars, industry shipments are expected to increase about 3 percent, while product shipments will increase more than 3 percent. Employment will rise only slightly. Exports are expected to rise to nearly $6 billion, and imports are projected to increase to $5 billion.

Long-Term Prospects

The drug market is expected to continue to expand over the next five years, but the rate of growth may be somewhat slower. During this period, $8 billion to $10 billion worth of brand-name drugs are set to come off-patent. How the generic producers market these drugs and how the brand-name drugs compete will influence the growth of the industry. Cost cutting efforts by hospitals, major health care institutions, the Federal Government and insurance companies will have important implications for the industry.

Medicinals and Botanicals

In 1991, shipments of medicinals and botanicals were valued at more than $5 billion, an increase of about 7 percent in constant dollars. Exports increased about 11 percent to more than $2 billion, while imports rose 24 percent to about $3 billion.

Medicinal and botanical establishments are primarily engaged in manufacturing bulk organic and inorganic medicinal chemicals and their derivatives and in processing bulk botanical drugs and herbs. As more product patents expire, the original patent holders have begun producing medicinal chemicals formerly covered under their patent and selling the chemicals to generic producers. This may increase domestic production of medicinal chemicals and reduce the level of imports in the future. These firms will continue to explore compounds among natural products to cure diseases and to develop new and more efficient approaches to new drug discovery.

Pharmaceutical Preparations

Shipments of pharmaceutical preparations were valued at nearly $49 billion in 1991, an increase of more than 3 percent in constant dollars. Exports and imports were more than $1 billion. The establishments in this industry are primarily engaged in manufacturing, fabricating, and processing drugs into pharmaceutical preparations for human or veterinary use. The products of this group usually finished in the form intended for final consumption.

Prescription drug costs in the U.S. continue to remain a much smaller percentage of total health care costs than in other industrialized countries. While spending on health care has been increasing rapidly as a percentage of the Gross National Product, spending on prescription drugs has remained substantially under 1 percent of GNP, just as it has for the past 25 years.

Senior citizens consume 30 percent of all prescription medication dispensed in the United States. The U.S. pharmaceutical industry continues to devote a considerable amount of its resources to discovering new medicines for the cure and treatment of diseases that debilitate older Americans, such Alzheimer's, arthritis, and osteoporosis.

In the veterinary sector, new products will be sought to enhance animal growth, to prevent bacterial contamination during processing of carcasses, and to reduce the amount of fat in meat while maintaining tenderness.

Diagnostic Substances

In 1991, shipments of diagnostics substances were valued at more than $2 billion, an increase of 1 percent in constant dollars. Exports for 1991 were more than $1 billion, an increase of 24 percent. Imports of $280 million were negligible by comparison.

Diagnostic firms are primarily engaged in manufacturing chemical, biological, and radioactive substances that are used in diagnosing or monitoring the state of human or veterinary health.

The blending of chemistry, biotechnology, and computer science is reshaping the diagnostics substances industry. Researchers are now able to magnify genes to the point where they see and copy their DNA sequences, a valuable tool in AIDS and cancer research.

In 1991, the U.S. Patent Office issued patents for oral diagnostic testing processes, including one for AIDS screening. Patents also were granted for several rapid diagnostic test formats, including rapid tests on whole-blood specimens, which produce results much faster than older methods.

The market for laboratory testing of genetic diseases is strong and promises to grow substantially over the next five years. More than 3,000 diseases are believed to be caused by genetic deformation, but gene sequences are known for only 100. Once a gene sequence is known, it can open the way to new treatment methods.

The world market for diagnostic test kits also is growing and is estimated to reach about $1 billion by 1996.

Biological Products

Shipments of biological products were valued at more than $2 billion in 1991, an increase of more than 3 percent in constant dollars. Exports in 1991 totaled $991 million, an increase of 2 percet over 1990. Imports were $314 million, an increase of 16 percent over 1990.

Biologicals establishments are primarily engaged in the production of bacterial and virus vaccines, toxoids, and analogous products (such as allergic extracts), serums, plasmas, and other blood derivatives for human or veterinary use. Vaccines continue to be one of the cheapest and most effective ways to eradicate certain diseases. The likelihood is that over the next five years vaccines will be developed to modify the body's immune response to chronic disease.

INFORMATION SERVICES AND DATA PROCESSING

Information services are a growing share of the U.S. economy, and they represent a strategic input to make their business customers more competitive internationally. Delivery of information by means of the newest electronic or photo-optic technologies is a large part of the infomation revolution. Information services Firms are finding innovative and cost-effective ways to create, store, manipulate, and cross-correlate information based increasingly on input from their customers.

The July, 1991 ruling by U.S. District Court Judge Harold Greene, now under appeal, which would allow the Bell Regional Holding Companies (usually known as RBOCs) to provide information services, has added a substantial dimension of uncertainty to all market planning within this sector. Nevertheless, in 1992 all subsectors are projected to show both positive real growth rates and growth above those of the national economy consistent with long-term trends.

Some subsectors will experience much greater employment turnover in 1992 in response to the national economic recovery. The best employment prospects are for UNIX-trained applications programmers, electronic data interchange (EDI) systems managers, computer trainers with foreign language capabilities, and consultants and systems analysts with foreign marketing experience.

The U.S. information services industry is well developed with 24,223 establishments competing in the marketplace, according to the Census Bureau's 1987 *Census of Service Industries*. The industry has nearly 1 million employees.

International Competitiveness

The U.S. information services industry has always had a positive balance of trade, and this trend is expected to continue. Finding new customers in foreign markets is essential if the industry is to maintain its leadership. The U.S. Government places a high prionty on removing barriers to trade and investment by U.S. information services companies, and this issue is being dealt with in U.S. discussions and negotiations with members of the General Agreement on Tariffs and Trade (GATT), the International Telecommunications Union (ITU), the Organization for Economic Cooperation and Development (OECD), as well as in bilateral talks with Mexico, Canada, the European Community (EC), and other countries.

The various trade associations representing the industry also play an important role in the globalizadon of information services. The Information Technology Association (formerly ADAPSO), the computer software and services industry association), the Information Industry Association, and the Electronic Data Interchange Association have established relationships with their overseas counterparts to promote the development of information services, to forge new commercial relationships, and to maintain open markets for trade and investment.

Electronic Information Services

The revenues of the eletronic information services industry are estimated to have grown by 18.5 percent in 1991 and amounted to $10.2 billion. Financial, credit, remarketing, and travel information services agree the most developed and accounted for the largest shares of the indutry's revenues. Companies offering videotex services aimed primarily at home consumers gained subscribers in 1991.

Electonic information services are provided by five means: online computer disk-read only memory (CD-ROM), magnetic tape, floppy disk, and auditex. Online delivery, which sends information from computers over telephone lines and broadcast systems to subscribers' personal computers or terminals, accounts for about 78 percent of thc electronic information services industry revenues. Audiotex and information on CD-ROM are the fastest growing media for the provision of electronic information services. Delivery of information services through magnetic tape and floppy disk is declining.

The amount of information available electronically continues to grow at a fast rate. According to Cuadra Associates, a company that publishes an annual database directory, the number of databases currently available worldwide is 6,200 (4,700 are available online and 1,500 are portable). In 1987, only 3,369 electronic databases were available. The United States is the largest producer and consumer of electronic information services. It produces more than 50 percent of the databases available in the world.

Outlook for 1992

Assuming that the U.S. economy and the economies of U.S.'s major trading partners remain healthy in 1992, the electronic information services industry is projected to grow by 20 percent in 1992, and revenues will amount to about $12 billion. Sales of information services on CD-ROM and through 900 telephone numbers will show the fastest growth. The 900 numbers will be used increasingly to provide reasonably priced, useful information to home customers. The demand for fast, accurate online information by businesses and professionals will grow modestly.

Long-Term Prospects

The long-term outlook for the electronic information services industry is generally favorable, but many difficult issues need to be resolved. Demand for industry services will be high if there are no serious downturns in the economies of industrialized countries. The growth rate of the industry is now projected at 20 percent annually through the next five years. The audiotex segment is expected to grow from $900 million in 1990 to $3 billion by 1993. The market for CD-ROM products is projected to reach $1.2 billion by 1993. During the 1990's, businesses will consider many electronic information services central to their operations rather than luxury services. The U.S. market is becoming saturated, and U.S. firms must find new overseas customers if they are to survive.

The EC and Japan are aggressively trying to develop their information services industries and are potentially a threat to U.S. leadership. They are making progress, although language barriers represent a serious problem. The different telecommunications policies and systems in the EC are a deterrent, but resolutions to this problem are under way. U.S. businesses have expressed concerns about aspects of the common telecommunications regulations that are being formulated and are consulting closely with EC officials about the future regulatory framework. The U.S. information services industry has to maintain a strong presence in the EC and Japan to take advantage of coming opportunities there.

Privacy protection, new rules for vendors of audiotex services, intellectual property protection for databases, and the participation of the Regional Bell Holding Companies (RBOCs) in the information services industry are the major policy issues resolution of these issues will take several years.

Consumer groups in the United States are demanding changes in the use of databases containing personal information. Complaints about the use of credit records for direct marketing purposes have already caused credit reporting companies to back away from this activity. The EC is in the process of drafting regulations that would limit the use of personal information. Developing databases through the use of automatic number identification also raises privacy concerns, and legislative solutions are being sought in this area.

The fraudulent and misleading practices of a limited number of providers of 900 services have caused the Federal Communications Commission (FCC) and Congress to draft regulations and guidelines for audiotex services to diminish these practices. The trade associations representing providers of 900 services have also established guidelines. These developments are viewed as positive because they will restore consumer confidence in using these services. The use of 900 services to obtain quick, useful information has great potential if some of the "ripoff artists" go out of business.

In March 1991, the Supreme Court ruled that the alphabetical listing of names and addresses in the white pages of a telephone directory was not protected by Federal copyright law. This decision could have a negative impact on information services providers because it could cheapen the value of databases and be a disincentive to produce them.

In July 1991, Judge Harold Greene reluctantly agreed to allow the RBOCs to provide information services to homes and business over their telephone networks. He stayed his order to allow for appeals to be filed. By September 1991, eight appeals have been filed by organizations opposing the decision because they feel that the regional companies will compete with them unfairly through cross-subsidizations and monopolies over local telephone networks. Some organizations are supportive of Judge Greene's decision because they believe that the RBOCs can be important in developing a mass market for consumer information services. The industry is anxiously awaiting the outcome of this case.

Data Processesing and Network Services

Despite the economic downturn in 1991, the data processing and network services industry as a whole performed well. The revenues of companies that provide services to depressed industry sectors such as the retail and construction industries grew at a slower rate, while the revenues of those that pursued new trends such as outsourcing and electronic commerce grew faster. In 1991, revenues of the data processing and network services industry grew by 14 percent and amounted to $35.6 billion.

The data processing and network services industry is experiencing steady growth for several reasons. Many sectors of the economy are heavily dependent on these services to remain competitive and, in some cases, are unable to do business without them. Revenues for transaction processing services, which includes such things as medical and insurance claims processing, utility billing, and credit card billing and approval, have the largest share of the industry's revenue. The revenues of this sector are stable and probably recession proof.

The trend toward outsourcing (contracting of services), especially in the banking and financing industry, is continuing. In the early 1980's, there was a surge in the acquisition of computers and software by companies and other organizations to set up data-processing facilities within firms. However, more organizations are now returning to outside sources for their data-processing and network-services needs. Outsourcing is occurring because of the inability of in-house operations to keep pace with technological changes, to acquire adequate technical staff, and to handle complex data-processing needs. Companies are also seeking to reduce their information technology budgets through outsourcing. The prime markets for outsourcing are government, banking and financial services, health care, transportation, and manufacturing.

Companies with networks for electronic data interchange (EDI) services are making an important contribution to the revenues of the data processing and network services industry. Expenditures on EDI services are growing at a rate of 56 percent annually and amounted to an estimated $500 million in 1990. EDI, which is the exchange of trade-related documents electronically, has been used successfully for several years in the transportation, retail, and grocery industries. Many more industries as well as government agencies are beginning to use EDI.

The highly competitive data processing and network services industry comprises more than 2,000 companies, which includes small businesses with fewer than 50 employees as well as global corporations. The industry employs nearly 300,000 persons.

Outlook for 1992

The outlook for the data processing and network services industry is for high growth. The revenues of the industry are projected to grow by 13.5 percent and amount to $40.4 billion. Data processing and network services vendors will continue to pursue outsourcing opportunities and business in overseas markets. Transaction processing is expected to remain stable, and the use of EDI will grow substantially.

Long-Term Prospects

The U.S. data processing and network services industry is expected to maintain an average annual growth rate of about 13 percent (in real terms) from 1992 to 1996. EDI and outsourcing are expected to remain high growth areas over the next five years. Barriers to the use of EDI, such as multiple standards, critical masses of computer users, and high costs are slowly being overcome.

At the same time, providers of EDI services are continually developing additional applications for EDI. For example, EDI will increasingly be used to make combined electronic document and payment transfers. One market research firm expects expenditures for EDI network services to reach $1.7 billion by 1993. Outsourcing of data processing and network services is projected to grow from $6 billion in 1990 to $15 billion by 1995.

Long-term international prospects are also good for dataprocessing and network service companies as more countries liberalize their telecommunications policies and develop their information services markets. Once improvements in telecommunications infrastructure are in place in Eastern Europe and Latin America, U.S. companies will be more aggressively pursuing opportunities in these regions. In Eastern Europe, some countries will have the necessary infrastructure within the next five years; others will not be ready for information services until the late 1990's. South Africa should also offer good opportunities if the country's social problems begin to be resolved.

Foreign markets for EDI services will be sizable. A market research firm specializing in the information services industry expects the Western European market for EDI to reach $250 million by 1992. Most major data processing and network companies will form strategic alliances with foreign firms, or enter overseas markets through acquisitions. Some companies will need to restructure their overseas operations during the next five years in order to be able to operate on a global basis. In some cases, firms will have to move their operations to other Western European countries. High-level local (rather than U.S.) managers will need to be hired, and more brochures and product materials will be in the local languages.

There are uncertainties about several policy issues that could affect the industry. These issues include Federal and state taxation of software and services, entry of RBOCs into the information services market (discussed in the Electronic Information section), imposition of access charges or fees by the FCC on information services providers, state regulation of information services providers, privacy, and intellectual property protection.

PROFESSIONAL SERVICES

Professional services include accounting, auditing, and bookkeeping services; executive search services; legal services; and management, consulting and public relations services.

The professional services sector has grown more rapidly than the economy over the past decade and the trend is expected to continue. However, the rate of growth over the next few years will not equal that of the 1980's, when professional services were frequently characterized by mergers and acquisitions. This has given way to a retrenchment which in all probability will continue throughout the 1990s.

The economic slowdown of 1990-91 was in sharp contrast to earlier downturns, when established professional services were still expanding and often shielded from the effect of recessionary forces. This time, there was an unusual wave of white-collar layoffs that could eventually streamline the professional services sector just as happened to the manufacturing sector when it was forced to retrench in the 1980's.

Over the past decade the public image of some professions has turned negative as accountants, auditors lawyers and others are held accountable for many of today's problems, such as the savings and loan crisis. Increasingly, professionals are targeted by goverment regulators and disgruntled clients and investors lookiny for scapegoats. The Securities and Exchange Commission (SEC), the Federal Trade Commission (FTC), the Department ot Justice (DOJ) and the Federal Deposit Insurance Corporation (FDIC) all have become more aggressive toward the professions. Even the marketplace has changed, as professionals engage in price cutting, and in other ways look for new business much more aggressively.

A continuing trend is the increased use of computers and specialized software. Personal computers, local area networks, electronic bulletin boards, and customized software are rapidly becoming pivotal tools of the trade. Practitioners who affectively employ such technology increase their productivity and cut costs and turnaround time. Customized software is now available even to the consumer, since accounting, legal and similar professional work can be handled through a wide variety of software on the market.

Professional services have a fragmented industry structure and concentration varies considerably among the many subsectors. At one end of the scale, large multinational firms dominate the market; at the other, firms tend to be specialized small to medium-sized companies and sole practitioners.

Although data on production and employment are limited because of difficulties in assessing services activity, conservative estimates suggest that total receipts in this sector exceeded $200 billion in 1990, with employment at 2.3 million. These figures are rough estimates, drawn from a variety of sources, and do not represent a consistant measure across all subsectors.

International Competitiveness

The United States is extremely competitive and has an edge in many professional service sectors The biggest competition comes from Japanese and European companies. In the global economy in which these firms operate, the competition will become more intense as the European Community (EC) nations merge into a single market, and as the North American Free Trade Agreement, joining the United States, Canada and Mexico, becomes a reality.

U.S., Japanese, and European companies are aggressively pursuing contracts in the EC in advertising, management, consulting and public relations services. U.S. legal and executive search firms are making major efforts to become more involved in Europe. U.S. and European accounting, auditing, and bookkeeping firms will expand in an effort to provide services to the emerging private sector in Eastern Europe, as will management, consulting, and public relations firms.

In the Far East, demand for professional services is increasing in Japan. Taiwan, and South Korea, as well as in Association of Southeast Asian Nations (ASEAN) memher countries: Brunei, Indonesia, Malaysia, the Philippines, Singapore, and Thailand. The demand for all professional services will continue to increase as the economies of these countries expand, diversify, and mature.

Many professional services companies are entering foreign markets through mergers and acquisitions of local firms. Foreign markets are less saturated than the U.S. markets. As a result, their growth potential is greater and foreign markets will grow at a more rapid rate than the U.S. market.

Long-Term Prospects

Professional services will continue to expand throughout the decade but at a lower rate than during the later half of the past decade. A major force behind this growth will be the increased use of computers, integrated systems, and other high-technology equipment. The professional services sector was significantly affected by the economic downturn of 1990-91. This is evidence that the professional services economy has matured to the extent that it is now susceptible to the same business conditions as the manufacturing sector, a fact of life the services companies must accept and assimilate.

Accounting, Auditing, and Bookkeeping

Receipts for accounting, auditing, and bookkeeping services for the 69,773 establishments with payrolls identified in the *Census of Service Industries* for 1987 reached an estimated $35 billion in 1991, an increase of only 2.2 percent from the previous year. The industry had approximately 545,000 employees in 1991, up 1.5 percent from 1990.

The mergers that restructured the largest firms of this sector will probably lead to additional merger activity among smaller firms. This, along with the retrenchment of the industry, the bankruptcy of one large firm, the disolution of another, and the reduction of partners at some Big Six accounting firms by 5 to 15 percent, will continue to reshape the industry.

Recent events have had a drastic effect on the way firms in this sector conduct business. For example, a majority of them have limited services they offer, and half of the firms have stopped doing business with such perceived high-risk clients as savings and loans. Almost all firms use engagement letters and many use disclaimers to limit their liability exposure.

Certified public accountants (CPAs) accept responsibility for the accuracy of their work and most acknowledge their responsibility to provide an independent evaluation of a client's financial position. However, most do not think they should be held accountable if they become victims when the firms they audit provide them with false information. Nor do they think that they should be held responsible for conclusions that investors and shareholders draw from their work. Most CPAs attribute investor lawsuits to a litigious society and the perception that accounting firms have deep pockets.

The economic downturn of 1990-91 created difficulties for accounting firms on the one hand and offered opportunities on the other. Bankrupcies increased to more than 782,000 in 1990 and were projected to exceed 900,000 in 1991. This is an increase of more than 100 percent in bankruptcy filings in just 10 years, much of which represents new business for accounting firms.

Ethical issues are an area of concern. In 1990, the FTC issued an order prohibiting CPAs from accepting commissions and other types of fees from audit clients.

Outlook for 1992

Demand for accounting, auditing, and bookkeeping services will increase, resulting in higher receipts and employment. Receipts are expected to increase 8.6 percent to an estimated $38 billion. Employment is forecast to reach 570,000 or 4.6 percent above the 1991 level.

Advertising

The advertising industry consists of establishments that prepare advertising (written copy, art, graphics, audio, video, and other creative work) for clients, and place the finished product in periodicals, newspapers, and broadcast media on a commission or fee basis.

Receipts for advertising firms with payrolls reached an estimated $2.5 billion in 1991, an increase of about 2.8 percent from 1990. The industry had approximately 240,000 employees on the payroll in 1991, up 0.8 percent from the previous year. The 1987 *Census of Service Industries* reported 17,199 firms engaged in this activity. The top ten advertising agencies in the world grossed $12.2 billion in 1990.

The economic downturn of 1990-1991 had a major impact on the advertising industry. Some industry sources lament that the advertising industry will never be the same. Advertising spending has declined from average annual increases of about 14 percent in the early 1980s to only 4 percent in the early 1990's. The same industry sources anticipate limited growth over the next few years.

This outlook may be overly bleak, but there is no expectation of a rapid recovery. Advertising spending usually recovers more slowly than the economy in general. For the larger international agencies the outlook for advertising outside the United States is more positive than at home.

Employment in advertising is expected to decline as a growing number of small and medium sized ad agencies close. In tough times, advertisers tend to move to larger, more established agencies with better track records and a more conservative approach.

On the other hand, small and medium-sized agencies are developing computer capabilities more rapidly than the larger agencies. This makes the smaller agencies more attractive because computerization provides greater control and efficiency in generating advertisements. It is estimated that an assignment that would take 12 to 13 hours to complete and costs $30,000 without computers now requires only six hours and costs $4,200 with the use of computers.

Advertisers are being cautious, going from making yearly budget commitments to quarterly commitments. Agencies also are being cautious by focusing on existing clients and trying to be more effective and efficient, adding value, utility, and service to their activities.

Outlook for 1992

Demand for adverising services will increase, resulting in higher receipts and employment. Receipts for advertising services are expected to reach $22 billion, a 7.3% percent increase over 1991. Employment is forecast to increase 4.2 percent to 250,000.

Executive Search

The executive search industry consists of companies that identify and recruit qualified candidates for executive-level positions. They assist employers seeking qualified candidates for specific employment opportunities.

Receipts for executive search firms reached an estimated $3.2 billion in 1991, an increase of about 3.2 percent from the previous year. The industry had about 31,000 on its payroll in 1991, of whom nearly half were professionals.

There are more than 2,000 firms in the United States that provide executive search services, and more than 90 percent of these firms have 10 or fewer professionals. The top 10 executive search firms had worldwide billings of $667.6 million in 1990.

Executive recruiting firms are retrenching in the wake of the economic downturn of 1990-91. The impact has been greatest on the smallest and the largest firms. The result has been the collapse of many small search firms and a reduction of fees. Also there has been an increase in services offered, and greater diversification by the largest firms.

To remain competitive, the leading executive search firms have lowered their fees for employers that request multiple searches, as well as offer additional services such as succession planning, managemnt audits, and executive pay advice. Expansion into the international marketplace is a high priority in light of recent performance. The U.S. market expanded only 2.8 percent in 1990, compared with the 21 percent increase in foreign operations that the nine largest firms experienced in the same period. Diversification and expansion are not risk-free. That is because diversifying may put executive search firms into direct competition with the big accounting firms, among others. Some firms use help-wanted advertisements outside the United States, a practice that has been successful in Europe. However, in the United States, this runs the risk of damaging their image because that is how employment agencies operate. In addition, U.S. firms are seeking to expand their operations by affiliating with foreign-based executive search organizations, but cultural and operational differences pose obstacles to this alternative.

Outlook for 1992

Demand for exeutive search services will grow in 1992, resulting in receipts increasing 6.3 percent, to $ 3.4 billion. Employment is forecast to reach 33,000 or 6.5 percent above the 1991 level.

Legal Services

Receipts for legel services establishments with payroll reached an estimated $100 billion in 1991, an increase of about 9.7 percent from 1990.

There were 950,000 employees on the payrolls in 1991, up 3.4 percent from the previous year. The 1987 *Census of Service Industries* reported 138,222 establishments engaged in this activity.

The legal profession is undergoing a major adjustment. One reason is the rapid rise in the number of lawyers over the past two decades. In the 1970's, the number of lawyers doubled, and in the 1980's their ranks increased 48 percent. In fact, the U.S. has 70 percent of the world's lawyers. This increase contrasts drastically with the decline of civil litigation including tort and personal injury filings. In addition, the economic downturn of 1990-91 increased the competition among lawyers and law firms, creating a "produce-business-or-perish" climate. Earnings for the majority of lawyers has been declining over the past two decades. The market has contracted to the extent that law schools report a 10 to 20 percent decline in job placements.

In a profession previously considered immune to economic conditions, firms are freezing rates, laying off associates, firing unproductive partners and hiring fewer new lawyers. The profession is benefiting from the increase in bankruptcy fillings and the savings and loan crisis, howevever. In 1990, legal costs for the saving and loan clean-up amounted to $733 million, of which $615 went to outside law firms. The remaining $118 million represented legal services provided by lawyers at the Federal Deposit Insurance Corporation and the Resolution Trust Corporation.

Malpractice suits against lawyers are becoming more common and are having a serious effect on the way many firms practice. The American Bar Association (ABA) estimates that 8 percent of the lawyers carrying malpractice insurance will be sued in 1991. However, as malpractice insurance rates increase --averaging 30 percent annually over the last few years -- fewer lawyers are carrying the coverage. It is estimated that 90 percent of the lawyers in practice were insured in the 1980's against only 60 percent today. But malpractice litigation costs remain high, and although lawyers win most cases, such suits adversely affect a lawyer's reputation.

The profession is debating the ethics of providing ancillary services and having non-lawyer partners. The ABA's House of Delegates recently voted to ban ancillary services. such as arranging financing for clients and giving business advice, unless the serviccs are provided under the direct supervision of a lawyer and are related to a client's legal business. However, many law firms own subsidiaries that offer ancillary services, and they intend to continue those operations. The firms consider the ABA vote merely a suggestion and will not comply unless the highest court in their individual jurisdiction adopts a ban. The ABA is also studying the issue of non-lawyer partnerships. Since law firms have branched into non-legal areas staffed by non-lawyers, the District of Columbia Court of Appeals has allowed non-lawyers to become partners, thus giving them a portion of the firm's profits and a role in its management. Lawyers and bar associations elsewhere are monitoring the effects of the District's rule closely.

Outlook for 1992

Demand for legal services will increase. Receipts are expected to reach $110 billion, or 10 percent above the 1991 level. Employment is forecast to rise 4.2 percent, to 990,000. The top 10 legal services firms in the United States billed $3.12 billion in 1990.

Management, Consulting, and Public Relations Services

The management, consulting, and public relations services industry provides information and expertise to a variety of clients on a contracted basis. There are five main categories: management and administration (business and facilities management, and other administrative services); public relations (including lobbyists); management consulting (marketing, personnel, and administrative consulting); economic and sociological research; and other consulting services.

Receipts for management, consulting, and public relations establishments with payrolls reached an estimated 65 billion in 1991, an increase of 6.2 percent from 1990. The industry had a payroll of about 665,000, up 6.9 percent. It is staffed primarily by such professional and technical personnel as accoutants, economists, industrial engineers, designers, and public relations specialists. The 1987 *Census of Service Industries* reported 65,623 establishments with payroll engaged in this activity.

Mergers and acquisitions have been prevalent in the consulting services sector in the past several years. Most occurred under positive economic conditions, but mergers and acquisitions also took place during the economic downturn of 1990-91, when times were harder for consultants than for most of their clients. Most of the consolidations were prompted by a desire to possess the information-technology skills that are required to adequately satisfy client needs.

In the recession of the early 1980's, consultants advised clients to cut staff in order to weather the storm. A decade later, those same clients understand that cost-cutting alone will not provide a lasting competitive edge. Today's generation of managers is better informed and more skeptical of simplistic solutions. Managers demand more sophisticated analyses of their problems as well as assistance in the implementation of proposals. In the past, consultants were outside agents; now the emphasis is on long-term client relationships. Formulating solutions is one thing and application of those solutions is another. In today's complex world of high technology, clients want the consultant to design or redesign their information-technology networks and manufacturing systems, put them in place, monitor their operation, and assess their effectiveness.

Information-technology expertise and implementation skills will allow consultants to survive, but new or redesigned ideas are required for success and growth. Large consulting firms are developing "knowledge networks" that are accessible by all of their consultants. Databases holding hundreds of thousands of documents are touted as a major source of information and assistance for any client's problem-solving demands.

Outlook for 1992

Management, consulting, and public relations services will grow at a significant pace. Receipts are expected to increase 7.8 percent to 70 billion. Employment in the industry is forecast to reach 715,000, or 7.5 percent above the 1991 level.

RETAILING

In 1989, total retail sales increased by 5 percent to $1.7 trillion. Apparel and accessory stores had the largest gain (7.1 percent), followed by food stores (7 percent), furniture group stores (6.9 percent), general merchandise (5.4 percent), and eating and drinking places (4.5 percent). Sales of durable goods store rose by 3.2 percent, and nondurable goods stores by 6.2 percent. By contrast, florist shops experienced 2.5 percent lower sales and variety stores sales were 0.4 percent lower. Sales of group II stores (companies with 11 or more units) accounted for 37 percent of all sales in 1989, with a total of $638 billion.

Turmoil in Retailing

Campeau Corp's declaration of bankruptcy in January, 1990, was the forerunner of the difficulties experienced by the entire retail industry, and the department store segment in particular.

Ames Department Stores also sought protection in 1990 under the bankruptcy laws as it attempted to integrate its acquisition of Zayre. Other significant events of 1990 were the sale of British American Tobacco's retail interests in the United States, including Saks and Marshall Field, and other major store properties.

In spite of major changes in the retail environment, department stores are expected to remain a viable, growing segment of the general merchandise group in the 1990's and beyond. This is based on the industry's past ability to adapt to changing economic and social conditions, to attract and retain capable management, and to finance expansions.

Technology

The retail industry increased the installation of automated checkout equipment in 1989 and 1990. The information thus gathered is vital to corporate managers to control inventory, to track the sale of individual items, and to gauge the success of sales campaigns. The competitiveness of the retail industry will require additional investment in these systems. The introduction of electronic data interchange (EDI) systems to enhance computer-to-computer reordering continues. The benefits of this technology will continue to increase as more retailers and manufacturers become familiar with EDI and the competitive advantages it provides.

J.C. Penney Co. appears to be poised to reap the benefits from its investment in equipment that will enable it to conduct about 80 percent of its transactions with merchandise suppliers electronically. The company also plans to convert 40,000 cash registers to bar-code scanner use. In addition, Penney's satellite broadcast system is being expanded to cover the entire store network. This will enable the company to beam 200 programs of merchandise presentations and permit the exchange of information that would entail 11,000 hours of transmission.

Long-Term Prospects

The political change in Eastern Europe and the liberalization in the former Soviet Union can have positive effects on the domestic retail economy. Import opportunities exist for selected categories of merchandise from countries where lower labor costs can be capitalized on to produce merchandise that is labor intensive and which stresses handwork, such as apparel and dolls. The attractiveness of direct investment via overseas stores will depend on a favorable investment climate, the potential for future sales, and freedom to repatriate earnings. As these nations return to a market economy with improved postal service and transportation, sales via mail-order may become practicable and profitable. For the foreseeable future, the domestic economy, aided by continued growth in disposable income and an upscale consumer bias, should enable the nation's retailer's continue to grow.

Department Stores

Between 1982 and 1987, the number of department stores with 25 or more employees increased from 10,163 to 11,069. In 1987, there were 10,041 department stores with 50 or more employees. Of the total, 2,425 were identified as conventional, 5,798 as discount or mass merchandising, and 1,818 as national chain stores.

The industry is continuing to consolidate, resulting in larger but fewer companies. Former regional companies, such as Dillard's and Wal-Mart, have become more national. Both companies have been highly successful in the past. Both have leadership, management, and the financing needed to realize planned expansion objectives.

Eating and Drinking Places

Sales of eating and drinking places increased by 4.5 percent in 1989, to $164.6 billion. Refreshment place (fast food) sales were $65.5 billion and accounted for 40 percent of the total. Sales of Group II eating places (companies with 11 or more units) were $42.2 billion, accounting for 26 percent of the total.

Between 1982 and 1987, the number of establishments increased from 352,000 to 391,000, aided by a 10 percent gain in the restaurant category and a 9 percent gain in refreshment place establishments.

With modest year-to-year overall sales increases, competition has become extremely keen, especially among the larger chains that feature hamburgers and chicken. Discount coupons and other price-reducing techniques are increasingly being used by companies of all sizes. Increasingly, too, the restaurant industry is offering the public a choice of healthier foods.

Several large American companies were recently sold, in some cases to foreign owners. The Japanese own Denny's Japan Co., a 343-store chain, and obtained the Japanese Mister Donut chain through a licensing arrangement. Burger King is owned by Britains Grand Metropolitan PLC.

Apparel Stores

The number of apparel establishments increased from 141,000 to 148,000 between 1982 and 1987. The number of stores increased in all segments of the industry, with the exception of the men's and boys' clothing groups. Their numbers declined from 18,600 stores in 1982 to 16,500 in 1987. The number of men's shoe stores also declined during the same period, from 4,400 to 3,900.

Sales of apparel stores increased 7.1 percent in 1989 over 1988. Shoe stores gained 8.5 percent and family clothing stores gained about 8.2 percent. Women's clothing specialty stores and furriers had a gain of 4.9 percent, and men's and boys clothing showed and increase of 0.5 percent.

Furniture

Furniture store sales totaled $28.3 billion in 1989, an increase of 1.4 percent over 1988.

Furniture retailers are discovering new sales opportunities overseas. In Japan, Drexel Heritage Furnishings Co. is selling furniture in concert with the Daimaru, Inc. store chain. The European Community (EC) is a potentially huge market of 325 million people with a Gross Domestic Product of $4.5 trillion and a per capita income of $13,770 in 1988.

Domestically, the industry continues to expand via acquisition of existing furniture chains as well as previously planned expansion strategies.

The baby boom generation is now stressing quality over price. Merchandise at the low end continues to sell well, however, in part because of improved quality.

Retail chains continue to mail out catalogs as an adjunct to store sales. Catalogs tend to interest consumers and draw them into stores.

Drug Stores

For the first five months of 1990, drug store sales were 7.9 percent above the same period a year ago.

The drug store industry continues to face significant competition from other non-drug store competitors. *Drug Store News* determined that in 1989, 40 supermarket chains owned 3,001 stores with pharmacies and a group of eight mass merchandisers had 2,102 stores with pharmacies. Other competitors are general merchandise retailers, including department and variety stores.

Drug store management is responding to increased competition by selling businesses not directly related to the pharmacy industry; refurbishing and upgrading existing profitable locations; accepting national credit cards; and expanding into areas with lower population densities. To maintain in-stock positions, warehouses and distribution centers are being added, and existing distribution centers are being upgraded with equipment that moves merchandise into and out of storage at a rapid pace.

Food Retailing

In 1990, total sales and services of the food retailing industry increased an estimated 7.2 percent, to about $381 billion. Sales by grocery stores, including convenience stores, reached $358 billion, an estimated 7.4 percent gain over 1989. Sales of the chain store segment of the grocery store group rose about 6.9 percent, to $209 billion. Sales of meat and seafood specialty stores rose almost 6 percent to $7.6 billion. Sales of retail bakeries turned up by 0.2 percent after declining in 1989 and 1988.

Long-Term Prospects

Adjusted for inflation, industry sales are forecast to rise by about one percent annually over the next five years. Spending for food and beverage consumption at home is likely to stabilize or even increase as a share of total personal consumption expenditures. Spending for food and drink outside the home will decrease proportionately. Consumers and retailers are expected to express renewed interest in generic products and private label goods. Brand-name food manufacturers will likely compete more aggressively for market share.

SEMICONDUCTOR MANUFACTURING

Electronic components are the primary building blocks for the U.S. electronics industry. These components, such as semiconductors, connectors, and printed circuit boards, support a domestic electronics industry that employs more than 2.5 million workers and accounts for about $300 billion in annual production. Component manufacturers provided their products to a wide range of end-users, including the computer, telecommunications, aerospace, medical, and automotive industries.

The wide range and differing economic cycles of end-user industries usually provides the component sector with a buffer against a downturn in any single end-user industry. However,the component industry faced a difficult first half of 1991 due to the general economic slump. The weak business conditions were reflected in decreased advertising revenue for industry publications and the cancellation of several trade exhibitions due to a lack of participants.

A general indicator for the difficult business conditions facing the sector was a decline in the venture capital financing available for the component area. In 1986, venture capital financing in the semiconductor industry totaled $165 million. By 1991, that had dropped to $63 million. Venture capital for passive electronic components fell from $47 million to $26 million during the same period.

The second half of 1991 did produce an upswing in orders and a firming in component pricing. Low semiconductor inventory levels among end-users were expected to quickly translate into increased orders when demand returned. Growth rates in component demand tracked overall economic trends.

Outlook for 1992

Shipments of electronic components will increase by about 4.7 percent in 1992 current-dollar terms, with semiconductor shipments rising 8 percent. A strengthened dollar and continued economic weakness in key European markets will combine to slow export growth. Sales to Southeast Asian countries will continue to be strong, and the area has become the most attractive regional export market.

Continued price reductions in consumer electronics products, personal computers, workstations, and other systems are expected as producers fight to maintain market share. This downward price pressure will affect component producers. An example is the personal computer (PC) market, which accounts for half the consumption of dynamic random access memory (DRAM) devices and 25 percent of micro processor consumption. Price reductions in the maturing PC market will increase pricing, competition among suppliers of PC components.

Long-Term Prospectss

Component industry shipments are forecast to grow at an annual rate of 5-7 percent through the mid-1990's. Component suppliers will face a constant demand for higher performance products. The increased complexity of the packaging and interconnection of high-performance systems places a premium on compatibility among components. Systems designers will select components that offer the best engineering solutions. Component suppliers will have to track technology and product developments carefully in their customer markets, and anticipate the needed changes in their own product development to ensure compatibility. A good example of the difficulty faced by component producers in anticipating which design will become the industry standard is semiconductor packaging. In 1980. the semiconductor industry packaged more than 90 percent of integrated circuit (IC) devices in dual-in-line packages (DIPs) By 1990, dozens of competing packaging styles, each with multiple variations, had evolved. Successful companies will be those best able to anticipate which technologies and product variants will be among the future industry standards

Semiconductors and Related Devices

The U.S. semiconductor industry experienced a market upswing in the second half of 1991, with year-end shipments increasing 7 percent over 1990 levels. The domestic book-to-bill ratio (a closely watched indicator of future industry health) rose above 1:1 for most of 1991, and shipments were expected to grow 8 percent in 1992. The strongest markets in 1991 were Japan and Southeast Asia, with 12 and 14 percent growth respectively.

U.S. semiconductor companies increased capital spending by about 15 percent in 1991 over the previous year's levels. reflecting an aggressive expansion during a year of business uncertanties. The industry prepared for the next expansion in demand, countering past tendencies to reduce spending during a downturn. Previously, the companies found themselves lagging competitors when the upturn began.

Competition in the semiconductor industry is not restricted R&D and marketing. but often occurs in the courtroom. Although these cases usually address infringements of intellectual property rights. with only a minor effect on a company's profitability, their outcome can sometimes determine survival. Some companies rely on royalty payments for innovations to remain financially viable.

A U.S. semiconductor producer, Texas Instruments, recently entered into a legal dispute with a Japanese competitor, Fujitsu, over a patent granted to the U.S. company in Japan in 1989. The Japanese company asserted that its products do not rely on the technology covered in the patent. In this specific case the final court ruling will affect hundreds of millions of dollars in royalty payments.

Intellectual property rights protection of semiconductor designs are addressed through intergovernmental negotiations. The Semiconductor Chip Protection Act of 1984, which was due to expire on July 1, 1991,has been extended until 1995. The legislation gives the Secretary of Commerce the authority to extend reciprocal protection of semiconductor mask works (a critical early step in semiconductor fabrication) to foreign companies in nations that protect U.S. designs.

Since 1984, the Commerce Department has extended this protection to semiconductor producers in 19 nations. These bilateral agreements are necessary because a fully satisfactory mutilateral chip protection agreement has not yet been reached in either the World Intellectual Property Organization (WIPO) or the General Agreement on Tariffs and Trade (GATT).

New alliances continue to be formed among semiconductor, computer, and software companies in the burgeoning domestic reduced instruction set computing (RISC) microprocessor business. RISC is a new technique, or system architecture, in which much of the software is embedded in the electronic hardware to speed information processing. Each alliance seeks to provide a full range of products centered around one RISC architecture in hopes of establishing it as the industry standard. Among the collaborative efforts under way are the Advanced Computing Environment (ACE) initiative, a consortium of more than 60 companies led by Hewlett-Packard, SPARC International, a competing consortium based on the Sun Microsystems architec-ure, and a recent alliance among IBM, Apple, and Motorola.

The National Advisory Council on Semiconductors (NACS), a congressionally established group of government and industry officials, issued its second annual report in 1991 and recommended actions to benefit the semiconductor industry: accelerate the depreciation schedule for semiconductor manufacturing equipment (SME); encourage formation of joint research consortia; develop an Intelligent Vehicle/Highway System, which would be a major user of advanced electronic components; and increase Federal funding for science and engineering education.

The issue of an accelerated depreciation schedule for SME is particularly critical for the semiconductor industry, which argues that the current five-year depreciation schedule no longer accurately reflects the economic life of the property. Parallel bills were introduced in both houses of Congress in 1991 to reclassify SME as "3-year property," but industry observers anticipate political activity before the issue can be resolved. The NACS has estimated that a three-year depreciation life for SME would increase the annual rate of capital investment in the industry by 11 percent.

Product Development

Research in microelectronics sometimes produces experimental results that promise to completely redefine the field. In mid-1991, IBM researchers demonstrated an "atom switch" that uses a scanning tunneling microscope to manipulate single atoms. This breakthrough would, in theory, make possible the creation of electronic circuits measured in nanometers (billionths of a meter), more than a thousand times smaller than today's circuits. However, the process is a long way from commercialization.

Unlike such revolutionary advances as the atom switch, most developments in the semiconductor industry are incremental. Designs and technologies are revised and adapted continuously to extend the product life. Semiconductor end-users have toi identify product cycles in order to incorporate new generations of semiconductor devices in their final products, while allowing enough flexibility in the design to accommodate semiconductor design upgrades. Semiconductor device life cycles usually follow a predictable pattern: R&D (1-3 years), introduction (3-12 months), growth to saturation (4-5 years), and finally decline and phaseout (3-4 years). Technology life cycles for the processes and materials used in manufacturing can reach 20-25 years and extend beyond specific product life cycles. Older technologies such as complementary metal oxide silicon (CMOS), in which individual elements on a device measure about 3 microns (millionths of a meter), are being phased out in favor of new technologies such as bipolar complementary metal oxide silicon (BiCMOS) with sub-micron feature sizes and correspondingly higher functional densities. Also, new materials with better electronic properties than silicon, such as gallium arsenide (GaAs) and indium phosphide (InP), are finding wider applications among end-users.

Semiconductor devices initially designed for different purposes sometimes gravitate into direct competition. This is the case with the conventional complex instruction set computing (CISC) architecture, which is being challenged by the new RISC microprocessors. RISC processors initially were tailored for the high-performance technical workstation market, but have since begun to compete directly with CISC-based PCs in the business applications market. CISC manufacturers are countering the RISC challenge by introducing faster, aggressively priced products.

A recent decision to use RISC microprocessors in the program to upgrade the U.S. Air Force's F-16 fighter aircraft illustrates the challenge this technology poses to the more mature CISC designs. RISC microprocessors have been designed into more than 100 prototype military systems in the past 2 years. This segment of the semiconductor industry faces increased technological competition as companies backing competing microprocessor architectures form strategic alliances to win future programs.

The semiconductor memory segment of the industry is grappling with questions of pricing and supply as well as design innovation. Spot shortages of 256K DRAMs and 64K static random access memory (SRAMs) are anticipated in 1992 as suppliers cut production in these maturing product lines. (DRAMs are called "dynamic" because they have to be electrically powered at all times; SRAMs do not and thus are "static." A 256K memory actually contains 262,144 bits and a 64K, 65,536.) Memory chip product configurations and packaging options will continue to expand. The design of 4 megabit (actually 4,194,304 bits) chips is gravitating toward more complex word configurations, such as 8 by 9 and 16 by 18 bits, and packaging options include zigzag-in-line packages (ZIP) and thin small-outline packages (TSOP) in order to achieve greater functional density.

A major technological innovation is the application specific integrated circuit (ASIC) in which standard ICs are customized for specific functions, thus taking advantage of the inherently lower cost of standard parts and the higher performance of custom ICs. One U.S. company has recently combined standard cell and gate array technology to bring high-density memory to gate arrays. Customers specify the amount of memory required and the supplier then develops an ASIC prototype. This combines the memory density of a standard cell ASIC with the production benefits of a gate array.

The traditional ASIC market includes such products as user-programmable devices (UPDs), programmable logic devices (PLDs), and field programmable gate arrays (FPGAs). The degree of customization can vary depending on the product. Now, an even broader category has been created: application specific standard products (ASSPs). These include chip sets, application specific DRAMs, and telecommunications ICs. These products target an entire market niche rather than a "one customer, one ASIC" approach. The close relationship between customer and supplier in the ASIC sector helps drive product development and makes U.S. products competitive in world markets.

International Competitiveness

The U.S. trade deficit in semiconductors was more than halved in 1991, dropping from the 1990 level of $1.3 billion to $580 million. The domestic semiconductor market was out performed in 1991 by the other major regional markets. This combination of slack domestic demand and increased demand abroad led to the sharp decline in the trade imbalance. The dominant regional trading partner continued to be East Asia, which accounted for $3.5 billion in exports and $4.8 billion in imports.

Western Europe

The Western European region is dominated economically by the members of the European Community (EC), but also includes the Scandinavian countries and Austria and Switzerland .Overall the economies of the EC were plagued by growing unemployment and stagnant economic growth in 1991. However, the European semiconductor industry held its own through uncertain economic times during the Persian Gulf conflict and has recently shown signs of recovery from the 1990 slump. The growth in the semiconductor market was dependent on growth in the major applications segments: electronic data processing (EDP). communications, consumer electronics. industrial transportation, and the military.

Due to falling memory prices and a downturn in PC production, semiconductor revenues from the European EDP segment declined. The communications segment demonstrated strong growth, with exchange switch equipment consuming high volumes of semiconductors. Growth remained steady for video cassette recorders (VCRs) and television sets, which boosted sales of semiconductors in consumer electronics applications. The industrial segment declined due to overall poor economic recovery and weaker prices. The growing electronics content of automobiles increased the consumption of semiconductors in the transportation segment. The military market remained weak during the second half of 1991 as nations made only incremental increases to defense spending levels to replace equipment used in the Persian Gulf and to prepare for future needs.

All regional semiconductor markets within Western Europe declined, when tabulated in terms of their local currencies. Germany, because of strong demand from its consumer and telecommunications sectors, was least affected by the economic downturn, with a decline of only 1.2 percent. Germany continued to be the single largest European semiconductor market and the second largest export outlet for U.S. semiconductor exports to Europe (after the United Kingdom, which accounted for twice the shipments as Germany in 1991). U.S. exports of a wide range of semiconductor products sold well in the German market: DRAMs, electrically erasable programmable read only memories (EEPROMs), MOS logic and memory, and discrete components.

The reunification of Germany greatly affected what used to be referred to as West Germany. The western German semiconductor companies benefited from reunification in 1990, based on the surge in demand for communications and consumer electronics products. The success of western German telecommunications companies in winning large contracts to rebuild eastern German communications gave the telecommunications segment a 14 percent boost over 1990. Similarly, the consumer electronics market expanded dramatically after reunification, with eastern German consumers buying newly available consumer electronics products. Dataquest, a market research firm in San Jose, CA, predicted serious overheating in the German economy by the beginning of 1992 as a result of the large infusion of capital from western German sources into the reunified eastern Germany. The German semiconductor market is expected to grow 11.3 percent in 1992.

The United Kingdom is the second largest semiconductor market in Western Europe, but has experienced extreme economic hardship in the past year. The British semiconductor industry has traditionally relied on the EDP market segment, which is dominated by U.S. multinational computer companies. If increased demand had not come from Far East office equipment, automotive, and consumer manufacturers, the British semiconductor industry would have declined in step with lower demand from the U.S. computer industry.

With the exception of Spain and Portugal, investment growth has leveled off in EC fabrication plants. This slowdown contrasts with trends of the past 2 years. Prior to the 1991 slowdown, industry analysts predicted significant investment growth in EC fabrication plants would continue through the initiation of the EC's 1992 economic unification. However, investment growth has been held down by the reality of a protracted world economic recession and inflated material and production costs in Europe. In addition, regional market expansion plans based on the economic transformation of the Eastern European economies are being delayed by uncertainty caused by the continued political volatility in several countries. Thus, many leading U.S. and Far East electronics companies have reined in plans for establishing a manufacturing presence in Europe.

European-owned companies' share of the world semiconductor market remained steady at 11 percent. Based on U.S. dollars, in 1991, the European semiconductor market grew 9.8percent. However, true market performance is only revealed when revenue is expressed in terms of the local currency. The European Currency Unit (ECU), a denominator for the currencies of the EC member nations, more accurately expresses market growth by factoring in the variance of each country's currency. According to Dataquest, the 1991 European semiconductor market actually contracted 6.1 percent, as measured in ECUs. The weakness of the U.S. dollar, coupled with an excess supply of memory devices, contributed to significantly lower unit prices. The European semiconductor market for 1990 was estimated at 51 billion ECUs, with European semiconductor companies maintaining 37 percent of their domestic market.

U.S. semiconductor companies that exported to Europe in 1991 fared well in sales to the region. As measured in U.S. dollars, export sales increased by 10 percent in the first half of 1991 over the same period of the previous year. U.S. companies,through a combination of exports and increased levels of local production, maintained 44 percent of the total Western European semiconductor market. Thus, although exports increased,the relative share of the total European semiconductor market held by U.S. firms remained unchanged.

The consolidation of the European electronics market was evidenced by the 1991 wave of mergers, acquisitions, and joint ventures. Meanwhile, the concept of "corporate partnering" was fast spreading through the industry sectors. Since 1985, increasing industrial concentration and the growing domination of merchant semiconductor markets (markets served by independent producers rather than the captive semiconductor divisions of equipment manufacturers) by vertically integrated manufacturers have caused concern for most participants in the European market. European, U.S., and Japanese electronics giants are positioning themselves for the market opportunities stemming from EC economic unification in 1992.

Since 1987, semiconductor firms have dramatically stepped up investment in European fabrication facilities. Semiconductor fabrication (fab) lines increased from 102 in that year to 124 in 1990. The investment boom in fab facilities has been dominated by East Asian electronics firms. The recent penetration by East Asian competitors raises concerns for both U.S. and European semiconductor producers.

The emergence of East Asian competitors in Europe is particularly significant for U.S. electronics firms, which have traditionally dominated the European market for electronic components, including semiconductors. U.S. market dominance is strongly challenged by increased semiconductor plant investment and more competitors for market share.

Another concern is the potential impact of new EC-wide regulations governing the electronics industry, specifically those related to investment and sourcing patterns. The two principal regulations at issue are: 1) the reinterpretation of the EC's rule of origin for ICs, and 2) a proposed value-added calculation for the origin of printed circuit board assemblies (PCBAs).

In February 1989, the EC changed its rule of origin for ICs by redefining the term, "place of last substantial transformation" by changing it from the stage of assembly and test to the stage of diffusion. Diffusion is a much earlier stage in the manufacturing process and is performed in a complete fab facility. Prior to 1989, only assembly and test facilities were necessary to meet the requirement of "substantial transformation." Thus it was unnecessary up to then for U.S. exporters to have a complete fabrication facility in the EC.

Also in 1989, the EC considered implementation of a Community-wide value-added rule of origin for PCBAs. The proposed regulation would replace the individual country of origin requirements, which had generally been satisfied by the assembly and test stage. The value-added proposal for PCBAs requires that at least 45 percent of the components on a board be of EC origin, which is a dramatic departure from most established sourcing patterns. After extensive consultations, the adoption of the PCBA rule was postponed in mid-1990, but not abandoned.

Since both ICs and PCBAs are fundamental products in the electronics product chain, the impact of such regulations could affect a large portion of the U.S. electronics industry. These regulations encourage EC sourcing of components at the expense of foreign suppliers that do not have European fabrication facilities.

Semiconductor producers are aware that their buyers may now prefer a European source for components to avoid both the current 14 percent tariff on semiconductors and the uncertainty caused by the new local content requirements in the rules of origin. These pressures are an impetus for foreign semiconductor suppliers to invest in EC manufacturing facilities or joint ventures.

Such manufacturing facilities require huge capital investment. However, many U.S. suppliers lack the necessary capital.A new fab facility costs $200 million-$300 million, and most small and medium sized U.S. firms cannot afford such an investment. Such large capital costs are prohibitive for even large firms if they want to manufacture all their product lines. Since each fabrication facility is generally devoted to specific product lines, extraordinary costs are involved in offering a European base for each product line.

Eastern Europe and the former Soviet Union

The dramatic social and political upheaval in Eastern Europe has highlighted the hurdles to be cleared in the transition from centrally planned to market economies. However, the recent significant increases in U.S. semiconductor exports suggests that buyer-supplier relationships are already being forged. It is only a matter of time before the economies of Poland and Hungary take off, according to industry analysts, and in 1991 these two countries were the best markets within Eastern Europe for U.S. semiconductors and other components. Exports to Eastern Europe of monolithic integrated circuits grew by 33 percent with MOS memory and logic chips leading exports. Overall, the markets showed signs of moderate growth for 1991, while the volume of trade remained under $1 million for the entire region.

Japan

The principal U.S.-Japan semiconductor trade issue in 1991 was the continuation of long-term efforts to increase U.S. and other foreign suppliers' access to the Japanese semiconductor market and to deter dumping (selling abroad at lower pricest than those in the domestic market) of Japanese semiconductorsin the United States. In 1991, the governments of the United States and Japan entered the fifth and final year of the U.S.-Japan Semiconductor Trade Arrangement, signed in 1986. Although the market access objectives of the arrangement had not been fully realized, the U.S. Government concluded that it had nonetheless provided major, concrete benefits to the U.S. semiconductor industry.

Previously, the United States determined that dumping of Japanese semiconductors had ceased, in compliance with the arrangement's anti-dumping provisions, and suspended anti-dumping sanctions on certain Japanese products. Prior to the scheduled July 31, 1991, expiration, the U.S. Government and the U.S. semiconductor and computer industries agreed that a new semiconductor arrangement would build upon progress in market access and maintain an effective deterrent to semiconductor dumping. Based on this consensus, the U.S. Government pursued a new agreement with Japan.

The two governments concluded a new Semiconductor Arrangement, which took effect August 1, 1991. The new arrangement followed the termination of the suspended anti-dumping investigation on 256K and larger DRAMs and the revision to the suspension agreement on erasable programmable read only memories (EPROMs). The arrangement will last five years, with the option to terminate after 3 years by mutual agreement of the two governments.

The new arrangement reflects U.S. expectations that foreign semiconductor makers can attain a 20 percent market share in Japan by 1992 through continued efforts both by foreign suppliers and Japanese users. The two governments agreed on a methodology for measuring foreign market share of the Japanese market. In announcing the new arrangement, the U.S. Government noted that "particular attention" would be given to market share in assessing market access progress. Furthermore, "specific consideration" would be given to the development of design-ins of new semiconductors for use in future products, long-term relationships between foreign suppliers and Japanese users, and overall efforts by these groups.

The new arrangement's anti-dumping provisions are expected to deter injurious dumping. Japanese semiconductor companies are to collect cost and price data and release the data to the U.S. Government on an expedited basis if a U.S. anti-dumping investigation is undertaken. These measures replace the export monitoring system of the 1986 arrangement administered by Japan' s Ministry of International Trade and Industry (MITI). Both governments also agreed to cooperate in any, GATT transactions concerning third-country dumping. The arrangement provides for third-country dumping consultations if the U.S. Government is petitioned to pursue such action in the GATT.

On August 1, 1991, with the beginning of the new arrangement, the U.S. Government suspended 100 percent tariffs on imports of certain Japanese computers and electropneumatic hammers. These duties were imposed in April 1987 for Japan's failure to comply with the 1986 arrangement's market access provisions. In announcing its determination, the Government cited Japan's progress in implementing its market access obligations under the 1986 arrangement, and the expectation that the market access objectives would be fully realized within the framework of a new arrangement.

Under the 1986 arrangement, U.S. and other foreign semiconductor suppliers participated in many market opening efforts. From the signing of the first arrangement in 1986 through July 1991, foreign market share in Japan increased from 9.27 percent to an estimated 13.6 percent. Semiconductor producers and Japanese semiconductor users undertook initiatives to accelerate foreign participation in the consumer. high definition television (HDTV), telecommunications, and automotive semiconductor end-use markets, and to increase the design-in (inclusion) of U.S and other foreign semiconductors in such products. U.S. firms pointed to some success stories: Japanese compact disc (CD) players incorporating U.S. advanced digital signal processors (DSPs), the design-in of U.S. ASICs into Japanese camcorders and transmission equipment, and Japanese auto firms' decisions to develop custom ICs with U.S. suppliers and to increase their purchases of U.S. and other foreign chips.

After the new semiconductor arrangement took effect, government-to-government consultations were held on such market access issues as continuing efforts to build long-term U.S.-Japanese relationships, enhancing opportunities for designing in U.S. and other foreign semiconductors, and means of accurately assessing foreign share in the Japanese semiconductor market. With respect to the dumping provisions of the arrangement, the consultations addressed product coverage.

In 1991, U.S. semiconductor exports to Japan rose 8.7 percent from $1.025 billion to $1.114 billion. Japanese demand for U.S. microprocessors and microcontrollers, DSPs, MOS logic, and EPROMs remains strong.

U.S. imports from Japan also increased in 1991, from $3.22 billion to $3.47 billion, serving to widen the U.S.-Japan semiconductor trade imbalance by 8 percent, from $2.19 billion to $2.36 billion. Imports of Japanese MOS memory chips rose 26 percent in 1991 due to increased demand from the U.S. computer industry. Such chips account for almost 40 percent of U.S. semiconductor imports from Japan.

Japanese demand, which accounts for 40 percent of the world semiconductor market, increased by 12 percent in 1991, with MOS logic and memory chips accounting for much of the growth. Demand by Japanese end-users is expected to flatten and taper off in the 1992-1994 period.

East Asia

The East Asian semiconductor market continued to be the fastest growing semiconductor market in the world in 1991 with a 15 percent increase over 1990 consumption figures. The East Asian market continued to be the primary U.S. export outlet for semiconductors, with export levels to East Asia (not including Japan) totaling three times that of Western Europe. The strongest East Asian export markets for U.S. semiconductors were Malaysia, Singapore, Taiwan, South Korea, Thailand. and Hong Kong.

East Asian electronics firms are becoming world-class suppliers of electronic components. The recent emergence of Malaysia, Singapore, and Thailand, and the sustained growth of Hong Kong, Taiwan, and South Korea, have resulted in the latest industry description for the region: the Dynamic Asian Economies (DAEs) The DAE governments are providing capital incentives for strategic development of their indigenous electronics manufacturers. According to Dataquest, East Asians have shifted in the last three to five years from imitation to innovation. The DAEs can no longer be strictly typified as "export-driven followers" since their reformed industrial strategies emphasize slower growth and consumption-oriented policies.

During the significant downturn in worldwide electronics equipment demand in 1990, the DAEs demonstrated increasing independence and resilience. According to Dataquest figures, when worldwide consumption grew a meager 1.8 percent in1990, the East Asian markets grew 17.6 percent. This strong market demand brought Malaysia, Thailand, and Singapore substantial amounts of North American, European, and Japanese investment into semiconductor fabrication facilities. Primary investment was in assembly and test operations.

U S suppliers of microprocessors, MOS logic, and analog integrated circuits have fared the best in East Asia. The MOS memory market grew by 56 percent in 1990 and continued at high rates in 1991. Data processing and consumer segments accounted for about 83 percent of semiconductor production for 1991 in the region. In the future, the transportation sector will be increasingly affected by automotive sales, with sales being driven by demand for electronic emission controls. If current trends persist, South Korea and China will probably expand their presence in consumer electronics, while the rest of East Asia focuses on data processing products.

Singapore and Malaysia are the prime offshore production locations for many U.S. and Japanese semiconductor companies. Many U.S. producers have established distributors in Singapore. Malaysia is home to at least 12 U.S firms, whose plants primarily perform test and assembly operations. Only one full wafer fabrication plant exists in Malaysia, and it is U.S.-owned. Singapore continues to maintain its traditional role as trade axis for the South East Asian region, with its advantages of geographical location, a pool of skilled labor, and an established international financial center.

Plans are being made to formalize Singapore's pivotal role through the proposal for the "Triangle of Growth," which establishes manufacturing and financial ties among Singapore. Malaysia's Johor Province, and Indonesia's Batam Islands. Development of an indigenous electronics manufacturing base is a high priority in the region. Thus, many incentives exist to attract capital and technology.

Due to the impact on the semiconductor industry from flat growth in the consumer electronics market segments and more competition from other Asian sources, South Korea and Taiwan are increasingly focusing on higher value electronic products. They have successfully forged world-class indigenous semiconductor industries that rival Japanese and U.S. suppliers in the memory market.

In the last five years, the South Koreans have invested more money in additional plant capacity than any other country in the world. While an increasing number of customers consider Korea as a primary source for advanced semiconductor technology, others view Korean sources as a hedge against potential supply shortages from U.S. and Japanese suppliers.

Although impressive strides have been made in Taiwan for semiconductor manufacturing, the industry is experiencing severe growing pains. Taiwanese companies are feeling the effects of overlapping production lines, under-utilized wafer fabrication facilities, and increasingly high capital costs.

Hong Kong's electronics industry has leveled off due to the political uncertainty of the return of the British crown colony to China in 1997 and saturation of demand in the electronic component market. However, Hong

Kong remains the key point of access to China, a crucial role for the long term in a potentially giant market.

Thailand's electronic components sector shows significant promise for expansion aa an outlet for U S. exports and as an off-shore production site. Various incentives exist to encourage the expansion of trade and investment with Thailand. For electronic components, there is a waiver on the 20 percent import duty for all electronics manufactured goods. However, beyond the prospects for continued expansion, there is concern that the Thai economy may overheat, since industrial growth is far outpacing Government spending on the infrastructure of services. The question remains whether Thailand will absorb imported technology and begin to innovate or simply continue to be an assembly site for foreign suppliers.

Outlook for 1992

The expected economic recovery should stimulate steady growth of U.S. semiconductor exports to most regions of the global semiconductor market. Export expansion in 1992 will be fueled by increased demand in the DAEs. In an increasingly competitive global environment, U.S. semiconductor manufacturers will need to emphasize improvement in product quality cost, delivery, and service. Domestic shipments are projected to grow by 8 percent in 1992.

Long-Term Prospects

In the long term, demand for semiconductors will be driven by consumption in four key markets: automotive, EDP, telecommnications, and consumer electronics. Shipments growth is expected to average 10 percent over the next 5 years. The growing interrelationships among semiconductor, computer, telecommunications, and consumer electronics industries will stimulate new technology growth and market opportunities in the 1990's. The time needed to introduce new products into the marketplace will continue to be the primary factor contributing to a company's success.

TELECOMMUNICATIONS

Revenues from domestic telecommunications services in 1990 increased 5.3 percent in current dollars and should increase about 4.9 percent in 1991. Revenues from international services, which rose 18.4 percent in 1990, will increase about 17.9 percent in 1991.

The telecommunications industry includes hundreds of companies providing telephone, telex, and telegraph services, international communications, microwave communications, satellite services, cellular mobile radio services, paging, private radio services, regional and metropolitan networks, data communications, and value-added services.

The U.S. national telecommunications network transmits local, long distance, and international text, video, and voice information. More than 2,000 companies provide public telecommunications services in the United States, switching more than 450 billion calls a year on a network linking 243 million telephones via 135 million local access lines and more than 15,689 central office switches. Each access line averages about 3,300 calls each year. Census Bureau data shows that as of March, 1990, 93.3 percent of the 94 million U.S. households had a telephone, up 0.3 percent from a year earlier, with 900,000 new homes added to the network.

Use of the network is increasing rapidly in the United States. Due to price decreases between 1984 and 1987, the average number of local calls per day increased from 1.11 billion to 1.50 billion, a 35.1 percent increase. Average daily long distance calls almost doubled, from 88 million to 162 million. By 1990, there were approximately 80 telephones per 100 U.S. inhabitants, compared with 63 telephones per 100 people in West Germany, 60 per 100 in France, and 53 per 100 in Japan and the United Kingdom.

Local telephone services are provided by seven Regional Bell Holding Companies (RHCs), which control 22 local Bell Operating Companies (BOCs); by GTE, United Telecom Centel; and by more than 1,400 smaller, independent local telephone companies. Many of these local companies operate as rural cooperatives. Long distance service is provided by AT&T and the RHCs are currently subject to price regulation by the Federal Communications Commission (FCC). Local telephone service is subject to regulation by state public utility commissions.

Local carriers are usually independent from long distance companies (United Telecom/Sprint being a notable exception); through FCC-regulated exchange access services, they make facilities available to long distance carriers for interstate calls. Intrastate long distance calls are regulated by state public utility commissions. Exchange access services will generate more than $28 billion in revenues for the local telephone carriers in 1991.

During 1991, the most significant trend in market structure will be the growing number of international joint ventures and strategic alliances. In addition, the growth of private corporate networks, operated by corporations for internal communications, will accelerate. The distinction between private and public telecommunications markets is eroding as regulatory constraints lessen and as technology allows for virtual networks that appear to be controlled by customers but are based on common-carrier networks. Many corporate customers can no longer justify wholly private bypass networks with facilities totally independent from the public network. Instead, large businesses will look for hybrid solutions, mixing public and private networks and applications. An economic slowdown may cause many corporations to cut costs by reducing the rate of growth of their telecommunications budgets. Corporate networks will, however, continue to be a growing market for telecommunications services. In 1991, for example, Ford Motor Company will continue expanding its already huge network to cover five continents, and AT&T will begin providing Pan American Airlines with services worldwide. In line with the growth of private corporate networks, telephone carriers will introduce even more sophisticated network management services, such as U.S. West's "self-healing" services, introduced in 1990, which ensure that such networks do not fail.

Global connectivity is the major force driving international alliances such as the service agreements between AT&T and KDD of Japan. More users are demanding access to sophisticated services on a worldwide basis, and telephone carriers in Europe, Japan, and North America are moving to address user needs for data connectivity. U.S. companies are focusing increasingly on the services markets in Europe as the European Community (EC) integrates its members' telecommunications policies and markets.

EC92 is the merger of 12 Western European countries, which constitute a single market of 325 million people with a Gross Domestic Products of $4.5 trillion and a per capita income of $13,770 in 1988. Although not expecting to be fully operational until 1992, the EC member countries are already gearing up for competition with other world markets, with telecommunications services and equipment a major component of EC plans. U.S. companies like IBM and Motorola are already involved in EC telecommunications markets, particularly for data communications and mobile radio services. Opportunities for other U.S. companies to increase their participation in the EC service markets are likely to increase as a result of EC market liberalization and reforms.

Telephone carriers will meet the demand for data communications and connectivity in part through services based on the integrated services digital network (ISDN). During 1990, ISDN services were deployed to roughly 150 corporate customers in the United States, and service will expand slowly during 1991. FCC data show that there were more than 6,100 ISDN

"D" channel circuits in the United States by 1990. Many ISDN users have been able to save 20 percent on telecommunications costs as they are able to consolidate leased line services, eliminate expensive rewiring problems, and allocate channels according to demand. However, ISDN will continue to face implementation problems during 1991 because of limited availability of terminal equipment and lack of connectivity nationwide among ISDN switches. The latter problem is called the "island" configuration, whereby carriers can provide ISDN services only from a single central office switch to a local calling area, rather than on a long distance basis between switches. The island configuration results from ISDN vendor incompatibilities and software that does not yet conform precisely to international standards.

Connectivity problems may be eased as carriers finish installing software for Signaling System 7 (SS7), which will be used to provide ISDN nationwide. The SS7 is being deployed rapidly, with some local exchange carriers contracting out to independent vendors for systems integration. Bell Atlantic and BellSouth equipped about 80 percent of their access lines with SS7 by early 1991, for example; by the end of the year, Bell Atlantic expects 65 percent of its switches to be capable of providing ISDN service. US Sprint began its introduction of ISDN service in 1990, while AT&T plans to introduce ISDN to more than 110 cities by 1991. MCI will begin implementation during 1991.

Local Services

In 1990, the total value of capital investment in local exchange communications plants and equipment was about $246 billion, with the largest investment, about $85 billion, being in central office switching. Of local carriers' 135 million access lines in 1990, 17 million were used for PBX and Centrex connections, 46 million for business customers, and about 87 million for residential subscribers.

Total revenues from local exchange services were about $76 billion in 1990, and are expected to grow at a 2.9 percent annual rate during 1991. Local telephone carriers had about $2.7 billion in revenues from private line services, of which local private lines generated more than $1 billion. Voice grade private line services other than data communications brought the local carriers about $476 million in revenue, while data services constituted almost $450 million. Toll (long distance) revenues from private line service were $1.5 billion. Total toll revenues for local exchange carriers were about $16 billion in 1990, indicating that about 15 percent of all local exchange carriers' revenues are derived from intrastate long distance telephone service. For the RHCs, the figure is about 25 percent. Access charges, paid by subscribers and long distance companies to the local exchange carriers, constituted about $28 billion, or an additional 25 percent of the local exchange carriers' revenues.

In one of the most significant mergers since divestiture, GTE and Contel agreed to a $6.2 billion deal to merge their operations. The combined company, with over 17.7 million access lines, will be larger than any one of the Regional Bell Holding companies. Bell Atlantic will be the second largest exchange carrier, with 171. million access lines.

Long Distance Services

Traffic growth in the long distance market segment will continue to exceed that of local exchange services, but price competition will keep revenue growth proportionately lower than actual increases in calling volume. An important strategic issue for the telephone carriers will be how to stabilize prices to maintain strong revenues while also remaining fully competitive. With the current level of merger and acquisition, the price cap system now in effect for AT&T--plus the lessening of time required for regulatory approval of rate reductions by the FCC--the industry is likely to achieve greater equilibrium over the next five years.

Revenues of the long distance telephone companies increased 7.3 percent in 1991, and are projected to grow 7.6 percent in 1992. Although the 1990-1991 recession contributed to lower growth in calling volume and helped result in reduced earnings to the industry, volume continued to increase at a rate far exceeding growth in the economy as a whole.

MCI, US Sprint, and other carriers will continue to gain market share from AT&T in 1992, but during 1991 AT&T fought aggressively to maintain its position and is likely to stabilize its dominant stance in the industry. During 1991, AT&T took over the long distance and international service operations of Alascom from Pacific Telecom Corp., significantly expanding their geographic coverage, and a Cable & Wireless (United Kingdom) U.S. acquisition made that firm this nation's fifth largest carrier. Other foreign carriers made inroads into the U.S. market as well, as Litel Communications sold a 20 percent share to Italcable, Italy's international carrier.

The product market for long distance services has several key segments, by far the largest of which is Message Telephone Service (MTS), used by most people to make direct-dial long distance calls. The MTS market is about $27 billion, and the annual growth rate is about 3.5 percent. Other important market categories are 800/900 WATS (inbound), outbound WATS analog and digital private leased circuits, and special services such as ISDN, Virtual Private Networks (VPN). Software Defined Networks (SDN), switched 56-Kbps data service, and others. In the operator services segment about 300 firms provide directory assistance services. However, only 50 were actual long distance carriers; the rest operate as resellers without purchasing network access.

The next largest revenue category for long distance services after MTS, is the market for 800 and 900 numbers, which totaled about $6.5 billion in 1991. However, the 800 number market is very mature. Steady traffic growth, heavy competition, and price erosion will lead to revenues remaining at the same level in 1992. Traffic from 800 number services actually accounts for about half of all long distance communications, with about 700,000 customers purchasing service. A key concern for 1992 in the 800 services market will be the issue of number portability. Portability will allow customers to switch form one long distance carrier to another without changing the 800 numbers for which they may have built significant public name recognition. There is no interim solution in sight, although Bellcore is developing a new number plan to be available by 1995.

The market for 900 services encountered severe difficulties and a downturn during 1991 because of problems with bill collection and negative public perception. Many state PUCs decided to prohibit disconnection for unpaid bills. As a result, such industry leaders as Telesphere Communications fared poorly. One estimate placed quarterly uncollected 900 number bills at about $66 million in 1991 (out of total quarterly billings of only $80 million). The estimated total 900 number market in 1992 will be in the range of $350 million to $400 million.

International Telephone Services

There are about 350 U.S. providers of international telephone services, carried both by satellites and by undersea cables of either copper or optical fiber.

Satellite services are provided through the Communications Satellite Corporation (COMSAT), a private company that is U.S. signatory to the International Telecommunications Satellite Organization (INTELSAT) and to the International Maritime Satellite Organization (INMARSAT). These are the global satellite cooperatives owned by the world's telephone companies. In the past few years, the FCC has authorized private undersea cable and satellite systems to compete with COMSAT and with traditional telephone carriers like AT&T.

Many developments during 1990 affected the structure of the international services market. AT&T, losing market share domestically but expanding in international markets, signed an agreement with the Ministry of Communications of the former Soviet Union to explore cooperation in telephone services. It also installed a new $12 million satellite earth station in California that will transpond with other earth stations in 12 Pacific Rim countries. And the company has introduced enhanced facsimile services to the United Kingdom and Japan, aided by a new U.S. trade agreement with Japan on international value-added services. AT&T's ownership of Istel, a British value-added service company, and its equipment alliance with Italtel, the Italian telecommunications company, will also provide inroads to the European services market. In partnership with Japan's KDD, AT&T also announced a deal to link the People's Republic of China to the United States and Japan with satellite and fiber optic cable facilities.

Other U.S. companies were also active overseas in 1990. Bell Atlantic and US West signed a letter of intent with Czechoslovakia to form a joint venture company to build a public packet-switched data network. These two companies also agreed to construct a national cellular telephone system and to work towards modernizing Czechoslovakia's overall network. Also, Ameritech and Bell Atlantic agreed to purchase New Zealand's state telephone company for $2.4 billion. Sweden and Hungary announced plans to privatize their telephone companies, an activity in which U.S. companies may have an opportunity to participate. Bell Atlantic won and then lost a contract to manage part of Argentina's telephone system, while Nynex now owns 50 percent of the telephone company in Gibraltar. Privatization is likely to increase in 1991.

For the first time, advanced services beyond basic telephone, telex, telegraph, and leased circuits, are now available internationally. For example, both AT&T and Japan's KDD began ISDN service to France in 1990 in cooperation with France Telecom. And MCI began providing its virtual private network service and its electronic mail services to Belgium.

Most international services, however, consist of basic switched services, including telephone, telex, and telegraph. In 1990, revenues collected by U.S. carriers from their customers for these international services originating in the United States, including services to Canada and Mexico, totaled about $8 billion. Switched telephone service accounts for at least 80 percent of that total.

In general, prices for international telephone and telex services are appreciably higher overseas than in the United States, so calls from a foreign country to the United States cost more than calls from the United States to that foreign country. This is one reason the United States generates more international calls than it receives. But since foreign companies charge more than U.S. companies for connecting international calls, the United States pays out more than it receives; the U.S. net settlements deficit for international telecommunications traffic rose from approximately $40 million in 1970 to more than $2 billion in 1990. The FCC estimates that $1 billion of this deficit is a direct subsidy paid by U.S. consumers to foreign telecommunications administrations that charge overly high prices to other telephone companies for completing international calls.

The deficit is produced almost entirely by telephone traffic, which is growing 20 percent a year, while telegraph and telex have been declining. The deficit is keeping pace with growth. With 20 percent compounded annually, the deficit will double about every 3.6 years. If the current growth rate and settlements practices are maintained, the deficit will be about $7 billion in seven years.

In 1990, the FCC opened an inquiry into the way international payments are established and suggested that it might encourage rate negotiations between U.S. and foreign carriers in order to lower accounting rates for services, thereby reducing the deficit.

International VANS Alliances

The trend toward global networking to meet multinational corporate demand is driving foreign investment in the United States and forcing U.S.

companies to forge overseas strategic alliances and joint ventures in the value-added and data communications market. During 1990, this trend was evident as General Electric Information Services (GEIS) announced plans to add Asia as a site for a fourth network to complement facilities in New Jersey, Paris, and London. GEIS also began voice mail service to England, and introduced an international video-conferencing service between London, the United States, and Japan. British Telecom acquired Tymnet from McDonell-Douglas for $355 million, while France Cables and Radio, a subsidiary of France Telecom, acquired 80 percent of Cylix Communications, a U.S. provider of value-added data communications services and of very small aperture terminal satellite networks. France Cables, through a U.S. holding company, also holds 14.9 percent of TRT/FTC Communications, an international carrier mostly owned by the U.S. company Pacific Telecon Cable.

MCI Communications purchased a 25 percent share in Infonet, a data networking company owned by telecommunications administrations in France, Germany, Belgium, Sweden and Spain. AT&T now owns Istel, a British value-added services provider, which will augment its ability to provide electronic mail and related services on a global basis. And Japan's NTT Data Communications opened a large facility in New Jersey. Also in the international arena, Canada and the United Kingdom opened their markets to competition for long-distance voice telephone services; the United States negotiated a new agreement further opening the value-added services market with Japan; and discussions continued in Geneva at the General Agreement on Tariffs and Trade (GATT) organization on whether to subject world trade in telecommunications services to the disciplines of international trade law, which could guarantee access to and use of basic telecommunications services worldwide.

Domestic VANS Alliances

Western Union and US Sprint joined together their E-Mail networks, while US Sprint folded its Telenet data communications subsidiary into its long-haul carrier organization, now called the Sprint Data Group. Sprint and BT Tymnet together control about 75 percent of the U.S. value-added public data services market.

In videotex services, there are more than two dozen commercial systems in operation in the United States. In 1990, there were nearly 1.7 million subscribers of videotex services, an increase of 20 percent over 1988. The market size is estimated at $99.9 million in 1987, $159.9 million in 1988, and about $200 million by 1991. Online databases and interactive services continue to experience significant growth, and provide a stimulus to the public data networks, which are used as a means of access. There are more than 4,500 databases available in the United States via at least 620 online services.

Rates and Tariffs

Despite the AT&T divestiture as of January 1984, and the competition stemming from more liberal FCC policies, subsidies in the form of access charges paid by long distance to local telephone carriers in the United States continue to be substantial, helping keep down the cost of local service. While U.S. inflation has averaged 6.1 percent annually since 1977, the increase in the cost of telephone service has averaged only 4.4 percent, according to the U.S. Bureau of Labor Statistics. Between 1977 and 1989, the inflation adjusted price of telephone service decreased by 24.3 percent. American consumers pay only about 2 percent of their income for telephone service, roughly the same percentage as in 1974.

Price changes have been most dramatic for long-distance telephone service, where (in current dollars) prices have risen 0.6 percent a year on average, less than one-tenth the overall rate of inflation. Real prices have fallen by 45.7 percent, while for interstate services alone the drop has been 59.7 percent since 1977. The real price of an intrastate telephone call was 26 percent less in 1989 than it was in 1983, while the price of an interstate long distance call is 46.3 percent less today.

For local telephone service, rates rose during the 1980s. Consumers pay about 5.9 percent more in real terms for local service than 10 years ago. However, the real price of local service has begun to decline recently, and since 1986 has fallen 3.0 percent.

The price for international calls has also decreased substantially and is well below that in other industrialized countries. Between 1977 and 1987, the average price per minute for an international call originating in the United States fell from $2.20 to $1.16. Adjusted for inflation, these data represent a 71.8 percent price decrease. In 1988, the price per minute for long distance calls originating in the United States and terminating in the 10 countries with the highest volume of U.S. traffic was 28 percent lower than for calls going in the opposite direction. Prices for international services will continue to fall during 1991.

During the first half of 1990, the Consumer Price Index for telephone service increased slightly, as increases in the cost of local service offset declines in the cost of long distance services. Local service prices rose at an annual rate of 4.4 percent, while the cost of interstate calling declined at a rate of 2.7 percent. As a result, the composite Consumer Price Index for telephone service increased at an annual rate of 1.9 percent. The nation's overall rate of inflation during the first half of 1990 was 6.1 percent. Thus, after adjusting for inflation, the real cost of telephone service fell at a rate of about 4 percent.

Telecommunications Policy Developments

In a major development, the Ninth Circuit Court of Appeals in California overturned the FCC's Third Computer Inquiry decision, throwing into question the issue of Open Network Architecture (ONA) and competition safeguards. In response, the FCC indicated it would continue its ONA program and open a new inquiry docket on the issue of competition policy and so-called non-structural safeguards that do not require AT&T and the RHCs to maintain separate subsidiaries for the provision of unregulated services.

The FCC also sought comments on a plan to lessen regulation of AT&T long distance services provided to large business customers, but maintain current policies for services provided to small business and residential customers. The FCC proposed that AT&T be permitted to provide customized, single-customer services to large business users under contract instead of tariff, or through private offerings not regulated by the FCC. In developments related to the AT&T divestiture, hearings were held in Congress during 1990 to investigate amending the Modified Final Judgement of the AT&T divestiture Consent Decree and lifting the line-of-business restrictions on the RHCs; this effort will continue in 1991. AT&T has been subject to greater regulation than other long-distance carriers since its divestiture because the FCC designated the company a "dominant" firm in the industry. As AT&T has lost considerable market share since divestiture, however, and the Regional Holding Companies now offer all long-distance carriers equal access to the local exchange network, the FCC proposes to reduce the level of regulation imposed on the company.

In a significant regulatory development, the FCC decided in October 1990 to impose a system of rate regulation known as price caps on GTE and the Bell Operating Companies' interstate access services, despite strong opposition from users and many long distance companies. In so doing, the FCC reduced the companies' allowable rate of return from 12 percent to 11.25 percent, but ruled that they can now retain additional profits from exchange access services. The plan will be voluntary for all other local exchange carriers, and its designed to provide the telephone companies with greater incentives to become more productive. The FCC estimates the plan will result in lower interstate access charges of $337 million in 1991, savings which long distance carriers can then pass on to their customers. Lower rates are likely to stimulate network usage, helping drive up carriers' revenues.

Cellular and Radio Services

Radio communications are becoming an increasingly dynamic force in the telecommunications services industry, spurred primarily by new technologies and strong demand.

The three most important new technologies are digital cellular, PCNs (personal communications networks), and CT-2 (advanced cordless systems). Cellular phones and PCNs handle 2-way communications; CT-2 handles only 1-way (outgoing) calls. Cellular is the only one that has permanent authorization from the FCC; a few CT-2 and PCN companies have been granted trials. Both PCNs and CT-2 have already been authorized in the United Kingdom.

Cellular technology involves cell sites located around a metropolitan area, and software that hands off calls from one site to another, enabling customers to travel without interrupting calls. Sixty percent of the cellular traffic is vehicular. Cellular also has the capacity of handling calls from hand-held portable units, but PCN and CT-2 companies are hoping to make in-roads in the pedestrian market with their less expensive customer units and service charges.

Cellular

Annual revenues from cellular telephone services were about $5.2 billion in 1990, with over $8 billion collected since service was first inaugurated in 1983. Revenue growth was about 50 percent in 1990. There were 4.4 million subscribers by mid-1990 and over 7 million subscribers expected by 1991, up from 3.5 million in 1989. Worldwide, there were more than 10 million users of mobile cellular telephone service in 1990. Service was available in all U.S. metropolitan areas and was being installed in many rural areas. There are about 375 companies that resell cellular telephone service; gross capital investment in the industry reached a cumulative level of more than $5.2 billion in mid-1990, up 16 percent in 6 months. The market research firm Dataquest estimates that cumulative revenues should be $7.6 billion by 1993, with the projected compound annual growth rate expected to increase to 22.6 percent.

The cellular industry's consolidation process, marked by two notable mergers in 1990, is expected to continue at a slower pace in 1991. The trend of large corporations expanding their cellular operations by combining with smaller firms is likely to predominate. In July 1990, GTE and Contel announced their intention to merge. If approved by the companies' boards and the FCC, this $6.2 billion deal would create the country's second largest cellular operator, with about 500,000 subscribers. Both companies had been aggressively acquiring cellular operations.

Similarly, Pacific Telesis and Cellular Communications Inc. (CCI) announced plans in August 1990 to combine cellular operations in the Midwest as part of an agreement that will allow Pacific Telesis to eventually buy out CCI. The initial $87 million agreement will create one of the three largest regional cellular networks with over 530,000 subscribers. If approved by the FCC and shareholders, the deal is expected to close in the second or third quarter of 1991. McCaw Communications provides cellular telephone service to more than 850,000 customers.

PCNs and CT-2

Spectrum shortage problems which have plagued the cellular industry will continue to worsen in 1990 due to experiments with new technologies for which no permanent spectrum has been allocated. Overcrowding of the finite radio spectrum, coupled with a surge of innovative proposals for new spectrum-dependent services such as CT-2 and PCNs, led to consideration of several possible resolutions. If the Emerging Telecommunications Technologies Act is passed in the final quarter of 1990, it would reassign 200 MHz of government spectrum to the private sector. Spectrum auctions and user fees also have been suggested. The FCC is likely to look most favorably on proposals demonstrating high spectrum-efficiency.

PCNs utilize personal handsets or cordless telephones that would operate in a variety of pedestrian, office, residential, and possibly vehicular settings, via microcell technology. This concept moved closer to reality in 1990 when the FCC approved experimental licenses for several PCN trials. Strong industry interest has also compelled the FCC to begin an inquiry into authorizing PCNs on a commercial basis. Entities interested in building PCNs expect that PCN products and services will be far less expensive than their cellular counterparts.

Several trials of these new technologies will begin in 1991, with CT-2 operating in New York and Florida at 940-941 MHz; and PCN trials running in Washington, D.C. (American Personal Communications), and in Houston and Orlando (Milicom subsidiary PCN America) at the 1.7 to 2.3 GHz frequency.

Satellite Services

In the satellite services industry, innovative proposals for new applications will generate growth in 1991. Annual revenues from the three broad areas of satellite services, Fixed Satellite Services (FSS), Mobile Satellite Services (MSS), and Direct Broadcast Satellite (DBS) services, are expected to rise from $800 million in 1990 to around $1 billion by 1992.

In 1990, 29 operational U.S. communications satellites were in orbit, run by six U.S. domestic satellite operators. These satellites carried approximately 588 transponders in 1990, thought to represent around 38 percent of civilian transponders available worldwide. Industry sources indicate that increases in demand are closing in on currently available transponder space, with the highest growth in demand coming from video services. Although most of these satellites will reach the end of their lifespan in the early 1990s, a number of planned satellite launches will augment transponder availability. In the latest (November 1988) FCC processing round for satellite system applicants, which will provide satellite capacity through the 1990s, seven companies applied for permission to construct and launch a total of 15 satellites plus 3 ground spares. The new transponder capacity of these 15 satellites will be roughly equivalent to 330 Ku-bank transponders and 144 C-band transponders, easing the tight supply.

Fixed Satellite Services

The Fixed Satellite Services area continues to be dominated by basic video broadcast services such as Cable TV (CATV) and other television markets. These services currently represent around 60 percent of all satellite revenues. Telephone services' contribution to satellite service revenue has been shrinking as fiber optic cable telephone systems gain an increasing share of the market.

U.S. revenues from international satellite services, both from the International Satellite Organization (INTELSAT) and from separate systems, continued to rise in 1990. COMSAT, the U.S. representative to INTELSAT, reported that its 1989 international revenues of $412 million represented an annual increase of more than 15 percent over 1988 satellite service revenues. COMSAT revenues from INTELSAT increased to $280 million in 1989, due primarily to an increase in voice circuit traffic and international business (private line) services. Video, voice, and data traffic to and from the United States rose 11 percent in 1989, with the strongest growth in voice-grade telephone traffic. However, the growth in voice transmission will likely to be offset by COMSAT's wider use of digital compression technology. COMSAT predicts an increase in the relative share of video and data, where digital compression technology is less prevalent.

International satellite systems separate from INTELSAT, owned either privately or by international consortia, continued to redefine their role in 1990. The only operational U.S. separate system was PanAmSat's PAS1, with Orion and Columbia--also U.S. owned--nearing launch dates. Four additional applicants have not yet secured the requisite foreign operating agreements for further FCC licensing. In July, 1990, PanAmSat petitioned the FCC to allow separate system operators to link with public switched telephone networks, arguing that increased competition with INTELSAT would lower the cost of such telephone services. PanAmSat, which provides video and data transmission for the U.S., South and Central America, and Europe, plans to launch an additional satellite system for the Pacific Rim by late 1993. Orion, the second U.S. operational separate system to win approval from INTEL-SAT, plans to launch its two-satellite private system into Atlantic orbital slots by late 1992 and has reportedly named European countries. However, the FCC has yet to approve Orion's construction and operating license, due to concerns regarding its ability to meet the equity financing criteria. Columbia recently won a court contest with COMSAT to use Tracking and Data Relay Satellite (TDRS) capacity on two NASA satellites, advancing its planned separate system.

Long-Term Prospects

The next decade is likely to be one of significant change for the telecommunications services industry, which may look quite different in terms of market structure within the next five years. The merging of public and private telecommunications networks, the explosion of new mobile communications technologies and services, the introduction of broadband transmission, ubiquitous digitization, and virtually cost-free bandwidth are some of the forces that will shape the change. For regulators, the convergence of technology and market forces means even greater difficulties in keeping unregulated activities distinct from tariffed services.

Public data networks in the United States will face increased competition during in 1990s from new technologies such as virtual private network services, software-defined data services, an advanced method of circuit and packet-switching known as frame relay that will allow simultaneous voice and data communications, fast-packet switching at high bandwidth that will also allow voice communications as well as data, optical fiber systems using SONET (fiber optic) technology, and broadband ISDN. SONET technology will experience an especially high growth rate, both in the United States and abroad. France Telecom plans to add the capability by 1992, for example. The overall trend for both value-added services and common carriers will be to integrate voice and data applications at very high speeds.

Voice messaging and speech recognition will also play a major role in the industry during the coming years, as will store-and-forward enhanced facsimile services, EDI and electronic mail. Carriers will attempt to integrate such services into single-service packages. In term of user applications, the penetration of such sophisticated telecommunications services into the residential market has been much slower than for business customers. However, it is likely that with the growing concerns over scarce energy resources and environmental quality, services oriented towards telecommuting will become more widespread during the 1990s, as workers increasingly spend more time away from the office. The growth of at-home work may spur the development of more advanced telecommunications business services into the residential market. Such trends were already evident during 1990, as AT&T and the state of Arizona planned a test to discover whether telecommuting can improve environmental quality, and may ultimately lead to a market convergence between business and home customers.

PART III

The Job Search

A JOB SEARCH PRIMER

The best way to obtain a better professional job is to contact the employer directly. Broad-based statistical studies by the Department of Labor show that job seekers have found employment more successfully by contacting employers directly, than by using any other method.

However, given the current diversity, and increased specialization of both industry and job tasks it is possible that in some situations other job seeking methods may prove at least equally successful. Three of the other most commonly used methods are: relying on personal contacts, using employment services, and following up help wanted advertisements. Many professionals have been successful in finding better jobs using one of these methods. However, the Direct Contact method has an overall success rate twice that of any other method and it has been successfully used by many more professionals. So unless you have specific reasons to believe that another method would work best for you, the Direct Contact method should form the foundation of your job search effort.

The Objective

With any business task, you must develop a strategy for meeting a goal. This is especially true when it comes to obtaining a better job. First you need to clearly define your objectives.

Setting your job objectives is better known as career planning (or life planning for those who wish to emphasize the importance of combining the two). Career planning has become a field of study in and of itself. Since most of our readers are probably well-entrenched in their career path, we will touch on career planning just briefly.

If you are thinking of choosing or switching careers, we particularly emphasize two things. First, choose a career where you will enjoy most of the day-to-day tasks. Sure, this sounds obvious, but most of us have at one point or another been attracted by a glamour industry or a prestigious sounding job without thinking of the most important consideration: Would we enjoy performing the everyday tasks the position entailed?

The second key consideration is that you are not merely choosing a career, but also a lifestyle. Career counselors indicate that one of the most common problems people encounter in job seeking is a lack of consideration for how well-suited they are for a particular position or career. For example, some people, attracted to management consulting by good salaries, early responsibility and high level corporate exposure, do not adapt well to the long hours, heavy travel demands, and the constant pressure to produce. So be sure to determine both for your career as a whole and for each position that you apply for, if you will easily adapt to both the day-to-day duties that the position entails and the working environment.

The Strategy

Assuming that you have now established your career objectives, the next step of the job search is to develop a strategy. If you don't take the time to develop a strategy and lay out a plan you will probably find yourself going in circles after several weeks making a random search for opportunities that always seem just beyond your reach.

Your strategy can be thought as having three simple elements:

1. Choosing a method of contacting employers.

2. Allocating your scarce resources (in most job searches the key scarce resource will be time, but financial considerations will become important in some searches too.)

3. Evaluating how the selected contact method is working and then considering adopting other methods.

We suggest you give serious consideration to using the Direct Contact method exclusively. However, we realize it is human nature to avoid putting all your eggs in one basket. So, if you prefer to use other methods as well, try to expend at least half your effort on the Direct Contact method, spending the rest on all of the other methods combined. Millions of other job seekers have already proven that Direct Contact has been twice as effective in obtaining employment, so why not benefit from their effort?

With your strategy in mind, the next step is to develop the details of the plan, or scheduling. Of course, job searches are not something that most people do regularly so it is difficult to estimate how long each step will take. Nonetheless, it is important to have a plan so that your effort can be allocated the way you have chosen, so that you can see yourself progressing, and to facilitate reconsideration of your chosen strategy.

It is important to have a realistic time frame in mind. If you will be job searching full-time, your search will probably take at least two months and very likely, substantially longer. If you can only devote part-time effort, it will probably take four months.

You probably know a few people who seem to spend their whole lives searching for a better job in their part time. Don't be one of them. Once you begin your job search on a part-time basis, give it your wholehearted effort. If you don't really feel like devoting a lot of energy to job seeking right now, then wait. Focus on enjoying your present position, performing your best on the job, and storing up energy for when you are really ready to begin your job search.

Those of you currently unemployed should remember that job hunting is tough work physically and emotionally. It is also intellectually demanding -- requiring your best. So don't tire yourself out by working on your job campaign around the clock. It would be counter-productive. At the same time, be sure to discipline yourself. The most logical approach to time management is to keep your regular working hours.

For those of you who are still employed, job searching will be particularly tiring because it must be done in addition to your regular duties. So don't work yourself to the point where you show up to interviews appearing exhausted and slip behind at your current job. But don't be tempted to quit! The long hours are worth it - it is much easier to sell your skills from a position of strength (as someone currently employed).

If you are searching full-time and have decided to choose a mixture of contact methods, we recommend that you divide up each week allowing some time for each method. For instance, you might devote Mondays to following up newspaper ads because most of them appear in Sunday papers. Then you might devote Tuesdays, and Wednesday mornings to working and developing the personal contacts you have, in addition to trying a few employment services. Then you could devote the rest of the week to the Direct Contact method. This is just one plan that may succeed for you.

By trying several methods at once, job-searching will be more interesting for you, and you will be able to evaluate how promising each of the methods seems, altering your time allocation accordingly. Be very careful in your evaluation, however, and don't judge the success of a particular method just by the sheer number of interviews you obtain. Positions advertised in the newspaper, for instance, are likely to generate many more interviews per opening than positions that are filled without being advertised.

If you are searching part-time and decide to try several different contact methods, we recommend that you try them sequentially. You simply won't have enough time to put a meaningful amount of effort into more than one method at once. So decide how long your job search might take. (Only a guess, of course.) And then allocate so many weeks or months for each contact method you choose to use. (We suggest that you try Direct Contact first.)

If you are expected to be in your office during the business day, then you have an additional time problem to deal with. How can you work interviews into the business day? And if you work in an open office, how can you even call to set up interviews? As much as possible you should keep up the effort and the appearances on your present job. So maximize your use of the lunch hour, early in the morning and late in the afternoon for calling. If you really keep trying you will be surprised how often you will be able to reach the executive you are trying to contact during your out-of-office hours.

The lunch hour for different executives will vary between 12 and 3. Also you can catch people as early as 8 AM and as late as 6 PM on frequent occasions. Jot out a plan each night on how you will be using each minute of your precious lunch break.

Your inability to interview at any time other than lunch just might work to your advantage. If you can, try to set up as many interviews as possible for your lunch hour. This will go a long way to creating a relaxed rapport. (Who isn't happy when eating?) But be sure the interviews don't stray too far from the agenda on hand.

Lunchtime interviews will be much easier for the person with substantial career experience to obtain. People with less experience will often find that they have no alternative other than taking time off for interviewing. If you have to take time off, you have to take time off. But try to do this as little as possible. Usually you should take the whole day off so that it is not blatantly obvious that you are job searching. Try to schedule in at least two, or at the most three, interviews for the same day. (It is very difficult to maintain an optimum level of energy at more than three interviews in one day.) Explain to the interviewer why you might have to juggle your interview schedule -- he/she should honor the respect you are showing your current employer by minimizing your days off and will probably appreciate the fact that another prospective employer is showing an interest in you.

Once again we need to emphasize if you are searching for a job, especially part-time, get out there and do the necessary tasks to the best of your ability and get it over with. Don't let your job search drag on endlessly.

Remember that all schedules are meant to be broken. The purpose of a schedule in your job search is not to rush you to your goal, its purpose is to map out the road ahead of you and evaluate the progress of your chosen strategy to date.

The Direct Contact Method

Once you have scheduled a time, you are ready to begin using the job search method that you have chosen. In the text we will restrict discussion to use of the Direct Contact method. Sideboards will comment briefly on developing your personal contacts and using newspaper advertisements.

The first step in preparing for Direct Contact is to develop a check list for categorizing the types of firms for which you would prefer working. You might categorize firms by their product line, their size, their customer-type (such as industrial or consumer), their growth prospects, or, of course by their geographical locations. Your list of important considerations might be very short. If it is, good! The shorter it is, the easier it will be to find appropriate firms.

DEVELOPING YOUR CONTACTS

Some career counselors feel that the best route to a better job is through somebody you already know or through somebody to whom you can be introduced. The counselors recommend you build your contact base beyond your current acquaintances by asking each one to introduce you, or refer you, to additional people in your field of interest.

The theory goes like this: You might start with 15 personal contacts, each of whom introduces you to 3 additional people, for a total 45 additional contacts. Then each of these people introduces you to three additional people which adds 135 additional contacts. Theoretically, you will soon know every person in the industry.

Of course, developing your personal contacts does not usually work quite as smoothly as the theory suggests because some people will not be able to introduce you to several relevant contacts. The further you stray from your initial contact base, the weaker your references may be. So, if you do try developing your own contacts, try to begin with as large an initial group of people you personally know as possible. Dig into your personal phone book and your holiday greeting card list and locate old classmates from school. Be particularly sure to approach people who perform your personal business such as your lawyer, accountant, banker, doctor, stockbroker, and insurance agent. These people develop a very broad contact base due to the nature of their professions.

Then try to decide at which firms you are most likely to be able to obtain employment. You might wish to consider to what degree your particular skills might be in demand, the degree of competition for employment, and the employment outlook at the firm.

Now you are ready to assemble your list of prospective employers. Build up your list to at least 100 prospects. Then separate your prospect list into three groups. The first tier of maybe 25 firms will be your primary target market, the second group of another 25 firms will be your secondary market, and remaining names you will keep in reserve.

This book will help you greatly in developing your prospect list. Refer to the company profile section of this book. You will notice that all companies are listed in straight alphabetical order. If you are interested in a particular industry or geographical location, then refer to the industrial and geographical indexes at the rear of the book.

At this stage, once you have gotten your prospect list together and have an idea of the firms for which you might wish to work, it is best to get to work on your resume. Refer to formats of the sample resumes included in the Resumes and Cover Letters section that follows this chapter.

Once your resume is at the printer, begin research for the first batch of 25 prospective employers. You will want to determine whether you would be happy working at the firms you are researching and also get a better idea of what their employment needs might be. You also need to obtain enough information to sound highly informed about the company during phone conversations and in mail correspondence. But don't go all out on your research yet! At some of these firms you probably will not be able to arrange interviews, so save your big research effort until you start to arrange interviews. Nevertheless, you should plan to spend about 3 or 4 hours, on average, researching each firm. Do your research in batches to save time and energy. Go into one resource at a time and find out what you can about each of the 25 firms in the batch. Start with the easiest resources to use (such as this book.) Keep organized. Maintain a folder on each firm.

If you discover something that really disturbs you about the firm (i.e. perhaps they are about to close their only local office) or if you discover that your chances of getting a job there are practically nil (i.e. perhaps they just instituted a hiring freeze) then cross them off your prospect list.

If possible, supplement your research efforts with contacts to individuals who know the firm well. Ideally you should make an informal contact with someone at the particular firm, but often a contact at a direct competitor, or a major supplier or customer will be able to supply you with just as much information. At the very least try to obtain whatever printed information that the company has available, not just annual reports, but product brochures and anything else. The company might very well have printed information about career opportunities.

Getting The Interview

Now it is time to arrange an interview, time to make the Direct Contact. If you have read many books on job searching you have probably noticed that virtually all tell you to avoid the personnel office like the plague. It is said that the personnel office never hires people, they just screen out candidates. In some cases you may be able to identify and contact the appropriate manager with the authority to hire you. However, this will take a lot of time and effort in each case. Often you'll be bounced back to personnel. So we suggest that you begin your Direct Contact campaign through personnel offices. If it seems that in the firms on your prospect list that little hiring is done through personnel, you might consider an alternative course of action.

The three obvious means of initiating Direct Contact are:

-Showing up unannounced
-Phone calls
-Mail

Cross out the first one right away. You should never show up to seek a professional position without an appointment. Even if you are somehow lucky enough to obtain an interview, you will appear so unprofessional that you will not even be seriously considered.

Mail contact seems to be a good choice if you have not been in the job market for a while. You can take your time to prepare a careful letter, say exactly what you want, tuck your resume in, and then the addressee can read the material at leisure. But employers receive many resumes every day. Don't be surprised if you do not get a response to your inquiry. So don't spend weeks waiting for responses that never come. If you do send a cover letter, follow it up (or precede it) with a phone call. This will increase your impact, and underscore both your interest in the firm and the fact that you are familiar with it (because of the initial research you did.)

Another alternative is to make a "Cover Call." Your Cover Call should be just like your cover letter: concise. Your first sentence should interest the employer in you. Then try to subtly mention your familiarity with the firm. Don't be overbearing; keep your introduction to three sentences or less. Be pleasant, self confident and relaxed. This will greatly increase the chances of the person at the other end of the line developing the conversation. But don't press. When you are asked to follow up "with something in the mail" don't try to prolong the conversation once it has ended. Don't ask what they want to receive in the mail. Always send your resume and a highly personalized follow-up letter, reminding the addressee of the phone conversation. Always include a cover letter even if you are requested to send a resume. (It is assumed that you will send a cover letter too.)

Unless you are in telephone sales, making smooth and relaxed cover calls will probably not come easily. Practice them on your own and then with your friends or relatives (friends are likely to be more objective and hence, better participants.)

If you obtain an interview over the telephone, be sure to send a thank you note reiterating the points you made during the conversation. You will appear more professional and increase your impact. However, don't mail your resume once an interview has been arranged unless it is specifically requested. Take it with you to the interview instead.

Preparing For The Interview

Once the interview has been arranged, begin your in-depth research. You have got to arrive at the interview knowing the company upside down and inside out. You need to know their products, their types of customers, their subsidiaries, their parent, their principal locations, their rank in the industry, their sales and profit trends, their type of ownership, their size, their current plans and much more. By this time you have probably narrowed your job search to one industry, but if you haven't then you need to be familiar with the trends in this firm's industry, the firm's principal competitors and their relative performance, and the direction that the industry leaders are headed. Dig into every resource you can! Read the company literature, the trade press, the business press, and if the company is public, call your stockbroker and ask for still additional information. If possible, speak to someone at the firm before the interview, or if not, speak to someone at a competing firm. Clearly the more time you spend, the better. Even if you feel extremely pressed for time, you should set aside at least 12 hours for pre-interview research.

If you have been out of the job market for some time, don't be surprised if you find yourself tense during your first few interviews. It will probably happen every time you re-enter the market, not just when you seek your first job after getting out of school.

Tension is natural during an interview, but if you can be relaxed you will have an advantage over the competition. Knowing you have done a thorough research job should help you relax for an interview. Also make a list of questions that you think might be asked in an interview. Think out your answers carefully. Then practice reviewing them with a friend. Tape record your responses to the questions he/she raises in the role as interviewer. If you feel particularly unsure of your interviewing skills, arrange your first interviews at firms in which you are not very interested. (But remember it is common courtesy to seem excited about the possiblity of working for any firm at which you interview.) Then practice again on your own after these first few interviews. Go over each of the questions that you were asked.

DON'T BOTHER WITH MASS MAILING OR BARRAGES OF PHONE CALLS

Direct Contact does not mean burying every firm within a hundred miles with mail and phone calls. Mass mailings rarely work in the job hunt. This also applies to those letters that are personalized -- but dehumanized -- on an automatic typewriter. Don't waste your time or money on such a project; you will fool no one but yourself.

The worst part of sending out mass mailings or making unplanned phone calls is that you are likely to be remembered as someone with little genuine interest in the firm, as someone who lacks sincerity, and as somebody that nobody wants to hire.

HELP WANTED ADVERTISEMENTS

Only a small fraction of professional job openings are advertised. Yet a majority of job seekers -- and a lot of people not in the job market -- spend a lot of time studying the help wanted ads. As a result, the competition for advertised openings is often much more severe.

A moderate-sized Manhattan employer told us about an experience advertising in the help wanted section of a major Sunday newspaper:

It was a disaster. We had over 500 responses from this relatively small ad in just one week. We have only two phone lines in this office and one was totally knocked out. We'll never advertise for professional help again.

If you insist on following up on help wanted ads, then research a firm before you reply to an ad so that you can ascertain if you would be a suitable candidate and that you would enjoy working at a particular firm. Also such preliminary research might help to separate you from all of the other professionals responding to that ad, many of whom will only have a passing interest in the opportunity. That said, your chances of obtaining a job through the want-ads are still much smaller than they are if you use the Direct Contact method.

How important is the proper dress for a job interview? Buying a complete wardrobe of Brooks Brothers pinstripes, donning new wing tip shoes and having your hair trimmed every morning is not enough to guarantee your obtaining a career position as an investment banker. But on the other hand, if you can't find a clean, conservative suit and a narrow tie, or won't take the time to polish your shoes and trim and wash your hair -- then you are just wasting your time by interviewing at all.

Very rarely will the final selection of candidates for a job opening be determined by dress. So don't spend a fortune on a new wardrobe. But be sure that your clothes are adequate. Men applying for any professional position should wear a suit; women should either wear a dress or a suit (not a pant suit.) Your clothes should be at least as formal or slightly more formal and more conservative than the position would suggest.

Top personal grooming is more important than finding the perfect clothes for a job interview. Careful grooming indicates both a sense of thoroughness and self-confidence.

Be sure that your clothes fit well and that they are immaculate. Hair must be neat and clean. Shoes should be newly polished. Women need to avoid excessive jewelry and excessive makeup. Men should be freshly shaven, even if the interview is late in the day.

Be complete. Everyone needs a watch and a pen and pad of paper (for taking notes.) Finally a briefcase or folder (containing extra copies of your resume) will help complete the look of professionalism.

Sometimes the interviewer will be running behind schedule. Don't be upset, be sympathetic. He/she might be under pressure to interview a lot of candidates and to quickly fill a demanding position. So be sure to come to your interview with good reading material to keep yourself occupied. This will help increase your patience and ease your tenseness.

The Interview

The very beginning of the interview is the most important part because it determines the rapport for the rest of it. Those first few moments are especially crucial. Do you smile when you meet? Do you establish enough eye contact, but not too much? Do you walk into the office with a self-assured and confident stride? Do you shake hands firmly? Do you make small talk easily without being garrulous? It is human nature to judge people by that first impression, so make sure it is a good one. But most of all, try to be yourself.

Often the interviewer will begin, after the small talk, by proceeding to tell you about the company, the division, the department, or perhaps, the position. Because of your detailed research, the information about the company will be repetitive for you and the interviewer would probably like nothing better than to avoid this regurgitation of the company biography. So if you can do so tactfully, indicate to the interviewer that you are very familiar

SOME FAVORITE INTERVIEW QUESTIONS

Tell me about yourself...

Why did you leave your last job?

What excites you in your current job?

What are your career goals?

Where would you like to be in 5 years?

What are your greatest strengths?

What are your greatest weaknesses?

Why do you wish to work for this firm?

Where else are you seeking employment?

Why should we hire you?

with the firm. If he/she seems intent on providing you with background information, despite your hints, then acquiesce. But be sure to remain attentive. If you can manage to generate a brief discussion of the company or the industry at this point, without being forceful, great. It will help to further build rapport, underscore your interests and increase your impact.

Soon (if it didn't begin that way) the interviewer will begin the questions. This period of the interview falls into one of two categories (or somewhere in between): either a structured interview, where the interviewer has a prescribed set of questions to ask; or an unstructured interview, where the interviewer will ask only leading questions to get you to talk about yourself, your experiences and your goals. Try to sense as quickly as possible which direction the interviewer wishes to proceed and follow along in the direction he/she seems to be leading. This will make the interviewer feel more relaxed and in control of the situation.

Many of the questions will be similar to the ones that you were expecting and you will have prepared answers. Remember to keep attuned to the interviewer and make the length of your answers appropriate to the situation. If you are really unsure as to how detailed a response the interviewer is seeking, then ask. Query if he/she would prefer more details of a particular aspect.

As the interview progresses, the interviewer will probably mention what he/she considers to be the most important responsibilities of the position. If applicable, draw parallels between your experience and the demands of the position as seen by the interviewer. Describe your past experience in the same manner that you did on your resume: emphasizing results and achievements and not merely describing activities. If you listen carefully (listening is a very important part of the interviewing process) the interviewer might very well mention or imply the skills in terms of what he/she is seeking. But don't exaggerate. Be on the level.

Try not to cover too much ground during the first interview. This interview is often the toughest, with many candidates being screened out. If you are interviewing for a very competitive position, you will have to make an impression that will last. Focus on a few of your greatest strengths that are relevant to the position. Develop these points carefully, state them again in other words, and then try to summarize them briefly at the end of the interview.

Often the interviewer will pause towards the end and ask if you have any questions. Particularly in a structured interview, this might be the one chance to really show your knowledge of and interest in the firm. Have prepared a list of specific questions that are of real interest to you. Let your questions subtly show your research and your knowledge of the firm's activities. It is wise to have an extensive list of questions, as several of them may have already been answered during the interview.

YOU'RE FIRED!!

You are not the first and will not be the last to go through this traumatic experience. Thousands of professionals are fired every week. Remember, being fired is not a reflection on you as a person. It is usually a reflection of your company's staffing needs and its perception of your recent job performance. Share the fact with your relatives and friends. Being fired is not something of which to be ashamed.

Don't start your job search with a flurry of unplanned activity. Start by choosing a strategy and working out a plan. Now is not the time for major changes in your life. If possible, remain in the same career and in the same geographical location, at least until you have been working again for a while. On the other hand, if the only industry for which you are trained is leaving, or is severely depressed in your area, then you should give prompt consideration to moving or switching careers.

Register for unemployment compensation immediately. A thorough job search could take months. After all, your employers have been contributing to unemployment insurance specifically for you ever since your first job. Don't be surprised to find other professionals collecting unemployment compensation as well. Unemployment compensation is for everybody who is between jobs.

Be prepared for the question, "Why were you fired?", during job interviews. Avoid mentioning you were fired while arranging interviews. Try especially hard not to speak negatively of your past employer and not to sound particularly worried about your status of being temporarily unemployed. But don't spend much time reflecting on why you were fired or how you might have avoided it. Look ahead. Think positively. And be sure to follow a careful plan during your job search.

Do not allow your opportunity to ask questions to become an interrogation. Avoid bringing your list of questions to the interview. And ask questions that you are fairly certain the interviewer can answer (remember how you feel when you cannot answer a question during an interview.)

Even if you are unable to determine the salary range beforehand, do not ask about it during the first interview. You can always ask about it later. Above all, don't ask about fringe benefits until you have been offered a position. (Then be sure to get all the details.) You should be able to determine the company's policy on fringe benefits relatively easily before the interview.

Try not to be negative about anything during the interview. (Particularly any past employer or any previous job.) Be cheerful. Everyone likes to work with someone who seems to be happy.

Don't let a tough question throw you off base. If you don't know the answer to a question, say so simply -- do not apologize. Just smile. Nobody can answer every question -- particularly some of the questions that are asked in job interviews.

Before your first interview, you may have been able to determine how many interviews the employer usually has for positions at your level. (Of course it may differ quite a bit within one firm.) Usually you can count on at least three or four interviews, although some firms, such as some of the professional partnerships, are well-known to give a minimum of six interviews for all professional postions.

Depending on what information you are able to obtain you might want to vary your strategy quite a bit from interview to interview. For instance if the first interview is a screening interview then try to have a few of your strengths really stand out. On the other hand, if later interviews are primarily with people who are in a position to veto your hiring, but not to push it forward (and few people are weeded out at these stages), then you should primarily focus on building rapport as opposed to reiterating and developing your key strengths.

If it looks as though your skills and background do not match the position your interviewer was hoping to fill, ask him or her if there is another division or subsidiary that perhaps could profit from your talents.

After The Interview

Write a follow-up letter immediately after the interview, while it is still fresh in the interviewer's mind. Then, if you have not heard from the interviewer within seven days, call him/her to stress your continued interest in the firm and the position and to request a second interview.

A parting word of advice. Again and again during your job search you will be rejected. You will be rejected when you apply for interviews. You will be rejected after interviews. For every job you finally receive you will probably have received a multitude of rejections. Don't let these rejections slow you down. Keep reminding yourself that the sooner you go out and get started on your job search and get those rejections flowing in, the closer you will be to obtaining the better job.

RESUMES AND COVER LETTERS

THIS SECTION CONTAINS:

1. Resume Preparation
2. Resume Format
3. Resume Content
4. Should You Hire A Resume Writer?
5. Cover Letters
6. Sample Resumes
7. General Model For A Cover Letter
8. Sample Cover Letters
9. General Model For A Follow-up Letter

RESUMES/OVERVIEW

When filling a position, a recruiter will often have 100 plus applicants, but time to interview only the 5 or 10 most promising ones. So he or she will have to reject most applicants after a brief skimming of their resume.

Unless you have phoned and talked to the recruiter -- which you should do whenever you can -- you will be chosen or rejected for an interview entirely on the basis of your resume and cover letter. So your resume must be outstanding. (But remember -- a resume is no substitute for a job search campaign. YOU must seek a job. Your resume is only one tool.)

RESUME PREPARATION

One page, usually.

Unless you have an unusually strong background with many years of experience and a large diversity of outstanding achievements, prepare a one page resume. Recruiters dislike long resumes.

8 1/2 x 11 Size

Recruiters often get resumes in batches of hundreds. If your resume is on small sized paper it is likely to get lost in the pile. If oversized, it is likely to get crumpled at the edges, and won't fit in their files.

Typesetting

Modern photocomposition typesetting gives you the clearest, sharpest image, a wide variety of type styles and effects such as italics, bold facing, and book-like justified margins. Typesetting is the best resume preparation process, but is also the most expensive.

Word Processing

The most flexible way to get your resume typed is on a good quality word processor. With word processing, you can make changes almost instantly because your resume will be stored on a magnetic disk and the computer will do all the re-typing automatically. A word processing service will usually offer you a variety of type styles in both regular and proportional spacing. You can have bold facing for emphasis, justified margins, and clear, sharp copies.

Typing

Household typewriters and office typewriters with nylon or other cloth ribbons are NOT good for typing the resume you will have printed. If you can't get word processing or typesetting, hire a professional with a high quality office typewriter with a plastic ribbon (usually called a "carbon ribbon.")

Printing

Find the best quality offset printing process available. DO NOT make your copies on an office photocopier. Only the personnel office may see the resume you mail. Everyone else may see only a copy of it. Copies of copies quickly become unreadable. Some professionally maintained, extra-high-quality photocopiers are of adequate quality, if you are in a rush. But top quality offset printing is best.

Proofread your resume

Whether you typed it yourself or had it written, typed, or typeset, mistakes on resumes can be embarrassing, particularly when something obvious such as your name is misspelled. No matter how much you paid someone else to type or write or typeset your resume, YOU lose if there is a mistake. So proofread it as carefully as possible. Get a friend to help you. Read your draft aloud as your friend checks the proof copy. Then have your friend read aloud while you check. Next, read it letter by letter to check spelling and punctuation.

If you are having it typed or typeset by a resume service or a printer, and you can't bring a friend or take the time during the day to proof it, pay for it and take it home. Proof it there and bring it back later to get it corrected and printed.

RESUME FORMAT

(See samples)

Basic data

Your name, phone number, and a complete address should be at the top of your resume. (If you are a university student, you should also show your home address and phone number.)

Separate your education and work experience

In general, list your experience first. If you have recently graduated, list your education first, unless your experience is more important than your education. (For example, if you have just graduated from a teaching school, have some business experience and are applying for a job in business you would list your business experience first.) If you have two or more years of college, you don't need to list high schools.

Reverse chronological order

To a recruiter your last job and your latest schooling are the most important. So put the last first and list the rest going back in time.

Show dates and locations

Put the dates of your employment and education on the left of the page. Put the names of the companies you worked for and the schools you attended a few spaces to the right of the dates. Put the city and state or city and country where you studied or worked to the right of the page.

Avoid sentences and large blocks of type

Your resume will be scanned, not read. Short, concise phrases are much more effective than long-winded sentences. Keep everything easy to find. Avoid paragraphs longer than six lines. Never go ten or more lines in a paragraph. If you have more than six lines of information about one job or school, put it in two or more paragraphs.

RESUME CONTENT

Be factual

In many companies, inaccurate information on a resume or other application material will get you fired as soon as the inaccuracy is discovered. Protect yourself.

Be positive

You are selling your skills and accomplishments in your resume. If you achieved something, say so. Put it in the best possible light. Don't hold back or be modest, no one else will. But don't exaggerate to the point of misrepresentation.

Be brief

Write down the important (and pertinent) things you have done, but do it in as few words as possible. The shorter your resume is, the more carefully it will be examined.

Work experience

Emphasize continued experience in a particular type of function or continued interest in a particular industry. De-emphasize irrelevant positions. Delete positions that you held for less than four months. (Unless you are a very recent college grad or still in school.)

Stress your results

Elaborate on how you contributed to your past employers. Did you increase sales, reduce costs, improve a product, implement a new program? Were you promoted?

Mention relevant skills and responsibilities

Be specific. Slant your past accomplishments toward the type of position that you hope to obtain. Example: Do you hope to supervise people? Then state how many people, performing what function, you have supervised.

Education

Keep it brief if you have more than two years of career experience. Elaborate more if you have less experience. Mention degrees received and any honors or special awards. Note individual courses or research projects that might be relevant for employers. For instance, if you are a liberal arts major, be sure to mention courses in such areas as: accounting, statistics, computer programming, or mathematics.

Job objective?

Leave it out. Even if you are certain of exactly the type of job that you desire, the inclusion of a job objective might eliminate you from consideration for other positions that a recruiter feels are a better match for your qualifications.

Personal data

Keep it very brief. Two lines maximum. A one-word mention of commonly practiced activities such as golf, skiing, sailing, chess, bridge, tennis, etc. can prove to be good way to open up a conversation during an interview. Do not include your age, weight, height, etc.

SHOULD YOU HIRE A RESUME WRITER?

If you write reasonably well, there are some advantages to writing your resume yourself. To write it well, you will have to review your experience and figure out how to explain your accomplishments in clear, brief phrases. This will help you when you explain your work to interviewers.

If your write your resume, everything in it will be in your own words -- it will sound like you. It will say what you want it to say. And you will be much more familiar with the contents. If you are a good writer, know yourself well and have a good idea of what parts of your background employers are looking for, you may be able to write your own resume better than anyone else can. If you write your resume yourself, you should have someone who can be objective (preferably not a close relative) review it with you.

When should you have your resume professionally written?

If you have difficulty writing in Resume Style (which is quite unlike normal written language), if you are unsure of which parts of your background you should emphasize, or if you think your resume would make your case better if it did not follow the standard form outlined here or in a book on resumes, then you should have it professionally written.

There are two reasons even some professional resume writers we know have had their resumes written with the help of fellow professionals. First, when they need the help of someone who can be objective about their background, and second, when they want an experienced sounding board to help focus their thoughts.

If you decide to hire a resume writer

The best way to choose a writer is by reputation -- the recommendation of a friend, a personnel director, your school placement officer or someone else knowledgeable in the field.

You should ask, "If I'm not satisfied with what you write, will you go over it with me and change it?"

You should ask, "How long has the person who will write my resume been writing resumes?"

There is no sure relation between price and quality, except that you are unlikely to get a good writer for less than $50 for an uncomplicated resume and you shouldn't have to pay more than $300 unless your experience is very extensive or complicated. There will be additional charges for printing.

Few resume services will give you a firm price over the phone, simply because some people's resumes are too complicated and take too long to do at any predetermined price. Some services will quote you a price that applies to almost all of their customers. Be sure to do some comparative shopping. Obtain a firm price before you engage their services and find out how expensive minor changes will be.

COVER LETTERS

Always mail a cover letter with your resume. In a cover letter you can show an interest in the company that you can't show in a resume. You can point out one or two skills or accomplishments the company can put to good use.

Make it personal

The more personal you can get, the better. If someone known to the person you are writing has recommended that you contact the company, get permission to include his/her name in the letter. If you have the name of a person to send the letter to, make sure you have the name spelled correctly and address it directly to that person. Be sure to put the person's name and title on both the letter and envelope. This will ensure that your letter will get through to the proper person, even if a new person now occupies this position. But even if you are addressing it to the "Personnel Director" or the "Hiring Partner," send a letter.

Type cover letters in full. Don't try the cheap and easy ways like photocopying the body of your letter and typing in the inside address and salutation. You will give the impression that you are mailing to a multitude of companies and have no particular interest in any one. Have your letters fully typed and signed with a pen.

Phone

Precede or follow your mailing with a phone call.

Bring extra copies of your resume to the interview

If the person interviewing you doesn't have your resume, be prepared. Carry copies of your own. Even if you have already forwarded your resume, be sure to take extra copies to the interview, as someone other than the interviewer(s) might now have the first copy you sent.

Chronological Resume
(Prepared on a Word Processor and Laser Printer.)

WALLACE R. RECTORIAN
412 Maple Court
Seattle, WA 98404
206/555-6584

EXPERIENCE

1984-present   THE CENTER COMPANY, Seattle, WA
Systems Analyst, design systems for the manufacturing unit. Specifically, physical inventory, program specifications, studies of lease buy decisions, selection of hardware the outside contractors and inside users. Wrote On-Site Computer Terminal Operators Manual. Adapted product mix problems to the LASPSP (Logistical Alternative Product Synthesis Program).

As *Industrial Engineer* from February 1984 to February 1986, computerized system design. Evaluated manufacturing operations operator efficiency productivity index and budget allocations. Analyzed material waste and recommended solutions.

ADDITIONAL EXPERIENCE

1980-1984   *Graduate Research Assistant* at New York State Institute of Technology.

1978-1980   *Graduate Teaching Assistant* at Salem State University.

EDUCATION

1982-1984   NEW YORK STATE INSTITUTE OF TECHNOLOGY, Albany, NY
M.S. in Operations Research. GPA: 3.6. Graduate courses included Advanced Location and Queueing Theories, Forecasting, Inventory and Material Flow Systems, Linear and Nonlinear Determination Models, Engineering Economics and Integer Programming.

1980-1982   M.S. in Information and Computer Sciences. GPA: 3.8
Curriculum included Digital Computer Organization & Programming. Information Structure & Process. Mathematical Logic, Computer Systems, Logic Design and Switching Theory.

1976-1980   SALEM STATE UNIVERSITY, Salem, OR
B.A. in Mathematics. GPA: 3.6.

AFFILIATIONS

Member of the American Institute of Computer Programmers, Association for Computing Machinery and the Operations Research Society of America.

PERSONAL

Married, three dependents, able to relocate.

Chronological Resume
(Prepared on a Word Processor and Laser Printer.)

DAMIEN W. PINCKNEY

U.S. Address:	Jamaican Address:
15606 Center Street	Oskarrataan Building, Room 1234
Bottineau, ND 58777	Hedonism II
701/555-9320	Negril, Jamaica
	809/555-6634

Experience

1984-present **HEDONISM II**, Negril, Jamaica
Resident Engineer for this publicly owned resort with main offices in Kingston. Responsibilities include:

Maintaining electrical generating and distribution equipment.

Supervising an eight-member staff in maintenance of refrigeration equipment, power and light generators, water purification plant, and general construction machinery.

1982-1984 **NEGRIL BEACH HOTEL**, Negril Beach, Jamaica
Resident Engineer for a privately held resort, assigned total responsibility for facility generating equipment.

Directed maintenance, operation and repair of diesel generating equipment.

1980-1982 Directed overhaul of turbo generating equipment in two Mid-Western localities and assisted in overhaul of a turbo generating unit in Mexico.

1975-1980 **CAPITAL CITY ELECTRIC**, Washington, DC
Service Engineer for the power generation service division of this regional power company, supervised the overhaul, maintenance and repair of large generators and associated auxiliary equipment.

Education

1972-1975 **FRANKLIN INSTITUTE**, Baltimore, MD
Awarded a degree of Associate of Engineering. Concentration in Mechanical Power Engineering Technology.

Personal Willing to travel and relocate.
Interested in sailing, scuba diving, deep sea fishing.

References available upon request.

Chronological Resume
(Prepared on a Word Processor and Laser Printer.)

Angela Weatherstone
1009 Kilminster Drive
Los Angeles, CA 90013
213/555-0987

Business experience

1988-present   PACIFIC COMPUTER LEASING, Los Angeles, CA
Manager of Debt Placement
* Responsible for developing and maintaining bank and institution-
al debt sources.
* Structured leases for maximum tax advantages.
* Have documented and closed $120,000,000 of secured loans.
* Work closely with investment bankers and bank and institutional
funding sources.

1981-1988   PRIME COMPUTER, INC., Natick, MA
Customer Finance Marketing Manager, North America
* Responsible for the profitable management of finance lease and
tax exempt installment programs in the United States and Mexico
used by government and business.
* Made certain pricing and documentation were suitable for sale of
portfolio to funding institutions. Typical transaction exceeded
$750,000.

1978-1981   COPPERBOTTOM INFORMATION SYSTEMS, Philadelphia, PA
Manager of Marketing Proposal Analysis, Atlanta, GA
* Advised field sales force in the initial stages of proposals with em-
phasis on the financial aspects of operating and finance leases, installment sales, and multi-party transactions.
Sectional Revenue Manager, Winston-Salem, NC
* Achieved planned lease purchase revenue mix, by appropriate
pricing policies and financial agreements with customers.
Sales Finance, Baltimore, MD
* Implemented and administered Copperbottom's finance lease program. Educated field sales personnel in financial plans. Handled
administration of equipment add-ons, replacements, handled contract amendments.

1975-1978   BAYBANK, N.A., Portland, OR
Branch Manager
* Responsible for the day-to-day operation of a branch bank.

Education
1970-1974   BABSON COLLEGE, Wellesley, MA
Bachelor of Science in Business Administration with a major in
financial management, minor in mathematics.

References   References will be supplied upon request.

Functional Resume
(Prepared on a Word Processor and Letter-Quality Printer.)

Michelle Hughes
430 Miller's Crossing
Essex Junction, VT 05452
802/555-9354

Solid background in plate making, separations, color matching, background definition, printing, mechanicals, color corrections, and supervision of personnel. A highly motivated manager and effective communicator. Proven ability to:

* **Create Commercial Graphics**
* **Produce Embossing Drawings**
* **Color Separate**
* **Analyze Consumer Acceptance**

* **Meet Graphic Deadlines**
* **Control Quality**
* **Resolve Printing Problems**
* **Expedite Printing Operations**

Qualifications

Printing: Black and white and color. Can judge acceptability of color reproduction by comparing it with original. Can make four or five color corrections on all media. Have long developed ability to restyle already reproduced four-color artwork. Can create perfect tone for black and white match fill-ins for resume cover letters.

Customer Relations: Work with customers to assure specifications are met and customers are satisfied. Can guide work through entire production process and strike a balance between technical printing capabilities and need for customer approval.

Management: Schedule work to meet deadlines. Direct staff in production procedures. Maintain quality control from inception of project through final approval for printing.

Specialties: Make silk screen overlays for a multitude of processes. Velo bind, GBC bind, perfect bind. Have knowledge to prepare posters, flyers, and personalized stationery.

Personnel Supervision: Foster an atmosphere that encourages highly talented artists to balance high level creativity with a maximum of production. Meet or beat production deadlines. Am continually instructing new employees, apprentices and students in both artistry and technical operations.

Experience

Professor of Graphic Arts, University of Vermont, Burlington, VT (1977-present).
Assistant Production Manager, Artsign Digraphics, Burlington, VT (1981-present) Part time.

Education

Massachusetts Conservatory of Art, PhD 1977
University of Massachusetts, B.A. 1974

Chronological Resume
(Prepared on an Office-Quality Typewriter.)

Lorraine Avakian
70 Monback Avenue
Oshkosh, WI 54901
Phone: 414/555-4629

Business Experience

1984-1991 **NATIONAL PACKAGING PRODUCTS,** Princeton, WI

1989-1991 **District Sales Manager.** Improved 28-member sales group from a company rank in the bottom thirty percent to the top twenty percent. Complete responsibility for personnel, including recruiting, hiring and training. Developed a comprehensive sales improvement program and advised its implementation in eight additional sales districts.

1986-1988 **Marketing Associate.** Responsible for research, analysis, and presentation of marketing issues related to long-term corporate strategy. Developed marketing perspective for capital investment opportunities and acquisition candidates, which was instrumental in finalizing decisions to make two major acquisitions and to construct a $35 million canning plant.

1984-1986 **Salesperson, Paper Division.** Responsible for a four-county territory in central Wisconsin. Increased sales from $700,000 to over $1,050,000 annually in a 15 month period. Developed six new accounts with incremental sales potential of $800,000. Only internal candidate selected for new marketing program.

AMERICAN PAPER PRODUCTS, INC., Oshkosh, WI
1983-1984 **Sales Trainee.** Completed the intensive six month training program and was promoted to salesperson status. Received the President's Award for superior performance in the sales training program.

HENDUKKAR SPORTING GOODS, INC., Oshkosh, WI
1983 **Assistant Store Manager.** Supervised six employees on the evening shift. Handled accounts receivable.

Education
1977-1982 **BELOIT COLLEGE,** Beloit, WI
Received Bachelor of Science Degree in Business Administration in June 1982. Varsity Volleyball. Financed 50% of educational costs through part-time and co-op program employment.

Personal Background
Able to relocate; Excellent health; Active in community activities.

Chronological Resume
(Prepared on a Word Processor and Laser Printer.)

Melvin Winter
43 Aspen Wall Lane
Wheaton, IL 60512
312/555-6923 (home)
312/555-3000 (work)

RELATED EXPERIENCE
1982-Present GREAT LAKES PUBLISHING COMPANY, Chicago, IL
<u>Operations Supervisor</u> (1986-present)
in the Engineering Division of this major trade publishing house, responsible for maintaining on line computerized customer files, title files, accounts receivable, inventory and sales files.

Organize department activities, establish priorities and train personnel. Provide corporate accounting with monthly reports of sales, earned income from journals, samples, inventory levels/value and sales and tax data. Divisional sales average $3 million annually.

<u>Senior Customer Service Representative</u> (1984-1986)
in the Construction Division. Answered customer service inquiries regarding orders and accounts receivable, issued return and shortage credits and expedited special sales orders for direct mail and sales to trade schools.

<u>Customer Service Representative</u> (1982-1983)
in the International Division. Same duties as for construction division except that sales were to retail stores and universities in Europe.

1980-1982 B. DALTON, BOOKSELLER, Salt Lake City, UT
<u>Assistant Manager</u> of this retail branch of a major domestic book seller, maintained all paperback inventories at necessary levels, deposited receipts daily and created window displays.

EDUCATION
1976-1980 UNIVERSITY OF MAINE, Orono, ME
Awarded a degree of Bachelor of Arts in French Literature.

LANGUAGES
Fluent in French. Able to write in French, German and Spanish.

PERSONAL
Willing to travel and relocate, particularly in Europe.

References available upon request.

General Model for a Cover Letter

```
                                          Your Address
                                          Date


Contact Person Name
Title
Company
Address



Dear Mr./Ms._____:


Immediately explain why your background makes you the best can-
didate for the position that you are applying for. Keep the
first paragraph short and hard-hitting.

Detail what you could contribute to this company. Show how
your qualifications will benefit this firm. Remember to keep
this letter short; few recruiters will read a cover letter
longer than half a page.

Describe your interest in the corporation. Subtly emphasize
your knowledge about this firm (the result of your research ef-
fort) and your familiarity with the industry. It is common
courtesy to act extremely eager to work for any company that
you interview.

In the closing paragraph you should specifically request an in-
terview. Include your phone number and the hours when you can
be reached. Alternatively, you might prefer to mention that
you will follow up with a phone call (to arrange an interview
at a mutually convenient time within the next several days).



                                          Sincerely,

                                          (signature)

                                          Your full name (typed)
```

Cover Letter

49 Chinwick Circle
Houston, TX 77031
October 5, 1993

Ms. Ruth Herman-George
V.P./Director of Personnel
Holly Rock Fire Insurance Group
444 Rolling Cloud Lane, Suite 24
Houston, TX 77035

Dear Ms. Herman-George:

I am a career-oriented individual who can successfully provide
technical direction and training to pension analysts in connection with FKLE system.

My major and most recent background is directly involved in
the administration of pension and profit sharing plans with
TRMZ. Furthermore, my extensive experience both as a Group Pension Pre-Scale Underwriter and as a Pension Underwriter involves data processing knowledge and overall pension
administration.

A prime function of mine is decision making with reference to
group pension business. You specifically seek an idividual who
can recommend changes and/or new procedures of plan administration and maintenance plus assistance in development of pension
administration kits for use by the field force at Holly Rock.
I feel that I possess the ability to fulfill your need dramatically.

I would welcome the practical opportunity to work directly
with general agents and plan trustees in qualifying, revising
and requalifying pension and profit sharing plans required by
TRMZ. You will note in my resume my background in working with
others in both an advisory and shirt-sleeve capacity.

I look forward to hearing from you.

Sincerely,

Henry Washington

Cover Letter

411 Looksee Avenue
Apt. 449
Medford, MA 02139
March 15, 1993

Mr. Benjamin Deiver
Sales Manager
Yankee Ski Products
456 Pillbox Lane
Denver, CO 80201

Dear Mr. Deiver:

I seek a position as a sales representative with Yankee Ski Products and I offer, in return, thorough industry experience and more than eleven years of solid practical background in sales.

As a sample of sales achievement, I increased my personal monthly gross sales volume to a point where it tripled the combined sales of three other full-time representatives for one ski manufacturer. Also, I have won numerous international and domestic sales awards.

As an experienced sales representative, I have succeeded in improving area or regional sales by employing a combination of aggressiveness, enthusiasm, and persistence, and I have been able to bring out these traits in those whom I have hired and trained in my capacity as National Sales Instructor for two companies.

I feel that your new line of competition skis offers an unbeatable price/performance combination for the serious racer. I am firmly convinced that I can improve your market penetration in the lucrative Upstate New York area at least to a top five position.

I am an avid skier. As such, I am familiar with not only the technical terms involved, but with the types of equipment available and the extent to which it is marketed.

I look forward to hearing from you.

Sincerely,

Christina Harges

Cover Letter

1286 136th Avenue
Newark, NJ 07101
December 10, 1992

Mr. Edward Buchanan
Personnel Manager
Caufield & Compson Engineering Services, Inc.
Central Park Square Building
New York, NY 10019

Dear Mr. Buchanan:

My diversity as well as my depth of engineering experience in
the wastewater treatment field could prove to be a particularly strong asset for Caufield & Compson given the firm's current and continued commitment to being a pioneering innovator
in the engineering and construction of wastewater treatment
facilities.

I offer an extensive background in investigating, reporting
and designing multimillion dollar wastewater treatment
facilities, pumping facilities and sewer lines in New Jersey
and in Puerto Rico. In addition, I have experience in coordinating engineering services during construction of sewers
and pumping facilities in Hawaii.

One of my basic strengths is my ability to act as liaison for
diverse engineering and non-engineering individuals and groups
to keep a project on schedule and in line with funding constraints.

I have come to a point in my career where I desire to expand
into areas where I might apply over 8 years of solid engineering experience. These areas include hazardous waste treatment,
industrial wastewater and water treatment, and water supply.

I will be glad to furnish any additional information you
desire. You may reach me during the day at 201/555-1100. I
look forward to hearing from you.

Sincerely,

Raymond A. Gatz

Enc. Resume

General Model for a Follow-Up Letter

```
                                              Your Address
                                              Date

Contact Person Name
Title
Company
Address

Dear Mr./Ms._____:

Remind the interviewer of the position for which you were in-
terviewed, as well as the date. Thank him/her for the inter-
view.

Confirm your interest in the opening and the organization. Use
specifics to emphasize both that you have researched the firm
in detail and considered how you would fit into the company
and the position.

Like in your cover letter, emphasize one or two of you
strongest qualifications and slant them toward the various
points that the interviewer considered the most important for
the position. Keep the letter brief, a half-page is plenty.

If appropriate, close with a suggestion for further action,
such as a desire to have additional interviews. Mention your
phone number and the hours that you can best be reached. Alter-
natively, you may prefer to mention that you will follow up
with a phone call in several days.


                                              Sincerely yours,

                                              (signature)

                                              Your full name (typed)
```

GEOGRAPHICAL INDEX OF EMPLOYERS

CALIFORNIA

Acuson
Adia Services
Adobe Systems
Advanced Logic Research
Alliance Imaging
Altera Corporation
Amdahl Corporation
American Biodyne
Amgen, Inc.
Anthem Electronics
Applied Materials, Inc.
Archive Corporation
AST Research
Autodesk Inc.
Bio-Rad Laboratories
Brajdas
Borland International
Bridgford Foods
Brooktree
Cadence Design Systems
California Energy
California Microwave
Centex Telemanagement
Century Medicorp
Cirrus Logic, Inc.
Cisco Systems
The Clorox Corporation
Coast Distribution Systems
Cohu
Community Psyciatric Centers
Compression Labs, Inc.
Conner Peripherals

ALABAMA

Alfa Corporation
Birmingham Steel Corporation
Bruno's Inc.
Comptronix
Durr-Fillauer Medical, Inc.
Healthsouth Rehabilitation Corp.
Intergraph Corporation
Nichols Research Corporation

ARIZONA

Artisoft Inc.
*Execu*Systems*
Phelps Dodge Corporation
Rockford Corporation
Sierra Tuscon Companies

ARKANSAS

Cannon Express, Inc.
Dillard Department Stores
J.B. Hunt Transport Services
TCBY
Tyson Foods
Wal-Mart Stores, Inc.

CXR Corporation
Cypress Semiconductor
DH Technology
Diagnostic Engineering
Diagnostic Products Corporation
Diceon Electronics
Digital Microwave Corporation
Dionex
Walt Disney Co.
Dreyer's Grand Ice Cream
Electronic Arts
Emcon
Everex Systems
Foundation Health Corporation
Franklin Resources
Frederick's of Hollywood
FRS, Inc.
Furon Company
The Gap
Genetech Inc.
Gish Biomedical Inc.
Harding Associates Inc.
Hewlett-Packard Company
Hexcel Corporation
IDB Communications Group
ILC Technology
Infrasonics, Inc.
Integrated Device Technology
Intel Corporation
International Technology Corporation
Intuit, Inc.
Jacobs Engineering Group
Kasler
Kaufman and Broad Home Corp.
Koll Management Services
Komag, Inc.
L.A. Gear
Laser Precision Corporation
P. Leiner Nutritional Products
Loredan Biomedical Inc.
LSI Logic Corporation
MacNeal-Schwendler Corp.
Mail Boxes Etc.
Marshall Industries
Maxim Integrated Products
MDT Corporation

Medex, Inc.
Medical Imaging Centers
Mercury General Corporation
Micro Technology, Inc.
Micronics Computers
Micropolis
MMI Medical, Inc.
Mobile Technologies Corporation
Molecular Biosystems
Mylex
Nantucket Corporation
National Education Corporation
Nellcor
Network Equipment Technologies
Neutrogena Corporation
Nichols Institute
Occup. Urgent Health Care Systems
Octel Communications Corporation
Oracle Systems Corporation
Pacificare Health Systems, Inc.
PDA Engineering
Prestige Leather
Price Company
PSICOR
Pyramid Technology Corporation
Quantum Corporation
Quicksilver, Inc.
Rainbow Technologies Inc.
Ranpac Engineering
Rexon
St. Ives Laboratories, Inc.
SBE, Inc.
Sci-Med Systems, Inc.
Seagate Technology, Inc.
Sigma Designs, Inc.
Silicon Graphics
Silicon Valley Group
Software Publishing
Software Toolworks, Inc.
Solectron
SPI Pharmaceuticals
State of the Art
Step Ahead Investments, Inc.
Sun Microsystems, Inc.
Sunrise Medical, Inc.
Supermail International Inc.

Sybase, Inc.
Symantec
Synoptics Communications
Syntex Corporation
Tandem Computers, Inc.
TCI International, Inc.
Tekelec
Teradata Corporation
3Com Corporation
Tokos Medical
Traditional Industries, Inc.
Tricare
Trimble Navigation, Ltd.
20th Century Industries
Verifone
Vestro Foods, Inc.
Viking Office Products
Vons Companies
Wet Seal, Inc.
Williams-Sonoma, Inc.
Xilinx, Inc.
Zenith National Insurance Corporation

COLORADO

Associated Natural Gas Company
Confertech International
Corporate Express
Hach
OEA
Plains Petroleum Company
Porter Mcleod
Tele-Communications
Triax Communications
USMX Inc.

CONNECTICUT

American Fructose
Baldwin Technology
Citizen's National Utilities
Dairy Mart Convenience Stores
Dianon Systems
The Dress Barn, Inc.

Duty Free International
General Electric Company
Hubbell, Inc.
Kaman Corporation
Lynch Corporation
Nac Re
Pitney Bowes, Inc.
Preferred Health Care Ltd.
Summagraphics
UPS
US Surgical Corporation

DELAWARE

Mercantile Stores Company, Inc.

DISTRICT OF COLUMBIA

Danaher Corporation
Marriott Corporation
MCI Communications Corporation
Student Loan Marketing Association

FLORIDA

All American Semiconductors
Blockbuster Entertainment
Cascade International Inc.
Catalina Lighting Inc.
Chico's
Devcon International Corporation
Dycom Industries
Encore Computer
Gale Group
Holiday RV Superstores, Inc.
Home Intensive Care
International Recovery Corporation
Ivax
JJW Construction
Kaydon
Killearn Properties
Kimmins Enivornmental Service Corp.
Knight-Ridder, Inc.

Loren Industries, Inc.
Mobile America Corporation
National Data Products, Inc.
Nutmeg Industries
Office Depot
Pharmacy Management Services
Ramsey HMO
Raymond James Financial
Riverside Group, Inc.
Sensormatic Electronics
Sound Advice, Inc.
Spec's Music Inc.
Stephan Company
Tech Data Corporation
Watsco, Inc.
Windmere Corporation

GEORGIA

Advanced Telecommunications
American Software
Atlantic Southeast Air
Crown Crafts, Inc.
Davis Water & Waste Industries, Inc.
First Financial Management
Genuine Parts Corporation
Gerber Alley & Associates
Graphic Industries, Inc.
John H. Harland Company
The Home Depot Inc.
Home Nutritional Services
Interface, Inc.
National Service Industries, Inc.
Prince Street Technologies
Shaw Industries Inc.
Superior Teletec Inc.
T^2 Medical
Total System Services
Video Display Corporation

IDAHO

Albertson's
Micron Technology, Inc.

Scientech
TJ International, Inc.

ILLINOIS

Abbott Laboratories
Ambitech Engineering
Archer-Daniels-Midland
Comark, Inc.
Comdisco, Inc.
R.R. Donnelley & Sons Co.
Arthur J. Gallagher
Healthcare Compare
Healthstaffers, Inc.
Illinois Tool Works, Inc.
Information Resources
Itel Corporation
Juno Lighting One
Landauer
Lawter International
McDonald's Corporation
Methode Electronics
Microenergy, Inc.
Molex
Newell Company
The Quaker Oats Company
Safety-Kleen
Sanford Corporation
Sara Lee
Service Master Limited Partnership
Stone Container Corporation
System Software Associates
Tootsie Roll Industries
Walgreen Co.
Wallace Computer Services, Inc.
Waste Management Inc.
Wm. Wrigley Jr. Co.
XL Datacomp, Inc.

INDIANA

Bindley Western Industries, Inc.
Biomet
Canonie Environmental Services Corp.

Conseco, Inc.
Excel Industries
Great Lakes Chemical Corporation
Hillenbrand Industries, Inc.
Eli Lilly and Company
Wabash National Corporation

IOWA

Art's-Way Manufacturing Company
Bandag, Inc.
Heartland Express Inc.

KANSAS

Britevoice Systems
Home Office Reference Laboratory
National Pizza Company
Sealright

KENTUCKY

Rally's
Vencor, Inc.

LOUISIANA

Freeport McMoran Resources
Marine Shale Processors

MAINE

Hannaford Brothers Company

MARYLAND

Bohdan Associates, Inc.
Computer Data Systems
Comsys Technical Services Inc.
Cosmetic Center

Dart Group
General Sciences Corporation
Giant Foods
Group 1 Software Inc.
Hechinger Company
Merry-Go-Round Enterprises
Micros Systems
NYMA, Inc.
Penril Datacom Networks
RJO Enterprises, Inc.
Rouse Co.
The Ryland Group
Statistica
Synergics
Technical & Management Services

MASSACHUSETTS

Banyan Systems
Bertucci's
Bolt Beranek & Newman
Boston Acoustics Inc.
Cambex
Candela Laser
Chipcom Corporation
Cognex
Corporate Software
Dynamics Research Corporation
Dynatech Corporation
Eaton Vance
EG&G
General Cinema
Haemonetics
IPL Systems Inc.
Keane, Inc.
Lifetime Corporation
Medchem Products, Inc.
Medisense Inc.
Mestek, Inc.
Microcom, Inc.
New England Business Services, Inc.
Octocom System
Progress Software Corporation
Reebok International
Software 2000 Inc.

Staples
Stratus Computer Inc.
Synetics
Thermo Electron Corporation
Thermo Instruments Systems
Watts Industries

MICHIGAN

Code-Alarm Inc.
Complete Business Solutions
Gainey Transportation Services
Gerber Products
Handleman Company
Kellogg Company
Masco Corporation
Medstat Systems, Inc.
Meyers Industries, Inc.
Oxford Energy
South Eastern Michigan Gas
        Enterprises, Inc.
Spartan Motors, Inc.
Stoneridge Resources, Inc.
Stryker Corporation
Tri-County Security
Trimas Corporation
Upjohn Co.
X-Rite

MINNESOTA

Airtran
Analysts International Corporation
Apogee Enterprises, Inc.
Bemis Corporation
Buffets
Cargill, Inc.
CNS, Inc.
Deluxe Corporation
Digi Internatioanl
EMPI
Fastenal Company
General Mills
Grist Mill Company

International Broadcasting Corporation
International Dairy Queen
Jostens, Inc.
Minnesota Mining & Manufacturing (3M)
MOCON
NWA, Inc.
Osmonics
St. Jude Medical
Super Valu Stores, Inc.
Techne
TSI, Inc.
Valspar Corp.
Zeos International

MISSISSIPPI

LDDS Communications

MISSOURI

H&R Block
Carpenter Healthcare Systems
Cencom Cable Associates
Emerson Electric Company
Hallmark Cards
Insituform Mid-America
La Petite Academy, Inc.
The May Department Stores Company
Medicine Shoppe International
Sigma-Aldrich Corporation
Stuart Hall Company, Inc.

NEBRASKA

Berkshire Hathaway
Conagra, Inc.
Isco
Werner Enterprises

NEVADA

International Game Technology

Show Boat Inc.
United Gaming, Inc.
Valmont Industries, Inc.

NEW HAMPSHIRE

Cabletron Systems
Chemical Fabrics
Salem Screen Printers, Inc.
Tyco Laboratories Inc.

NEW JERSEY

A.L. Laboratories
Alpine Lace Brands
Applied Bioscience International
Automatic Data Processing, Inc.
C.R. Bard, Inc.
Champion Mortgage Company
Convergent Solutions Inc.
Dataflex Corporation
Datascope Corporation
Fedders Corporation
Handex
Harmony Schools
Hooper Holmes
J&J Snack Foods
Johnson & Johnson
King World Productions, Inc.
Lechters
Medco Containment Services
Merck & Co., Inc.
Micro Healthsystems
Mid-Atlantic Medical Services, Inc.
New York Style Bagel Chip
NMR of America, Inc.
Ogden Projects
Par Pharmaceutical, Inc.
Programming & Systems
Regency Cruises Inc.
Schering-Plough
Score Board
Telerate
Toys 'R' US

Ultimate Corporation
Vital Signs
Warner-Lambert

NEW MEXICO

Advanced Sciences
Diagnostek, Inc.
Vivigen Inc.

NEW YORK

A&W Brands
Allou Health & Beauty Care
American Home Products Corporation
American International Group
American Precision Industries
Artistic Greetings
Borden, Inc.
Bristol-Meyers Squibb Company
Carter-Wallace, Inc.
Cheyenne Software
Liz Claiborne
Comptek Research
Computer Associates International
Corning, Inc.
CPAC Inc.
Dow Jones & Co.
Dun & Bradstreet Corporation
Ecology and Environment
Esquire Radio & Electronics
Forest Laboratories
Frontier Insurance Group
General Transportation Services
Geraghty and Miller Inc.
Instrument Systems
International Flavors & Fragrances
International Paper Company
Jaco Electronics
JWP
Estee Lauder
Liuski International
Mark IV Industries
Marsh & McLennan Cos.

MBIA
McGrath Industries
Melville Corporation
Merchants Group
Metro Mobile CTS
National Patent Development Corporation
New Line Cinema
Olsten Corporation
Pall Corporation
Paxar Corporation
Paychex, Inc.
Pfizer
Ply-Gem Industries, Inc.
Sbarro, Inc.
Sequa Corporation
Shorewood Packaging Corporation
State-O-Maine
Symbol Technologies, Inc.
Tambrands, Inc.
Time-Warner
Trigen Energy Corporation
Uniforce Temp Personnel, Inc.
Viacom Inc.
Viatech, Inc.

NORTH CAROLINA

Cape Fear Insulation, Inc.
CEM Corporation
Communication Cable
Food Lion, Inc.
Lance, Inc.
Vanguard Cellular Systems

OHIO

Agency Ret-A-Car
Cardinal Distribution Inc.
Cintas Corporation
Comair Holdings, Inc.
Cooper Tire & Rubber
Duriron
Bob Evans Farms, Inc.
Future Now

M.A. Hanna Co.
LDI
The Limited, Inc.
Mid-America Waste Systems
Modern Technologies Corporation
Myers Industries Inc.
Ohm Corporation
Progressive Corporation
Royal Appliance Manufacturing Co.
RPM, Inc.
Rubbermaid, Inc.
Sherwin-Williams Co.
The J.M. Smucker Company
State Auto Financial
Structural Dynamics Research
Telxon
Tranzonic Companies
Venture Lighting International
Waxman Industries, Inc.

OREGON

Mentor Graphics
Microware, Inc.
Nike, Inc.
Oregon Metallurgical Corporation
Precision Castparts Corporation
Sequent Computer Systems Inc.

PENNSYLVANIA

Alco Health Services
AMP
Autoclave Engineers
Michael Baker
C-Cor Electronics
Chambers Development Company, Inc.
Charming Shoppes
Comcast Corporation
CSS Industries
PH Glatfelter Company
Healthcare Services Group
H.J. Heinz Company
Hershey Foods Corporation

Intelligent Electronics
Magic Years Child Care
Novacare
Pep Boys-Manny, Moe, and Jack
Respironics
Safeguard Scientifics, Inc.
SEI
Super Rite Foods
Surgical Laser Technologies
Technitrol Inc.
US Healthcare, Inc.
Vallen Corporation
Vishay Intertechnology

RHODE ISLAND

American Power Conversion
Astro-Med, Inc.

SOUTH CAROLINA

Am-Pro Protective Agency
Colonial Companies
One Price Clothing Stores Inc.
Policy Management Systems
Ryan's Family Steak Houses, Inc.
Sonoco Products Co.
Span America Medical Systems, Inc.

SOUTH DAKOTA

Gateway 2000
Raven Industries

TENNESSEE

Clayton Homes
Coventry Corporation
Cracker Barrel Old Country Store, Inc.
Danek Group
Federal Express Corporation
National Safety Associates

Surgical Care Affiliates

TEXAS

Allwaste, Inc.
American Medical Electronics
American Oil and Gas Corporation
Babbages
Banctec, Inc.
Berne Group
BMC Software
Brinker International
Browning-Ferris Industries
Calidad Electronics
Cash America Investments
Columbia Hospital Corporation
Compucom Systems
Critical Industries, Inc.
Daisytek
Dallas Semiconductor Corporation
Dell Computer
Destec Energy, Inc.
Enclean Inc.
Energy Ventures
Ennis Business Forms, Inc.
Entertainment Marketing
Frozen Food Express Industries
Gainsco
Gundle Environmental Systems
Helen of Troy
Hitox Corporation
Inter Voice Inc.
Kent Electronics
Kimberly-Clark
Kirby Corporation
Landmark Graphics
Luby's Cafeterias Inc.
Maxxam
Offshore Pipelines, Inc.
O.I.
J.C. Penny
Seagull Energy
Serv-Tech
Service Corporation International
Software Spectrum

Spaghetti Warehouse, Inc.
Swift Energy Company
Sysco
Tandy Corporation
Tetra Technologies
Trinity Industries

UTAH

Ballard Medical Products
EFI Electronics Corporation
Franklin International Institute
Nature's Sunshine Products, Inc.
Novell, Inc.
Research Industries
Utah Medical Products, Inc.
Wordperfect

VERMONT

Ben & Jerry's Homemade

VIRGINIA

American Management Systems
Circuit City Stores, Inc.
Comprehensive Technologies Int'l
Dibrell Brothers, Inc.
Diversified Technology
Dual & Associates
Ethyl Corporation
Gannett Company, Inc.
Government Technology Services
Green Thumb Enterprises
Heilig-Myers Company
ICF International
JAK Construction
Landmark Systems Corporation
Legent Corporation
Mars, Inc.
Metters Industries
Orbital Sciences Corporation
Owens & Minor, Inc.

SRA International
Universal Corporation

WASHINGTON

Airborne Freight Corporation
Alaska Air Group
Aldus Corporation
Arctic Alaska Fisheries
The Boeing Co.
Egghead, Inc.
Expeditors International
Microsoft Corporation
Nordstom
Univar Corporation
Utilx

WISCONSIN

Capitol Transamerica
Costco Wholesale Corporation
Harley-Davidson, Inc.
Harnischefeger Industries, Inc.
Johnson Controls
Regal Beloit Corporation
Snap On Tools
Sullivan Dental Products
Terex Corporation
Universal Medical Buildings L.P.
Value Merchants

WYOMING

Ehman

INDUSTRIAL INDEX

BUSINESS SERVICES

Adia Services
Cintas Corporation
Information Resources
Olsten Corporation
Right Management Consultants
Telerate
Total System Services
Uniforce Temporary Personnel

CHEMICAL

Applied Bioscience International
Chemical Fabrics
CPAC, Inc.
Dionex
Duriron
Freeport McMoran Reseources
Great Lakes Chemical Corporation
M.A. Hanna Company
National Service Industries
Univar Corporation

COMPUTERS: HARDWARE, SOFTWARE & SERVICES

Adobe Systems
Advanced Logic Reserch
Aldus Corporation

Amdahl Corporation
American Management Systems
American Software
Analysts International Corporation
Archive Corporation
Artisoft
AST Research
Autodesk, Inc.
Automatic Data Processing
Banctec
Banyan Systems
BMC Software
Bohdan Associates
Bolt, Beranek & Newman
Borland International
Brooktree
Cabletron Systems
Cadence Systems
Cambex
Cheyenne Software
Chipcom Corporation
Cisco systems
Comark, Inc.
Comdisco, Inc.
Complete Business Solutions
Comptronix
Compucom Systems
Computer Associates International
Computer Data Systems
Comsys Technical Services
Conner Peripherals
Convergent Solutions
Corporate Software
Daisytek
Dataflex Corporation
Dell Computer

DH Technology
Digi International
Ehman
Electronic Arts
Encore Computer
Everex Systems
FRS, Inc.
Gateway 2000
General Sciences Corporation
Government Technology Services
Group 1 Software, Inc.
Hewlett-Packard Corporation
Intergraph Corporation
Intuit
IPL Systems
JWP
Keane, Inc.
Komag, Inc.
LDI
Legent Corporation
Liuski International
MacNeal-Schwendler Corporation
Mentor Graphics
Micro Healthsystems
Micro Technology, Inc.
Microcom
Micronics Computers
Micropolis
Micros Systems
Microsoft Corporation
Microware
Mylex Corporation
National Data Products, Inc.
Nellcor
Network Equipment
Novell, Inc.
NYMA, Inc.
Oracle Systems Corporation
Paychex
PDA Engineering
Policy Management Systems
Programming & Systems
Progress Software Corporation
Pyramid Technology Corporation
Quantum Corporation
Rainbow Technologies

Rexon
RJO Enterprises
SBE, Inc.
Scientech
Seagate Technology
Sequent Computer Systems
Sigma Designs
Silicon Graphics
Software Publishing
Software Spectrum
Software Toolworks
Software 2000
State of the Art
Statistica
Stratus Computer
Structural Dynamics Research
Summagraphics
Sun Microsystems
Sybase
Symantec
Symbol Technologies
Synoptics Communications
System Software Associates
Tandem Computers
Tech Data Corporation
Technical and Management Services
Telxon
Teradata Corporation
3Com Corporation
Ultimate Corporation
Verdix Corporation
Wordperfect
XL Datacomp
Zeos International

CONSTRUCTION/REAL ESTATE

Apogee Enterprises
Cape Fear Insulation
Clayton Homes
Devcon International Corporation
Execu*Systems

Insituform Mid-America
Jacobs Engineering Group
JAK Construction
JJW Construction
Kasler
Kaufman and Broad
Killearn Properties
Koll Management Services
Landmark Graphics
Masco Corporation
McGrath Industries
Porter McLeod
Riverside Group
Rouse Co.
The Ryland Group
Sanford Corporation
Stoneridge Resources
Terex Corporation

CONSUMER PRODUCTS MANUFACTURING

Allou Health & Beauty Care
American Home Products Corporation
Artistic Greetings
Berkshire Hathaway
Bristol-Meyers Squibb Co.
Cascade International
Catalina Lighting, Inc.
Clorox Corporation
Coast Distribution Systems
Crown Crafts
CSS Industries
Danaher Corporation
Dibrell Brothers
Walt Disney Company
Fedders Corporation
General Electric Co.
Gerber Products
Handleman Co.
Helen of Troy
Hillenbrand Industries
Interface, Inc.

International Flavors & Fragrances
Jostens
Johnson & Johnson
Juno Lighting One
Kimberly-Clark Corporation
L.A. Gear
Estee Lauder
P. Leiner Nutritional Products
Loren Industries
Meyers Industries
Minnesota Mining & Manufacturing Co. (3M)
National Safety Associates
Nature's Sunshine Products
Neutrogena
Newell Co.
Nike, Inc.
Nutmeg Industries
Philip Morris
Prince St. Technologies
Reebok International
Rockford Corporation
Royal Appliance Manufacturing
Rubbermaid
St. Ives Laboratories
The Score Board
Shaw Industries
Sherwin-Williams
Snap-On Tools
Stephan Company
Tambrands
TJ International
Tranzonic Companies
Universal Corporation
Viking Office Products
Windmere Corporation
Wm. Wrigley Jr. Co.

ELECTRONICS

All American Semiconductors
Altera Corporation
American Power Conversion

American Precision Industries
AMP, Inc.
Anthem Electronics
Applied Materials, Inc.
Astro-Med
Boston Acoustics
Brajdas
Calidad Electronics
C-COR Electronics
Cirrus Logic
Code-Alarm, Inc.
Cognex
Cohu
Communication Cable
Compression Labs
Comtek Research
Comptronix
Cypress Semiconductor
Dallas Semiconductor Corporation
Diceon Electronics
Dynatech Corporation
EFI Electronics Corporation
EG&G
Emerson Electric Co.
Entertainment Marketing
General Electric Co.
Hubbell, Inc.
ILC Technology
Instrument Systems
Integrated Device Technology
Intel Corporation
Jaco Electronics
Johnson Controls
Juno Lighting One
Kent Electronics
LSI Logic Corporation
Marshall Industries
Maxim Integrated Products
Methode Electronics
Microenergy, Inc.
Micron Technology
Molex
Pitney Bowes
Quicksilver
Raven Industries
Sensormatic Electronics

Silicon Valley Group
Solectron
Technitrol, Inc.
Trimble Navigation
Verifone
Video Display Corporation
Vishay Intertechnology
Xilinx
X-Rite

ENERGY

American Oil and Gas Corporation
California Energy
Citizen's National Utilities
Destec Energy
Energy Ventures
Landmark Graphics
Offshore Pipelines, Inc.
Oxford Energy
Plains Petroleum Company
Seagull Energy
Southeastern Michigan Gas Enterprises
Trigen Energy Corp.

ENGINEERING

Advanced Sciences
Ambitech Engineering
Autoclave Engineers
Michael Baker
Comprehensive Technologies International
Diversified Technology
Dynamics Research Corporation
EG&G
Metters Industries
Modern Technologies Corporation
Ranpac Engineering
Synetics
Viatech, Inc.

ENTERTAINMENT/ BROADCASTING

Blockbuster Entertainment
Cencom Cable Associates
Comcast Corporation
Walt Disney Company
General Cinema
IDB Communications Group
International Broadcasting Corporation
International Game Technology
King World Productions
Lynch Corporation
New Line Cinema
Tele-Communications
Time-Warner
Triax
United Gaming
Viacom

ENVIRONMENTAL SERVICES

Allwaste
Browning-Ferris Industries
Canonie Environmental Services
Corporation
Chambers Development Company
Critical Industries, Inc.
Davis Water & Waste Industries
Diagnostic Engineering
Ecology & Environment
Emcon
Enclean
Geraghty & Miller
Gundle Environmental Services
Hach
Handex Environ Recovery
Harding Associates
ICF International
International Technology Corporation
Kimmins Environmental Service
Corporation
Landauer

Marine Shale Processors
Mid-America Waste Systems
Ogden Projects
OHM Corporation
O.I. Corporation
Safety-Kleen
Tetra Technologies
Thermo Electron Corp.
Thermo Instrument Systems
Waste Management

FINANCIAL SERVICES/INSURANCE

Alfa Corporation
American International Group
Berkshire Hathaway
H&R Block
Capitol Transamerica
Champion Mortgage Company
Colonial Companies
Conseco
Dow Jones & Co.
Dun & Bradstreet Corporation
Eaton Vance
First Financial Management
Franklin Resources
Frontier Insurance Group
Gainsco
Arthur J. Gallagher
General Electric Co.
Healthcare Compare
Kirby Corporation
Marsh & McLennan Companies, Inc.
MBIA
McKinsey & Co.
Merchants Group
Mercury General Corporation
Mobile America Corporation
NAC Re
Pharmacy Management
Progressive Corp.
Raymond James Financial

SEI
Student Loan Marketing
20th Century Industries
Zenith National Insurance

FOOD & BEVERAGES

A&W Brands
Alpine Lace Brands
American Fructose
Archer-Daniels-Midland Co.
Arctic Alaska Fisheries
Ben & Jerry's Homemade, Inc.
Borden, Inc.
Bridgeford Foods
Cargill, Inc.
Conagra
Dreyer's Grand Ice Cream
General Mills
Gerber Products
Grist Mill Company
H.J. Heinz
Hershey Foods Corporation
International Dairy Queen
J&J Snack Foods
Kellogg Company
Lance, Inc.
Mars, Inc.
New York Style Bagel Chip
Philip Morris
The Quaker Oats Company
Sara Lee
Sealright
The J.M. Smucker Company
Super Rite Foods
Sysco Corporation
Tootsie Roll
Tyson Foods
Vestro Foods

HEALTH CARE: MEDICAL SERVICES, EQUIPMENT & PHARMACEUTICALS/ BIOTECHNOLOGY

Abbott Laboratories
Acuson
AL Laboratories
Alco Health Services
Alliance Imaging
American Biodyne
American Medical Electronics
Amgen
Ballard Medical Products
C.R. Bard, Inc.
Bindley Western Industries
Biomet
Bio-Rad Laboratories
Bristol-Meyers Squibb Co.
Cabot Medical
Candela Laser
Cardinal Distribution, Inc
Carpenter Healthcare Systems
Carter-Wallace, Inc.
CEM Corporation
Century Medicorp
CNS, Inc.
Columbia Hospital Corporation
Community Psychiatric Centers
Coventry Corporation
Danek Group
Datascope Corporation
Diagnostek, Inc.
Diagnostic Products
Dianon Systems
Durr-Fillauer Medical, Inc.
Empi
Forest Laboratories
Foundation Health Corporation
Genentech
Gerber Alley & Associates
Gish Biomedical
Haemonetics
Heathcare Compare
Healthsouth Rehabilitation Corporation
Healthstaffers, Inc.

Home Intensive Care, Inc.
Home Nutritional Services
Home Office Reference Laboratory
Hooper Holmes
Infrasonics
Ivax Corporation
Johnson & Johnson
Lifetime Corporation
Eli Lilly
P. Leiner Nutritional Products
Loredan Biomedical
MDT Corporation
Medchem Products
Medco Containment Services
Medex, Inc.
Medical Imaging Centers of America
Medisense, Inc.
Medstat Systems, Inc.
Merck & Co.
MMI Medical, Inc.
Molecular Biosystems
National Patent Development Corp.
Nature's Sunshine Products
Nellcor
Nichols Institute
NMR of America
Novacare
Occupational-Urgent Care Health Systems
Owens & Minor
Pacificare Health Systems
Par Pharmaceutical
Pfizer
Preferred Health Care
Psicor
Ramsey HMO
Research Industries
Respironics
Rhone-Poulenc Rorer
St. Jude Medical
Schering-Plough
Sci-Med Life Systems
Sierra Tuscon Companies
Sigma-Aldrich
Span America Medical
SPI Pharmaceuticals
Stryker Corporation

Sullivan Dental Products
Sunrise Medical
Surgical Care Affiliates
Surgical Laser Technologies
Syntex Corporation
T^2 Medical
Techne Corporation
Tokos Medical
Tricare
Universal Medical Buildings
The Upjohn Company
US Healthcare
US Surgical Corporation
Utah Medical Products
Vencor
Vital Signs
Vivigen
Warner-Lambert Company

INDUSTRIAL PRODUCTS MANUFACTURING

Art's-Way Manufacturing Company
Bemis Corporation
Chemical Fabrics
Cooper Tire & Rubber
Danaher Corporation
DUAL & Associates
Furon Company
Gale Group
General Electric Co.
Harnischefeger Industries
Hexcel Corporation
Hitox Corporation
Illinois Tool Company
International Paper Co.
Isco
Kaydon Corporation
Laser Precision Corporation
Lynch Corporation
Mark IV Industries
Maxxam
Mestek, Inc.

MOCON (Modern Controls)
Modern Technologies Corp.
Myers Industires
OEA
Oregon Metallurgical
Osmonics
Pall Corporation
Paxar Corporation
Phelps Dodge Corp.
Precision Castparts Corp.
Regal-Beloit Corp.
RPM
Sequa
Shorewood Packaging
Sonoco Products Co.
Stone Container Corp.
Trimas Corporation
TSI
Tyco Laboratories
USMX
Vallen Corporation
Valmont Industries
Valspar Corp.
Viatech
Watsco
Watts Industries
Waxman Industries

PRINTING & PUBLISHING

Baldwin Technology
Berkshire Hathaway
Deluxe Corporation
R.R. Donnelly & Sons
Dow Jones & Co.
Dun & Bradstreet Corporation
Ennis Business Forms
Gannett Company
General Cinema
P.H. Glatfelter Co.
Graphic Industries, Inc.
Hallmark Cards
John H. Harland Company
Knight-Ridder, Inc.
Lawter International
National Education Corporation
New England Business Service
The Reader's Digest Assn.
Salem Screen Printers
Stuart Hall Company
Time-Warner
Traditional Industries

MISCELLANEOUS SERVICES

Agency Rent-A-Car
Am-Pro Protective Agency
Green Thumb Enterprises
The Harmony School
La Petite Academy
Magic Years Child Care & Learning
Centers
Mail Boxes, Etc.
National Education Corporation
Service Corporation International
ServiceMaster Limited Partnership
Supermail International
Tri-County Security

RETAILERS, HOTELS & RESTAURANTS

Albertson's
Babbages
Berne Group
Bertucci's
Blockbuster Entertainment
Brinker International
Bruno's, Inc.
Buffets
Cash America Investments
Charming Shoppes
Chico's

Circuit City Stores
Corporate Express
Cosmetic Center
Costco Wholesale Corporation
Cracker Barrel Old Country Store
Dairy Mart Convenience Stores
Dart Group
Dillard Department Stores
The Dress Barn
Duty Free International
Egghead, Inc.
Bob Evans Farms
Fastenal Company
Food Lion
Frederick's of Hollywood
Future Now
The Gap
General Cinema
Giant Foods
Hannaford Bros. Co.
Hechinger Co.
Heilig-Myers Co.
Holiday RV Superstores
The Home Depot
International Dairy Queen
Lechter's
The Limited
Longs Drug Stores
Luby's Cafeterias
Marriott Corporation
May Department Stores
McDonald's Coporation
Medicine Shoppe International
Melville Corporation
Mercantile Stores Company
Merry-Go-Round Enterprises
National Pizza Company
Nordstrom
Office Depot
One Price Clothing Stores
J.C. Penney
Pep Boys-Manny, Moe, & Jack
Price Company
Publix Super Markets
Rally's
Ryan's Family Steak Houses

Sbarro
Showboat
Sound Advice
Spaghetti Warehouse
Spec's Music
Staples
Step Ahead Investments
Super Valu Stores
Tandy Corporation
TCBY Enterprises
Toys 'R' Us
Value Merchants
Vons Companies
Walgreen Co.
Wal-Mart Stores
Wet Seal
Williams-Sonoma

TELECOMMUNICATIONS

Advanced Telecommunications
Corporation
Brightvoice Systems
California Microwave
Centex Telemanagement
Comcast Corporation
CXR Corporation
Digital Microwave Corporation
Dycom Industries
Esquire Radio & Electronics
Inter Voice, Inc.
LDDS Communications
Lynch Corporation
MCI Communications
Metro Mobile CTS
Mobile Technologies Corporation
SRA International
Superior Teletec
Tekelec
Vanguard

TRANSPORTATION/ AEROSPACE/SHIPPING

Airborne Freight Corporation
Airtran
Alaska Air Group
Atlantic Southeast Air
Bandag
The Boeing Company
Cannon Express
Comair Holdings
Confertech International
Cooper Tire & Rubber
Excel Industries
Expeditors International
Federal Express Corporation
Frozen Food Express Industries
Gainey Transportation Services
General Transportation Services
Genuine Parts Corporation
Harley-Davidson
Heartland Express
J.B. Hunt TransportServices
Intelligent Electronics
International Recovery Corporation
Itel Corporation
Kaman Corporation
Kirby Corporation
Lynch Corporation
NWA
Orbital Sciences Corporation
Regency Cruises
Spartan Motors
Trinity Industries
United Parcel Service of America
Wabash National Corporation
Werner Enterprises

AVAILABLE AT YOUR LOCAL BOOKSTORE

Knock 'em Dead With Great Answers to Tough Interview Questions
Will you have the answers when the recruiter asks: Why do you want to work here? What can you do for us that someone else cannot? How much money do you want? Why do you want to change jobs? In *Knock 'em Dead*, Martin Yate gives you not only the best answers to these and scores of more difficult questions, but also the best way to answer--so that you'll be able to field any tough question, and get the job and salary that you deserve. 6x9 inches, 204 pages, paperback, $7.95.

Resumes that Knock 'em Dead
In *Resumes that Knock 'em Dead*, Martin Yate reviews the marks of a great resume: what type of resume is right for each applicant, what always goes in, what always stays out, and why. Every single resume in *Resumes that Knock 'em Dead* was used by a real individual to successfully obtain a job. No other book provides the hard facts for producing an exemplary resume. 8 1/2x11 inches, 216 pages, $7.95.

Cover Letters that Knock 'em Dead
Cover Letters that Knock 'em Dead shows not just how to write a "correct" cover letter, but how to write a cover letter that offers a powerful competitive advantage in today's tough job market. *Cover Letters that Knock 'em Dead* gives the essential information on composing a cover that wins attention, interest and job offers. 8 1/2x11 inches, 184 pages, $7.95.

ALSO OF INTEREST...
The JobBank Series
There are now 18 *JobBank* books, each providing extensive, up-to-date employment information on hundreds of the largest employers in each job market. Recommended as an excellent place to begin your job search by *The New York Times, The Los Angeles Times, The Boston Globe, The Chicago Tribune,* and many other publications, *JobBank* books have been used by hundreds of thousands of people to find jobs.

Books available: *The Atlanta JobBank--The Boston JobBank--The Chicago JobBank--The Dallas-Ft. Worth JobBank--The Denver JobBank--The Detroit JobBank--The Florida JobBank--The Houston JobBank--The Los Angeles JobBank--The Minneapolis JobBank--The New York JobBank--The Ohio JobBank--The Philadelphia JobBank--The Phoenix JobBank--The St. Louis JobBank--The San Franciso JobBank--The Seattle JobBank--The Washington DC JobBank.* Each book is 6x9 inches, over 250 pages, paperback, $12.95.

If you cannot find a book at your local bookstore, you may order it directly from the publisher. Please send payment including $3.75 for shipping and handling (for the entire order) to : Bob Adams, Inc., 260 Center Street, Holbrook, MA 02343. Credit card holders may call 1-800-USA-JOBS (in Massachusetts, 617-767-8100). Please first check at your local bookstore.